FREE $TUFF
for SENIORS

By Matthew Lesko
with Mary Ann Martello

Publisher's Note

This book is for general information only. It does not constitute medical, legal, or financial advice or practice. We cannot guarantee the safety or effectiveness of any treatment or advice mentioned. Some of these tips may not be effective for everyone. Readers are urged to consult with their personal financial advisors, lawyers, and health-care professionals.

"Consider it pure joy, my brothers, whenever you face trials of many kinds, because you know that the testing of your faith develops perseverance."

- James 1:2-3 (NIV)

Free Stuff For Seniors and all material contained therein copyright © 1997 by Matthew Lesko with Mary Ann Martello. All rights reserved. Printed in the United States of America.

This book or any portion thereof may not be reproduced or distributed in any form or by any means without written permission of the publisher. For information, or to order copies, contact:

FC&A Publishing
103 Clover Green
Peachtree City, GA 30269

Produced by the staff of FC&A
Cover images ©1996 PhotoDisc, Inc.
Sixth Printing January 2000
ISBN 1-890957-31-3

Contents

Neat Things to Do With Your Free Time.............. 39

Money-Saving Household Hints 103

Pamper Your Pets for Pennies 117

Help With Diet And Exercise 123

Healthy Living for Less... 135

Cut Your Legal Costs 227

Gifts, Bargains, and How to Find Them

Showing respect for your elders used to mean you stood up when adults entered the room. You said, "Yes, sir," and "No, sir" to your grandpa. And you wrote formal thank-you notes to Great Aunt Lucille when she sent you handkerchiefs for your birthday.

But times have changed. Those old-fashioned courtesies have pretty much gone out of style. When you visit your grandkids, chances are they come running with hands outstretched, asking what you brought them. Then they give you a hug and tell you how cool you are for taking them to that neat science museum where they saw the dinosaur bones.

Today we show respect for maturity differently. And it's not just in our families. The perks of seniority from businesses and the government are getting better all the time. And the truth is, that's how it should be. After all, you've worked hard, raised your children well, and contributed your talents and skills to your community.

As a senior citizen, you continue to share your wisdom and experience in ways that make this world a better place. So use your senior citizens' status proudly when you get dollars off your dinner or entertain your grandson at the Natural Science Museum. Accept the gifts and discounts as a pat on the back. You deserve it!

Time for Bargains

The old saying, "time is money," takes on a new meaning in retirement. Life no longer sends you rushing to work, juggling appointments, or feeling guilty about staying in bed when you are sick. Now you have the time to be patient and flexible. You are willing to change your plans for dinner out on Friday night if a new restaurant offers a "seniors' special" on Tuesday night. Maybe Saturday used to be your favorite time to go to the movies, but with retirement, every day is like Saturday. The "seniors' matinee" on Thursday is just as good a time as any to hold hands with your favorite sweetheart while watching the latest flick.

You're in no hurry at a U.S. Postal Service sale as you wade through all the stuff you don't want until you uncover a real gem. And you have the patience to wait until that fishing rod you've been wanting goes on sale for 50 percent off at the sporting goods store.

The Free Stuff Way of Life

Are you in the market for a new sofa or love seat? While you are in the furniture store, take a good look around. If you see a lamp or a couple of pillows that match the piece you've selected, ask the salesperson to throw them in for free. Sometimes he's happy to sweeten the deal with one or more of those items.

Always remember this when buying any big-ticket item. With a computer purchase, ask for a box of floppy disks, an attractive mouse pad, or even a supply of printer paper. If you are buying a new stereo system, ask for some free CDs or cassette tapes. Your success will depend on how much freedom the salesperson has and how badly the store wants to move the merchandise.

You are more likely to make a deal in an independently-owned store than in a chain store whose policies come from upper management far away. But sometimes you can have good luck even in a large chain store; you won't know unless you ask. You could save some bucks on items you would otherwise wind up paying for.

You Get What You Ask For

In a restaurant, at the movies, or wherever you go, always ask for the senior citizens' gifts and discounts. Even if you look your age (and, of course, you don't) the waiter or sales clerk may not want to ask if you're a senior citizen. If you are a member of American Association of Retired Persons (AARP), just show your membership card. (Read more about AARP in Chapter 17, *Organizations for People Over Fifty.*) Be sure to let businesses know that you appreciate the special treatment. That encourages them to keep the policies that benefit seniors.

A good place to start is with Wolf Camera's Wolfpack club. This membership costs younger folks $12.99 a year. But if you are 62 or older or are a member of AARP, ask for the free lifetime membership. This entitles you to a free second set of prints, a 25 percent discount on developing, or free use of their photonet service as a way of sharing photos with friends and relatives on the Internet. It also gives you a 10 percent discount on film, frames, enlargements, and other products and services.

And for even more savings, Wolf lets you use discount coupons in combination with your Wolfpack membership. So watch for their ads. Recently, their web site offered a 33 percent discount on film developing. All you had to do was print the coupon and take it in or mail it in with your film. Add that to the 25 percent Wolfpack discount and you would save a whopping 58 percent!

To find the store nearest you, call 888-644-WOLF (9653). Learn more at their web site <www.wolfcamera.com>. (For information on using the Internet as a resource, read on.)

Finding Freebies

We made numerous phone calls and searched a lot of places so we could pack this book with information about free stuff and how to get your hands on it. We found out, for example, that Uncle Sam has a golden passport just for you. It gives you free admission to some great vacation spots and it's good for a lifetime. You'll read about it in the next chapter, *Passport to Travel Savings*.

And we learned the U.S. Government has a lot of other goodies it doesn't advertise. You won't see signs in Washington saying "Free Firewood," "Travel Free Overseas," or "Take Free College Courses," but in fact these opportunities do exist. There are over 2,500 government sources you can turn to for money, services, and valuable information about your health, your finances, and your legal rights. We'll tell you how to get amazing deals on everything from clothing and jewelry to luxury cars and real estate at government sales and auctions.

We also located a lot of free stuff from private businesses, as well — gifts, samples, and discounts. How about free cosmetics, free food for your pet, and free recipes for a healthier diet? We'll show you how you can attend free performances at your local theatre, celebrate a special occasion with free gifts, or take a free vacation.

Within the pages of this book you'll find the phone numbers and addresses you need to take advantage of all these opportunities and many more. You'll also find tips on how to discover additional bargains and freebies and ways to get them quickly and easily.

Warning: This Book Is Out of Date

We live in a rapidly changing world. Your phone book is out of date as soon as you get it. Much of your newspaper is even out of date when it hits the streets. Supplies of free samples run out and discount policies are sometimes changed. There is no way anyone in book publishing can have only the most current information in print. So please be patient if you find that a telephone number, program, or policy has changed.

For a wrong number you can call the information operator in the city where the business or organization is located and ask for the new listing. If you call for a free sample and are told they have run out, ask if they have something else to offer. Chances are they'll at least send you some free or cents-off coupons. If you contact an agency and find the program you are interested in has changed, be sure to ask if they know of any other programs that might satisfy your request.

Free Stuff by Mail

A lot of neat freebies and valuable information can be ordered through the mail. It's just a matter of taking the time to write for them. But to avoid disappointment, it's important to be clear about what you are requesting and accurate in addressing the envelope. Read any requirements closely and follow them to the letter. Watch these things carefully:

RETURN CARDS AND ENVELOPES: Some of these offers may come to you with a return card or envelope already addressed. You just neatly fill in the required information. Others will require you to provide the envelope and address it. Take care to be absolutely accurate when you copy the address onto the center of the envelope. Write your return address clearly in the top left-hand corner. To be sure your writing is legible, it's usually better to print, using blue or black ink.

THE SASE (SELF-ADDRESSED STAMPED ENVELOPE): Often the instructions ask for an SASE or LSASE (long SASE). In either case, a #10 business envelope (about nine and one-half inches long) is the best size to send. Write your own address (not that of the company or organization you are writing to) both in the center and in the left hand top corner of the envelope. Write neatly in black or blue ink. Unless asked to do otherwise, put one regular postage stamp on it. Do not seal it, but it's OK to fold it to fit inside the other envelope.

WHAT ELSE GOES INSIDE? Write a clear statement of the item you are requesting. If you are sending money for postage and handling, whenever possible, write a check. If cash must be sent, try to make it bills. If coins are necessary, tape them to the letter so they won't slide around. Put these and the SASE inside the envelope addressed to the place you are mailing it. Then just seal it, stamp it, and mail it.

Sometimes a company you are writing to may have run out of supplies by the time they receive your request. If a box number was set up just for that item, your letter may be returned as undeliverable. Or they may send you free or cents-off coupons or an item similar to the one you ordered. You'll probably get something just as good or better than what you requested. But to avoid disappointment, if you have the phone number, you might want to call first to see if the offer is still good.

Write for a Sampling of Freebies

Here are some free gifts and samples you might like to have.

SPICE UP YOUR BEDROOM WITH SCENTED DRAWER LINERS. Get them from Eleni's Garden, 396 East Center, Shelley, ID 83274. Send $1.00 postage and handing.

GET A FREE RECIPE PLACE MAT FOR YOUR TABLE. You won't forget hamburger recipes when they are printed on your place mat. Just read them again while you're eating. Write to: Mine's Gotta Have Heinz, PO Box 57, Pittsburgh, PA 15230-0057.

SURPRISE YOURSELF. Maybe you'll get a sponge filled with shampoo and wax to quickly clean and shine your car. Or it might be a replica of a Chinese tapestry mounted on a plastic pin. Find out when you send a dollar for postage and handling to Surprise Gift of the Month Club, PO Box 11, Garnerville, NY 10923.

READ HELPFUL HEALTH INFO FOR MATURE ADULTS. This free booklet will help you maintain good health into the later years. Order it from

Pfizer Pharmaceuticals, PO Box 3852, Grand Central Station, New York, NY 10163.

ELVIS HAS LEFT THE POST OFFICE BUILDING. But you can attract him to your refrigerator. The Elvis stamp as a magnet is yours when you send 75 cents to Hicks Specialities, 1398 68th Lane North, Brooklyn Center, Minneapolis, MN 55430.

SEND FOR FREE DECORATIVE STICKERS. You'll receive a pack of photo memories stickers when you mail a self-addressed, stamped envelope to Fiskars, 7811 West Stewart Ave., Wausau, WI 54401.

LEARN MORE ABOUT SHOPPING FROM HOME. Do you know what your rights are under the F.T.C.'s Mail Order Merchandise Rule? You can find out when you order a free booklet, *Shopping by Phone and Mail*, from Department P, Federal Trade Commission, Washington, DC 20580.

DECORATE YOUR REFRIGERATOR DOOR. You'll be delighted with this pretty little potpourri straw hat, tied with satin ribbon, flowers, and lace. Send 50 cents for postage and handling to Valerie's Hattery, Inc., 13435 S. Cedar St., Cedar, MI 49621.

BE CRAFTY WITH YOUR CELEBRATIONS. Enjoy creating 10 projects to celebrate birthdays, Christmas, Easter and other occasions. Order this book from Crafts and Things Celebrations, 2400 Devon, Suite 375, Dept. PP397, Des Plaines, IL 60018.

☆☆☆

Toll-Free Phoning for Freebies

Just by picking up your phone you can order all kinds of samples, recipes, magazines, free coupons, and other goodies. More and more businesses can now be reached for free by dialing 1-800, 1-888, or 1-877 and the company number. Once you reach the number, it may require some more patience. But waiting through the recordings with all those choices of extensions often pays off in some really neat gifts.

Sometimes you may not hear a choice that seems to be the one you want. Usually if you just remain on the line, a real live person will talk to you. Be prepared to give your mailing address and your phone number. They may have other questions as well, such as how you learned about their product.

If they say they no longer have the sample or gift you are requesting, ask them if they have something else for free. If you hit it lucky, you might get something even better than what you called about.

Call for This Free Stuff

Here are some of the many gifts and samples that are available to you just for picking up the phone.

PRELIEF: This dietary supplement is designed to prevent heartburn by neutralizing acidic foods while you eat. For a free sample call 800-994-4711.

BIOGIME SKIN CONDITIONER: Just call 800-443-8604 to leave your name and address and you'll be sent a sample. Tell them if you want the sample for men or for women.

"HEART HEALTH IN A CAPSULE": That's what Heart Foods Company, Inc., calls this herbal supplement. They will send you a five-day supply. That's 15 capsules in a reusable pocket-size container. The capsules contain African Birdseye and East Indian Blend cayenne, garlic, hawthorn berries, onion, ginger, and lecithin. Call 800-229-3663.

REMBRANDT TOOTHPASTE: To get a free sample, call 800-548-3663. Or, if you prefer, write to Den-Mat Corporation, PO Box 1729, Santa Maria, CA 93456.

WORX: Are you getting your hands dirty from some of those hobbies you now have time to enjoy: gardening, calligraphy, maybe restoring an antique automobile? Remove the ink, grease, and grime when you get a free sample of this organic, 100-percent-biodegradable hand cleaner. Call 800-610-5907.

ALOE VERA: The Aspen Group, Inc., carries a line of natural supplements and herbal products developed by women for women. To receive a free sample of an aloe vera product, call their toll-free number 888-227-7361. For a complete listing of their merchandise, you can visit them online at <www.aspengrp.com>.

PICK-A-MEAL WHEEL: Just what you need when you are searching for an idea for a quick meal. Nabisco and Grey Poupon have designed a wheel with a selection of dinners you can prepare in 30 minutes. Call 888-476-8766.

FREE MAGAZINES: A lot of your favorite publications will give you a free sample copy. *Antique Week Magazine*, for example, will send one free when you call 800-876-5133. In some cases they do this as an introduction to a subscription. If you don't want to continue getting the magazine and paying for it, be sure to write "cancel" on the bill and return it.

CAMOCARE GOLD. Refresh your skin with products made from camomile and other natural ingredients. Call 212-860-8358 for free samples. They'll also send you $2.00-off coupons that you can use on future purchases.

Watch for other offers of free samples and gifts. You'll find them in the mail, in magazines, and on the radio or television. If there's a product you've been thinking of buying, give the company a call and ask if they have free samples you could try out first.

A Word About the Internet

In addition to the regular ("snail mail") addresses and telephone numbers, you'll find Internet addresses in this book. That's because more and more of you are finding out how exciting and beneficial going online with your computer can be. In fact, seniors make up the fastest growing population of Internet users.

If you haven't tried the Internet yet, don't feel you are being left behind. Throughout your life you have mastered many new technologies; the computer can be next. And you don't even have to have your own computer. Use one for free at your public library. They have them all hooked up, ready and waiting for you. Write down a few interesting web addresses, maybe some of the ones listed below. Take them in and ask a librarian, or media specialist, to show you how to find them. It's a very easy process once you "jump in and get your feet wet."

Or better yet, ask a grandchild to teach you. This is a great way to spend quality time together. And what a self-esteem builder for a pre-teen who can teach something new to the granddad or grandmother who has taught her so much! Let her show off her skills while you have fun learning to "surf the net."

If you already use the Internet, you'll make even better use of it with the resources in this book. But please be aware that web sites change frequently. Some may no longer exist; others may have changed addresses. Usually they'll give you the new one on the screen when they tell you the old one has changed. Internet addresses are given between the marks < and > throughout the book for both web sites and e-mail address-es. These enclosure marks are not part of the address.

There are a number of Internet web sites devoted to the more mature browser. Here are a few you'll probably enjoy checking out.

LEARN MORE ABOUT CRUISING THE INTERNET. Are you thinking about going online for the first time with your own computer or Web TV? If so, you'll get answers to most of your questions with "A Seniors' Guide to Going Online." This web site is located at <www.qni.com/~shepherd/online.htm>.

AARP (AMERICAN ASSOCIATION OF RETIRED PERSONS). offers senior benefits. AARP is the most popular membership organization for adults who are 50 and older. Find out how to join at their web site. You'll also find other interesting information as well as links to other web sites for seniors. Go to <www.aarp.org>.

REGISTER TO WIN A FREE BOOK. At the FC&A web site you can learn about our company and our other publications. While you are there, put your name in the pot for our monthly drawing for a free book. Go to <www.fca.com>.

LAUGH AT LIFE FROM A MATURE POINT OF VIEW. "The Geezer Brigade" web site is devoted to humor for older folks. Get your free laughs at web site <www.thegeezerbrigade.com>.

HAVE FUN WITH ADVENTUROUS ELDERS. "Senior Frolic" promotes itself by stating it is not a place to get advice about how to lead a more pro-ductive life during the golden years. Its menu includes entertainment, hobbies, shopping, and intrigue. Under hobbies, you can learn how to turn your dog's hair into yarn for making a vest! You'll definitely want to check out this free foolishness at <www.geocities.com/Heartland/4474/>.

MAKE YOUR POINTS FOR FREE MERCHANDISE. When you know you are ready to spend a good bit of time on the Internet, you might want to sign onto the "My Points Program." You can get points for things like clicking on an advertisement, taking a brief survey, or visiting a web site. It takes a while to accumulate points. But eventually they can be traded for merchandise and services from companies like Marriott, Sony, Barnes and Noble, Marshall's, Spiegel, T.J. Maxx, Olive Garden, and Red Lobster. To start making points, go to <www.ppi-free.com>

Find Free Magazines on the Web

Magazines frequently offer a free trial copy, hoping you'll like it and subscribe. At the time of this writing, *Sports Illustrated* is offering not one, but four free issues of their magazine. And if you subscribe, they'll give you a long sleeve, mock turtleneck shirt. This may turn out to be a short term offer, so don't be too disappointed it you get there and find the offer has changed. If this is so, they are likely to have something else for you. Be patient. There's a lot of other free stuff on the web. Go to <www.CNNSI.com>.

Another web site that regularly features free magazines recently had a free trial issue of *Catholic Digest.*. If you subscribe at a 40 percent discount, you also get a 32-page booklet *All About Angels*. See what else is available at <www.ppi-free.com>.

Good "Scents" About Samples

At the cosmetic counter in your favorite department store you can get samples of lotions, creams, and other skin care and beauty products. If the salesperson hands you just one, ask for more. With a week's supply of hand cream, for example, you can try it every day. Then you'll be better able to tell if you like it enough to buy it. (Explain that to the salesclerk, and she'll probably give you a whole handful.)

When shopping for gifts, watch for free items that come with a purchase. You'll often find those specials right before Christmas and Mother's Day. And by the way, men's cosmetics are usually about 20 percent cheaper than those made for women. So if you are a female, check out the products made for him. If you find one you like, buy it for yourself and save money.

Playtime Goodies

Do you enjoy playing board games but find that your bank is running low in Monopoly money? Or is it getting hard to make high points in Scrabble because the K's and some of the U's are missing? Before you run out and buy a whole new game, check with the manufacturer for replacement pieces.

Hasbro will send you up to 10 Scrabble tiles for free. And if a youngster in your life is missing a mustache or nose from Mr. Potato Head, they'll provide an inexpensive replacement. While you are helping the kids out, ask Bandai to send free replacements of swords and lazer guns for Power Rangers.

You can get a full pack of Monopoly money for $2. Barbie shoes, for you collectors and grandmas, can be replaced for 50 cents. If you are persistent, you'll be able to get other pieces for free or at a small price.

Call Hasbro, Kenner, and Tonka at 800-327-8264; Milton Bradley and Parker Brothers at 888-836-7025; Mattel and Tyco at 800-524-8697; Bandai at 714-816-9561. (See also chapter 18, *Freebies for Kids and Grandkids.*)

Write to the Stars

Maybe you'd like to write a fan letter or get a free autograph or photograph of a favorite celebrity. But, unfortunately, you don't know how to reach them. Chances are good you can locate them on the Internet. Here are a few addresses you might be looking for:

Alan Alda, 641 Lexington Ave., #1400, New York, NY 10022

Woody Allen, 930 5th Ave., New York, NY 10018

Kathy Bates, 6220 Del Valle, Los Angeles, CA 90048

The Honorable President Jimmy and Rosalyn Carter, 1 Woodlawn Dr., Plains, GA 31780

Annette Funicello, 16102 Sandy Lane, Encino, CA 91316

The Rev. Billy Graham, PO BOX 779, Minneapolis, MN 55440

Tom Hanks, PO Box 900, Beverly Hills, CA 90213

Sophia Loren, La Concordia Ranch, 1151 Hidden Valley Rd., Thousand Oaks, CA 91361

Denzel Washington, 4701 Sancola, Toluca Lake, CA 91602

Henry Winkler, 1122 S. Robertson Blvd., #15, Los Angeles, CA 90035

You'll also find lots more addresses at this web site <www.addresses.site2go.com>.

If you prefer to write, you can get 10 celebrity addresses for free by mail. Just send a long, self-addressed, stamped envelope to Michael

Levine, The Address Book, Los Angeles, Ca 90036.

A Potpourri of Sachet Recipes

Fill small cotton, linen, or silk bags with rosebuds and petals, cinnamon chips, and other sweet-smelling ingredients. Tie them with ribbon or Victorian lace and place them in your drawers or on your shelves. Or give them as lovely gifts to friends who'll think of you when they open their closet doors. For over 40 free potpourri recipes, go to <www.sfherb.com> or call 415-861-4440.

Sample Some Sumptuous Treats

How would you like to receive free samples of special foods from gourmet shops in New York City? Every month three lucky winners get goodies delivered to their homes. And there's no delivery charge. You become eligible to win when you sign the guest book at <www.nycfood.com>.

Fix Your Car for Free

More than 500 secret automobile warranties are deliberately being kept from the public, according to the Center for Auto Safety (CAS) in Washington, D.C. These warranties cover defects in specific cars that the manufacturer knew about — but didn't necessarily tell you about — when you bought the car. And the manufacturer should fix those problems for free. Why are these valuable warranties kept secret? Because, in all but four states, there are no laws requiring the automaker to tell you about them. That's where the Center for Auto Safety comes in. The Center is a non-profit organization that fights for your rights as a consumer. They have a record of every secret warranty out there and will gladly share this information with you whether your car's gone kaput or not.

To find out if your car company is keeping secrets from you, check the CAS website at <www.autosafety.org> or send a self-addressed, business-size envelope (stamped with 55 cents postage) to CAS Consumer Packets,

2001 S Street NW, Washington, D.C. 20009. Include a note that lists the year, make, and model of the car as well as a description of the problem your car is having (if any).

If you discover that your car's problem is covered by a secret warranty, talk to your dealer, show him the report, and ask him to fix it for free. If your dealer refuses, call the manufacturer's customer service number.

If you feel you haven't been treated fairly, contact The Center for Auto Safety for additional assistance. Or try one of the car manufacturing customer service numbers listed below. You may have more coming to you than you think.

Buick	1-800-521-7300	**Nissan**	1-800-647-7261
Cadillac	1-800-458-8006	**Oldsmobile**	1-800-442-6537
Chevrolet	1-800-222-1020	**Pontiac**	1-800-762-2737
Ford	1-800-392-3673	**Saturn**	1-800-553-6000
GMC	1-800-462-8782	**Toyota**	1-800-331-4331
Lincoln	1-800-521-4140		

A Surprise for a Special Occasion

When someone you know is celebrating a special birthday or anniversary, delight them with a letter from the President of the United States. The recipient must be celebrating a 50th or later wedding anniversary or at least an 80th birthday. Such a letter, signed and embossed with the Presidential seal, will also be sent at the birth of a new baby. Allow four weeks advance notice. Write to The Greetings Office, The White House, Washington, DC 20500.

Gobble Some Goodies

Get in the habit of looking for samples. They usually aren't just for seniors, of course. But you have the advantage of the time and the patience to watch for them. Start at the grocery store. Go by the deli section and ask for free samples of a meat or cheese you'd like to try. Or shop late in the morning on the day your supermarket puts out samples of cheese, crackers, dips, sliced fruits and vegetables, and other goodies. Munch your way through the store and skip lunch.

★★★

At-Home Tour of the White House

If you can't visit the White House, then let the White House come to you. Free at your request is a book called *The White House, The House of the People*. It contains a room-by-room tour with beautiful full-color photographs. It also has historical information about this home of the Presidents. Write to The White House, Washington, DC 20500. For an online tour, go to the web site at <www.whitehouse.gov>.

Have Fun Making Free Holiday Ornaments

Do you like making some of your own Christmas decorations? You'll brighten your holidays when you create ornaments with these patterns and materials. They are free, but a small postage and handling fee is required.

WOODEN HOLIDAY CUTOUTS: You'll get a snowman, Christmas tree, gingerbread man, and a pumpkin to paint and decorate. Plus, you'll receive a $1.00 coupon you can use with future orders. Send $2.00 for postage and handling to AMC Woodworking, 14111 Cleobrook, Houston, TX 77070.

DOUGH DOLL ORNAMENT: Would you believe a pregnant dough doll? She's six inches long and comes with instructions for creating more dolls just like her. What a neat gift for an expectant mother! Send $1.00 to Dough Doll, PO Box 4020, Traverse City, MI 49685.

ANGEL DECORATION: With just a little painting and gluing, you can create this wooden ornament. (Paint and glue are not included.) Send a 32-cent stamp and $1.00 to Tigger's Sandbox Crafts, 1159 Miles Rd., Harlem, GA 30814.

CHRISTMAS SAMPLER: You'll get half a skein of silk floss and an instruction chart for making this handsome sampler. Just send $1.00 and a long SASE to Krenik, 3106 Timaunus Lane 101, Baltimore, MD 21244.

Free Photos of Bill, Hill, and Socks

Maybe you are a fan of the first family. Or perhaps you like just like collecting photographs of famous personalities. Whatever your reasons, you can get free photos of the President and the First Lady. You can even ask for an 8 x 10 of First Feline Socks. Or maybe you'd like a picture of Buddy, the President's canine pal. All you need to do is send a letter with your request to Presidential Correspondence, White House, Photo Department, Attention Stephen Nolet, Old Executive Office Building, Room 94, Washington, DC 20502.

View Videos of African Art

If you visit The Smithsonian's National Museum of African Art you will find a collection of over 300,000 photographic prints. But with so many choices, how do you know where to start? Before you go there in person, (or instead) you might like to borrow from their videotape collection through the education department. All you pay is the return postage. Limit your request to two videotapes. You may keep them for up to three weeks. Allow two weeks for delivery. Some titles you might choose from are:

"The Hands of the Potter"
"Masters of Brass: Lost-Wax Casting in Ghana"
"Nagayati: Arts and Architecture among the Gabra Nomads of Kenya"
"Togu Na and Cheko: Change and Continuity in the Art of Mali"

Contact the National Museum of African Art, 950 Independence Ave., SW, Washington, DC 20560; or call 202-357-4654.

Look Over Your Van Goghs and Monets

Did you know you own some of the most valuable art in the world? Well, you do. That is, you and all the other citizens of the United States. You can visit your holdings at the National Gallery of Art. But if you can't get there to see them in person, you can at least borrow slides and videos about them. The Gallery's extension programs cover topics on painting, sculpture, and architecture from different cultures. They include artists' biographies and studies of particular styles of art. These video and slide programs are available for free to groups and individuals. You may keep them for up to five days and must provide return postage. For an Extensions Program catalogue, write to the Department of Education

Resources, Extension Programs Section, National Gallery of Art, Washington, DC 20565.

Fly a Flag for a Friend

No need to struggle looking for the right present for a patriotic friend or relative. As a special gift, you can purchase an American flag and have it flown over the Capitol in his or her honor. It comes with a certificate verifying the date on which the flag was flown and the name of the person it was flown for.

You can request a specific date, such as a birthday or anniversary. Although these flags are not free, they are a good bargain. They cost between $6.50 and $18.50, depending on the size and material. There are some additional charges as well. For the flying and certifying, add $4.05, and for mailing, $3.25. They can be purchased by contacting the office of your Senator or Representative at The Capitol, Washington, DC 20510; or call 202-224-3121. If you need the name of your senator or representative, you can get it at this number.

Uncle Sam Will Keep You Warm This Winter

Free firewood is yours for the asking from one of the 154 National Forests and other public lands. Simply call your local forest ranger to find out how to go about claiming it.

You can also check with builders on nearby construction sites. They frequently have to cut down trees to make way for a new house or other building. They may be happy to have you take the wood away. Even if you have to pay someone to help you cut and haul it home, you'll still get a bargain.

Do you want to know more about how to select and get the best use from firewood? The National Forest Service can help you out with free information. Write Firewood #559, Forest Service, PO Box 2417, Washington, DC 20013.

☆☆☆

Get the Dirt and More

Did you ever watch one of those big shovels scooping up great mounds of dirt while digging a basement or foundation for a new home? How would you like to have some of that fill dirt — maybe even some top soil for your garden? Why not ask? Chances are, the builder would be happy for you to take it away.

And are you looking for free fertilizer for your plants? Manure, too, may be yours for the asking. Check with your county extension agent, especially if the circus has just come to town, or with your local zoo. They often have free fertilizer you can haul away for home use.

Could you use some more trees for shade or to beautify your property? If you live in a city with a beautification program, they might provide some trees for free. Call City Hall to find out. While you are at it, check on any Arbor Day events, which usually include free seedling giveaways. And some cities will give you seedlings when you take in your Christmas tree for recycling after the holidays.

☆☆☆

Shopping With Uncle Sam

Now that you have time to hunt down bargains, it's a good time to check out those government sales you hear about. The truth is, the government has a lot of surplus and confiscated property that it passes on to the public at these sales and auctions. They attract a lot of people, and you might as well be among them. Here are some of the main ones. You can get more information about these and other government sales at the web site <www.treas.gov>.

GOING ONCE, GOING TWICE— SOLD! Whatever you are looking for, chances are good you'll find it at one of Uncle Sam's auctions. They have fancy cars and luxury homes confiscated by the IRS, U.S. Customs Service, and other government agencies from drug dealers and tax dodgers. You'll find diamond rings, fine linens, coins, carpets, electronics, and clothing. Look for airplanes, boats, and commercial real estate as well. Sometimes the prices are amazingly low!

Regularly scheduled auctions are held approximately every nine weeks at sales centers in the following cities: Edison, New Jersey; Miami or Fort Lauderdale, Florida; El Paso, Texas; Los Angeles , California, and Nogales, Arizona. Vehicle auctions are held every four weeks in Chula

17

Vista, California. Other sales are held in other locations from time to time as well. Flyers are mailed every two weeks to subscribers to the Subscription Program. For information contact EG&G Dynatrend, 3702 Pender Dr., Suite 400, Fairfax, VA 22030; phone 703-273-7373; or online at <www.treas.gov/auctions/>.

DEFEND YOUR RIGHT TO SAVE. What the Department of Defense has for sale might surprise you. With all the cutbacks taking place, you can now buy tents, sporting equipment, computers, horses, furniture, telephone systems, and photographic equipment. They even have B-52s and entire military bases for sale! The merchandise is sold at over 200 locations worldwide.

Information on local and national sales is available in the free booklet *How To Buy Surplus Personal Property From DoD.* To obtain your booklet, write Battlecreek Federal Center, Marketing Dept., 74 Washington Ave. North, Battlecreek, MI 49017-3084. (Be sure to give the title of the publication along with your name and address.) Or you can call 888-352-9333 (press 2).

YOUR SAVINGS ARE IN THE MAIL. You can get great bargains at Mail Recovery Centers. At one time or another, almost everything is shipped by mail, including the latest CDs, videos, books, toys, ostrich eggs, and even suits of armor. When items are damaged or the U.S. Postal Service can't deliver packages, they collect in the back of post offices and eventually get auctioned off. To find out when auctions are being held, write to the manager of the Mail Recovery Center listed below that is nearest you.

Atlanta Mail Recovery Center, PO Box 4416, Atlanta, GA 30336-9590

San Francisco Mail Recovery Center, PO Box 7872, San Francisco, CA 94120-7872

St. Paul Mail Recovery Center, 443 Fillmore Ave. E, St. Paul, MN 55107-9607

CASH IN ON BANKING PROBLEMS. Tired of putting money into a bank and not seeing much in return? The Federal Deposit Insurance Corporation (FDIC) sells a wide variety of assets from failed banks including loans, real estate such as undeveloped land, hotels, shopping malls, single-family homes, condominiums, and apartment complexes. They even sell personal property including computers, phone systems, furniture, fixtures, plants, and more.

For information about the sales, contact the FDIC, 550 17th St., NW, Washington, DC 20429-9990; phone 202-736-0000.

☆☆☆

Someone's Loss Is Your Treasure

Have you ever lost something valuable while traveling by plane: an expensive camera, a leather briefcase, a piece of designer jewelry, or maybe a pair of skis? It seems hard to believe that good stuff like that could get lost and never be claimed, but it does. And a lot of it winds up in Scottsboro, Alabama at the Unclaimed Baggage Center. They handle over a million lost items each year. You'll get some good deals on used, but valuable, items. This is not, however, the place to call if you are trying to locate a lost item. By the time it reaches them there is no way the original owner can be identified. To find out more, especially about their special sales, contact them at 509 West Willow Street, Scottsboro, AL 35768; phone 256-259-1525; or online at <www.unclaimedbaggage.com>.

Passport to Travel Savings

You can learn what John Glenn discovered at age 77: It's never too late to travel. Of course you can't expect to cover the miles our senior astronaut logged aboard the space shuttle Discovery. But wherever you travel far or near, whether you take to the skies or head out on the highways, the retirement years are a great time for exploration.

Perhaps you want to return to where you were born or pay a visit to the grandkids. Maybe friends from long ago have invited you to visit. On the other hand, maybe you are looking for adventure with no particular destination in mind. Whatever your reason to travel, at long last you have the free time to do it.

With this new freedom to come and go as you please you have more choices. You can relax quietly in a favorite get-away spot while the crowds swarm to the major tourist attractions. You can wait for the end of the season to avoid those long lines and take advantage of cooler weather and discounted prices.

But wait a minute. You don't have to wait for the off-season to get bargains anymore. You can get free opportunities and discounted prices year-round. No matter what the season, your biggest decision is, "Where do I want to go next?"

With all the possibilities at home and abroad, your neighbors will wonder where you moved to! So get busy planning your itinerary. And bon voyage!

Come on and Take a Free Ride

The view from the air will be even more exciting when you are traveling free or at a low fare. Over the years you've probably developed the patience to wait for just the right deal. Well, here are some to watch for and maybe wait for.

GET FREE FLIGHTS BY BUILDING UP FREQUENT FLYER MILES. You may think that you don't fly often enough to build up bonus miles. But you never know. If you fly once, chances are, in this changing world, you'll fly again. And it may be sooner than you think. So tell your travel agent you want to accumulate miles. Or call the airline you are using and tell them you'd like to sign up for their frequent flyer program.

If you do a lot of flying, you might want to use a credit card that gives free frequent flyer miles. But watch out for high interest rates on these cards. Because they tend to be as much as 40 percent higher than some credit cards, you'd need to use it a lot or pay it off every month to come out ahead.

"BUMP" INTO A FUTURE FREE FLIGHT. Airlines often sell more seats than they have on a particular flight. That's because some people make a reservation and then don't show up. If everyone does show up, there's not enough room. So sometimes while you are waiting for a flight you'll hear an announcement that the flight is overbooked. They'll ask for volunteers to give up their seats. They give these passengers seats on the next flight to their destination. Usually they also get a free ticket for another trip on that airline, and it's generally good for a full year.

So why not try to get "bumped" on a flight when you aren't in a particular hurry? Here's how you can increase your chances. When you call for reservations, ask which flight is already most nearly full. Reserve a seat on that one. Then arrive early at the gate and tell the agent that you are willing to give up your seat if the flight is overloaded.

Odds are you'll be delayed only a few hours in getting to your destination. And you'll arrive with a free ticket for a future flight in hand.

FLY AS A COURIER. Sometimes international companies need to ship packages quickly. They can avoid delays by sending items as a passenger's baggage rather than shipping them as cargo. So they buy a ticket and send a courier who sits in a seat but gives up their baggage allowance for the company's use.

Some companies hire full-time couriers who fly absolutely free. But they usually deliver a package and return home immediately. They also use individuals who want to get a vacation out of the deal. These couriers generally pay something for the ticket. But it's still a bargain. The only catch is you must manage to get by with taking only what you can put in a carry-on bag. (This is easier when traveling in warm rather than cold climates. Those winter clothes take up a lot of space.)

You may even be able to convince the courier company, if they are in a pinch, to give you a free ticket. Look in your phone book under "Air courier service" for the names of local companies. Give them a call to see how you can sign up as a courier.

WIN A FREE TICKET, BUT BE SURE IT'S ON THE LEVEL. Last night you got a call about a free weekend in Las Vegas. The caller seemed so sincere and the trip sure sounded like fun. But not all cheap vacation offers turn out to be good deals. So before you sign up and fly across the country, get some free advice about dealing with travel schemes.

The Federal Trade Commission will send you this advice in a free pamphlet, *Telemarketing Travel Fraud*. It provides information and tips to help prevent your being taken in by swindlers who are interested in only one thing — your money. Contact Public Reference, Room 130, Federal Trade Commission, 600 Pennsylvania Ave. NW, Washington, DC 20580; 202-326-2222; or online at <www.ftc.gov>.

AIRLINE DISCOUNTS. Most airlines offer a 10 percent discount to seniors. But you may get bigger savings by joining an airline's discount club. In most cases you buy a book of coupons that save you quite a bit more than 10 percent. Costs and policies (days when you can and can't travel, required length of stay, companion fares) change from time to time. So call the airline that flies from your city to the locations you want to visit.

Sometimes they may say they aren't currently accepting new members. In that case, ask to be put on their waiting list. To get the details, call:

AActive American Traveler Club, American Airlines, 800-421-5600

Senior Citizen Desk, Continental Airlines, 800-441-1135

Skywise, Delta Airlines, 800-325-3750

Silver Wings, United Airlines, 800-720-1765

Compassionate fares are available with most major airlines in case of an emergency involving serious illness or death. Discounts range from 35 to 70 percent.

Know Your Rights and Check Their Wrongs

Don't assume that the airlines will offer you everything that's due you if there are problems getting you to your destination. The free booklet *Fly Rights: A Consumer's Guide to Air Travel* will tell you what your rights are so you can ask for what you are entitled to by law. Write Superintendent of Documents, PO Box 371954, Pittsburgh, PA 15250-7954. Phone 202-512-1800.

And if you want to know the statistics about an airline's delayed and canceled flights, lost luggage, and customer complaints, write for the free booklet *Air Travel Consumer Report*. Get it from the Aviation Consumer Protection Division, US Department of Transportation, C-75

Room 4107, Washington, DC 20590. Phone 202-366-2220.

All Aboard for 15% Discounts

Traveling by train can make getting there a lot of fun. So park the car in the garage and climb aboard. No worrying about maps or empty gas tanks. Sit back, relax, and enjoy the view of our beautiful countryside.

If you are 62 or older you can save 15 percent on the lowest available fare to wherever you want to go on AMTRAK. Call their toll-free hotline for a free travel planner. It tells about their services and includes a listing of their special vacation packages. And it offers travel tips as well. Contact AMTRAK Customer Relations, 60 Massachusetts Ave., NE, Washington, DC 20002; 800-USA-RAIL.

And when you arrive at a destination, check on discount fares with the local transportation system. In Atlanta, for example, MARTA, the rapid transit system, offers a half-fare card for seniors 65 and over.

Free as a Breeze

Does a cruise aboard a luxury liner seem exciting, but you think it's too expensive for your pocketbook? Well, think again. You can cruise absolutely free. There are several ways to do it. One is to get a job as a crew member. But chances are, you love your freedom too much to make that kind of commitment. Well, there are other ways that don't tie you to a long-term schedule.

People on cruises are on the ship a lot of hours between stops at ports-of-call. They can't spend all that time eating and looking at the water. The cruise directors need a wide variety of activities to keep passengers happy. So they look for people who can entertain or teach something. Do you know a foreign language or how to arrange dried flowers? Are you an expert in money management or can you show slides and talk about growing herbs in your garden? Are you a whiz at embroidery or interior decorating? Or maybe you're more of an entertainer, experienced in singing, dancing, or telling jokes. If you have a skill or a talent, why not share it with others on a cruise ship? Then you can freely enjoy the rest of your cruise time.

It's even easier if you are a charming, well groomed older male. You can sign on as a gentleman escort. There are a lot more golden-age women than men on most cruises. So extra men are frequently given free passage in exchange for socializing with the female guests. You must be a good dancer and able to carry on an interesting conversation. Being a good bridge player helps, too.

Don't worry that this is a shady deal of some sort. Escorts are counseled not to give too much attention to any one passenger. They are expected to be gracious and friendly with everyone and to be gentlemen at all times.

For more information, call one of these cruise lines or ask a travel agent to recommend others.

American Classic Voyages, 312-466-6000

Bergen Line, 212-319-1300

Carnival Cruise Lines, 305-599-2600

Crystal Cruises, 310-785-9300

Princess Cruises, 310-553-1770

"Sea" Your Way Clearly

A cruise sounds like the ideal vacation. But your "free and easy" spirit finds the idea of spending even part of your time working too confining. You prefer to kick back, enjoy the breeze, maybe dance until dawn, even if you have to pay for it. Okay, but be sure you ask for a seniors' discount.

To find out how to get the most from your cruise, order the free information in *101 Tips for the Mature Traveler* from Grand Circle Travel, 347 Congress St., Boston, MA 02210. Phone 800-248-3737.

Another number to call for a free vacation planner is 888-Y-CRUISE (927-8473).

Live Like the Locals for Free

Travel is much more fascinating when you get to know how people live in the area you are visiting. It's fun to meet everyday people in the local shops, at a community festival, or at a church service. One of the best ways to do this, and get free lodging at the same time, is to do a home swap. You stay in someone's home in another city, state, or country, and they travel to where you live and stay in your home.

Nobody pays for lodging. There are three main ways to do this:

SWAP WITH SOMEONE YOU KNOW. Do you have a friend or relative who lives in a place you'd like to visit? Make arrangements to coordinate your vacations for a home exchange. Or perhaps your next-door neighbor has relatives who live across the country. Maybe you could swap houses with them for a week or two. Your neighbors would probably love this arrangement — having relatives nearby but not underfoot. So they are likely to do everything they can to help you work out the details.

PLACE A CLASSIFIED AD IN THE PAPER in the town you'd like to visit. State the dates you can come, how many people you'll bring, and any other requirements (like being close to public transportation). Mention what you have to offer in exchange. Tell what's unique about your home or town and how many people your house will comfortably accommodate. Include any specific requirements or limitations — like no pets, for example.

JOIN A HOME-EXCHANGE CLUB. These membership groups don't actually arrange the exchange for you. They just publish the information in a directory. You pay a fee and your information is published and you receive the next issue or issues for a year. It is your responsibility to contact the owners of a home that interests you or to respond to those who contact you. (Some will let you list your RV as well.)

Try one of these:

Intervac US, 30 Corte San Fernando, Tiburon, CA 94920. Call 415-435-3497 or 800-756-4663. E-mail < IntervacUSaol.com> (Offers a discount to seniors and will send a free info packet.)

Trading Homes International, PO Box 787, Hermosa Beach, CA 90254. Phone 800-877-8723. <www.trading-homes.com>

Homelink International, PO Box 650, Key West, FL 33041. Phone 800-638-3841. < www.swapnow.com>

Free Speech, Free Travel

Did you know that the government might pay you $50 a day to teach kids in Tanzania to throw a shot putt, or $100 a day to talk about women's rights in Bangladesh? And they'll foot the bill for your round-trip airfare as well.

If you have had a unique American experience or hold a particular expertise, you can join the likes of Sandra Day O'Connor, Sally Ride, and John Updike. They are just a few of those who have taken part in the U.S. Speakers Program. You will get a chance to meet with government officials, journalists, labor leaders, students, entrepreneurs, and anyone who wants to know more about the United States.

Every year about 600 Americans are sent overseas for short-term speaking programs. If selected, you could be eligible to receive $100 a day, plus expenses. A U.S. Speaker's tour generally includes informal lectures or discussions, followed by questions and answers with a small group of experts.

No, you cannot teach golf in Paris. This program is for bonafide experts in a field. For more information, contact U.S. Speakers Program, U.S. Information Agency, 301 4th St., SW, Room Fourth Floor North, Washington, DC 20547; 202-619-4764.

Play the Leading Lady

You don't have to be an expert in travel or in anything else to act as a travel tour guide. This is a great way to get to travel abroad and get paid for it. You may have the idea that these are jobs for younger folk. But the fact is, most companies prefer the over 50 female. Sorry, fellas. You may have to do a harder selling job to land one of these tour guide positions.

Managers say they prefer someone who has a lot of enthusiasm for helping people. So when you apply, stress your nurturing qualities and experiences. This is what they are looking for more than your love for travel.

These are mostly seasonal opportunities, which is great if you prefer part-time work. For more information check with these companies:

Collette Tours, 180 Middle Street, Pawtucket, RI 02860, 401-727-9000.

Maupintour, 1421 Research Park Drive, Suite 300, Lawrence, KS 66049, 785-331-1000.

Allied Tours, 165 West 46th Street, 10th Floor, New York, NY 10036, 212-869-5100.

Globus & Cosmos, 5301 S. Federal Circle, Littleton, CO 80123, 800-851-0728

Still the Toughest Job You'll Ever Love

When President Kennedy began the Peace Corps in 1961, perhaps you were tempted to join, but you already had family responsibilities. Now that you're retired, you have free time and guess what? The Peace Corps is still around, and still asking for volunteers. It's a great way to see the world for free and make a contribution to global unity. Don't let your age hold you back, either. The Peace Corps isn't just for college students. Today, seven percent of volunteers are over age 50.

As a volunteer you will serve for two years, living among the native people and becoming part of the community. The Peace Corps sends volunteers throughout Latin America, Africa, the Near East, Asia, the Pacific, and Eastern Europe to share their expertise in education, agriculture, health, economic development, urban development, and the environment.

To learn more about serving the world, contact Peace Corps, 1990 K St., NW, Washington, DC 20526; 800-424-8580; or online at <www.peacecorps.gov>.

If you have already been a Peace Corps volunteer, the Corps could use your help again. Returning volunteers can contact Peace Corps — Crisis Corps, 1111 20th St. NW, Washington, DC 20526; e-mail: <crisiscorps @peacecorps.gov>; phone 800-424-8580, extension 2.

Learning: a Life-Long Pursuit

Lots of seniors are proving that you can continue to learn as long as you live. Every year over 270,000 Americans who are 55 years of age or older participate in study-travel programs as part of Elderhostel.

Nearly 2,000 educational institutions offer Elderhostel programs which include classes, field trips, and social activities. Participants can study topics from astronomy to zoology, both in the U.S. and abroad. The cost of participation varies, but includes accommodations, meals, instruction, and field trips at bargain prices.

If you know any sharp and deserving but needy older persons, suggest they look into "Hostelships." These scholarships pay all expenses for those who meet the requirements.

Contact: Elderhostel, 75 Federal Street, Boston, MA 02110-1941. Call toll-free at 877-426-8056. <www.elderhostel.org>.

Traveling in the Land of the Free

Being a senior citizen in the USA opens up a lot of opportunities to enjoy the natural wonders and historic places of our country. And Uncle Sam foots the bill for a lot of it. So enjoy exploring the charms of our 50 states!

THE GOLDEN AGE PASSPORT will get you Yellowstone, Yosemite, Mount Rainier, and a great deal more for $10. Now that's quite a bargain! But it's true. Seniors aged 62 or older pay only $10 for a lifetime pass to the National Park Service's parks, monuments, historic sites, recreation areas, and national wildlife refuges.

You must purchase this pass in person at any National Park Service entrance fee area. If you enter in a private vehicle, the Golden Age Passport admits you and the other passengers. Otherwise, the pass covers the entry fee for you, your spouse, your children, and your parents.

The Golden Age Passport also entitles you to a 50 percent discount on most fees for facilities and services, such as camping, swimming, parking, boat launching, and cave tours.

The National Parks Service also operates campgrounds and other visitor facilities at the parks. Reservations can be made by calling 800-365-2267.

You can use the Internet to learn more about the National Parks and other government recreational facilities listed below, at a very user-friendly site: <www.recreation.gov>.

For a complete catalog of publications about the various parks, including a map and guide, contact the National Park Service, Office of Information, PO Box 37127, Washington, DC 20013; 202-208-4747; or online at <www. nps.gov>.

THE U.S. ARMY CORPS OF ENGINEERS owns thousands of square miles of some of the best recreational areas in the country. Now, who would have thought that spending time on property owned and operated by the U.S. Army could be fun? Boot camp for seniors? Far from it. You can relax and enjoy picnic areas, swimming beaches and hiking trails. Or maybe you'd prefer canoeing, ice fishing, hunting, or snowmobiling.

For a kit that includes maps and information about services and phone numbers at each recreational site, contact U.S. Army Corps of Engineers, Directorate of Civil Works, Natural Resources Management Branch, CECW-ON, 20 Massachusetts Ave., NW, Washington, DC 20314-1000; 202-761-0247. <www.recreation.gov>.

TWO NATIONAL WILDLIFE RESERVES, in Oklahoma and Nebraska, provide the chance to see buffalo, Texas longhorn cattle, deer, elk, and other wildlife in their natural habitat.

For more information, contact Fort Niobrara National Wildlife Refuge, Hidden Timber Route, HC 14, Box 67, Valentine, NE 69201, 402-376-3789; or Wichita Mountains Wildlife Refuge, Rt. 1, Box 448, Indiahoma, OK 73552; 405-429-3221. Another resource is National Bison Range, Moise, MT 59824; 406-644-2211.

NATIONAL FOREST RECREATION SITES offer a good place to pull in for a night where you can enjoy the sights and sounds of nature. (Who needs marble bathrooms, a king-size bed, or room service to have an ideal vacation?)

You can phone the Forest Service toll-free hotline to make a reservation at one of the 156 National Forests. There are over 100,000 miles of trails and 10,000 recreation sites where you can hike, fish, camp, ski, or just relax. Call the toll-free number to make reservations for any of the National Forests at 800-280-CAMP; or online at <www.fs.fed.us>.

THE BUREAU OF LAND MANAGEMENT (BLM) PUBLIC LANDS include campgrounds, visitors' centers, national wild and scenic rivers, national wilderness areas, and national historic and scenic trails.

For a recreation guide, contact Office of Public Affairs, Bureau of Land Management, U.S. Department of the Interior, 18th and C Sts., NW, Washington, DC 20240; 202-452-5125; or online at <www.blm.gov>.

See it for Free in D.C.

You've sent a lot of tax dollars to Washington, D.C. over the years. Why not spend a vacation with some of the fruits of your taxes? This city probably has more things to do for free than any other city in the U.S., so go visit what you helped pay for.

MAKE A MILLION DOLLARS. Or watch someone else do it — literally. Take a free self-guided tour at the Bureau of Engraving and Printing. There you'll see money being printed, cut, and counted right before your eyes. Although the armed guards discourage sampling the goods, you can still enjoy yourself by buying uncut sheets of currency, engraved prints, small bags of shredded currency, and other neat stuff.

For more information, contact the Bureau of Engraving and Printing, U.S. Department of Treasury, 14th and C Sts., SW, Washington, DC 20228;

202-874-3019; or online at <www.dep.treas.gov>.

TAKE A VIP TOUR OF THE WHITE HOUSE. Don't stand in that long line at the White House waiting to see the First Lady's china pattern, or the Prez's jogging shoes. Do what the insiders do: call your member of Congress and join the special VIP tours. They are held every Tuesday through Saturday from 10:00 a.m. to 12 noon, unless the White House is closed for some official function. Who knows? You might even see Newt Gingrich's mother waiting in line with you.

To learn about the White House tours, contact White House, 1600 Pennsylvania Ave., NW, Washington, DC 20500; 202-456-7041. To make a reservation, contact your Senator or Representative, The Capitol, Washington, DC 20515; 202-224-3121; or online at <www.whitehouse.gov>.

MOSEY THROUGH MUSEUMS. You can view dresses worn by the nation's First Ladies and see paintings by famous artists. You'll find impressive portraits of prominent people from history and admire antique cars and airplanes.

Sixteen museums, galleries, and the National Zoo make up The Smithsonian Institution. Most are open daily, year-round except Christmas, from 10:00 a.m. to 5:30 p.m. Call 202-357-2700 for general information. For recorded information, call Dial-a-Museum at 202-357-2020.

WATCH YOUR CONGRESSMAN AT WORK. The U.S. House of Representatives meets in the House Chamber in the south wing of the Capitol. You can be seated in the side or rear gallery while Congress debates the pros and cons of bills they are considering.

Seats are available to those who secure passes from their Representative on a first come, first served basis. Contact your member of Congress, U.S. House of Representatives, Washington, DC 20515; 202-224-3121; or online at <www. house.gov>.

HEAR FREE CONCERTS. If listening to five hours of debate over Social Security isn't music to your ears, then you might want to check out the American Festival/Concerts at the Capitol performed by the National Symphony during the spring and summer months.

The Armed Service bands and choral groups of the Air Force, Army, Marine Corps, and Navy also provide summer nighttime entertainment. Concerts are free, seating is on the lawn, and picnics are in order. Contact Architect of the Capitol's Office, Room SB-15, U.S. Capitol Bldg., Washington, DC 20515; 202-228-1793.

FROLIC AMONG THE FLOWERS. Take a break from traffic and history-in-the-making with at least a pleasant stroll (if not a frolic) through the

Botanic Garden. It is open to the public from 9:00 a.m. to 9:00 p.m. daily, June through August, and from 9:00 a.m. to 5:00 p.m. the rest of the year.

Contact Public Programs Office, U.S. Botanic Garden, 245 1st St., SW, Washington, DC 20024; 202-226-4082.

Magicard Saves Money at the Magic Kingdom

When making your plans to visit Disneyworld and other attractions in that vicinity, call the Orlando city tourist office for the free, money-saving Magicard. It is valid for up to six people and will save you 10 to 50 percent on admissions and purchases at 76 stores, restaurants, and attractions. You can get $2 off the Kennedy Space Center's Mission Pass. (Admission to the Space Center's Visitor's Complex is free.) And you save $3 off each admission to Sea World. As you can see, the savings can add up quickly.

You can pick up the card in person, but if you order it in advance you'll be able to plan better. Not only will they send you this free discount card, they will include a visitor's information packet containing the Official Visitor's Guide. Ask them to send a copy of the Free or Bargain ($10 and Under) list as well.

Official Visitor Center, 8723 International Drive, Orlando, FL 23819-9318. Call 800-551-0181 or e-mail them at <info@orlandocvb.com>.

☆☆☆

What Your Travel Agent Won't Tell You About Foreign Travel

Wouldn't it have been nice if someone had told you before you went to Rome that you should not keep your money and your wallet together in your purse? Who knew that those little kids didn't really want to take your picture in front of St. Peter's but wanted your money instead?

Your travel agent may not tell you things that might discourage you from traveling. But you know that if you are well informed you'll have a smoother and safer trip. So prepare yourself with the facts.

Travel Tips for Seniors is a free publication with basic information on insurance, medication, travel warnings, and passports. The pamphlet also includes information on the kinds of assistance you can expect from U.S. embassies and consulates around the world if you run into problems overseas.

For your copy, contact Overseas Citizens Services, U.S. Department of State, 2201 C St., NW, Room 4817, Washington, DC 20520; 202-647-5225; or online at <www.travel.state.gov>.

And when planning travel outside the U.S., you'll want to know about any disease outbreaks in the countries you'll be visiting. In some cases you may need to get a vaccination.

The Centers for Disease Control's Voice Information System allows anyone using a touchtone phone to get pre-recorded information on International Travelers' health issues. The system is available 24 hours a day. Contact Centers for Disease Control at 888-232-3228; or online at <www.cdc.gov>.

☆☆☆

Free Passports for Families
of Deceased Veterans

Unfortunately there isn't a discount for seniors on the cost of a passport. But did you know that you can get one free of charge if you are a member of a family visiting the overseas grave site of a veteran?

To be eligible for a free passport, you must be the spouse, parent, child, sister, brother, or guardian of the deceased who is buried or commemorated in a permanent American military cemetery on foreign soil.

The American Battle Monuments Commission maintains cemeteries around the world where 124,921 U.S. war dead are interred. Each year the Commission publishes free pamphlets which highlight individual memorials. They include locations, site descriptions and photographs, and brief histories of the battles in which the deceased fought. You'll also get directions to the sites from the nearest major airports.

For additional information, write to the American Battle Monuments Commission, 2300 Clarendon Blvd., Suite 500, Arlington, VA 22201; 703-696-6897.

Take a Free Read

A number of travel magazines and newsletters will send you a free issue if you write or call with your request. Check out some of these:

Consumer Reports Travel Letter, PO Box 53629, Boulder, CO 80322-3629; 800-234-1970.

La Belle France, PO Box 3485, Charlottesville, VA 22903; 800-225-7825.

Passport, 401 North Franklin St, Third Floor, Chicago, IL 60610; 312-464-0300.

Scenic Walking, 703 Palomar Airport Rd.,Suite 200,Carlsbad, CA 92009; 800-473-1210

Travel Smart, 40 Beechdale Rd., Dobbs Ferry, NY 10522; 800-327-3633.

Pick a Free Vacation Pack

A lot of places will send you packets of information about a particular type of travel. Check out some of these and look for more in magazines and at travel agencies.

Vacation Directory to the Cherokee Indian Reservation in the Great Smoky Mountains National Park on the Blue Ridge Parkway. Contact: Cherokee Indian Reservation, PO Box 460-78, Cherokee, NC 28719; 800-438-1601; <www.cherokee-nc.com>.

The Best of Golf in Scotland, Ireland, England, and Portugal, Owenoak International, 40 Richards Ave., Norwalk, CT 06854; 800-426-4498.

Caribbean Vacation Planner, Caribbean Coalition for Tourism, 800-356-9999, ext. 450.

Europe Through the Back Door has information about Europasses, Eurail passes, and other passes for most countries of Europe. ETBD, Box 2009, Edmonds, WA 98020.

Travel to Africa and Turkey tells you about trips that take you to out-of-the-way places you might otherwise miss. Overseas Adventure Travel, 625 Mt. Auburn St., Cambridge, MA 02138.

Hotlines for Some Hot Places

Is it your dream to spend your vacation seeing the sights of New York City, visiting Native American festivals in the pueblos of New Mexico, or checking out Bill Clinton's birthplace in Arkansas? Whatever U.S. state or territory you are planning to visit, begin with a call to the Travel and Tourism Office hotline listed below.

As you scout out a particular city, they'll help you find hotels, restaurants, movie theaters, supermarkets, drug stores, churches, and historic places of interest. And they can tell you about special discounts and programs for seniors.

Other information from state tourism offices might include highway conditions and weather advice. In general, each state will provide an information package containing a travel guide, a calendar of events, state maps, and brochures from private, state, and regional tourist attractions.

State Tourism Offices

Alabama
334-242-4169, 800-ALABAMA,
< www.touralabama.org>

Alaska
907-465-2012, <www.commerce.
state.ak.us>

American Samoa
684-633-1091-2-3

Arizona
602-230-7733, 800-824-8257,
<www.arizonaguide.com>

Arkansas
501-682-1088, 800-NATURAL,
<www.ono.com/arkansas>

California
916-322-2881, 800-TO-CALIF,
<gocalif.ca.gov>

Colorado
303-592-5510, 800-COLORADO
<www.state.co.us>

Connecticut
800-CT-BOUND,
<www.state.ct.us/tourism. htm>

Delaware
800-441-8846, 302-739-4271,
<www.de.state.us>

District of Columbia
202-789-7000,
<www.washington.org>

Florida
904-488-5607, 888-735-2872,
<www.fla.us.com>

Georgia
404-656-3553, 800-VISIT-GA,
<www.georgiaonmymind. com>

Guam
671-66-5278-79, 800-US3-GUAM

Hawaii
808-586-2550,

Idaho
208-334-2470, 800-635-7820,
<www.visitid.org>

Illinois
312-814-4732, 800-226-6632,
<www.enjoyillinois.com>

Indiana
317-232-8860, 800-824-8376,
<www.indianatourism.com>

Iowa
515-242-4705, 800-345-4692,
<www.state.ia.us/tourism>

Kansas
913-296-2009, 800-2KANSAS,
<www.kansascommerce.com>

Kentucky
502-564-4930, 800-225-TRIP,
<www.state.ky.us./tour/
tour.htm>

Louisiana
504-568-6968, 800-33-GUMBO,
<www.louisianatravel.com>

Maine
207-289-5710, 800-533-9595
<www.state.me.us>

Marianas
670-234-8327

Maryland
410-767-6277, 800-543-1036,
<www.mdisfun.org>

Massachusetts
617-727-3201, 800-447-MASS,
<www.mass_travel.com>

Michigan
517-373-0670, 800-543-2937,
<www.michigan.org>

Minnesota
612-296-2755, 800-657-3700,
<www.exploreminnesota. com>

Mississippi
800-WARMEST, 601-359-3297,
<www.mississippi.org>

Missouri
573-751-4133, 800-877-1234
<www.missouritourism.org>

Montana
406-444-2654, 800-VISIT-MT,
<www.travel.mt.gov>

Nebraska
402-471-3794, 800-228-4307,
<www.ded.state.ne.us/tourism>

Nevada
702-687-4322, 800-NEVADA8
<www.travelnevada.com>

New Hampshire
603-271-2665, 800-FUNINNH,
<www.visitnh.gov>

New Jersey
609-292-6963, 800-JERSEY7,
<www.state.nj.us>

New Mexico
800-545-2040, 505-827-7400,
<www.newmexico.org>

New York
518-474-4116, 800-CALL-NYS,
<iloveny.state.ny.us>

North Carolina
919-733-4171, 800-VISIT-NC,
<www.visitnc.com>

North Dakota
800-437-2077, 701-328-2525,
<www.ndtourism.com>

Ohio
614-466-8844, 800-BUCKEYE,

Oklahoma
405-521-3981, 800-652-6552,
<www.otrd.state.ok.us>

Oregon
800-547-7842,
<www.traveloregon.com>

Pennsylvania
717-787-5453, 800-VISIT-PA,
<www.state.pa.us>

Puerto Rico
89-721-1576-2402, 800-866-
STAR, <www.discoverpr.com>

Rhode Island
800-845-2000, 401-277-2601,
<www.visitrhodeisland.com>

South Carolina
803-734-0122, 800-364-3634,
<www.prt.state.sc.us/sc>

South Dakota
800-SDAKOTA, 605-773-3301,
<www.state.sd.us>

Tennessee
615-741-2158
<www.state.tn.us/tourdev>

Texas
512-462-9191, 800-8888-TEX,

<www.traveltex.com>

Utah
801-538-1030, 800-200-1160,
<www.utah.com>

Vermont
802-828-3236, 800-VERMONT,
<www.vermont.com>

Virginia
804-786-2051, 800-VISITVA,
<www.virginia.org>

Virgin Islands
809-774-8784, 800-372-8784
<www.usvi.net>

Washington
360-753-5600, 800-544-1800,
<www.tourism.wa.gov>

West Virginia
304-558-2286, 800-CALL-WVA,
<www.state.wv.us/tourism>

Wisconsin
608-266-2345, 800-432-TRIP,
<www.landsend.com>

Wyoming
307-777-7777, 800-225-5996,
<www.state.wy.us/
commerce/tourism/index.htm>

Tourism Offices Worldwide Directory

If you want tourism information on international destinations, visit the Tourism Offices Worldwide Directory on the Internet at: <www.mbnet.mb.ca/lucas/travel/tourism-offices.html>

Neat Things to Do With Your Free Time

You worked hard all your life and you've earned a leisurely retirement. You planned for it financially, and probably looked forward eagerly to all that free time. Now, however, you may have more free time on your hands than you know what to do with. Even if you've continued to work, perhaps you could use some fresh ideas on what to do with your spare time, without spending a lot of money. This chapter has lots of fun ideas for activities that are free or low-cost.

And remember, whenever you're out having fun — at dinner, the movies, the theater — don't forget to ask if they offer a senior discount. You might save enough to pay for the next enjoyable event.

Take a Company Tour

Going to an amusement park just doesn't excite you the way it did when you were a kid, and shelling out the outrageous ticket price really turns you off. However, you still like to be entertained. There are plenty of tours and free-to-the-public attractions that are interesting and maybe even exciting. Would you like to get a behind-the-scenes look at a company in your area? Call and see if they give tours. Here is just a sampling of a few companies that offer free or almost-free tours.

CHOCOLATE WORLD: Chocoholics beware! This tour through the world of chocolate making might just send you over the edge. Learn the history of chocolate and the Hershey company, and even get some free samples afterward. Chocolate World, 400 Park Blvd., Hershey, Pa.; free to the public, and usually open daily from 9 to 5. Phone 717-534-4900.

HARLEY DAVIDSON FACTORY: Even if you're not a leather-wearing biker, you can appreciate the craftsmanship and interesting background of the Harley Davidson motorcycle. Tours through the plant and museum are free. Call for details at 717-848-1177; Harley Davidson, 1425 Eden Rd., York, Pa.

FEDERAL RESERVE BANK: If you and some of your friends are interested in learning more about the banking system or the history of money, the Federal Reserve Bank offers tours to groups of 10 to 30 people who are high school age or older. Guided tours are by reservation only, but the Monetary Museum is open to the public on weekdays.

HERE ARE THE LOCATIONS YOU CAN VISIT:

Atlanta: 104 Marietta Street, NW, Atlanta, GA 30303-2713; phone 404-521-8267

Birmingham: 1801 Fifth Avenue, North Birmingham, AL 35203; phone 205-731-8553

Jacksonville: 800 West Water Street, Jacksonville, FL 32204; phone 904-632-1091

Miami: 9100 NW 36th Street, Miami, FL 33178-2425; phone 305-471-6290

Nashville: 301 Eighth Avenue, North, Nashville, TN 37203-4407; phone 615-251-7160

New Orleans: 525 St. Charles Avenue, New Orleans, LA 70130; phone 504-593-3246

ANHEUSER-BUSCH: Have a tee-totally good time at the Anheuser-Busch factory. You can see the famous Clydesdales in the flesh, and tour the brewing and bottling facility. Free to the public Monday through Saturday from 9 to 4; phone 314-577-2333. Located at 13th and Lynch Street, St. Louis, Mo.

THE FREEDOM CENTER: The Tribune Company, which publishes the *Chicago Tribune*, offers free tours of its printing facility. You can watch a film on the history of the *Chicago Tribune*, and then see the presses rolling. It's located at 777 W. Chicago Ave., Chicago, Ill.; reservations required; 312-222-2116.

CELESTIAL SEASONINGS: This tour may be just your cup of tea. You can even sample some of the delicious soothing varieties. Located at 4600 Sleepytime Drive, Boulder, Colo.; Monday through Saturday 10 to 3, Sunday 11 to 3; phone 800-525-0347.

BEN & JERRY'S: Do you flip for Chunky Monkey or is Cherry Garcia your favorite? If you love ice cream (and who doesn't?), you'll love this ice cream factory tour. The price is $2.00 for adults, but half the admission price is donated to charity. The factory is at Rt. 100, Waterbury, Vt. For more information call 802-244-5641.

Catch Museum Mania

You may not be able to jet to Paris to see the Mona Lisa, but it's a sure bet there are some great museums right in your area. While most will accept a donation if you want to give it, many are free to the public, and some that aren't free offer a senior discount. If you're not an art fan, don't worry; theme museums abound to appeal to all tastes. Are you interested in Native American history, geology, aviation, or oceanography? Perhaps your favorite person in history has a museum dedicated just to him or her. There may be a free museum right in your area that you need to visit, or plan to see a few on your next vacation. Here's just a sample of some free museums. For more information on museums and other attractions, call the State Tourism Offices listed at the end of the *Passport to Travel Savings* chapter.

ALASKA

Heritage Library and Museum, Northern Lights Blvd., Anchorage, Alaska; weekdays 12 to 4; 907-271-2834.

Carrie McLain Memorial Museum, 200 E. Front St., Nome, Alaska; summer: daily 9 to 6; fall, winter, and spring: Tuesday through Friday 10 to 5, Saturday 12 to 5, closed December through January; 907-443-2566.

ALABAMA

Birmingham Museum of Art, 2000 8th Avenue N., Birmingham Ala.; Tuesday through Saturday 10 to 5, Sunday 12 to 5; phone 205-254-2566.

Ft. McClellan Women's Army Corps Museum, US 431 and SR 21, Anniston, Ala.; weekdays 8 to 4, weekends by appointment; 205-237-4011.

U.S. Army Aviation Museum, SR 249, Building 6000, Fort Rucker. Ala.; open daily 9 to 4; phone 334-255-2893.

Carver Museum (George Washington Carver), Tuskegee Institute, US 29, Tuskegee Ala.; open daily 9 to 5; phone 334-727-3200.

ARIZONA

Colorado River Indian Tribes Museum and Library, 2nd and Mohave Sts, Parker, Ariz.; weekdays 8 to 5, Saturday 10 to 3; call 520-669-9211, extension 335.

Arizona Mining and Mineral Museum, 1502 West Washington St., Phoenix, Ariz.; weekdays 8 to 5, Saturday 1 to 5; phone 602-255-3791.

Phoenix Museum of History, 1002 West Van Buren St., Phoenix, Ariz.; Tuesday through Saturday 10 to 4, Sunday 12 to 4; phone 602-253-2734.

Navajo Tribal Museum, SR 264, Window Rock, Ariz.; April through October: Monday through Saturday 8 to 6; November through March:

weekdays 9 to 6; phone 520-871-6673.

Scottsdale Center for the Arts, Civic Center Plaza, Scottsdale, Ariz.; Monday through Saturday 10 to 5, Sunday 12 to 5; phone 602-994-2707.

ARKANSAS

Arkansas Arts Center, MacArthur Park, 9th & Commerce, Little Rock, Ark.; Monday through Saturday 10 to 5, Sunday 12 to 5; phone 501-372-4000.

Stuttgart Agricultural Museum, 921 East 4th St., Stuttgart, Ark.; Tuesday through Saturday 10 to 4, Sunday 1:30 to 4:30; phone 501-673-7001.

Southeast Arkansas Arts and Science Center, 200 East 8th St., Pine Bluff, Ark.; weekdays 8 to 5, Saturday 1 to 4; phone 501-536-3375.

CALIFORNIA

California Museum of Science and Industry, 700 State Dr., Los Angeles, Calif.; daily 10 to 5; phone 213-744-7400.

Marin Museum of the American Indian, Miwok Park, 2200 Novato Boulevard, Novato, Calif.; Tuesday through Friday 10 to 3, weekends 12 to 4; phone 415-897-4064.

Cable Car Museum and Powerhouse Viewing Gallery, 1201 Mason St., San Francisco, Calif.; April through October: daily 10 to 6; November through March: daily 10 to 5.

Los Angeles Maritime Museum, Berth 84, Sixth St., San Pedro, Calif.; Tuesday through Sunday 10 to 5; phone 310-458-7618.

Gatekeeper's Log Cabin Museum, SR 89, Tahoe City, Calif.; summer: daily 11 to 5; spring and fall: Wednesday through Sunday 11 to 5; phone 916-583-1762.

Albinger Archaeological Museum, 113 East Main St., Ventura, Calif.; summer: Wednesday through Sunday 10 to 4; fall, winter, and spring: weekends 10 to 4; phone 805-648-5823.

COLORADO

Leanin' Tree Museum of Western Art, 6055 Longbow Dr., Boulder, Colo.; weekdays 8 to 4:30, Saturday 10 to 4; phone 303-530-1442.

Colorado Springs Pioneer Museum, 215 S. Tejon St., Colorado Springs, Colo.; May through October: Tuesday through Saturday 10 to 5, Sunday 1 to 5; phone 719-578-6650.

Museum of the American Numismatic Association, 818 North Cascade Ave., Colorado Springs, Colo.; weekdays 8:30 to 4; phone 719-632-2646.

Peterson Air and Space Museum, US 24, Colorado Springs, Colo.; Tuesday through Friday 8:30 to 4:30, Saturday 9:30 to 4:30; phone 719-556-4915.

World Figure Skating Hall of Fame Museum, 20 First St., Colorado Springs, Colo.; summer: Monday through Saturday 10 to 4; fall, winter and spring: weekdays 10 to 4; phone 719-635-5200.

Jack Dempsey Museum, 410 Main St., Manassa, Colo.; summer: Monday through Saturday 9 to 5; phone 719-843-5207.

CONNECTICUT

Historic Ship Nautilus/Submarine Force Museum, SR 12, Groton, Conn.; daily 9 to 5, closed Tuesdays in winter; phone 800-343-0079.

Eli Whitney Museum, 915 Whitney Ave., Hamden Conn.; Wednesday through Friday and Sunday 12 to 5, Saturday 10 to 3; phone 203-777-1833.

Museum of American Political Life, 200 Bloomfield Ave., West Hartford, Conn.; Tuesday through Saturday 11 to 4; phone 860-768-4090.

DELAWARE

Zwaanendael Museum, Savannah Rd. and King's Hwy., Lewes, Del.; Tuesday through Saturday 10 to 4:30, Sunday 1:30 to 4:30; 302-645-1148.

Messick Agricultural Museum, Walt Messick Rd., Harrington, Del.; weekdays 7:30 to 5, weekends by appointment; 302-398-3729.

FLORIDA

Southeast Museum of Photography, 1200 International Speedway Blvd., Daytona Beach, Fla.; Friday 10 to 3, Tuesday 5 to 7, weekends 1 to 4; phone 904-254-4475.

National Museum of Naval Aviation, NAS Pensacola, Fla.; daily 9 to 5; phone 800-327-5002.

Water Ski Museum and Hall of Fame, 799 Overlook Drive SE, Winter Haven, Fla.; weekdays 10 to 5; phone 941-324-2472.

GEORGIA

The High Museum of Folk Art and Photography Gallery, 30 John Wesley Dobbs Ave., Atlanta, Ga.; weekdays 11 to 5; phone 404-577-6940.

Confederate Naval Museum, 202 4th-Victory Dr., Columbus, Ga.; Tuesday through Friday 10 to 5, weekends 1 to 5; phone 706-327-9798.

HAWAII

Honolulu Academy of Arts, 900 S. Beretania St., Honolulu, Hawaii; Tuesday through Saturday 10 to 4:30, Sunday 1 to 5; 808-538-3593.

ILLINOIS

Museum of Broadcast Com-munication, Chicago Cultural Center, 78 E. Washington, Chicago, Ill.; Monday through Saturday 10 to 4:30, Sunday 12 to 5; phone 312-629-6000.

Illinois Art Gallery, 100 W. Randolph St., Chicago, Ill.; weekdays 9 to 5:30; phone 312-413-5353.

Wheels Through Time Museum, Waltonville Rd., Mount Vernon, Ill.; Weekdays 8 to 5 (closed Wednesday), Saturday 8 to 4; 618-244-4116.

Moweaqua Coal Mine Museum, 129 S. Main St., Moweaqua, Ill.; April through October: daily 1 to 4; November through March: weekends 1 to 4; phone 217-768-3019.

Illinois State Museum, Capitol Complex, Springfield, Ill.; Monday through Saturday 8:30 to 5, Sunday

12 to 5; phone 217-0492-4150.

INDIANA

Evansville Museum of Arts and Science, 411 SE Riverside Dr., Evansville, Ind.; Tuesday through Saturday 10 to 5, Sunday 12 to 5; phone 812-425-2406.

National Art Museum of Sports, 850 W. Michigan St., Indianapolis, Ind.; weekdays 8 to 5; phone 317-274-2700.

Circus City Festival Museum, 154 N. Broadway, Peru, Ind.; Weekdays 9 to 4; phone 317-472-3918.

IOWA

The Farm House Museum, Knoll Rd., Ames, Iowa; March through December: Tuesday, Thursday, and Sunday 12 to 4; phone 515-294-3342.

National Balloon Museum, 1601 N. Jefferson Ave., Indianola, Iowa; weekdays 9 to 4, Saturday 10 to 4, Sunday 1 to 4; phone 515-961-3714.

Telephone Museum, 105 W. Harrison St., Jefferson, Iowa; weekdays 9 to 5; phone 515-386-2626.

Iowa Great Lakes Maritime Museum, US 71 & Lake St., Okoboji, Iowa; summer: daily 10 to 8:30; fall, winter, and spring: weekends 1 to 4; phone 712-332-5159.

KANSAS

Greyhound Racing Hall of Fame, 407 Buckeye Ave., Abilene, Kan.; April through November: daily 9 to 8; December through March: daily 9 to 5; phone 913-263-3000.

United States Cavalry Museum, Building 205, Sheridan & Custer Ave., Fort Riley, Kan.; Monday through Saturday 9 to 4:30, Sunday 12 to 4:30; phone 913-239-2737.

Frontier Army Museum, Gibbon and Reynolds Ave., Leavenworth, Kan.; weekdays 9 to 4, Saturday 10 to 4, Sunday 12 to 4; phone 913-684-3767.

KENTUCKY

Bardstown Historical Museum, 114 N. 5th St., Bardstown, Ky.; May through October: Monday through Saturday 9 to 5, Sunday 1 to 5; November through April: Monday through Saturday 10 to 4, Sunday 1 to 4; phone 502-348-2999.

Colonel Sanders Cafe and Museum, US 25, Corbin, Ky.; daily 7 am to 11 pm; phone 606-528-2163.

Patton Museum of Cavalry and Armor, 4554 Fayette Ave., Fort Knox, Ky.; summer: weekdays 9 to 4:30, weekends 10 to 6; fall, winter, and spring: weekdays 9 to 4:30, weekends 10 to 4:30; phone 502-624-3812.

Colonel Harland Sanders Museum, 1441 Gardiner Ln., Louisville, Ky.; Monday through Thursday 8:30 to 4:30, Friday 8 to 3; phone 502-456-8353.

Appalshop, 306 Madison St., Whitesburg, Ky.; weekdays 9 to 5; phone 606-633-0108.

LOUISIANA

Heritage Museum, 1606 Main St., Baker, La.; Tuesday through

Thursday 8:30 to 4:30, Sunday through Monday 12:30 to 4:30; phone 504-774-1776.

De Quincy Railroad Museum, 400 Lake Charles Ave., De Quincy, La.; weekdays 9 to 4, weekends 12 to 4; phone 318-786-2823.

Masur Museum of Art, 1400 S. Grand St., Monroe, La.; Tuesday through Thursday 9 to 5, Friday through Sunday 2 to 5; phone 318-329-2237.

Historic New Orleans Collection, 533 Royal St., New Orleans, La.; Tuesday through Saturday 10 to 4:45; phone 504-523-4662.

MAINE

Fisherman's Museum, Lighthouse Park, SR 130, Pemaquid Point, Maine; summer: Monday through Saturday 10 to 5, Sunday 11 to 5; phone 207-677-2494.

Marshall Point Lighthouse Museum, Marshall Point Rd., Port Clyde, Maine; summer: Tuesday through Sunday 1 to 5; May and October: weekends 1 to 5; phone 207-372-6450.

Shore Village Museum, 104 Limerock St., Rockland, Maine; June through October: daily 10 to 4; phone 207-594-0311.

Maine Coast Artists' Gallery, Russell Ave., Rockport, Maine; June through October: daily 10 to 5; November through May: Tuesday through Saturday 10 to 5; phone 207-236-2875.

MARYLAND

Maritime Museum, 77 Main St., Annapolis, Md.; daily 9 to 5; phone 410-268-5576.

Bufano Sculpture Garden, Johns Hopkins University, Baltimore, Md.; open daily 24 hours.

Fire Museum of the Baltimore Equitable Society, 21 N. Eutaw St., Baltimore, Md.; weekdays 9 to 4; phone 410-727-1794.

Historical Electronics Museum, 1745 W. Nursery Rd., Linthicum Heights, Md.; weekdays 9 to 3, Saturday 10 to 2; phone 410-765-3803.

MASSACHUSETTS

Addison Gallery of American Art, Chapel Ave., Andover, Mass.; September through July: Tuesday through Saturday 10 to 5, Sunday 1 to 5; phone 617-749-4015.

Robert S. Peabody Museum of Archeology, Phillips and Main, Andover, Mass.; Tuesday through Saturday 12 to 5, Saturday 10 to 1, August: closed; phone 508-749-4490.

USS Constitution Museum, Charlestown Navy Yard, Charlestown, Mass.; November through March: daily 10 to 5; May through October: daily 9 to 6; phone 617-426-1912.

The Titanic Historical Society Museum, 208 Main St., Springfield, Mass.; weekdays 10 to 4, Saturday 10 to 3; phone 413-543-4770.

Woods Hole Oceanographic Institution Exhibit Center, 15

School St., Woods Hole, Mass.; May through October: Tuesday through Saturday 10 to 4:30, Sunday 12 to 4; March, April, November, and December: Friday through Sunday 10 to 4:30; phone 508-289-2663.

MICHIGAN

Art Center of Battle Creek, 265 E. Emmett St., Battle Creek, Mich.; September through July: Tuesday through Friday 10 to 5, Weekends 1 to 4; phone 616-962-9511.

Museum of African American History, 301 Frederick Douglass, Detroit, Mich.; Wednesday through Saturday 9:30 to 5, Sunday 1 to 5; phone 313-833-9800.

Automotive Hall of Fame, 3225 Cook Rd., Midland, Mich.; weekdays 9 to 4; phone 517-631-5760.

Michigan Iron Industry Museum, Forge Rd., Muskegon, Mich.; May through October: daily 9:30 to 4:30; phone 906-475-7857.

Saginaw Art Museum, 1126 N. Michigan Ave., Saginaw, Mich.; Tuesday through Saturday 10 to 5, Sunday 1 to 5; phone 517-754-2491.

MINNESOTA

Museum of Questionable Medical Devices, 219 Main St., Minneapolis, Minn.; Tuesday through Thursday 5 to 9, Friday 5 to 10, Saturday 12 to 10, Sunday 12 to 5; phone 612-379-4046.

Rochester Art Center, 320 E. Center St., Rochester, Minn.; Tuesday through Saturday 10 to 5, Sunday 12 to 5; phone 507-282-8629.

Minnesota's Machinery Museum, SR 23, Hanley Falls, Minn.; Summer: Tuesday through Sunday 1 to 5; phone 507-768-3522.

MISSISSIPPI

Meridian Museum of Art, 628 25th Ave., Meridian, Miss.; Tuesday through Sunday 1 to 5; phone 601-693-1501.

Scranton Floating Museum, Pascagoula River Park, US 90, Pascagoula, Miss.; Tuesday through Saturday 10 to 5; phone 601-762-6017.

Mississippi Museum of Natural Science, 111 N. Jefferson St., Jackson, Miss.; weekdays 8 to 5, Saturday 9:30 to 4:30; phone 601-354-7303.

MISSOURI

Legler Barn Museum, 14907 W. 87th St. Pkwy., Lenexa, Mo.; Tuesday through Saturday 10 to 4, Sunday 1 to 4; phone 913-492-0038.

History Museum, Jefferson Memorial Building, Forest Park, St. Louis, Mo.; Tuesday through Sunday 9:30 to 5; phone 314-746-4599.

Mercantile Money Museum, Mercantile Tower, 7th and Washington, St. Louis, Mo.; daily 9 to 4; phone 314-421-1819.

National Video Game and Coin-Op Museum, 801 N. Second St., St. Louis, Mo.; March through September: Monday through Saturday 10 to 10, Sunday 12 to 8; October through February: Thursday through Saturday 12 to 10, Sunday through

Wednesday 12 to 8; phone 314-621-2900.

Soldiers' Memorial Military Museum, 1315 Chestnut St., St. Louis, Mo.; daily 9 to 4:30.

Springfield Art Museum, 1111 E. Brookside Dr., Springfield, Mo.; Tuesday through Saturday 9 to 5 (Thursday 9 to 8), Sunday 1 to 5; phone 417-866-2716.

MONTANA

Museum of the Plains Indians, US 2 and 89, Browning, Mont.; Summer: daily 9 to 5; fall, winter, and spring: weekdays 10 to 4:30; phone 406-338-2230.

Mineral Museum, Park Street, Butte, Mont.; summer: daily 8 to 5; fall, winter, and spring: weekdays 8 to 5, Sunday 1 to 5; phone 406-496-4414.

Frontier Gateway Museum, Belle Prairie Dr., Glendive, Mont.; summer: Monday through Saturday 9 to 5, Sunday 1 to 5; May and September: daily 1 to 5; phone 406-365-8168.

Missoula Museum of the Arts, 335 N. Patee St. Missoula, Mont.; Monday through Saturday 12 to 5; phone 406-728-0447.

NEBRASKA

Trails and Rails Museum, 710 W. 11th St., Kearney, Neb.; summer: Monday 10 to 5, Tuesday through Saturday 10 to 8, Sunday 1 to 5; phone 308-234-3041.

National Museum of Roller Skating, 4730 South St., Lincoln, Neb.; weekdays 9 to 5; phone 402-483-7551.

Sod House Museum, SR 47, Gothenburg, Neb.; daily 8 am to 9 pm, May and September: daily 9 to 6; phone 308-57-2680.

Museum of Nebraska Art, 2401 Central Ave., Kearney, Neb.; Tuesday through Saturday 11 to 5, Sunday 1 to 5; phone 308-865-8559.

NEVADA

Comstock Firemen's Museum, 125 South C St., Virginia City, Nev.; June through October, daily 10 to 5; phone 702-847-0717.

Stewart Indian Museum, 5366 Snyder Ave., Carson City, Nev.; Monday through Saturday 9 to 5, Sunday 9 to 4; phone 702-882-1808.

NEW HAMPSHIRE

New England Ski Museum, Parkway exit 2, Franconia, N.H.; Thursday through Tuesday 12 to 5; November and April: closed; phone 603-823-7177.

Sandwich Historical Society Museum, SR 109 and 133, Center Sandwich, N.H.; summer: Tuesday through Saturday 11 to 5; phone 603-284-6269.

NEW JERSEY

New Jersey State Museum, 205 W. State St., Trenton, N.J.; Tuesday through Saturday 9 to 4:45, Sunday 12 to 5; phone 609-292-6464.

Bergen Museum of Art and Science, Ridgewood & Fairview,

Paramus, N.J.; Tuesday through Saturday 10 to 5, Sunday 1 to 5; phone 201-265-1248.

NEW MEXICO

National Atomic Museum, Kirtland Air Force Base, Albuquerque, N.M.; daily 9 to 5; phone 505-845-6670.

Rough Riders Memorial and City Museum, 725 N. Grand Ave., Las Vegas, N.M.; Monday through Saturday 9 to 4; phone 505-425-8726.

Wheelwright Museum of the American Indian, Camino Lejo, Santa Fe, N.M.; Monday through Saturday 10 to 5, Sunday 1 to 5; phone 505-982-4636.

Meteorite Museum, 200 Yale Blvd, Albuquerque, N.M.; weekdays 9 to 4; phone 505-277-2747.

Silver City Museum, 312 W. Broadway, Silver City, N.M.; weekends 10 to 4; phone 505-538-5921.

Center for Contemporary Arts of Santa Fe, 291 E. Barcelona Rd., Santa Fe, N.M.; weekdays 10 to 5, Saturday 12 to 4; phone 505-982-1338.

NEW YORK

American Museum of Firefighting, 125 Harry Howard Ave, Hudson, N.Y.; daily 9 to 4:30; phone 518-828-7695.

Hispanic Society of America Museum, 613 W. 155th St., Manhattan, N.Y.; Tuesday through Saturday 10 to 4:30, Sunday 1 to 4; phone 212-926-2234.

Museum of American Financial History, 24 Broadway, Manhattan, N.Y.; weekdays 11:30 to 2:30; phone 212-908-4519.

Society of Illustrators Museum of American Illustration, 128 E. 63rd St., Manhattan, N.Y.; Tuesday 10 to 8, Wednesday through Friday 10 to 5, Saturday 12 to 4; phone 212-838-2560.

New York State Museum, Empire State Plaza, Albany, N.Y.; daily 10 to 5; phone 518-474-5877.

NORTH CAROLINA

The Appalachian Heritage Museum, US 221/321, Blowing Rock, N.C.; summer: daily 9 to 6; fall, winter, and spring: daily 9 to 5; phone 800-438-7500.

North Carolina Maritime Museum, 315 Front St., Beaufort, N.C.; weekdays 9 to 5, Saturday 10 to 5, Sunday 1 to 5; phone 919-728-7317.

Ava Gardner Museum, 205 S. Third St., Smithfield, N.C.; daily 1 to 6; phone 919-934-5830.

North Carolina Museum of Art, 2110 Blue Ridge Rd., Raleigh, N.C.; Tuesday through Saturday 9 to 5, Sunday 11 to 6; phone 919-833-1935.

North Carolina Museum of History, 1 East Edenton St., Raleigh, N.C.; Tuesday through Saturday, Sunday 1 to 6; phone 919-715-0200.

NORTH DAKOTA

Roger Maris Baseball Museum, I-29 & 13th Ave., Fargo, N.D.; weekdays 10 to 9, Saturday 10 to 7,

Sunday 12 to 6; phone 701-282-2222.

North Dakota Museum of Art, University of North Dakota, Grand Forks, N.D.; weekdays 9 to 5, weekends 1 to 5; phone 701-777-4159.

North Dakota Heritage Center and State Historical Museum, Capitol Mall, Bismarck, N.D.; weekdays 8 to 5, Saturday 9 to 5, Sunday 1 to 5; phone 710-224-2666.

OHIO

Goodyear World of Rubber, 1201 E. Market St., Akron, Ohio; weekdays 8 to 4:30; phone 330-796-7117.

Wyandot Popcorn Museum, 169 E. Church St., Marion, Ohio; May through October: Wednesday through Sunday 1 to 4; November through April: weekends 1 to 4; phone 614-387-4255.

Dittrick Museum of Medical History, 11000 Euclid Ave., Cleveland, Ohio; weekdays 10 to 5; phone 216-368-3648.

Dayton Art Institute, 456 Belmonte Park N., Dayton, Ohio; daily 9 to 5; phone 937-223-5277.

OKLAHOMA

National Hall of Fame for Famous American Indians, US 62, Anadarko, Okla.; Monday through Saturday 9 to 5, Sunday 1 to 5; phone 405-247-5555.

J.M. Davis Gun Museum, 333 N. Lynn Riggs Blvd., Claremore, Okla.; phone 918-341-5707.

Seminole National Museum, 524 S. Wewoka Ave., Wewoka, Okla. ; February through December: Tuesday through Sunday 1 to 5; phone 405-257-5580.

Museum of the Western Prairie, 1100 N. Hightower St., Altus, Okla.; Tuesday through Friday 9 to 5, weekends 2 to 5; phone 405-482-1044.

Will Rogers Memorial, SR 88, Claremore, Okla.; daily 8 to 5; phone 918-341-0719.

Pioneer Woman Museum, 701 Monument Rd., Ponca City, Okla.; Tuesday through Saturday 9 to 5, Sunday 1 to 5; phone 405-765-6108.

Osage Tribal Museum, 819 N. Grandview Ave., Pawhuska, Okla.; Tuesday through Saturday 10 to 5; phone 918-287-4622.

Fenster Museum of Jewish Art, B'nai Emunah Synagogue, 1223 E. 17th St., Tulsa, Okla.; Sunday through Thursday 10 to 4; phone 918-582-3732.

OREGON

Siuslaw Pioneer Museum, US 101, Florence, Ore.; Tuesday through Sunday 10 to 4, closed December; phone 541-883-4208.

Hatfield Marine Science Center, Marine Science Dr., Newport Ore.; summer: daily 10 to 6; fall, winter, and spring: daily 10 to 4; phone 541-867-0226.

Kerbyville Museum, US 199, Cave Junction, Ore.; summer: Monday through Saturday 10 to 5, Sunday 1 to 5; phone 503-592-2076.

49

PENNSYLVANIA

Trout Art Gallery, High Street, Dickinson College, Carlisle, Pa.; Academic year: Tuesday through Saturday 10 to 4; phone 717-245-1711.

Zane Grey Museum, Scenic Dr., Lackawaxen, Pa.; summer: daily 12 to 5; spring and fall: weekends 12 to 4; phone 717-685-4871.

Bob Hoffman's Weightlifting and Softball Hall of Fame, 3300 Board Rd., York, Pa.; weekdays 9 to 4, Saturday 9 to 3; phone 717-767-6481.

Southern Alleghenies Museum of Art, St. Francis College, Loretto, Pa.; weekdays 10 to 4, weekends 1:30 to 4:30; phone 814-472-6400.

American Freedom Museum, E. State St., Hermitage, Pa.; May through December: daily 10 to 5; phone 412-346-0444.

Greenville Railroad Museum, 314 Main St., Greenville, Pa.; summer: daily 12 to 5; spring and fall: Friday through Sunday 12 to 5; phone 412-588-4009.

Indian Steps Museum, Indian Steps Rd., Airville, Pa.; April through October, Thursday through Friday 10 to 4, weekends 10 to 5; phone 717-862-3948.

RHODE ISLAND

Rhode Island Watercolor Society, Slater Memorial Park, Pawtucket, R.I.; Tuesday through Saturday 10 to 4, Sunday 1 to 5; phone 401-726-1876.

Naval War College Museum, Founders Hall, Coasters Harbor Island, Newport, R.I.; summer: weekdays 10 to 4, weekends 12 to 4; fall, winter, and spring: weekdays 10 to 4; phone 401-841-4052.

SOUTH CAROLINA

Hopelands Gardens and Thoroughbred Racing Hall of Fame, 149 Dupree Place, Aiken, S.C.; September through June: Tuesday through Sunday 2 to 5 (Gardens open daily 10 to dusk); phone 803-642-7630.

The Citadel Museum, Moultrie St., Charleston, S.C.; Sunday through Friday 2 to 5, Saturday 12 to 5; phone 803-953-6846.

Parris Island Museum, Building 111, Marine Corps Recruit Depot, Parris Island, S.C.; daily 10 to 4:30 (Thursday 10 to 7); phone 803-525-2951.

Sumter Gallery of Art, 421 N. Main St., Sumter S.C., Tuesday through Friday 12 to 5, weekends 2 to 5; closed July; phone 803-775-0543.

SOUTH DAKOTA

Sioux Indian Museum, 515 W. Boulevard, Sioux Falls, S.D.; summer: Monday through Saturday 9 to 5, Sunday 11 to 4; fall, winter and spring: Monday through Saturday 9 to 5, closed Sunday; phone 605-348-0557.

Dakota Sunset Museum, 205 W. Commercial Ave., Gettysburg, S.D.; summer: daily 1 to 5; fall, winter, and spring: closed Wednesday and Sunday; phone 605-765-9480.

Dacotah Prairie Museum, Main St., Aberdeen, S.D.; Tuesday through Friday 9 to 5, weekends 1 to 4; phone 605-626-7117.

Akta Lakota Museum and Cultural Center, St. Joseph's Indian School, Chamberlain, S.D.; summer: Monday through Saturday 8 to 6, Sunday 1 to 5; fall, winter, and spring: weekdays 8 to 4:30; phone 605-734-3455.

TENNESSEE

National Bird Dog Museum, SR 18, Grand Junction, Tenn.; Tuesday through Friday 10 to 2, Saturday 10 to 2, Sunday 1 to 4; phone 901-764-2058.

Memphis Police Museum, 159 Beale St., Memphis, Tenn.; daily 24 hours; phone 901-528-2370.

Museum of Science and Energy, 300 S. Tulane Ave., Oak Ridge, Tenn.; daily 9 to 5; phone 423-576-3200.

Museum of Tobacco Art and History, 8th Ave. N. & Harrison St., Nashville, Tenn.; Monday through Saturday 9 to 4; phone 615-271-2349.

National Medal of Honor Museum of Military History, 4th St. and Georgia Ave., Chattanooga, Tenn.; Monday through Saturday 9 to 4:30; phone 423-267-1737.

TEXAS

O. Henry Museum, 409 E. 5th St., Austin, Texas; Wednesday through Sunday 12 to 5; phone 512-472-1903.

Cattleman's Museum, 1301 W. 7th St., Fort Worth, Texas; weekdays 8:30 to 4:30; phone 817-332-7064.

Museum of Printing History, 1324 W. Clay, Houston, Texas; Tuesday through Saturday 9 to 5; phone 713-522-4652.

El Paso Museum of History, I-10, El Paso, Texas; Tuesday through Sunday 9 to 4:30; phone 915-858-1928.

Asian Culture Museum and Educational Center, 5858 S. Padre Island Dr., Corpus Christi, Texas; Tuesday through Saturday 12 to 6; phone 512-993-3963.

Sid Richardson Collection of Western Art, 309 Main St., Fort Worth, Texas; Tuesday through Wednesday 10 to 5, Thursday through Friday 10 to 8, Saturday 11 to 8, Sunday 1 to 5; phone 817-332-6554.

The Presidential Museum, 622 N. Lee St., Odessa, Texas; Tuesday through Saturday 10 to 5; phone 915-332-7123.

UTAH

Western Mining and Railroad Museum, 296 S. Main St., Helper, Utah; summer: Monday through Saturday 9 to 5; fall, winter, and spring: Tuesday through Saturday 11 to 4; phone 801-472-3009.

College of Eastern Utah Prehistoric Museum, 155 E. Main St., Price, Utah; April through September: daily 9 to 6; October through February: Monday through Saturday 9 to 5; phone 435-637-5060.

Fairview Museum of History and Art, 85 N. 100 St., Fairview, Utah; March through September: Monday through Saturday 10 to 6, Sunday 2 to 6; phone 801-427-9216.

Great Basin Museum, 328 W. 100 N., Delta, Utah; Monday through Saturday 10 to 4; phone 801-864-5013.

VERMONT

Bread and Puppet Museum, SR 122, Glover, Vt.; May through October: daily 10 to 6; phone 802-525-3031.

Mary Bryan Memorial Art Gallery, Main St., Jeffersonville, Vt.; June through October: daily 11 to 5; phone 802-644-5100.

VIRGINIA

Reedville Fishermen's Museum, US 360, Reedville, Va.; summer: Monday through Sunday 10:30 to 4:30; phone 804-453-6529.

Lancaster Train and Toy Museum, 5661 Shoulder Hill Rd., Suffolk, Va.; November through December: daily 10 to 9; January through October: daily 10 to 6; phone 804-484-4224.

Virginia Sports Hall of Fame, 420 High St., Portsmouth, Va.; Tuesday through Saturday 10 to 5, Sunday 1 to 5; phone 804-393-8031.

Collingwood Library and Museum on Americanism, 8301 E. Boulevard Dr., Alexandria, Va.; Monday through Saturday 10 to 4, Sunday 1 to 4; closed Tuesday; phone 703-765-1652.

Virginia Museum of Fine Arts, 2800 Grove Ave., Richmond, Va.; Tuesday through Sunday 11 to 5, Thursday 11 to 8; phone 804-367-0844.

WASHINGTON

Coast Guard Museum Northwest, Pier 36, 1519 Alaska Way S., Seattle, Wash.; Monday, Wednesday, and Friday 9 to 3, weekends 1 to 5; phone 206-217-6993.

Big Rock Garden of Art, 2900 Sylvan St., Bellingham, Wash.; March through October, Wednesday through Sunday 11 to 5; phone 360-671-1069.

Hanford Museum of Science and History, 825 Jadwin, Richland, Wash.; weekdays 8 to 5, Saturday 9 to 5; phone 509-376-6374.

WEST VIRGINIA

West Virginia State Farm Museum, SR 62, Point Pleasant, W. Va.; April through November: Tuesday through Saturday 9 to 5, Sunday 1 to 5; phone 304-675-5737.

Eastern Regional Coal Archives, Craft Memorial Library, 600 E. Commerce St., Bluefield, W. Va.; weekdays 9:30 to 5, weekends by appointment; phone 304-325-3943.

WISCONSIN

Rhinelander Logging Museum, Rt. 8, Rhinelander, Wis.; summer: daily 10 to 5; phone 414-636-9177.

Wisconsin Folk Museum, 100 S. Second St., Mount Horeb, Wis.; summer: daily 12 to 5; fall: weekends 12 to 5; phone 608-437-4742.

Hoard Historical Museum and Dairy Shrine, 407 Merchants Ave., Fort Arkinson, Wis.; summer: Tuesday through Saturday 9:30 to 4:30, Sunday 1 to 5; fall, winter, and spring: Tuesday through Saturday 9:30 to 3:30; phone 414-563-7769.

State Historical Museum, 30 N. Carroll St., Madison, Wis.; Tuesday through Saturday 10 to 5, Sunday 12 to 5; phone 608-264-6555.

WYOMING

Medicine Bow Museum, US 30, Medicine Bow, Wyo.; summer: Monday through Saturday 10 to 5, Sunday 12 to 5; phone 307-379-2383.

Tate Mineralogical Museum, 125 College Dr., Casper, Wyo.; week-days 10 to 12; phone 307-268-2447.

Grand Encampment Museum, Encampment, Wyo.; summer: Monday through Saturday 10 to 5, Sunday 1 to 5; fall: daily 1 to 5; phone 307-327-5308.

Greybull Museum, 325 Greybull Ave., Greybull Wyo.; summer: daily 10 to 8; fall: weekdays 12 to 6; spring: weekdays 1 to 4; winter: Monday, Wednesday, and Friday 1 to 4; phone 307-765-2002.

Homesteader Museum, 135 S. Clark St., Powell, Wyo.; summer: Friday through Saturday 10 to 5; fall, winter, and spring: Tuesday through Friday 1 to 5, Saturday 10 to 5; phone 307-754-9481.

✩✩✩

Some Crafty Suggestions for Your Free Time

Idle hands are the Devil's workshop, but put a needle in those hands, and you can make heavenly creations while keeping busy. If quilting, crocheting, sewing, or other crafts are your passion, or if you'd like to learn some new crafts, there's plenty of free stuff for crafters available.

If free information is what you're looking for, your local craft or fabric shop is the place to be. They often offer free demonstrations on crafting techniques. They can also direct you to local quilting guilds or other craft groups. Join one of these groups, and you'll be rewarded by meeting nice people who share your interests, and are willing to share their knowledge.

Free information is priceless, but if crafting is your game, you can get even more. You can also find free samples, patterns, and publications. Here are just a few freebies for crafters.

MEDIEVAL NEEDLEWORK PATTERN: Medieval, Gaelic, and Renaissance needlework designs. Send a long, self-addressed, stamped envelope for a free brochure and sample pattern to: Guinevere's Crucible, 1915B Chain Bridge Rd., Suite 701M, McLean, VA 22102.

CRAFT MAGAZINE: Get a free trial issue of *Crafts 'n Things* magazine. If you don't like the sample issue, just write cancel on your invoice. You still get to keep the trial issue. If you do like it, and want to subscribe, the price is $14.97 for 10 issues, plus $2.00 postage and handling. Write to: Crafts 'n Things Magazine, PO Box 5026, Dept. F794C11P, Des Plaines, IL 60017; online: <www.afree.com/craftsub.htm>

CRAFT NEWSLETTER: Get *Crafty Ladies Newsletter* and a catalog featuring scrapbook supplies for free. Send a long self-addressed, stamped envelope (two stamps) to: Design Originals, 2425 Cullen St., Fort Worth, TX 76107.

TEDDY BEAR CUTOUT: Get a free wooden teddy bear cutout to paint, and a coupon good for $1.00 toward future purchases. Send a long self-addressed, stamped envelope and $1.00 postage and handling to: AMC Woodworking, 14111 Cleobrook, Houston, TX 77070.

CROSS STITCH SAMPLE: Get a free cross stitch wall hanger. Choose a theme of friendship, flowers, home, love, or religion and send $2.00 postage and handling to: You-Nique Creations, 194 Homewood St., Bacabille, CA 95688.

POLY-FIL PROJECT: Poly-fil is good for more than just stuffing pillows. Get a surprise craft pattern for free when you write to: Fairfield Processing Corporation, PO Box 1130, Danbury, CT 06813.

SNOWMAN CROSS STITCH: Get a free snowman cross stitch by sending a long self-addressed, stamped envelope to: Kreinik, 3106 Timanus Lane #101, Baltimore, MD 21244.

CROCHET SNOWFLAKES: Crochet solid snowflakes or snowflakes to frame photos. This free 20-page booklet also includes cross stitch charts for personalizing photos. Send $2.00 postage and handling to: Helen Haywood, 1492 Ridout Lane, Annapolis, MD 21401.

CROCHET MAGAZINES: Get a free trial issue of a crochet magazine, and keep the sample issue even if you decide not to subscribe. Subscription cost: $11.97 for 4 issues. Write to: Crochet Digest, PO Box 9015, Big Sandy, TX 75755, and/or Old Time Crochet, PO Box 9009, Big Sandy TX 75755.

WOODWORKING PROJECTS: Get 30 to 40 project sheets for Forster woodworking projects. Send $2.00 postage and handling to: Forster, Inc., PO Box 657, Wilton, ME 04294.

BOWMAKER: Make your own bows to brighten up your gift-giving. Get one Bowmaker, five feet of ribbon, and instructions for only $2.00 postage and handling. Write to: Holiday Offer - BMO6, 602 S. LaSalle St., Suite H448, Chicago, IL 60605.

SEWING BASICS: If you've never even mended a pair of slacks, don't worry. You can learn to sew with these simple step-by-step instructions for an elastic waist skirt from the Sewing Fashion Council. Send $2.50 postage and handling to: Sewing Fashion Council, 1350 Broadway, Suite 1601, New York, NY 10018.

Free Sewing Classes

You never know when it will come in handy to know 100 things to do with a yard of fabric. If you are using your retirement time to get back into sewing, or even want to teach sewing classes to kids, a great resource is your County Cooperative Extension Office. They frequently offer courses, workbooks, and even videos about how to sew. Some even focus on certain projects like Christmas gifts or draperies.

To learn more about what is available in your area, look in the blue pages of your phone book for the office nearest you. For more information, contact Extension Service, U.S. Department of Agriculture, Room 3328, Washington, DC 20250; 202-720-3029; or online at <www.reeusda.gov>.

Can't Get Enough Catalogs

If you have a hobby, there's a catalog out there just for you. And many of them are free. After all, the manufacturers want you to buy their merchandise. You can find everything you need to while away the hours happily working on your favorite craft, sport, or collectible. And if you're a "window shopper", you can look and dream without even spending the gas to drive to the shopping center. Here are just a few examples of free catalogs.

POSTAGE STAMP CATALOG FROM THE U.S. POSTAL SERVICE: Pick up an order card at your local post office, or write to: Free Stamp Catalogs, United States Postal Service, PO Box 57, Grand Rapids, MN 55744-9926.

TOYS AND MINI-REPLICAS FROM THE PAST: Foreign and U.S. reproductions. Tin trains, die-cast cars, trucks, planes, etc. Lilliput Motor Co., Ltd., Box 447, Yerington, NV 89447.

BILLIARDS AND DARTS: Everything you need from cue sticks to dartboards. Mueller Sporting Goods, 4825 S. 16 St., Lincoln, NE 68512; phone 402-423-8888.

NEEDLECRAFTS: Cross stitch, latch hook, needlepoint and more at <www.Herrschners.com>; 800-441-0838.

WOODCRAFTS AND SUPPLIES: 405 East Indiana Street, Oblong, IL 62449; Order Phone 800-592-4907; Info Phone 618-592-4907; fax 618-592-4902; Internet web site <www.woodcraftssupplies.com>; e-mail <info @woodcraftssupplies.com>.

SCI-FI CATALOG: Books, t-shirts, posters, collectibles, etc. Perfect for fans of *X-Files, Star Trek, Lost in Space,* and other sci-fi classics. 800-Trekker, Inc.; 800-873-5537.

CRAFTS: Handmade by craft students at Berea College: kitchen and office accessories, children's games, candlestick holders, and more. Berea College Crafts, CPO 2347, Berea, Kentucky 40404; phone 606-986-9341.

BOOKS: Low-priced books in all fields, including children's books, crafts, literature, puzzles, and more. Dover Publications, 31 E. Second St., Mineola, NY 11501; phone 516-294-7000.

BOOKS ON TAPE: If you prefer to listen to your favorite books, you can get them on tape. Call 800-88-BOOKS (800-882-6657) and ask for your catalog of books to buy or rent. The cost of the catalog is $5.00, which is applied to your first order.

SEEDS: Burpee Seed Co., 032763 Burpee Building, Warminster, PA 18974; phone 800-888-1447; fax 800-487-5530.

TOMATOES: Totally Tomatoes, Department 83, PO Box 1626, Augusta, GA 30903.

GARDENING TOOLS AND ACCESSORIES: Gardener's Supply Company, 128 Intervale Road, Burlington, VT 05401.

Help for Model Ship Builders

If miniature ship building is a pastime for you, then turn to the National Archives for help in making your replicas accurate. The brochure *Pictures of United States Navy Ships: 1775-1941* lists pictures available covering sailing ships to submarines, in addition to steamships, aircraft carriers, battleships, cruisers, destroyers, and torpedo boats.

For the brochure and ordering information, contact the National Archives and Records Administration, Product Development and Distribution Staff (NWCP), Room G-7, 700 Pennsylvania Ave. NW, Washington, DC 20408-0001. Requests may also be faxed to 202-501-7170. Reach them online at <www.nara.gov/publications/avrecs.html >.

Free Videos of the One That Got Away

Back up your fishing adventures with evidence. The Fish and Wildlife Service lends slides and still photos to lend credibility to even the tallest tale that you can dream up to tell your buddies.

The Audio Visual Department of the Fish and Wildlife Service has a collection of both black and white pictures and color slides of fish and wildlife and there is no charge for their lending service. You can even contact your regional Fish and Wildlife office for free loaner films and videos to get you excited about the upcoming fishing season.

Contact Broadcast and Audio Visuals, Fish and Wildlife Service, 18th and C Sts., NW, Washington, DC 20240; 202-208-5611; or online at <www.fws.gov>.

A Fisherman's Dream

Did the movie *A River Runs Through It* excite you about fly fishing? Do you buy every fancy lure and gadget you can find? Do you spend hours at the lake or river, only to come home empty-handed? Maybe you should spend some time reading up on the topic, and improve your technique.

A free shopping list of government fishing publications (document # SB209) is available which provides information on fisheries and fish research, and another list (document # SB57) provides information on charts and marine posters.

For your copies, contact Superintendent of Documents, Government Printing Office, Washington, DC 20402; 202-512-1800.

If you're more serious about your fishing dreams, "Pathway to Fishing" is a 12-part, hour-long instructional program covering fish biology, aquatic ecology, angler ethics, methods for handling fish, and information about where to go fishing.

Although a bit pricey at $61, it's packed with a user's guide, 12 support posters and an instructional video. Contact the Fish and Wildlife Service, Pathway To Fishing, 1849 C St., NW, ARLSQ-820, Washington, DC 20240; 202-208-5611.

Attention Aspiring Archeologists

Have you always dreamed of being like Indiana Jones and finding rare artifacts? Go ahead and indulge your dream. A small home study course might help you get started. *Participate in Archeology* is a free brochure which provides some basic information on archeology, and lists magazines, books, videos, and agencies and organizations through which you can receive additional information.

Contact the Publications, *Archeology* and *Ethnography Program* (2275), National Park Service, 1849 C St. NW, Washington, DC 20240; 202-343-4101; or online at <www.cr.nps.gov/aad/aepubs.htm>.

Join a Free Archeological Dig

Never liked staying on the sidelines? Well then, dig in. "Passport In Time" helps you open a window on the past by allowing you to join activities such as archeological excavation, site mapping, drafting, laboratory and art work, collecting oral histories, restoration, and much more.

Projects vary in length and there is no registration cost or fee. You may even receive a small stipend to offset your living expenses.

For information on upcoming opportunities, contact Passport In Time Clearinghouse, PO Box 31315, Tucson, AZ 85751-1315; 800-281-9176; or online at <www.fs.fed.us/recreation/opp_to_vol.html>; fax 520-298-7044; e-mail <sriarc@aol.com>.

Learn About Endangered Species

You actually may not need to go any farther than your own backyard to find rare and wonderful things. If you are a card-carrying bird watcher, the Fish and Wildlife Service has information booklets on attracting birds to your yard, and even information on different homes for birds.

If you are worried about endangered species, they can provide you with information on the Endangered Species Act, a list of endangered and threatened species, as well as information sheets on many species. Contact U.S. Fish and Wildlife Service, 4401 N. Fairfax Dr., Arlington, VA 22203; 703-358-1711; or online at <www.fws.gov>.

Make a Difference With Your Free Time

You can fill a need as you fill in your empty hours when you volunteer. Volunteer opportunities abound in many fields. Everyone has a particular talent or expertise. Why not share your knowledge and experience? You'll be making a contribution, gaining satisfaction, and probably having a lot of fun to boot.

HELP OUT A FELLOW SENIOR. Sometimes seniors end up in nursing homes simply because they don't have the small amount of help they need to remain in their own homes. You can share your time and open your heart to a less fortunate senior. Over half a million seniors like you volunteer each year to deliver meals to shut-ins, help others get to doctor's appointments — whatever is needed to keep them functioning in their homes and communities.

The Senior Companion program matches seniors who need a little extra support with those who have extra support to give. You could be the key to helping a fellow senior remain independent, and you might gain a friend in the bargain. For more information, contact National Senior Service Corps, 1201 New York Ave., NW, Washington, DC 20525; 800-424-8867; or online at <www.whitehouse.gov/WH/EOP/cns/html/senior.html>.

The Eldercare Locator is a nationwide, directory assistance service designed to help older persons and caregivers locate local support resources for aging Americans. If you have the time and want to get involved, or if you know someone who needs help, contact Eldercare Locator, Administration on Aging, 330 Independence Ave., SW, Washington, DC 20201; 202-629-0641; 800-677-1116; or online at

<www.ageinfo.org/elderloc/elderloc.html>.

STAY YOUNG BY HELPING CHILDREN. The Foster Grandparent Program matches low-income seniors with young people who need various kinds of special help. Volunteers serve as mentors, tutors, and caregivers for children and young kids with special needs, and can also work in schools, hospitals, and recreation centers in their communities. Volunteers work twenty hours per week, and receive a small paycheck and other benefits such as transportation costs or uniforms. If you think you are up to a challenge like this, contact National Senior Service Corps, 1201 New York Ave., NW, Washington, DC 20525; 800-424-8867; or online at <www.whitehouse.gov/WH/EOP/cns/html/senior.html>.

SHARE YOUR KNOW-HOW. You may be retired, but the years of experience you've accumulated didn't just disappear on your last day at work. You can lend that expertise to businesses or nonprofit groups trying to get a start, or share your knowledge with young people in your field.

The Retired Senior Volunteer Program (RSVP) gives retired people a chance to continue using their professional experience by working with local service organizations doing such things as conducting employment workshops and acting as consultants to nonprofit organizations. Contact National Senior Service Corps, 1201 New York Ave., NW, Washington, DC 20525; 800-424-8867; or online at <www.whitehouse.gov/WH/EOP/cns/html/senior.html>.

If business is your field of expertise, consider volunteering with SCORE, Service Corps of Retired Executives. SCORE volunteers are usually retired business professionals who want to share their knowledge with the next generation of business owners. If you are interested in becoming one of over 13,000 SCORE members nationwide, contact them at SCORE, 409 Third St., SW, Fourth Floor, Washington, DC 20024; 202-205-6762; 800-634-0245; or online at <www.score.org>.

HAVE SOME FUN IN THE GREAT OUTDOORS. If you're an outdoors kind of person, and you care about helping preserve wildlife, maybe you should volunteer at one of our national forests or parks, or for the wildlife service. Volunteers are essential in managing our nation's natural resources.

For a list of national forests nearest you, contact U.S. Forest Service, U.S. Department of Agriculture, Human Resource Programs, PO Box 96090, Washington, DC 20090; 703-235-8855; or online at <www.fs.fed.us>.

Get in touch with your nearest National Park to discover an interesting way to spend your free time or to receive a free brochure. Contact the Office of Public Inquiries, National Park Service, U.S. Department of the Interior, PO Box 37127, Washington, DC 20013; 202-208-4747; or online at <www.nps.gov/volunteer/>.

To find out about volunteer opportunities at your local Fish and Wildlife Office, look in the blue pages of your phone book, or contact U.S. Fish and Wildlife Service, U.S. Department of the Interior, 4401 N. Fairfax Dr., Arlington, VA 22203. You may also request a brochure titled *Volunteers: Your Wildlife Opportunity* by calling 304-876-7203, or send a request by fax to 304-876-7689. Visit their web site at <www.fws.gov>.

CLEAN UP YOUR ENVIRONMENT. The Army Corps of Engineers cares for almost 12 million acres of public land. That's quite a job! To do it right, they need lots of volunteers. You get to work outdoors, meet new people, and maybe learn some new skills.

Some of the duties Corps volunteers may be assigned include: serving as campground hosts, maintaining trails and facilities, restoring wildlife habitats, recovering archeological artifacts, staffing visitor centers, and restoring or preserving historic structures. For more information, write to: U.S. Army Corps of Engineers, Volunteer Clearinghouse, PO Box 1070, Nashville, TN 37202-1070, or call 800-VOL-TEER.

☆ ☆ ☆

Flash in the Pan Prospecting

When you watch old westerns, are you more interested in the old prospector with his mule than in the handsome hero? Does the idea of searching for gold appeal to you? If so, you should know that you can prospect on government land. For information, just send a card to the Forest Service at this address: Minerals and Geology Staff, Forest Service DOA, PO Box 2417, Washington, DC 20013.

Bountiful Botany

Do you have a green thumb or does everything you touch wither and turn brown? If you want to grow plants, there's plenty of free information to help your garden grow.

The Horticulture Services Division of the Smithsonian Institution has a series of fact sheets that can answer some of your plant questions. From ferns to poinsettias, these brochures include information on how to help your plants grow, how to spot and avoid potential problems, and details on fertilization and cultivation. For more information, contact the Horticulture Services Division, Arts and Industries Building, Room 2282, MRC 420, Smithsonian Institution, Washington, DC 20560; 202-357-1926.

If you don't have a clue about how to start a garden, the John Deere Company may help. Write to them and ask for *Starting Your Own Garden Booklet,* John Deere Company, 1400 Third Avenue, Moline, IL 61265.

Ready to redo your garden? Get a free "Yard & Garden Remodeling Kit". Send $1.00 for postage and handling to The Garden Council, 500 N. Michigan Ave., Suite 1400, Chicago, IL 60611.

Take care of your trees with the information in the booklet *Spunky's Tree Care Check List.* Send a long, self-addressed, stamped envelope to American Forestry, PO Box 2000, Washington, D C 20013.

Crazy about roses? Get tips on selecting, planting, and caring for your roses. Send a self-addressed, stamped envelope and $1.00 postage and handling to: All America Rose Selections, 221 North LaSalle, Suite 3500, Chicago, IL 60601.

Bring Me Your Tired, Sick, and Decaying Plants ...

Almost all Cooperative Extension Service offices (which are located in most counties) have a horticulture hotline, where you can talk to gardening experts and bring in samples of your plants for diagnoses. There is usually no fee for this service.

They can even help you deal with squirrels digging up your bulbs and deer eating your trees. Look in the blue pages of your phone book for the office nearest you. The office may be listed by a slightly different name; just look for the key word "extension" in the title.

For more information, contact the Extension Service, U.S. Department of Agriculture, Room 3328, Washington, DC 20250; 202-720-4111; or online at <www.reeusda.gov>.

☆☆☆

Help Your Garden Grow

You're proud of your fresh-from-your-own-garden vegetables. They're delicious and healthy, but you're concerned about all the products you use to enhance their growth and protect them from pests. Are you cancelling out all the healthy benefits by using chemicals? Don't worry, your vegetables and flowers can still be the talk of the neighborhood — without using potentially harmful pesticides.

You can learn how to fertilize and protect your plants without adding harmful chemicals with some help from the Environmental Protection Agency. They have fact sheets and information booklets on pesticides, organic gardening, and even composting.

To learn more, contact the Public Information Center, U.S. Environmental Protection Agency, 401 M St. SW, 3404, Washington, DC 20460; 202-260-5922; or online at <www.epa.gov>.

A Seed Sampler

Whether you're a gardening novice or a master gardener, a few free seeds to get you started or try out some new plants would be a welcome arrival in your mail box. Here are a few companies that offer free seed samples.

Sprinkle some color in your yard for free. Get a sample of annual flower seeds from Alberta Nurseries, PO Box 20, Bowden, Alberta, Canada TOM-OKO.

There's nothing in the world like home-grown tomatoes. Unless it's free home-grown tomatoes. Get free tomato seeds by sending 25 cents for postage and handling to Stakeless Tomato Seed Offer, Gurney Seed Company, 3101 Page Street, Yankton, SD 57079.

Have a little green in your yard year-round. Get free evergreen tree seeds and planting instructions. Send 50 cents for postage and handling to: Reynolds Wrap Entertaining Ease, PO Box 1820, Waukesha, WI 53187, and ask for Colorado Spruce Tree Seeds.

Can't afford a vacation in Hawaii? Bring a bit of the tropics to your backyard with free tropical Hawaiian plant seeds. Send $1.00 for postage and handling to: Hawaiian Ti Plant, PO Box 34989, San Rafael, CA 94902.

Another Elvis Sighting

You may think you've seen Elvis around town, but don't think you're all that special — so have millions of others. What you probably saw was

Elvis' face on millions of envelopes. Elvis did a favor for the Post Office — he made stamp collecting even more the rage.

Join the crowd with some help from the U.S. Postal Service, and request their free brochure, *Introduction to Stamp Collecting*, which will help you learn how to start and maintain a collection. Contact your local post office or write U.S. Postal Service, 475 L'Enfant Plaza West, SW, Washington, DC 20260; phone 800-STAMP-24 (800-782-6724); or visit online at <www.usps.gov>.

Help Digging Up Your Roots

Gathering up all those branches, limbs, and splinters can be an incredible treasure hunt. If you are putting together your family tree, let the National Archives help you along. They maintain ship passenger arrival records, census records, immigration and naturalization records, and military records.

To help with your genealogy research, the National Archives offers a number of free publications from the Product Development and Distribution Staff (NWCP), National Archives and Records Administration, Room G-7, Seventh Street and Pennsylvania Avenue, NW, Washington, DC 20408; phone 202-501-5235 or 1-800-234-8861; fax 202-501-7170. Visit their web site at <www.nara.gov/genealogy/genindex.html>.

Native American Activities

Are you the granddaughter of a great Indian chief? Or are you just interested in learning more about Native American culture? The Bureau of Indian Affairs runs three museums full of all kinds of Indian folk art. They'll send you free pamphlets and brochures about their respective programs and exhibition activities.

Contact the museums directly at Southern Plains Indian Museum, PO Box 749, Anadarko, OK 73005; 405-247-6221; Museum of the Plains Indian, PO Box 400, Browning, MT 59417; 406-338-2230; or Sioux Indian Museum, PO Box 1504, Rapid City, SD 57709; 605-348-0557.

A Hotline for Your Cool Boat

You finally bought that boat you've been dreaming about for years. But before you embark on the first of many leisurely cruises, it might be a good idea to get the latest facts on licensing and safety issues.

The Boating Safety Hotline can provide you with information on such topics of interest to boaters as safety recalls, publications, Coast Guard department contacts and addresses, public education courses, and free Coast Guard services. A free consumer information packet is available. The hotline also takes consumer complaints about safety defects and violations.

Contact Boating Safety Hotline, Consumer and Regulatory Affairs Branch (G-NAB-5), Office of National Safety and Waterways Services, U.S. Coast Guard, 2100 2nd St., SW, Room 1109, Washington, DC 20593; 800-368-5647; or online at <www.dot. gov/dotinfo/uscg/>.

Online Books

If you'd like to fill up your free time with lots of good books, you probably know where to look — the library. However, what do you do if you just can't make it to the library, or if the library doesn't have the book you want? If you have a computer and an Internet connection, you can get books online. Several web sites offer literary classics in their entirety for you to download and enjoy. One such site is Project Gutenberg at <www.gutenberg.net>. And the best part is, there's no late fee for forgetting to return them!

Meet the Author

You've always been an avid reader, and you'd like to know more about your favorite authors. Watch the arts section of your local newspaper and check out your local bookstores for book signings. Usually authors will do a book tour just as a new book is released. You can hear them talk about their book, ask them questions, and get their autograph.

☆☆☆

Watch TV Tapings

Instead of sitting on your couch watching television, you could be right where the action is — at the taping. Many television shows that are filmed before live audiences offer free tickets. Send a long, self-addressed, stamped envelope for a calendar of television program taping schedules to: Audiences Unlimited, 100 Universal City Plaza, Building 153, Universal City, CA 91608. Or call your local television station to see if any locally-filmed shows offer free tickets.

Start a Local Theater or Dance Company

Have you always had a flair for theater or art? Joining a local arts group can give you an outlet for your creativity. And if your arts group develops work reflective of your own community, you may be eligible for grants.

These grants are to professionally directed arts organizations that are rooted in culturally diverse, inner-city, rural, or tribal communities. Matching grants are available to help create, exhibit, or present works representative of the culture of a community, and to provide a community with access to all types of quality art.

To learn more about eligibility requirements, contact Public Information Office, National Endowment for the Arts, 1100 Pennsylvania Ave., NW, Washington, DC 20506; 202-682-5400; or look online at <arts.endow.gov>.

$10,000 for Craftspeople and Storytellers

If you create works in a traditional art form, then look to the Heritage and Preservation Program for assistance. This program supports traditional arts that have grown through time within the many groups that make up our nation — groups that share the same ethnic heritage, language, occupation, religion, or geographic area.

These folk arts include music, dance, poetry, tales, oratory, crafts, and various types of visual art forms. Money can be used for festivals, tours, workshops, residencies, exhibits, and more.

To learn about eligibility, contact the Heritage and Preservation Program, National Endowment For The Arts, Room 710, 1100 Pennsylvania Ave., NW, Washington, DC 20506; 202-682-5449.

Get a Smithsonian Exhibit for a Fundraiser

The Smithsonian can bring art to you, whether you live in a major metropolitan area or a rural one. The Smithsonian Institute Traveling Exhibition Services (SITES) sponsors 80 to 100 different exhibits at any given time in museums and other locations around the country.

The participation fee varies from $500 to $20,000. The exhibitions range from popular culture to fine arts, photography, historical exhibits, or topics of interest to children. The collections are most frequently sent to other museums, libraries, historic homes, or even schools and community centers.

Request a free *SITES Updates* catalog to see what is currently available. Contact Smithsonian Institute Traveling Exhibition Service, Smithsonian Institution, 1100 Jefferson Dr., SW, Room 3146, Washington, DC 20560; 202-357-3168.

Kick Up Your Heels

Put your dancing boots on and slap a hat on your head. Even people with two left feet can learn to do country line dancing. You can get easy-to-follow instructions for six popular dances. Just send $1.00 postage and handling to: Lisa Harmel, 12351 Wade Way, El Cajon, CA 92021.

Usher in Good Times

You can see many theatrical productions and concerts for free when you take part in an usher program. You will have to work for the privilege, but showing people to their seats is a small price to pay for seeing quality productions, often to sold-out shows that you couldn't have gotten a ticket for anyway. Call your local theater or concert arena and ask if they have an usher program.

Another possible way to see your favorite shows for free or almost free is to call and ask if dress rehearsals are open to the public. Many theater companies like to have a real audience for their dress rehearsals, but don't charge admission. Of course, the performance won't be as polished, but sometimes seeing the "bloopers" is even more fun!

Cheap Seats ... Discounts on Theater Tickets

Take advantage of some special deals for those that hit the magic age of seniority. Many ballets, orchestras, museums, and art galleries offer discounted admission to senior citizens.

Here's a sample of nonprofit cultural organizations across the country that have received funding from state arts councils or the National Endowment for the Arts and provide programs geared specifically toward older adults.

ARKANSAS

The Arkansas Symphony Orchestra (ASO), PO Box 7328, Little Rock, AR 72717; 501-666-1761. The ASO provides discounted tickets to senior citizens. The Quapaw String Quartet performs in retirement communities and community centers.

CALIFORNIA

National Institute of Art and Disabilities, 551 23rd St., Richmond, CA 94804; 510-620-0290; Director: Carol Weinstein. National Institute of Art and Disabilities provides an ongoing, full-time art program for adults with developmental disabilities, many of whom are older and are developing careers as visual artists. Participants' work is facilitated by master artists and teachers.

GEORGIA

The Woodruff Arts Center, 1280 Peachtree St., NE., Atlanta, GA 30309; 404-733-4200. The Woodruff Arts Center provides discounted theater and museum tickets for people over age 65.

KENTUCKY

Appalshop, 306 Madison St., Whitesburg, KY 41858; 606-633-0108. Appalshop provides programs that seek to break down cultural stereotypes of the Appalachian people. They have several programs that target older citizens. The Roadside Theater program draws together diverse groups to examine local heritage. The community radio program features programs such as "Deep in Tradition," an old-time mountain music show.

ElderSprites, 1816 Frankfort Ave., Louisville, KY 40205; 502-451-7302;

Attn: Mary Ann Maier. Elder Dance Express, 1442 Rufer Ave., Louisville, KY 40204; 502-581-1976; Attn: Chris Doerflinger. ElderSprites, a theater troupe of older adults; and Elder Dance Express, an ensemble of older dancers, perform in schools, senior centers, and community centers, as well as in theaters throughout Kentucky.

MASSACHUSETTS

Boston-Fenway, Inc., Elder Arts Project, 590 Huntington Ave., Boston, MA 02115; 617-445-0047; Attn: Juanda Drumgold. This initiative involves older adults in the activities of the Boston Symphony Orchestra, New England Conservatory of Music, Huntington Theater, Stewart Garden and Museum, and Boston Museum of Fine Arts. The program provides complimentary tickets and transportation to selected events and performances. The more than 500 older adults participating in the program live in elder care centers or low-income housing complexes in Boston's Roxbury and Back Bay neighborhoods.

MINNESOTA

St. Paul's Chamber Orchestra, Hamm Building, 408 St. Peters St., Suite 300, St. Paul, MN 55102; 612-292-3248. The Saint Paul Chamber Orchestra provides "The Morning Coffee Series," which is geared toward older people, and is comprised of eight morning Baroque concerts opening with informative concert previews.

NEW MEXICO

Very Special Arts New Mexico, PO Box 7784, Albuquerque, NM; 505-768-5188. Very Special Arts New Mexico features the Buen Viaje Dancers, a modern dance troupe of all ages with multiple disabilities. They received a grant to produce, market, and distribute a video on teaching dance to individuals with disabilities.

NEW YORK

Performance Space 122, 150 1st Ave., New York, NY; 212-477-5288. Performance Space 122 provides dance tickets for events at a cost of $8 for eligible seniors.

Theater Development Fund, 1501 Broadway Ave., New York, NY 10036; 212-221-0013 (recorded message); 212-221-0885 (staff). The Theater Development Fund provides discounted theater and dance tickets to individuals and nonprofit community and senior centers.

Elders Share the Arts (ESTA), 57 Willoughby St., Brooklyn, NY 11201; 718-488-8565; Attn: Susan Pearlstein. Elders Share the Arts produces living history theater workshops and performances throughout New York's five boroughs. Elders tour and perform at city-wide festivals, schools, museums, and community and senior centers.

Bronx Arts Ensemble, c/o Gulf House, Van Courtland Park, Bronx, NY 10471; 718-601-7399. The Bronx Arts Ensemble provides occasional free concerts and a series of concerts at reduced rates that are available to senior adults.

NORTH CAROLINA

Greensboro Symphony Society, PO Box 20303, Greensboro, NC 27420; 910-333-7490. The Greensboro Symphony Orchestra provides discounted tickets to senior citizens.

Grass Roots Art and Community Effort (GRACE), PO Box 324, Saint Johnsbury, VT 05819; 802-472-6857. GRACE discovers, develops, and promotes visual art produced primarily by older self-taught artists in rural Vermont. GRACE has involved older adults in arts programs, many of whom are in nursing homes and other residential centers.

WASHINGTON, D.C.

Washington D.C. International Film Festival, PO Box 21396, Washington, DC 20009; 202-274-6810. The Washington D.C. International Film Festival provides two free matinee screenings for senior citizens at the Kennedy Center for Performing Arts during their May film festival each year.

Sports Fans Alert

Whether you're a baseball fan, a football fan, or just a fan of sports in general, watching your favorite team can be a pleasant way to spend a few free hours. You don't have to camp out in front of the television, though. Go on out to the ballpark. Most teams offer senior discounts, or give freebies (caps, pennants, etc.) to seniors who come to the games and ask for them. Most teams also offer a free fan package that includes photos, decals, and more — and you don't even have to be a senior to get it. Usually you just have to send in a post card or a self-addressed, stamped envelope and ask for it. Here's a sampling of team addresses. If your favorite team isn't listed, you can look it up in your local phone book, or call or write the league headquarters.

FOOTBALL

Arizona Cardinals, PO Box 888, Phoenix, AZ 85001-0888

Atlanta Falcons, 2745 Burnette Rd, Suwanee, GA 30174

Buffalo Bills, PR Dept, Memorial Stadium, 1000 East 33rd St., Baltimore, MD 21218

Carolina Panthers, 227 West Trade St., Charlotte, NC 28202

Chicago Bears, 250 N. Washington Rd., Lake Forest, IL 60045

Cincinnati Bengals, PR Dept., 200 Riverfront Stadium, Cincinnati, OH 45202

Dallas Cowboys, PR Dept., One Cowboys Parkway, Irving, TX 75063

Denver Broncos, 13655 Broncos Parkway, Englewood, CO 80122

Detroit Lions, Pontiac Silverdome, 1200 Featherstone Rd, Pontiac, MI 48342

Green Bay Packers, PR Dept., 1265 Lombardi Ave., Green Bay, WI 54304

Indianapolis Colts, PO Box 535000, West 56th St., Indianapolis, IN 46253

Jacksonville Jaguars, One Stadium Place, Jacksonville, FL 32202

Kansas City Chiefs, PR Dept., One Arrowhead Dr., Kansas City, MO 64129

Miami Dolphins, PR Dept., 2269 NW 199th St., Miami, FL 33056

Minnesota Vikings, PR Dept., 9520 Viking Dr., Eden Prairie, MN 55344

New England Patriots, 60 Washington St., Foxboro, MA 02035

New Orleans Saints, 6928 Saints Dr., Metairie, LA 70003

New York Giants, PR Dept., Giants Stadium, East Rutherford, NJ 07073

New York Jets, 1000 Fulton Avenue, Hempstead, NY 11550

Oakland Raiders, PR Dept., 332 Center St., El Segundo, CA 90245

Philadelphia Eagles, 3501 S. Broad St., Philadelphia, PA 19148

Pittsburgh Steelers, 300 Stadium Circle, Pittsburgh, PA 15212

San Diego Chargers, PO Box 609609, San Diego, CA 92160

San Francisco 49ers, 4949 Centennial Boulevard, Santa Clara, CA 95054

Seattle Seahawks, 11220 NE 53rd St., Kirkland, WA 98033

St. Louis Rams, 100 N. Broadway, Suite 2100, St. Louis, MO 63102

Tampa Bay Buccaneers, One Buccaneer Place, Tampa, FL 33607

Washington Redskins, 21300 Redskin Park Dr., Ashburn, VA 22011.

BASEBALL

Atlanta Braves, PO Box 4064, Atlanta, GA 30302

Baltimore Orioles, 333 W. Camden St., Baltimore, MD 21230

Boston Red Sox, Fenway Park, Boston, MA 02115

California Angels, 2000 Gene Autry Way, Anaheim, CA 92806

Chicago Cubs, Wrigley Field, 1060 W. Addison St., Chicago, IL 60613

Chicago White Sox, 333 W. 35th St., Chicago, IL 60616

Cincinnati Reds, 100 Riverfront Stadium, Cincinnati, OH 45202

Cleveland Indians, Jacobs Field, 2401 Ontario Sr., Cleveland, OH 44115

Colorado Rockies, 2001 Blake St., Denver, CO 80205

Detroit Tigers, 2121 Trumbull Ave., Detroit, MI 48216

Florida Marlins, 100 NE Third Avenue, Third Floor, Fort Lauderdale, FL 33301

Houston Astros, PO Box 288, Houston, TX 77001-0288

Kansas City Royals, Kauffman Stadium, 1 Royal Way, Kansas City, MO 64129

Los Angeles Dodgers, Dodger Stadium, 1000 Elysian Park Dr., Los Angeles, CA 90012

Milwaukee Brewers, PO Box 3099, Milwaukee, WI 53201

Minnesota Twins, 501 Chicago Ave. S., Minneapolis, MN 55415

Montreal Expos, PO Box 500, Station "M", Olympic Stadium, Montreal Quebec, Canada H1V 3P2

New York Mets, Shea Stadium, 126th St. and Roosevelt Ave., Flushing, NY 11368

New York Yankees, Yankee Stadium, Bronx, NY 10451

Oakland A's, Oakland Coliseum, Oakland, CA 94621

Philadelphia Phillies, Veterans Stadium, PO Box 7575, Philadelphia, PA 19101

Pittsburgh Pirates, 600 Stadium Circle, Pittsburgh, PA 15212

St. Louis Cardinals, 250 Stadium Plaza, St. Louis, MO 63102

San Diego Padres, PO Box 2000, San Diego, CA 92112-2000

San Francisco Giants, Candlestick Park, San Francisco, CA 94124

Seattle Mariners, PO Box 4100, Seattle, WA 98104

Texas Rangers, 1000 Ballpark Way, Arlington, TX 76011

Toronto Bluejays, PO Box 7777, Adelaide St. Post Office, Exhibition Stadium, Toronto, Ontario, Canada, M5C 2K7

BASKETBALL

Atlanta Hawks, PR Dept., One CNN Center, Suite 405, Atlanta, GA 30303

Boston Celtics, 151 Merrimac St., 5th Floor, Boston, MA 02114 Attn: Fan Mail Dept.

Charlotte Hornets, Hive Drive, Charlotte, NC 29217

Chicago Bulls, 1901 W. Madison St., Chicago, IL 60612-2459

Cleveland Cavaliers, 1 Center Court, Cleveland, OH 44115-4001, Attn: Fan Mail Dept.

Dallas Mavericks, Reunion Arena, 777 Sports St., Dallas, TX 75207

Denver Nuggets, PR Dept., 1635 Clay St., Denver, CO 80204

Detroit Pistons, Palace of Auburn Hills, Two Champion Dr., Auburn Hills, MI 48057, Attn: Fan Mail Dept.

Golden State Warriors, Oakland Coliseum Arena, Oakland, CA 94621-1995

Houston Rockets, PR Dept., PO Box 272349, Houston, TX 77277

Indiana Pacers, 300 East Market St., Indianapolis, IN 46204

Los Angeles Clippers, Los Angeles Sports Arena, 3939 S. Figueroa, Los Angeles, CA 90037

Los Angeles Lakers, PR Dept., PO Box 10, Inglewood, CA 90306

Miami Heat, Miami Arena, Miami, FL 33136-4102

Milwaukee Bucks, PR Dept., 1001 N. Fourth St., Milwaukee, WI 53203-1312

Minnesota Timberwolves, 600 First Ave. North, Minneapolis, MN 55403

New Jersey Nets, Brendan Byrne Arena, East Rutherford, NJ 07073

New York Knickerbockers, Two Pennsylvania Plaza, New York, NY 10001

Orlando Magic, PO Box 76, Orlando, FL 32802, Attn: Fan Mail Dept.

Philadelphia 76ers, Veterans Stadium, PO Box 25040, Philadelphia, PA 19147

Phoenix Suns, PR Dept., PO Box 1369, Phoenix, AZ 85001

Portland Trailblazers, 700 NE Multnomah St., Suite 600, Portland, OR 97232

Sacramento Kings, PR Dept., One Sports Parkway, Sacramento, CA 95843

San Antonio Spurs, The Alamodome, 100 Montana St., San Antonio, TX 78205

Seattle Supersonics, PR Dept., Box C900911, Seattle, WA 98109

Toronto Raptors, 20 Bay St., Suite 1702, Toronto, Ontario, Canada M5J WN8

Utah Jazz, 5 Triad Center, 5th Floor, Salt Lake City, Utah 84180

Vancouver Grizzlies, General Motors Plaza, 800 Griffiths Way, Vancouver, British Columbia, Canada V6B 6G1

Washington Bullets, PR Dept., Capital Center, One Harry S. Truman Dr., Landover, MD 20785

HOCKEY

Anaheim Mighty Ducks, Arrowhead Pond of Anaheim, 2695 Katella Ave., Anaheim, CA 92086

Boston Bruins, 1 Fleet Center, Suite 250, Boston, MA 02114

Buffalo Sabres, Memorial Auditorium, 140 Main St., Buffalo, NY 14202

Calgary Flames, Olympic Saddledome, PO Box 1540, Station M, Calgary, Alberta, Canada T2P 3B9

Carolina Hurricanes, 5000 Aerial Center, Suite 100, Morrisville, NC 27560

Chicago Blackhawks, 1901 W. Madison, Chicago, IL 60612

Colorado Avalanche, 1635 Clay St., Denver, CO 80204

Dallas Stars, 211 Cowboys Pkwy., Irving, TX 75063

Detroit Redwings, Joe Louis Arena, 600 Civic Center Dr., Detroit, MI 48226

Edmonton Oilers, Northland Coliseum, 7424-118 Ave., Edmonton, Alberta, Canada, T5B 4M9

Florida Panthers, Miami Arena, 100 NE Third Ave., 10th Floor, Ft. Lauderdale, FL 33301

Los Angeles Kings, PO Box 17013, Inglewood, CA 90308

Montreal Canadians, 2313 St. Catherine St. West, Montreal, Quebec, Canada H3H 1N2

New Jersey Devils, Byrne Meadowlands Arena, PO Box 504, E. Rutherford, NJ 07073

New York Islanders, Nassau Coliseum, Uniondale, NY 11553

New York Rangers, Madison Square Garden, 4 Penn Plaza, New York, NY 10001

Ottawa Senators, 301 Moodie Dr., Suite 200, Nepean, Ontario, Canada K2H 9C4

Philadelphia Flyers, The Spectrum, Pattison Place, Phildelphia, PA 19148

Pittsburgh Penguins, Civic Arena, Gate No. 9, Pittsburgh, PA 15129

St. Louis Blues, PO Box 66792, St. Louis, MO 63166-6792

San Jose Sharks, San Jose Arena, 525 W. Santa Clara St., San Jose, CA 95113

Tampa Bay Lightning, 501 E. Kennedy Blvd., Suite 175, Tampa, FL 33602

Toronto Maple Leafs, Maple Leaf Gardens, 60 Carlton St., Toronto, Ontario, Canada M5B 1L1

Vancouver Canucks, Pacific Coliseum, 100 N. Renfrew St., Vancouver, B.C., Canada V5K 3N7

Washington Capitols, U.S. Air Arena, Landover, MD 20785

Winnipeg Jets, 10th Floor, 1661 Portage Ave., Winnipeg, Manitoba, Canada R3J 3T7

Free Books on Tape

Is reading becoming more difficult due to temporary or permanent changes in your eyesight? If so, you'll want to check out what the National Library Service (NLS) has to offer. They maintain a large collection of books, magazines, and journals in large type as well as in Braille. And if you prefer listening to someone read your favorite selections, they have lots of books and other reading materials on records and cassette tapes. Books in the collection include bestsellers, biographies, fiction, and how-to manuals.

The NLS distributes these recordings and the necessary playback equipment through a national network of cooperating libraries. Call your local library to find out what's available. Or you may contact Handicapped Readers Reference Section, National Library Service for the Blind and Physically Handicapped, Library of Congress, Washington, DC 20542; 202-707-5100. To get information online, go to <http://lcweb.loc.gov/nls/nls.html>.

Lower Your Housing Expenses

One of the biggest concerns we face as we get older is where — and how — we are going to live. Millions of senior citizens are faced with this important issue every day. Maybe you've owned your home for 30 years but find taxes harder to pay now that you're on a fixed income. Perhaps your pension isn't enough to cover your rent as well as your other living expenses. Or maybe you're just worried that someday getting around will be a little tougher than it used to be.

Whatever your situation, there's no need to despair. We live in a country that provides older adults with many living options. Look through this chapter to find the programs and benefits that can help with your situation. There may be tax breaks you're not aware of, low-profile loan or rent subsidy programs, or even a new type of living arrangement you've never considered. Not every opportunity listed here will apply to you, but many of the items can be potential lifesavers if you find yourself in a situation you did not anticipate.

Uncle Sam Has Done His Homework —
and You Can Benefit

An important function of any government — and one that our government is pretty good at — is keeping track of information about how its people live. They do this so they can make people aware of their options and also figure out what types of programs need to be developed. But they're not going to come to you with this wealth of information; you have to go to them.

Maybe you're interested in the most affordable or popular living arrangement for American seniors. Or perhaps you're curious about the pros and cons of congregate housing for the elderly. You may not even know what "congregate housing" is. Your task is simple: Go ask Uncle Sam.

Your first step is to contact your Congressman. He keeps up to date by reading reports prepared by the Congressional Research Service (CRS).

These reports are written by experts in various fields at the request of Congress. They provide an understandable overview of each topic as well as relevant newspaper articles and sources for even more information. While these packages are prepared specifically for Congress, they are great resources for anyone who can get their hands on them. And how do you do that? Your Congressman will send them to you. For free.

CRS reports dealing with housing include:
- *Congregate Housing: The Federal Program and Examples of State Programs (86-918E)*
- *Description of Residential Facilities for the Elderly (84-19 EPW)*
- *Elderly and Handicapped Housing: Recent Developments in Section 202 (89-667E)*
- *Evolution of Section 202: Housing for the Elderly (93-645-E)*
- *Federal Housing Programs Affecting Elderly People (88-576E)*
- *Housing for the Elderly and Handicapped: Section 202, Issue Brief (IB84038)*
- *Housing for Older Persons Act of 1995: HR 660 (95-443E)*

You can get these and other reports by contacting Your Senator or Representative, The Capitol, Washington, DC 20510; phone 202-224-3121.

Choosing the Best Way to Live

One thing about life that never changes is that life never stops changing. A living arrangement that works for you today might be completely unmanageable tomorrow. Maybe your house is too large to keep up by yourself. Maybe you need a hand now and then with chores like shopping or snow shoveling. Or maybe a roommate's the answer.

A brochure called *Your Home, Your Choice (Living Choices for Older Americans)* will help you make the right decision and show you where to get more help for any decision you make.

For your free copy, contact Public Reference, 6th & Pennsylvania Ave. NW, Room 130, Federal Trade Commission, Washington, DC 20580; phone 202-326-2222; or online <www.ftc.gov>.

Did You Really Say ... Roommate?

Sure. Maybe you haven't had a roommate other than your spouse since college, but it may be time to reconsider. Many seniors these days are taking advantage of the added security and companionship that a roommate can provide. According to recent statistics, 670,000 people over 65 share housing with nonrelatives; that's a 35 percent increase from over a decade ago.

There are a number of shared housing projects in existence today. One of the largest is called Operation Match, which is a division of the housing office of many cities. It helps match people looking for an affordable place to live with those who have space in their homes and are looking for someone to aid with their housing expenses.

To learn more about this type of program, contact the housing office in your area (you can find it in the blue pages of your phone book), or contact the ElderCare Hotline for a referral to an appropriate agency. The phone number is 800-677-1116; online is <www.ageinfo.org/elderloc/elderloc.html>.

Your Home Cash Machine

You've been putting money into your house for years; how about taking some money out of it for a change? You don't have to sell your home to make it work for you financially. Your commitment to home ownership over the years entitles you to some programs that are not available to renters.

The Federal Trade Commission publishes several free brochures that explain how you can convert the value of your home into ready cash. You can use this cash just about any way you want, from remodeling your home to investing in your portfolio to enjoying a nice trip to the Bahamas. But you must follow strict guidelines. Your options are explained in these free publications:
- *Home Equity Credit Lines*
- *Home Financing Primer*
- *Mortgage Money Guide*
- *Reverse Mortgages*

To get your copies or for more information, contact Public Reference, 6th & Pennsylvania Ave. NW, Room 130, Federal Trade Commission,

Washington, DC 20580; phone 202-326-2222; or online <www.ftc.gov>.

Mortgage Your House, Not Your Future

The mortgage on your house is probably your single largest financial commitment. Is it working for you the way it should? Many people don't take the time to set up the type of mortgage that will best serve their needs; they just go along with whatever the bank says. As usual, a little research can often save you a lot of money.

For a free handbook on what kinds of mortgages are available, different payment plans and options, and other valuable information, request *Buyers Beware* from the Federal Trade Commission. Write to 600 Pennsylvania Avenue NW, Washington, DC 20580, or call 202-326-2222.

Get Cash From Your Home

One of the best ways to take advantage of your status as a homeowner is to use your house as financial leverage. If you need money for repairs, medical bills, or any number of other reasons, getting a loan can be much easier if you own your own home. Being a senior citizen doesn't hurt, either.

A Home Equity Conversion Mortgage (HECM) enables older Americans to continue living independently in their own homes. The HECM program allows homeowners 62 and older to borrow against the equity in their home and get cash for just about any manner of living expenses. Loans do not have to be repaid until the homeowner moves from the home, sells the home, or dies. This program is now available in 47 states and is often referred to as a reverse mortgage.

If you would like more information on applying for a reverse mortgage, contact the HUD field office nearest you or the Assistant Secretary for Single Family Housing, U.S. Department of Housing and Urban Development, 451 7th St. SW, Room 9100, Washington, DC 20410; phone 888-466-3487; or online <www.hud.gov/rvrsmort.html>.

Low-Cost Loans for Veterans

America will forever owe a debt of gratitude to its fighting men. One way that the government acknowledges this debt is by offering certain benefits for veterans and their families. If you are a veteran or an unmarried surviving spouse of a vet, you may be eligible for a loan guarantee for the purchase or refinancing of a house, condo, or manufactured home.

Under this program, Veterans Affairs (VA) guarantees part of the total loan so a veteran may obtain a mortgage on a home or condominium with a competitive interest rate — and without a down payment if the lender agrees. VA does, however, require a down payment for the purchase of a manufactured home.

To learn who can qualify, details of financing and more, contact Veterans Assistance Office, U.S. Department of Veterans Affairs, 810 Vermont Ave., NW, Washington, DC 20420; phone 800-827-1000; or online <www.va.gov>.

How to Bring Your Down Payment ... Well ... Down

A lot of people go through life making rent payments that aren't much less than what mortgage payments would be on a similar property. Often, what stops these people from buying a home is the imposing reality of the initial down payment. But depending on the buyer, the lender, and the mortgage, there are various way to get around this hurdle.

Contact the Consumer Information Center for the free booklet, *How To Buy A Home With A Low Down Payment.* When ordering, request booklet number 566E. Write CIC-8D, PO Box 100, Pueblo, CO 81002, or call 888-878-3265.

☆☆☆

Let the State Pay Your Property Taxes

Many seniors face this frustrating dilemma: They've spent years paying off the mortgage on their houses so they could live rent-free in retirement, only to have property taxes raised to the point where a fixed, retirement income can't cover them. If this sounds familiar, a tax deferral might be the answer you're looking for.

Property tax deferral programs have been set up in many states to allow older homeowners to postpone paying their taxes until they sell their homes or die. The state will pay taxes on the property to the local government, secured by the owner's equity in the home. These payments accrue with interest as a loan from the state to the homeowner, and when the homeowner either dies or sells the home, the loan is repaid out of the proceeds of the sale of the estate.

For more details about this program, as well as information on other types of property tax relief available to seniors, contact your state's Department of Taxation.

Save Your House Profit From the Tax Man

Say you want to sell your house in Ohio for $150,000 and buy a condo in Florida for $30,000. You'll probably take a big hit on capital gains tax, right? Not necessarily.

There are new laws in place that allow you to keep that money for yourself. The Internal Revenue Service has done away with the one-time exclusion rule for those over the age of 55. Now when you sell your home you can exclude from your income any profit up to $500,000. There are several rules you have to meet to enjoy this new benefit, however. For example, you must have owned and lived in the home for two out of the last five years. For this reason, you can only take advantage of this benefit every two years. But how many times are you planning to move, anyway?

To find out what other restrictions apply, request Publication 523, *Selling Your Home*, from the Internal Revenue Forms Line at 800-829-3676; or online at <www.irs.gov>.

Make the Best of a Taxing Situation

Most people get a bit nervous when you mention the IRS. They generally don't want to mess with taxes — just pay them quietly and hope they don't go up. But the truth is, neither the IRS nor your local government is all-powerful. They do make mistakes, and sometimes they even admit them.

According to the American Homeowners Association, four out of five homeowners who challenge their property tax assessments end up getting their taxes reduced. Depending on your property, this could mean saving a big chunk of money. You've got nothing to lose, and according to the statistics, you've also got a great chance of success. If you suspect you may be paying too much in property tax, call your local assessor's office right away.

Just What Are You Sitting On?

OK, you've decided to sell the old homestead. Maybe you're moving to another part of the country or into a smaller place. Or maybe you're just thinking about it. One of the first things you're going to need to know is how much you can get for the place.

You might have no idea how much your home is worth, especially if you bought it a long time ago. Property values can go way up or down depending on many factors. Before you try to sell, it's important to know what a reasonable asking price will be. Even if you're not selling, getting a feel for your home's worth can help you decide whether your property is being taxed too highly and whether you've got enough homeowner's insurance.

Help is just a phone call away. For a $5 charge, a company called Home Price Check will look up recent sale prices for houses like yours in your neighborhood. Depending on their search and the number of sales in your area, they can turn up prices on at least one, or as many as 18 different properties. The search takes only a few minutes, so you can have your information right away. Give them a call at 800-487-6534.

Free Real Estate Resources

Has the house gotten too big now that the kids are gone? Do you want to move to a more comfortable neighborhood in, say, Florida? Whatever your reason for seeking a new house, you'll want to take your time with the househunting process and cover all the bases.

For free help in organizing your search, request a copy of the *Househunter's Scorecard*. This handy reference will outline all the things you need to consider when looking for your new place and remind you of certain aspects of buying a house that are frequently overlooked. Take advantage of this free resource by calling 312-223-2000, or writing to the Chicago Title Insurance Company, Consumer Affairs, 111 West Washington Street, Chicago, IL 60602.

☆☆☆

More Dollars for Your Domicile

If you're buying a new house, chances are you'll need to sell the old one. But just like buying, the selling process is also time-consuming and complicated. It's the Consumer Information Center to the rescue again.

CIC will send you its free reference manual, *Selling A Home* (#568E) to help you get the best deal for your home. It will give you tips on fixing up your house for showing, finding good realtors and legal assistance, and taking care of the tax issues that will arise. Give the CIC a call at 888-878-3265, or write to PO Box 100, Pueblo, CO 81002.

Money to Pay the Rent

It's no secret that when you retire your financial situation can change dramatically. Many people find that their budgets tend to get a little tighter. This is particularly true for the 25 percent of seniors who rent. For those who don't own a home, monthly rent payments can take a big bite out of a fixed income. This doesn't necessarily mean trouble if you live intelligently and know where to look for help.

Depending on your situation, you may be eligible for some sort of government assistance. A variety of programs are available for those living on a low income. One of the agencies set up for this purpose is the Department of Housing and Urban Development (HUD).

If you are struggling to pay rent, several HUD programs may be able to help you. For instance, under the Section 8 Rental Assistance Program, low-income renters can receive special vouchers to cover part of their rent.

Remember, low-income doesn't have to mean poor. In some parts of Ohio, for example, the eligible income for a single person can range up to $24,700. With the vouchers, the most you would have to pay is 30 percent of your adjusted income for rent.

To apply for this type of assistance, contact your local public housing agency (look in the blue pages of your phone book), or the HUD field office for your state. Information on the Section 8 program can be found online at <www.hud.gov/progdesc/voucher.html>.

Don't Leave Home Without It

If you rent an apartment, you probably had to put down a security deposit when you first signed your lease. Now that you're moving, the management should give it back to you if you haven't damaged the property. But sometimes you have to remind them.

Always ask for your security deposit back when you move or even if you just renew your lease. Most people know that, but here's something you may not know. In many states, you're not only entitled to a refund of your deposit, you are also entitled to the interest that collected while the deposit was held by the management. Even if you have damaged the property and aren't getting the deposit back, you should still demand to be paid the interest. That was your money building the interest, after all.

More Help From HUD

Want to find an apartment you can afford in a building filled with people your own age? No need to look any further than your local public housing office. It has a special program called Supportive Housing for the Elderly (Section 202).

If you meet certain income guidelines, your rent will be no higher than 10 to 30 percent of your adjusted income. An added plus is that many of these buildings also offer the benefit of a Service Coordinator, a sort of concierge of special services for seniors. They can hook you up with special transportation, medical programs, food assistance, and more.

If you are involved with a nonprofit or consumer cooperative, and you sense a need for housing services for elderly persons, you can take advantage of the Section 202 program. Capital advances are made to eligible private, nonprofit sponsors to finance the development of rental housing with supportive services for the elderly.

The advance is interest free and does not have to be repaid as long as the housing remains available for very low-income elderly persons for at least 40 years. You can also take advantage of the fact that the Service Coordinators are an eligible expense under this program. Contact the HUD field office nearest you to learn how you can apply, or check the program out online at <www.hud.gov/progdesc/2eldrl14.html>.

Small Town Rent Money

Big city life has its advantages, but living in the country can have some pretty good perks, too. There are special programs designed to lend assistance to seniors depending on where they live. If you live in a rural area and need some help with rent, contact the Rural Housing and Community Development Services (formerly Farmers Home Administration), which provides payments to make up the difference between the tenants' payments and the Rural Housing-approved rents for the housing.

To be eligible, low-income families must occupy Rural Rental Housing, Rural Cooperative Housing, or Farm Labor Housing projects financed by the Rural Housing and Community Development Services.

Contact your local office of Rural Housing and Community Development Services (look in the blue pages), or Rural Housing Services, U.S. Department of Agriculture, 14th and Independence Ave. SW, Room 5321, Washington, DC 20250; phone 202-720-1599; or online <www.rurdev.usda.gov/agency/rhs/rhsprog.html>.

Enjoy the Fresh Country Air

You can move away from congestion, nosy neighbors, and smog by checking out a program designed to help you get a home in the country. The program is called Section 502, and it's set up just for low-income families to buy new or existing houses in rural areas. Borrowers may reduce the interest rate to as low as 1 percent, and for some borrowers the loan term may be as long as 38 years. There are income requirements you must meet to qualify.

For information on the loans and eligibility requirements, contact your local Rural Housing office (formerly Farmers Home Administration) or Rural Housing Services, U.S. Department of Agriculture, 14th & Independence Ave. SW, Room 5334, Washington, DC 20250; phone 202-720-1474; or online <www.rurdev.usda.gov/agency/rhs/rhsprog.html>.

$1,600 to Keep You Warm This Winter

One of the best ways to keep out Old Man Winter is by taking good care of Old Man House. Storm windows, insulation, and even weather stripping can help reduce your fuel bill. And if you meet certain income guidelines, you can receive assistance in weatherizing your home or apartment at no charge. States allocate dollars to nonprofit agencies for purchasing and installing energy-related repairs, with the average grant being $1,600 per year.

Contact your State Energy Office or the Weatherization Assistance Programs Branch, 5E066, U.S. Department of Energy, 1000 Independence Ave., SW, Washington, DC 20585; phone 202-586-8295; or online <www.eren.doe.gov>.

★★★

Kill the Chill That Kills Your Bills

If you want to cut your housing expenses, start with your energy bill. Most of us waste a good deal of energy in our homes just by being lazy and not making little changes that could save us a tidy sum each month.

Learn how to take a bite out of the heating bill with the tips on insulation, weatherization, lighting, and much more that you will find in *Energy Savers: Tips on Saving Energy & Money At Home.* Priced at 50 cents, this book could pay for itself even if you just tossed it in the fireplace for heat. Order through the Consumer Information Center, PO Box 100, Pueblo, CO 81002, or call 888-878-3265.

★★★

Let the Pink Panther Help Protect Your Home

If you want expert advice on something, to whom do you turn? That's right, the expert. For years, Owens Corning has been a leader in the field of home insulation and sound control. Now the company is willing to share its expertise with you.

Call 800-GET-PINK for a free information packet about how to best protect your home against the elements. The Home Energy Savings Kit will arrive within 10 business days, complete with household tips about roofing, weather protection, conserving energy, home exterior design, and safe methods for do-it-yourself home improvement. Of course, the company promotes its own products (with a little help from the Pink Panther cartoon), but the good information it provides is well worth it.

Want to Save Energy? Turn on Your Computer

Chances are, your house is heated by conventional fuel, and your microwave is powered by electricity that comes from the power plant a few miles away. But perhaps this won't be the case forever. More and more, researchers concerned with saving our natural resources are looking to alternative sources of power such as the sun and wind. These sources aren't right for or available to everyone, but you can find out all about them by looking on the Internet.

The U.S. Department of Energy sponsors a web site called the Energy Efficiency and Renewable Energy Network (EREN) that provides a great deal of information on energy options that can save you money now and in the future. You can find the site at <www.eren.doe.gov/consumerinfo/>. While you're there, check out its free list of energy savers: *Tips on Saving Energy and Money at Home.*

If you're not yet online, you can get this information by writing to the Department of Energy at US DOE Energy Efficiency and Renewable Energy Clearinghouse (EREC), PO Box 3048, Merrifield, VA 22116, or call 800-363-3732.

Can't Pay Your Energy Bill?

There's help out there for the asking if you're having trouble with the high cost of heating and cooling. More than 1,500,000 seniors, both home-owners and renters, take part in the Low Income Home Energy Assistance Program (LIHEAP).

Although eligibility requirements vary from state to state, the house-hold's income must not exceed 150 percent of the poverty level or 60 percent of the state median income. Payments may be made directly to eligible households or to home energy suppliers and may take the form of cash, vouchers, or payments to third parties, such as utility companies or fuel dealers.

To learn more about the program, you may contact the state LIHEAP coordinator from the list below, or Administration for Children and Families, 370 L'Enfant Promenade, 5th Floor West, Suite 509, Washington, DC 20444.

LIHEAP Coordinators

Alabama: Mr. Willie D. Whitehead, Economic and Community Affairs; 334-242-5365

Alaska: Ms. Mary Riggen-Ver, Department of Health and Social Services; 907-465-3058

Arizona: Ms. Juanita Garcia, Community Services Administration; 602-542-6611

Arkansas: LIHEAP Unit, Department of Human Services; 501-682-8726

California: Ms. Toni Curtis, Department of Economic Opportunity; 916-323-8694, 800-433-4327 (in CA only)

Colorado: Ms. Ann Peden, Department of Social Services; 303-866-5972

Connecticut: Ms. Marion Wojick, Department of Social Services; 860-424-5891

Delaware: Ms. Leslie Lee, Div. of State Service Centers; 302-577-3491

District of Columbia: Mr. Richard Kirby, DC Energy Office; 202-673-6700

Florida: Mr. Robert Lakin, Bureau of Community Assistance; 850-488-7541

Georgia: Mr. Preston Weaver, Office of Community Services; 404-656-6697

Hawaii: Ms. Patricia Williams, Hawaii Department of Human Services; 808-586-5734

Idaho: Ms. Neva Kaufman, Department of Health and Welfare; 208-334-5732

Illinois: Ms. Kathy Hauger, Office of Human Services; 217-524-8029

Indiana: Ms. Maria Larson, Family and Social Services Administration; 317-232-7015

Iowa: Ms. Sue Downey, Bureau of Energy Assistance; 515-281-3838/3943

Kansas: Ms. Kathy Valentine, Division of Income Maintenance, DSRS; 913-296-3349

Kentucky: Mr. Patrick Bishop, Dept. of Social Insurance; 502-564-4847

Louisiana: Mr. Lonnie Didier, Office of Community Services; 504-342-2274

Maine: Ms. Jo-Ann Choate, Maine State Housing Authority; 207-626-4600

Maryland: Ms. Sandra Brown, Community Services Administration; 410-767-7218

Massachusetts: Mr. James A. Hays, EOCD/BEP; 617-727-7004, ext. 533

Michigan: Ms. Shirley Nowakowski, Department of Social Services; 517-335-3588

Minnesota: Mr. Mark D. Kaszynski, Div. of Community Based Services; 612-297-2590

Mississippi: Mr. Godwin Agulanna, Department of

Human Services; 601-359-4769

Missouri: Mr. Charles F. Wright, Division of Family Services; 314-751-0472

Montana: Mr. Jim Nolan, Dept. of Social and Rehabilitation Services; 406-447-4260

Nebraska: Mr. Bill Davenport, Department of Social Services; 402-471-9172

Nevada: Ms. Vickie DeKoekkoek, Department of Human Services; 702-687-6919

New Hampshire: Richard Johnson, Energy and Community Services; 603-271-2611

New Jersey: Mr. John R. Simzak, Division of Family Development; 609-588-2488

New Mexico: Ms. Loretta Williams, NM Human Services Department; 505-841-2693

New York: Mr. Steven Ptak, Bureau of Energy Programs; 518-474-9321

North Carolina: Ms. Alice Smith, Division of Social Services; 919-733-7831

North Dakota: Mr. Ron Knutsen, Department of Human Services; 701-328-4882

Ohio: Ms. Vicky Mroczek, Home Energy Assistance; 614-644-6858, 614-728-6832

Oklahoma: Mr. Ron Amos, Dept. of Human Services; 405-521-4089

Oregon: Ms. Linda Marquam, Oregon Housing and Community Services; 503-986-2094

Pennsylvania: Ms. Joan Brenner, Div. of Cash Assistance; 717-772-7902

Puerto Rico: Ms. Lucila B. Rivera, Department of Social Services; 809-722-7361

Rhode Island: Mr. Matteo Guglielmetti, Division of Central Services; 401-277-6920

South Carolina: Mr. Michael Hawkins, Div. of Economic Opportunity; 803-734-0662

South Dakota: Ms. Abbie Rathbun, Office of Energy Assistance; 605-773-4131

Tennessee: Mr. Steve Neece, Department of Human Services; 615-313-4764

Texas: Mr. J. Al Almaguer, Dept. of Housing and Community Affairs; 512-475-3951

Utah: Mr. Sherm Roquiero, Office of Family Support Administration; 801-538-8644

Vermont: Mrs. Judy Rosenstrike, Department of Social Welfare; 802-241-2889

Virgin Islands: Ms. Kathryn C. Mills, Dept. of Human Services; 809-774-1166

Virginia: Ms. Charlene Chapman, Virginia Department of Social Services; 804-692-1750

Washington: Mr. William Graham, Dept. of Community Development; 360-753-3403

West Virginia: Mr. Robert Kent, Dept. of Health and Human Resources; 304-558-8290

Wisconsin: Mr. Steve Tryon, Department of Health and Social Services; 608-266-7601

Wyoming: Ms. Evon Williams, Department of Family Services; 307-777-6095

Park It in a Trailer Park

Home ownership can be very expensive, and yet many people feel crowded in apartments. But is there any other option? For well over a million American seniors, the answer is yes. The solution: trailer homes.

Many older adults live in trailer homes for the convenience, the mobility, and the camaraderie of trailer park living. Many also take advantage of the U.S. Department of Housing and Urban Development (HUD), which will insure loans for people to finance the purchase of manufactured homes and/or lots. The loans, called Title 1, are made by private lending institutions and are available to any person able to make the cash investment and the loan payments.

To learn more about this insurance program, contact the HUD Field office near you, or Assistant Secretary for Housing, Federal Housing Commissioner, U.S. Department of Housing and Urban Development, 451 7th St. SW, Room 9100, Washington, DC 20410; phone 202-708-3600; or online <www.hud.gov>.

Helping Hands Can Keep You in Your Home

As we get older, living on our own can become more challenging. Some of the things we used to do for ourselves may just be too much to handle. But this doesn't necessarily mean it's time for a nursing home.

Maybe it is time to look into a new program called HOPE for Elderly Independence. This program was designed to help seniors live at home longer by providing help with personal needs such as dressing, bathing, and grooming, as well as functional needs around the house like cooking and cleaning. It can also help with the rent through Section 8 rental certificates. These services are provided at a low cost, and can often mean the difference between staying in your home and seeking new arrangements.

To learn if the project is currently underway in your town, contact your local public housing office, or you may contact the Rental Assistance

Division, Office of the Assistant Secretary for Public and Indian Housing, U.S. Department of Housing and Urban Development, Operations Division, 451 7th St. SW, Room 4220, Washington, DC 20410.

A Little Help Around the Homestead

Another great program that helps seniors manage their home life and maintain their independence is the Congregate Housing Services Program (CHSP). This is similar to the HOPE program, but instead of homeowners, this one focuses on those who live in rented dwellings.

Some public housing agencies and nonprofit Section 202 sponsor meals and other support services such as housekeeping, aid in grooming, dressing, and other activities for elderly or handicapped residents. Each participant must pay 10 to 20 percent of their income for the meals program, plus they may have to pay a flat fee for other supportive services. But total fees can add up to no more than 20 percent of the resident's adjusted income.

Below you will find a listing of those who participate in the program as well as the local U.S. Department of Housing and Urban Development or Rural Housing and Community Development Service offices. Keep in mind that many other senior citizen housing facilities offer similar services to residents.

For more information, contact the program nearest you from the list below, or contact Assistant Secretary for Housing-Federal Housing Commissioner, U.S. Department of Housing and Urban Development, 451 7th St. SW, Room 9100, Washington, DC 20410; phone 202-708-3600.

Congregate Housing Services Program Grantee List

ARKANSAS

North Arkansas Human Services, PO Box 2578, Batesville, AR 72503; phone 501-793-8934

CALIFORNIA

Community Development Commission, 2 Coral Circle, Monterey Park, CA 91755; phone 213-890-7125

Marin County HA, 30 N. San Pedro Rd., PO Box 4282, San Rafael, CA 94913; phone 415-491-2348

Spanish Speaking Unity Council, 1900 Fruitvale Ave., Suite 2A, Oakland, CA 94601-2468; phone 510-535-6913

COLORADO

Archdiocesan Housing Committee,

1580 Logan, #700, Denver, CO 80203; phone 303-830-0215

Francis Heights, Inc., 2626 Osceola St., Denver, CO 80212-1258; phone 303-433-6268, ext. 224

CONNECTICUT

Mansfield Retirement Community, One Silo Circle, Storrs, CT 06268-2018; phone 860-429-9933

State of Connecticut, Department of Social Services, 25 Sigourney St., 10th Floor, Hartford, CT 06106; phone 860-424-5283

DELAWARE

Wilmington Housing Authority, 400 N. Walnut St., Wilmington, DE 19801; phone 302-429-6775

FLORIDA

Ft. Pierce Housing Authority, 707 N. 7th St., Fort Pierce, FL 34950-4501; phone 561-461-7281

Dade County HUD, PO Box 350250, Miami, FL 33135-0250; phone 305-644-5290

Dowling Park Home Inc., PO Box 4307, Dowling Park, FL 32060; phone 904-658-3333

Dowling Park Apartments Inc., PO Box 4307, Dowling Park, FL 32060; phone 904-658-3333

Kinneret Inc. & Kinneret II, 515 S. Delaney Ave., Orlando, FL 32801-3841; phone 407-425-4537

HAWAII

Hale Mahaolu, 200 Hina Ave.,

Kahului, Maui, HI 96732-1821; phone 808-871-4792

Opportunities for the Disabled, Inc., 64-1510 Kamehameha Hwy., Wahiawa, HI 96786; phone 808-622-3929, ext. 123

ILLINOIS

The Lambs, Inc., PO Box 520, Libertyville, IL 60048-0520; phone 847-362-4636

Bloomington Housing Authority, 104 E. Wood St., Bloomington, IL 61701-6768; phone 309-829-3360, ext. 214

INDIANA

Muncie Housing Authority Agency, 409 E. First St., Muncie, IN 47302; phone 317-288-9242

IOWA

Waterloo Housing Authority, 620 Mulberry St. Carnegie, Waterloo, IA 50703; phone 319-233-0201

Ecumenical Housing, Inc., 2671 Owen Court, Dubuque, IA 52002; phone 319-556-5125

Alverno Apartments, Inc., 3525 Winsor Ave., Dubuque, IA 52001-0419; phone 319-582-2364

Charles City Housing Commission, 1000 S. Grand Ave., Charles City, IA 50616; phone 515-228-6661

KANSAS

Housing Authority of the City of Atchison, 103 S. 7th St., Atchison, KS 66002; phone 913-367-3323

LOUISIANA

Village de Memoire I/NCSCHMC, 1001 N. Reed St., Ville Platte, LA 70581; phone 318-363-0162

MAINE

Methodist Conference Home, 46 Summer St., Rockland, ME 04841-2939; phone 207-596-6477

Old Town Housing Authority, 100 S. Main St., PO Box 404, Old Town, ME 04468-1572; phone 207-827-6151

Brunswick Housing Authority, PO Box A, Brunswick, ME 04011-1541; phone 207-725-8711

Summer Street Housing Preservation, Inc., 46 Summer St., Rockland, ME 04841-2939; phone 207-596-6477

MARYLAND

Housing Authority of Baltimore City, 417 E. Fayette St., Room 265, Baltimore, MD 21202-3431; phone 410-396-4271

The Arc of Southern Maryland, PO Box 1860, Prince Frederick, MD 20678; phone 410-535-2413

MASSACHUSETTS

Bethany Homes, 10-12 Phoenix Row, Haverhill, MA 01832; phone 508-374-2160

MI Residential, 189 Maple St., Lawrence, MA 01841-3761; phone 508-682-7575

Jewish Community Housing, 30 Wallingford Rd., Brighton, MA 02135-4753; phone 617-254-1861

MICHIGAN

Jewish Federation Apts., Inc., 6700 W. Maple Rd., West Bloomfield, MI 48322; phone 810-661-5220

Plymouth Opportunity, Non-Profit Housing, 593 Deer St., Plymouth, MI 48170-1701; phone 313-422-1020

Jewish Federation Apts., Inc., 15100 W. Ten Mile Rd., Oak Park, MI 48237; phone 810-967-4240

Moore Non-Profit Housing Corp., 401 W. Jolly Rd., Lansing, MI 48910-6607; phone 517-393-4442

Detroit Int. Stake Adult Housing, 16651 Labser Rd., Detroit, MI 48219; phone 313-538-0360

Potential Development Homes, PO Box 1978, Jackson, MI 49204; phone 517-784-4426

MINNESOTA

St. Paul Housing Authority, 480 Cedar St., Suite 600, St. Paul, MN 55101-2240; phone 612-298-5664, ext. 3083

Duluth Housing Redevelopment Authority, 222 E. Second St., Duluth, MN 55816-0900; phone 218-726-2857

HRA City of South St. Paul, 125 Third Ave. North, South St. Paul, MN 55075-2097; phone 612-455-1560

St. Paul Public Housing Agency, 480 Cedar St., Suite 600, St. Paul, MN 55101-2240; phone 512-298-5665, ext. 3083

MISSISSIPPI

Mississippi Regional HA, No. 5, PO Box 419, Newton, MS 39345-0419; phone 601-683-3371

MISSOURI

Crown Center for Senior Living, 8350 Delcrest Dr., St. Louis, MO 63124-2166; phone 314-991-2055, ext. 222

St. Louis Housing Authority, 5655 Kingsbury, St. Louis, MO 63112; phone 314-367-1686

Murphy-Blair Senior Commons, 2600 Hadley St., St. Louis, MO 63106; phone 314-539-9625

MONTANA

Northern Cheyenne Tribe, PO Box 128, Lame Deer, MT 59043; phone 406-477-6284

NEBRASKA

Falls City Housing Authority, 800 E. 21st St., Falls City, NE 68355-2349; phone 402-245-4204

Lincoln Area Agency on Aging, 129 N. 10th St., Room 222, Lincoln, NE 68508; phone 402-441-6175

NEW HAMPSHIRE

Manchester Housing Authority, 198 Hanover St., Manchester, NH 03104-6125; phone 603-624-2146

Laconia HRA, 25 Union Ave., Laconia, NH 03246-3558; phone 603-524-2112

Keene Housing Authority, 105 Castle St., Keene, NH 03431; phone 603-352-6161

Somersworth Housing Authority, 9 Bartlett Ave., PO Box 31, Somersworth, NH 03878; phone 603-692-2357

Nashua Housing Authority, 101 Major Dr., Nashua, NH 03060-4783; phone 603-883-5661

NEW JERSEY

Plainfield Housing Authority, 510 E. Front St., Plainfield, NJ 07060-1424; phone 908-769-6335

Trent Center, 511 Greenwood Ave., Trenton, NJ 08609-2108; phone 609-394-0093

NEW YORK

New York City Housing Authority, 250 Broadway, Room 1503, New York, NY 10007; phone 212-306-3330

Schenectady Municipal HA, 375 Broadway, Schenectady, NY 12305-2519; phone 518-382-8651

NORTH CAROLINA

Bell House, Inc., 2400 Summit Ave., Greensboro, NC 27405-5014; phone 910-621-0938

High Point Housing Authority, 500 E. Russell Ave., PO Box 1779, High Point, NC 27261-1779; phone 910-887-2661, ext. 60/35

East Salem Homes, Inc., 8 W. Third St., Suite 400, Winston Salem, NC 27101; phone 910-725-3564

NORTH DAKOTA

Fargo Housing Authority, 2525 N. Broadway, Fargo, ND 58102-1439; phone 701-293-7870

Senior Meals and Services, Inc., PO Box 713, Devil's Lake, ND 58301; phone 701-662-5061

OHIO

Cincinnati Metrop Housing Authority, 16 W. Central Pkwy., Zone 10, Cincinnati, OH 45210; phone 513-675-5585

Alpha Phi Alpha Homes, 695 Dunbar Dr., Akron, OH 44311-1315; phone 216-376-8787

Central Ohio Area Agency on Aging, 174 E. Long St., Columbus, OH 43215; phone 614-645-3886

OKLAHOMA

Cherokee Nation Housing Authority, PO Box 948, Tahlequah, OK 74465-0948; phone 918-456-0671, ext. 241

Muskogee Fairhaven Manor, Phase I, 500 Dayton, Muskogee, OK 74403; phone 918-682-4300

OREGON

Housing Authority of Portland, 135 SW Ash St., Portland, OR 97204; phone 503-273-4522

PENNSYLVANIA

Philadelphia Housing Authority, 801 Arch St., 5th Floor, Philadelphia, PA 19107; phone 215-684-4421

OIC Housing, 1717 W. Hunting Park Ave., Philadelphia, PA 19140; phone 215-229-9000

Riverview Towers, Phase I Inc., 52 Garetta St., Pittsburgh, PA 15217-3231; phone 412-521-7876

East Brady Heights, 106 E. North St., New Castle, PA 16101; phone 412-654-8659

RHODE ISLAND

United Methodist Retirement Center, 40 Irving Ave., East Providence, RI 02914; phone 401-438-4456

SOUTH DAKOTA

South Dakota HDA, 221 South Central, Pierre, SD 57501; phone 605-773-4532

TENNESSEE

St. Peter Manor, 108 N. Auburndale, Memphis, TN 38104-6405; phone 901-278-8200

Orange Grove Center, 615 Derby St., PO Box 3249, Chattanooga, TN 37404-0249; phone 423-493-2919

TEXAS

W. Leo Daniels Towers, 8826 Harrell St., Houston, TX 77093; phone 713-692-8541

REAL, Inc., 301 Lucero, Alice, TX 78332; phone 512-668-3158

UTAH

St. Mark's Gardens, 514 North 300 West, Kaysville, UT 84037-3103; phone 801-544-4231

WISCONSIN

Residential Care, 424 Washington Ave., Oshkosh, WI 54901; phone 414-236-6560

WYOMING

RENEW, 2 North Main, Suite 406, Sheridan, WY 82801; phone 307-674-4200

The Continuing Care Compromise

For some seniors, maintaining a household becomes too much trouble, but the thought of nursing home life is unappealing. There is an option, however, called continuing care retirement communities (CCRCs), that combines the best of both worlds.

Typically these communities provide housing, personal care, healthcare, and a range of social and recreation services as well as group meals. Residents contract with the community to pay an entrance fee and monthly fees in exchange for benefits and services. The contract is usually effective for the remainder of a resident's life.

The definition of these communities continues to be confusing and inconsistent due to the wide range of services offered, differing types of housing units, and different contracts. Some problems have developed regarding refunds or contract cancellation when people have changed their minds. It is important to take your time when looking into any living option, and be sure that you understand all the details of a contract before signing it.

The American Association of Homes for the Aging has a consumer guidebook that provides information about the various contracts and services and also outlines the benefits and risks. *Continuing Care Retirement Communities Guidebook* is available for $6.95 by contacting American Association of Homes and Services for the Aging, Suite 500, 901 E St., NW, Washington, DC 20004; phone 202-783-2242, or calling the Publication Dept. at 800-508-9442.

Choosing a Nursing Home

About 5 percent of all senior citizens reside in nursing homes, and for many, making the choice is a difficult decision. There are many prejudices against this style of living, but depending on the facility, it can be a pleasant and efficient way to live.

As more and more older adults look toward this option, the number and variety of nursing homes is greatly increasing. Competition for residents should help drive the quality of nursing care up and bring the cost down. If you're considering a nursing home as your place of residence, be sure to shop around and do a little homework.

At about $30,000 per year, nursing home living can be expensive. However, the special attention and facilities available at most nursing homes are sometimes practical necessities. Questions about what type of care is most essential and how to pay for it can be answered by looking into the various government resources that are available on this topic.

Free Workshops to Help You Decide

Choosing a nursing home is never easy, but with some preparation the move can go smoothly. Many County Cooperative Extension offices offer pamphlets or workshops on selecting a nursing home and planning for it financially. Some local offices have information on estate planning and the pros and cons of nursing home insurance.

To learn more about what your local County Cooperative Extension office has for seniors, look in the blue pages of your phone book for the office nearest you, or contact Cooperative State Research Education and Extension Service, U.S. Department of Agriculture, Room 3328, Washington, DC 20250; phone 202-720-3029; or online <www.reeusda.gov>.

Nursing Home Shopping List

If you're shopping around for a nursing home, chances are you don't know exactly what to look for. What are the options and benefits that you're going to want? What are some of the danger signs that you should be aware of? How do you know you'll be getting your money's worth?

During your search, you might start by asking a few simple questions. When touring any facility, keep these preliminary questions in mind: Do residents seem well cared for and generally content? Is there an activity room? Is the home certified for Medicare and Medicaid programs? Does the home have a security system to prevent confused residents from wandering away?

These are just some of the questions you will find listed on the nursing home checklist provided in the free publication, *When You Need A Nursing Home*. To receive your copy, contact National Institute on Aging, Information Center, PO Box 8057, Gaithersburg, MD 20898; phone 800-222-2225; or online <www.nih.gov/nia/>.

The Medicare Hotline also distributes a free publication titled, *A Guide to Choosing a Nursing Home,* which provides you with information and questions you should ask when looking at facilities. Contact the Medicare Hotline at 800-638-6833; or online at <www.hcfa.gov/medicare/medicare.htm>.

Get Married and Move to Arizona

It may sound like strange advice, but according to statistics, this is what you should do if you never want to live in a nursing home. Arizona has the lowest rate of nursing home residence, and research shows that people who have been married are less likely to use a nursing home than those who haven't.

The group that compiles these and other statistics about nursing homes is called the Agency for Health Care Policy and Research (AHCPR). Through its research, this agency has gathered a wealth of information on the subject of senior citizen care, their options, and their tendencies. The AHCPR is willing to share its findings with you if you're trying to decide what residential options to pursue. Some of its free publications include:

- *Characteristics of Nursing Homes that Affect Resident Outcomes*
- *A Lifetime Perspective on Proposals For Financing Nursing Home Care*
- *Long-Term Care Arrangements for Elderly Persons with Disabilities: Private and Public Roles*
- *Nursing Home Reform and the Mentally Ill*
- *Nursing Home Use After 65 in the United States*
- *Nursing Home Use and Costs*
- *Public and Private Responsibility for Financing Nursing Home Care*
- *Quality of Board Care Homes Serving Low-Income Elderly*
- *Lifetime Use of Nursing Home Care*
- *The Risk of Nursing Home Use in Later Life*
- *Use of Formal and Informal Home Care by the Disabled Elderly*
- *Use of Psychoactive Drugs in Nursing Homes*

For your free copies or more information, contact Agency for Health Care Policy and Research, PO Box 88547, Silver Spring, MD 20907; phone 800-358-9295; or online <www.ahcpr.gov>.

Who's Really Picking Up the Check?

A recent government study has discovered that a disturbingly large number of seniors who buy long-term care insurance will actually stop paying their premiums long before they get to the point where they need the insurance coverage the most. This trend is especially alarming given the fact that the price of nursing home care is expected to double in the next 25 years.

Don't let this happen to you. To find out more about this study and others on long-term care issues, contact the General Accounting Office (GAO). The GAO has a series of reports that deal with long-term care issues including:

- *Long-Term Care Insurance: High Percentage of Policyholders Drop Policies (GAO/HRD 93-129)*
- *Long-Term Care: The Need for Geriatric Assessment in Publicly Funded Home and Community-Based Programs (T-PEMD 94-20)*
- *Long-Term Care: Demography, Dollars, and Dissatisfaction Drive Reform (T-HEHS 94-140)*
- *Long-Term Care Insurance: Tax Preferences Reduce Costs More for Those in Higher Tax Brackets (GAO/GGD 93-110)*

All reports are free and can be requested by contacting the U.S. General Accounting Office, PO Box 6015, Gaithersburg, MD 20884; phone 202-512-6000; or online <www.gao.gov>.

Your Nursing Care Rights — Get What You Pay For

Living in a nursing home is sometimes the best option, but it is hardly ever cheap. You worked hard for many years so you could afford to be taken care of in your later years. Knowing your rights as a resident will help you know what you should and should not expect and help you keep your caregivers on their toes.

The Nursing Home Reform Amendments were passed to protect your rights, and every state in the country has specific regulations that outline how a nursing home must treat its residents. For example, you cannot be denied admittance to a nursing home simply because you have Medicare or Medicaid benefits. As a resident, you are entitled to free visitation, choice of doctors, and to keep any of your belongings as long as they do not create a health risk. Other areas covered are privacy issues, filing of grievances, and reasons for discharge.

Nursing home violations should be reported. Taking action not only improves your quality of life, it makes the whole system better in the long run. For more specific information on your rights as a nursing home resident, contact the AARP Foundation's National Training Project, 601 E Street, NW, Washington, DC 20049. Another good source is the National Citizen's Coalition for Nursing Home Reform, 1424 16th Street, NW, Suite 202, Washington, DC 20036; phone 202-332-2275.

Don't Take Poor Treatment Lying Down

Occasionally, an exposé on TV will show the story of a nursing home that's not doing much nursing. Reports about nursing home abuses are disturbing, and while this type of problem isn't common, it does occur.

If you believe that you or a family member are being mistreated or are not getting what you paid for, it's time to take action. The best way to start is by making a call to your state's Nursing Home Ombudsman. The Ombudsman Program is designed to investigate and resolve complaints made by or on behalf of residents of long-term care facilities. They also make sure these places are running properly and up to code. The Ombudsmen can help you with anything from being denied admission to a nursing home to complaints about quality of the food you are being served. They can even help report stolen property.

Ombudsmen act as mediators, but they are not enforcement agencies. They cannot force a nursing home to change or correct its practices. But it is in the best interest of the nursing home to work with you before you refer your complaint elsewhere (which the Ombudsman can assist you with).

To locate the Nursing Home Ombudsman in your state, contact your state capitol, or check the Directory of State Information at the end of this book.

Money-Saving Household Hints

Does it seem like nobody's willing to help around the house? Do you sometimes feel like it's just you alone out there, standing against the dust bunnies, the wobbly banister, and the mysterious purple stain on the carpet?

Well, fear not. There are people who are willing to lend a hand, often for free. You can get great samples of household products, big discounts on home improvement supplies, and scads of free information simply by learning where to look. The government, private companies, and consumer groups all have ways to save you money, but you have to ask in order to receive.

Often, a company will offer free information and samples in the hopes that you will remember their generosity when purchase time rolls around. But just because an informative brochure has a corporate logo on it, or is written with a promotional slant, doesn't mean that it can't provide you with a great deal of valuable knowledge.

So if you've got a cleaning showdown looming around the old homestead, saddle up that spray bottle, draw your paint brush, and pull out your *Free Stuff For Seniors*. Your posse of eager helpers might be just a page away.

How Safe Is Your Home?

The world is a dangerous place. Violent crime, crazy traffic, extreme weather — sometimes it's enough to make you want to lock yourself away in the safety of your own home. But be careful if you do. Your home comes equipped with its own built-in, quieter dangers. Every day we see stories in the paper about the dangers of lead paint, radon, and carbon dioxide. These dangerous elements could be in your home right now, and unless you know how to detect them, they could cause serious health problems.

The Environmental Protection Agency is the office of our government responsible for controlling environmental pollution, and can answer all your questions about such household dangers. They have brochures and pamphlets describing how to check for radon and what should be done about it; the proper use of pesticides; how to garden without chemicals; recycling; how to find and use safe drinking water; and indoor and outdoor air pollution.

For all your environmental questions, contact Public Information Center 3404, U.S. Environmental Protection Agency, 401 M St., SW, Washington, DC 20460; 202-260-5922; or online at <www.epa.gov>.

Make Like Noah and Plan Ahead

You're a smart homeowner. You've planned ahead. You know that disaster can strike at any time in the form of fire, burglar, or even tornado. But what about torrential rain that turns into a flood?

The scary truth is that most home insurance policies do not cover damage caused by flood. For whatever reason, most companies insist that if you want to be covered against this particular natural disaster, you must get a separate policy. And even if they realize this, most people simply don't do it. Perhaps you should.

Houses that are built on flood plains, close to rivers, or at very low elevations are particularly susceptible to rising water. It is important to evaluate your property and figure out your level of risk. For free information on setting up a workable insurance plan, or deciding if you need one, call the National Flood Insurance Program at 800-611-6123 and ask for extension 490.

For further information, you can contact the Federal Emergency Management Agency (FEMA).Write to FEMA/CTI, PO Box 1395, Jessup, MD 20797. You can also visit FEMA online at <www.fema.gov/nfip> or call 888-CALL-FLOOD and ask for Extension 758.

☆☆☆

A Watchdog Whose Bark You Should Heed

You wouldn't invite a dangerous criminal to live in your home, would you? Of course not. But each year, millions of Americans do the next best thing, by purchasing products with design flaws that can make them deadly. Of course, you have no way of knowing what products are going to go bad and be potential killers. That's why your Uncle

Sam has a watchdog to help keep you safe.

The U.S. Consumer Product Safety Commission keeps a constant eye on these things for you. Every month, they put out a new batch of press releases that offer home safety tips, describe dangerous items, and announce product recalls. In one recent month alone, such recalls included portable heaters, clothes irons, sandals, home audio theater systems, and many more. Check out their current posting at <www.cpsc.gov> or write to them at the U.S. Consumer Product Safety Commission, Washington, DC 20207.

Walk for Safety

How would you like to take a special walk that could save your life without ever having to leave your home? A home safety tour might not sound like an exciting way to spend an afternoon, but it can make a big difference to your family's well-being.

There are many people out there who can help you secure your home. You can call a home safety specialist and pay him a big chunk of money to inspect your house. Or, if you prefer, call for any or all of the free do-it-yourself inspections listed below to do essentially the same thing.

YOUR HOUSE: The U.S. Consumer Product Safety Commission has prepared an extensive, 15-page safety checklist. It will take a bit of time to complete, but you'll feel — and actually be — a whole lot safer when you're done. This worksheet is also available to download from their web site at <www.cpsc.gov>. Or you can write to them at the U.S. Consumer Product Safety Commission, Washington, DC 20207.

FIRE: Call the MetLife Consumer Education Center for their booklet *About Keeping Your Home Safer*. It talks about fire prevention and what to do in case a fire breaks out. The number is 800-638-5433.

ELECTRICAL: Find out if your cords, fuses, or electric blankets are putting you at risk. Get the do-it-yourself test by sending a self-addressed, stamped envelope and 55 cents to the National Electrical Safety Foundation, 1300 N. 17 Street, Suite 1847, Rosslyn, VA 22209.

BREAK-INS: Is your home safe from prowlers? Take the New England Lock Company's home security test by calling 203-866-9283 or writing them at Box 544, South Norwalk, CT 06856.

Burning Issues

Some of the most common and dangerous household injuries are burns. Yet, despite their frequency, most of us don't know how to treat them. We've been told to put everything from water to ice to cold cream on burns, but what is right? In a pinch, you're really going to want to know.

The people at the Boston Burn Clinic of Shriners Hospital know, and they're happy to share this critical information with you free of charge. They'll send you a package of information that includes ways to prevent every kind of household burn, steps to take for fire safety, and first aid. You'll even get a bright yellow sticker that you can put on your refrigerator that tells you just what to do — and what not to do — in case of an emergency. Call them today at 800-255-1916.

Getting Ready to Paint

The first step in repainting anything is removing the old paint. But if you don't know what you're doing, stripping can cause serious damage to the surface, cause the new paint job to look shoddy, and even make you sick. Save yourself the expense of major repairs and having to do things twice. Get it right the first time by ordering the Consumer Information Center's book *Stripping Paint from Wood*. Write CIC, Department 571Y, Pueblo, CO 81009.

Paint Like an Artist in Your Own Home

Even a past master would tell you that you don't start a project until you know what it's going to involve. One of the most common — and most expensive — mistakes that do-it-yourselfers make is jumping into a major project without any real idea of how they plan to finish it.

Save time and money by starting out with free plans. *The Prep, Paint and Protect Technique Guide* will walk you through the steps of a successful painting project, from selecting your tools to slapping on the final coat. Send your request to Delta, 2550 Pellissier Place, Whittier, CA 90601.

$15,000 to Spruce Up Your Home

What do you do when your beloved house starts to show her age? Maybe funds are short, but you know your home needs a new furnace, roof, water heater, or even plumbing. Don't let your castle crumble around you.

If you live in a small town and don't make much money, you can apply for a grant to fix up your home from the Rural Housing Preservation Grants (Section 504). The average grant is $7,500, but you can get up to $15,000. This is government money, but is distributed to local groups who in turn give it out to local homeowners.

To learn more about the program, to identify local groups that are giving out the money, or to learn eligibility requirements, contact your local Rural Housing and Community Development Services (formerly Farmers Home Administration). You may also contact Multiple Family Housing Loan Division, Rural Housing Services, U.S. Department of Agriculture, AG Box 7081, Washington, DC 20250; 202-720-1606; or online at <www.rurdev.usda.gov/agency/rhs/rhsprog.html>.

A Thousand-Dollar Home Face Lift

Need cash to refurbish or fix up your home? As part of the HOME Investment Partnership Program, the HOME Repair/Modification Programs For Elderly Homeowners program makes low interest loans available to low-income individuals for home repair services. Money is distributed through over 500 sites, so to locate the closest program and application information, write to Community Connections, PO Box 7189, Gaithersburg, MD 20898; or call 800-998-9999.

⭐⭐⭐

Find the Right Man for the Job — Free!

Unless your name is Bob Vila, you're probably not going to want to tackle major remodeling jobs without at least a little help. While saving money through do-it-yourself projects is a good idea, sometimes you'll save more money — and prevent damage to your house and yourself — by having the right professional do it for you.

But with so many carpenters and builders and contractors out there, how do you know which ones are the good ones, and which ones will just try to rip you off? What kind of credentials or references should you look for? What questions should you ask, and what decisions should you make before even talking to a contractor?

Get the dirt on building from the people who keep their eyes on the industry. The National Association of Home Builders offers a series of articles that give you the low-down, and teach you what you need to know to make an informed, safe choice. If you send them a self-addressed, stamped, business-size envelope, they'll send you their article "How to Find a Professional Remodeler." Be sure to mention the article by name in your request, and send it to the National Association of Home Builders, Remodeler's Council, Dept. SW, 1201 15 Street NW, Washington, DC, 20005-2800. Or give them a call at 800-223-2665.

★★★

Pay Less by Planning Smart

Making big renovations to your home can be costly, in terms of both time and money. Possibly the best thing you can do to conserve both of these important resources is to plan ahead. Get the facts, compare, know what to expect and what you are talking about. Only then should you go ahead and tear down a wall.

If you don't know enough to even ask the right questions, ask the folks who do. Call the National Association of the Remodeling Industry at 800-440-6274. They'll send you their brochure, *The Master Plan for Professional Home Remodeling,* absolutely free. Inside, you'll learn what to expect from a professional builder, which one to pick, and how to budget the financial end of a big project. You'll also get advice on selecting products to use, realistic timelines for certain projects, and other valuable information that can help you stay within your limitations of time and money.

The Consumer Information Center offers free advice in the form of a 13-page booklet appropriately titled *Home Improvement* (Code #570E). This resource provides information on how to finance repairs, the ways in which remodeling can be a drain or a boon to the value of your home, and how to choose the best and most affordable professionals to help you. Don't let your ambitious projects turn your house into a money pit. Get the free information today by writing to the CIC, PO Box 100, Pueblo, CO 81002; 888-878-3265.

50-Cent Solutions From the CIC

As you've already learned, the Consumer Information Center in Pueblo, Colorado is an information clearinghouse that works with the government to put valuable knowledge in the hands of Americans. If your particular hands aren't very "handy," the CIC can help. They have hundreds of brochures and packages to help guide you every step of the way on improvements around your house and yard.

The average cost for these brochures is about 50 cents. Many are free, and some cost as much as a few bucks. Below are listed some of the best for helping you get things done around the house. To order, use the listed code number. Or to request a full listing of everything they offer, call them up at 888-878-3265, or write CIC, PO Box 100, Pueblo, CO 81002.

Code 335E: (50 cents) *Fixing Up Your Home and How to Finance It.* This information sheet shows you the hows and whys of doing it yourself, hiring a professional, and loans that are available to make your projects financially feasible.

Code 336E: (50 cents) *Healthy Lawn, Healthy Environment.* Everything you need to know about getting your hands dirty if you weren't born with a green thumb.

Code 338E: (50 cents) *Home Water Treatment Units.* Don't be fooled by clever sales tactics. This tells you how to choose the right kind of water purification system for your home and your family's needs.

Code 119E: ($1.00) *Selecting a New Water Heater.* The features needed in a water heater will vary from household to household. Which type is right for you?

Code 117E: ($1.50) *How to Prune Trees.* Use a saw or shears? How close should you cut? How can I keep branches off my roof? These answers and more are found in this 19-page, illustrated manual.

Code 573E: (Free) *Protect Your Family from Lead in Your Home.* Safeguard your home against the dangerous effects of lead. Learn what to look for and how to correct the problems.

Code 133E: ($2.00) *Should You Have the Air Ducts in Your Home Cleaned?* Know where to turn for professional cleaning services, when you need to call them, and how to keep your ducts in clean and working order.

Tips on Towels and More

Who knows more about cleaning than the quicker-picker-upper people at Bounty? Put their years of cleaning experience to work in your home by ordering their free booklet on innovative household cleaning techniques. Call 888-463-9785.

When the Bills Add Up

If you're having an unusually hard time paying your utility bills, don't despair. Most people — particularly seniors — who are living on a low income are eligible for special programs that ease the burden of high electric or water bills. Even if the utility company has threatened to shut off your power because of non-payment, give them a call. Let them know you are a senior and need to know about their discount programs. Very often, they will not cut off your service, but instead will try to work something out with you.

For additional help or advice, or if you can't manage to fix things with the utility company, contact your State Public Utilities Commission (PUC), in some states called the Public Service Commission (PSC). It's their job to regulate matters in the utility field, helping people who are having problems with their energy, gas, water, or phone service. The PUC or PSC is a division of your state government.

When the Meter Reader
Needs His Glasses Checked

Another time to turn to the Public Utilities Commission or Public Service Commission is when you are having a problem with your utility company and you just can't seem to work it out. Sometimes big corporations such as those that provide power, gas, and telephone service seem to give the little guy the run-around, and it can get downright frustrating. If you think your problem is not being taken seriously — anything from being overcharged on your bill to having trouble getting a repairman to show up — take your beef to this Commission.

The PUC or PSC is empowered to regulate the utilities and keep an eye on their rates and level of customer service. If you can't seem to get the water company's attention, they will be happy to do it for you. Find the Commission office nearest you by looking in the state information listings in the blue pages of your local phone book.

A Room Fit for a King

While most people have plenty of ideas about how to fix up or redesign the living room, refurbishing plans often fall short in the bath. Fixing up your bathroom can really add to the value of your home, as well as making your daily visits much more pleasant.

To help you get started, visit American Standard's comprehensive web site at <www.americanstandard.com>. Here you'll find all sorts of innovative ideas to inspire your creative flair in bathroom decor. They also have lots of information on products and ideas to help renovate your kitchen or even install a whirlpool. If you're not online, get the same free information by calling 800-524-9797 and asking for Extension 692. If you prefer to write, send your request to American Standard, PO Box 90218, Richmond, VA 23230-9031.

Treat Your Windows to Window Treatments

Many homeowners don't realize the value of good windows. When fix-up time comes around, many people concentrate on things like making the lawn look nice or fixing that runny toilet. But as any good Realtor will tell you, high-quality, well-maintained windows can save you money now and make you money later.

Poorly maintained windows are eyesores that can drain your house of heat in winter and make your air conditioner work too hard in summer. That can be murder on your utility bills, and it won't do you any favors when it's time to sell the house. Windows are one of the best investments you can make in your home, but being able to tell the difference between the type that will save you lots of money and the type that will just cost you a lot of money is a matter of being informed. The smart consumer knows where to look for this information, and how to get it free.

Window panes are the first line of defense in keeping you warm in winter, cool in summer. But they can be expensive. Find out about the add-on window pane option by ordering a free color brochure. Call 800-382-7263 and ask for Department CWD.

Believe it or not, what you dress your window with on the inside — blinds, drapes, etc. — can also affect your utility bills. Learn all about energy efficiency and other window treatment concerns such as safety, style, and privacy by ordering a free book from Hunter Douglas Window Fashions. Get the information by calling 800-238-3883, extension 101, and requesting *What to Wear if You're a Window.*

Blinds are a popular and versatile option for enhancing your home's privacy while letting in light. The American Blind & Wallpaper Factory offers all sorts of blinds through the mail at prices up to 82 percent off. Visit their web site at <www.abwf.com>. A catalog will set you back $2.00, but will also entitle you to an additional 10 percent off your order if you decide to purchase from them. Call 800-735-5300.

Your Own Personal Style Consultant

It's time to spruce up the old homestead, but you don't know the first thing about interior design. Time to hire some high-priced, snooty advisor, right? Not on your life.

Call the Decorating Den at 800-428-1366, and the professionals will come to you, free of charge. When you call, the Den will set up an appointment for a professional designer in your area to come to your home within just a few days. They'll bring a huge inventory of samples for you to consider without obligation. Furniture, wallpaper, carpeting, just about everything you'll need to give your home a complete makeover. Your personal decorator will also have info on special deals that will save you money when it's time to start buying. So what are you waiting for? Sign up for your free "style profile" today.

More Literature Than a Library,
Without the Hassle of Returning It

What if you had a library dedicated solely to home decorating ideas and techniques right across the street from your house, and at this particular library, you never had to return the books you borrowed? You'd probably get yourself a library card. But guess what? At this library you don't need a card, and it's closer than across the street. It's right at your fingertips.

Build yourself your own home improvement reference section without spending a dime by just lifting your finger and the phone. The references below have literature available free of charge that will set you up with ideas and resources for getting your project underway.

COUNTERS, TUBS & FLOORS: Call Wilson Art Flooring at 800-710-8846, extension 2717, or see their web site at <www.wilsonart.com>.

HOME DECOR. Broyhill offers a 24-page decorating workbook free of charge. Their number is 800-327-6944. Allow four to five weeks for delivery.

FLOORING CONCEPTS: Contact Columbia Flooring by dialing 800-654-8796, or go to the web site at <www.columbiaforestproducts.com>.

WALLPAPER: This one actually is kind of like a library, but it's worth it. For a deposit of $14.95, the National Blind & Wallpaper Factory will send you a CD-ROM that displays hundreds of wallpaper samples, often priced at up to 80 percent off. They'll return your deposit when you return the CD. Call 800-477-8000.

FURNITURE: LA-Z-BOY will send you a home furnishing kit, which includes decorating guides and a grid that helps you map out different room arrangements. Visit their web site at <www.lazyboy.com> or call 800-625-3246.

CARPET: Everything you ever wanted to know about floor coverings, but were afraid to ask. Call the Carpet & Rug Institute at 800-882-8846, and they'll send you more information about carpeting than you'll know what to do with. Learn how to install, maintain, and remove spots from your carpets & rugs, as well as what steps you can take toward improving the quality of the air in your home.

Green Acres Without a Green Thumb

Want to make your yard and garden look their best, but don't have a lot of extra green to spend? Get a little free help from the seed people.

The folks at the Park Seed Company will send you their manual called *The Gardener's Handbook* free with any order you place. Get a catalog of available items by dropping a postcard to the George W. Park Seed Company, Inc., 254 Cokebury Road, Greenwood, SC 29647, or by e-mail at <orders@parkseed.com>.

If that's not free enough for you, check out the company's comprehensive web site at <www.parkseed.com>. The entire text of *The Gardener's Handbook* is available for your cyber-gardening enlightenment.

All Aboard the Stain Train

What do Lady MacBeth and a kid with measles have in common? They both have spots they can't seem to get rid of. Fortunately, you won't have to deal with such problems if you send for *Good Riddance: An Emergency Spot Removal Guide.*

The guide showcases homemade removers that you can use, as well as offering instructions on how to get spots out of your carpet, drapes, furniture, and more. To get the dirt on getting out the dirt, send a self-addressed, stamped envelope to Coit Services, Inc., 897 Hinckley Road, Burlingame, CA 94010.

Someone's in the Kitchen With Savings

Without a doubt, many wonderful aromas have drifted out of your kitchen over the years, but what smells sweeter than saving money? Well, maybe fresh-baked cookies on a cold day.

While there aren't a lot of people out there giving away free cookies (would you?), there are plenty of ways to get free stuff for your kitchen. Looking for free samples of products offered in magazine ads and store displays is always a good idea. Clipping coupons and saving UPC symbols can put money back in your pocket, too. For more savings, get in touch with some of the people below. And then get cooking!

COOKWARE: Betty Crocker can mix up a good cake, but she can also save you money. If you are a fan of General Mills products, you can start saving Betty Crocker Points right away. Look for them on over 200 of the company's items, then request the Betty Crocker Savings Catalog. You can redeem your points for discounts of up to 75 percent on things like cookbooks, dinnerware, kitchen gadgets, even toys for the grandkids. For a copy of the catalog, write to Betty Crocker Catalog, PO Box 5284, Minneapolis, MN 55460-5284.

FOOD SAFETY: Good eating is safe eating, so be sure to stay up-to-date on current food safety information. For a free booklet on safe food preparation and handling from the Industry Council on Food Safety, call 800-266-5762.

HOTLINES: For quick, free information on food storage and sanitation, call the tip hotline at 800-995-9765. Or if you're a "cyber" chef, click over to the web site of the Food Marketing Institute at <www.fmi.org/foodkeeper>.

FIVE-DOLLAR BONUS: Get a free chef's catalog that contains anything and everything you'll ever need to whip up masterpieces in the kitchen by calling 800-727-8114. Be sure to mention Code CC844, and they'll give you a $5.00 discount on your first order.

Hey, Who Invited You?

Everything is perfect. You've repaired the roof, redesigned the dining room, gotten the spot out of the carpet, and prepared a wonderful, healthy, four-course meal. The kids and the grandkids are around the table and you're carefully placing the last sprig of parsley on the turkey. You smile as you contemplate the peaceful gathering.

And then the phone rings. "Hello? No, this is not a good time. No, I don't want new aluminum siding. Yes, I'm happy with my phone company."

Telemarketers seem to have a mystical talent for knowing just the wrong time to call. You're probably much too nice a person to scream at them, and even if you did, they'd still call back and disrupt another family dinner. So what can you do?

Stop the disruption of telemarketing in your home by following a couple of simple steps. First, write a note that includes your name, address, and phone number to Telephone Preference Service, Direct Marketing Association, PO Box 9014, Farmingdale, NY 11735-9014. Tell them you don't want your name used for sales purposes, and many of your calls will stop.

Also, when ordering anything by mail or by phone, insist that your information not be added to any mailing or calling lists. Many companies trade information about their customers, but will honor your request to be excluded. Now you can enjoy that next holiday meal without interruption.

Pamper Your Pets for Pennies

Owning a pet can really hit you in the pocketbook. Food, supplies, toys, and other accessories quickly add up to an average of $800 per year per family, making pet ownership the country's top leisure expense. Even so, animals have found a permanent place in our hearts and homes. Their undying love and devotion are especially appreciated by older adults who may be alone in their later years. Studies have found that pets can help relieve depression, lower blood pressure, and just make life all-around more pleasant. So how do you take care of your faithful friend without taking out a small loan? Here are some easy ways to lower your pet-care costs.

Take a 'Pound Puppy' Home Today

When looking for a pet, head to the nearest animal pound or humane shelter. For a nominal fee, you can adopt an animal that will give you every bit as much love and devotion as an expensive purebred, and possibly fewer problems. That's because some breeds are more susceptible to certain health problems that don't seem to affect mixed breeds. But be sure to check the animal's health and disposition before you take him home. He should look bright-eyed and alert and be reasonably friendly. If he doesn't move around, or tries to hide or run you down, keep looking.

How to Care for Your Cat (or Cow)

Many County Cooperative Extension Service Offices have information pamphlets, classes, or even videos on the care and feeding of animals. And you may be surprised to find that they're not just limited to livestock.

Want to learn how to take better care of your pet? What about dog-training classes? To learn what your local Extension Service has to offer, look in the blue pages of your phone book for the office nearest you.

For more information, contact the Extension Service, U.S. Department of Agriculture, Room 3328, Washington, D.C. 20250; 202-720-4111.

If you're looking for information on how to care for your adorable new kitten, you can join Purina's Kitten Care Club for free coupons and more. To join, call 800-KITTENS (548-8367).

Don't forget two other sources if your pet needs some obedience training. Local recreation departments usually offer classes that are much cheaper than private instruction. And your public library has books, and sometimes even videos, that give step-by-step instructions on teaching basic commands.

Know What To Do When They're Sick

If you're like most pet owners, you treat your pet like a child. You worry about what they eat, and you especially worry when they are sick.

The Center for Veterinary Medicine can answer all your pet food and nutrition questions. They have fact sheets and articles about choosing food for your pets, as well as information sheets on common pet illnesses and veterinary terms.

To receive free copies of these fact sheets, contact the Center for Veterinary Medicine, Food and Drug Administration, 7500 Standish Place, Rockville, MD 20855; 301-594-1755; or online at <www.fda.gov/cvm>.

Another web site that provides information on keeping your dog or cat healthy is <www.healthypet.com>. For a free healthy pet sticker and brochure about pet health exams, write to American Animal Hospital Association, PO Box 150899, Denver, CO 80215. Include a business-sized self-addressed stamped envelope.

Avoid Expensive Vet Visits

Trips to the vet can take a big chunk out of your savings. But certain things can be taken care of at home. Is your pet scratching or pawing at its ears a lot? It may have ear mites. Mineral oil is a great natural remedy for ear mites in cats and dogs. Just apply with a dropper or well-soaked cotton ball. Fold outer ear over ear opening and massage gently to get oil down into ear canal. Repeat every four or five days for a few weeks in order to kill newly hatched mites.

If your pet's scratching is due to fleas, save yourself the expense of flea dips and medication, and make your own remedy. How about a lemon tonic? Slice a whole lemon, and place it in a pint of almost boiling water. Let it sit overnight. Next morning, apply it to the pet's skin with a soft cloth. Repeat daily as needed for bad infestations. (Don't use this remedy on skin that's irritated or broken from too much scratching.)

If your pet suffers from chronic itching, scratching, and flaky skin, you may find that an over-the-counter lotion will help. Lipiderm is a natural formula that stops skin irritations without using harmful steroids. The company will send you dollars-off coupons to try its products if you call 800-889-1853.

Any routine maintenance you can perform on your pet will help save you money. Clip your pet's nails with special animal clippers you can buy at the store. Ask your vet to show you how to do it and which clippers to use. And take care of dental problems by brushing your pet's teeth once a week with a little baking soda on a moistened cloth.

Easy Savings on Pet Food

If you regularly buy commercial pet food, try the large discount stores like Kmart or Wal-Mart for about a 20 percent savings over supermarket and pet store prices. Warehouse clubs like Sam's Club can save you even more. But for the best savings, try a commercial feed store. These stores usually sell a wide range of pet foods at a substantial discount. And remember, the larger the bag, the more you'll save.

Savings Through the Mail

You can cut your pet-care expenses drastically by ordering from a national mail-order discounter. Among those that offer up to 75 percent savings are The Pet Warehouse, for owners of tropical fish, dogs, cats, birds, gerbils, and other small animals, 800-443-1160, or online at <www.pet-whse.com>; R.C. Steele, offering mainly dog supplies, 800-872-3773; and Doctors Foster and Smith, for small and large animals, 800-826-7206.

Free Food for Fido and Friends

Need some puppy food to get your new friend started on a nutritious diet? Or maybe you'd like to try a different brand of pet food. You can obtain a free sample of Pedigree Puppy dog food by calling 800-362-5700.

Ralston Purina will send you free dog food, and you can choose chicken and rice, lamb and rice, Purina light, or lamb and rice for puppies. Or, if you're a cat owner, you can obtain a free sample of Purina One cat food with a choice of salmon, tuna, or chicken and rice. Call 800-787-0078 or 800-699-1380.

And if you're a fish owner, you're in luck, too. Ocean Nutrition will give you free fish food if you send a self-addressed stamped envelope. Write to Ocean Nutrition, Attn: Free Sample Request, 1124 Bay Boulevard, Chula Vista, CA, 91911; 619-628-1050.

Free Litter (Literally!)

If you're tired of paying high prices for cat litter, here's an idea that will help your environment as well as your cats. Recycle your daily newspaper into a cheap, plentiful source of cat litter. Simply cut or shred it, and lay it in your pet's litter box. One note of caution: Newspaper may contain dyes that are toxic to small animals. So if you have kittens in the house, you're better off sticking with store-bought brands.

If you're looking for a quick and easy clean-up, how about some liners for your litter box? AAC lets you try a free sample before ordering. Just send a business-sized self-addressed stamped envelope with 55 cents postage to AAC, 9 Ivy Place, Howell, NJ 07731.

Inexpensive Ideas for Playtime

What interesting, amusing things occupy your puppy's time? They can be the key to finding an inexpensive toy for your playful pet. Does he like to chew or carry around bones? Try cutting a piece of hard plastic tubing from the hardware store as a replacement. Is tug-of-war the game of choice? Many rubber belts from the hardware store will work well for the wrestling match. The replacement items will probably last much longer than expensive, store-bought toys.

Give your dog a special treat by checking out the stuffed toys the next time you're at a garage sale. You can probably get poochie a toy for just 25 or 50 cents — a fraction of the cost of new ones in the pet store. A spot or stain won't bother your dog. Just be sure to look for toys that are sturdy and don't have parts that could be chewed off.

If you own a cat, you have infinite possibilities for free toys. Try some laundry bottle caps, cardboard boxes, straws, ping pong balls, or tennis balls. An especially clever homemade toy is a shoe box with a golf ball inside. Tape the lid on and cut holes in the top and sides large enough for a cat to get a paw in but not big enough for the ball to fall out. Your cat will enjoy hours of entertainment.

Stop Scratching Your Head
Over Your Cat's Behavior

If you have an indoor cat that's driving you crazy scratching your belongings to shreds, you can make a simple, sturdy scratching post from items you usually have around the house. Using old scrap wood, make a square base. (Make sure it doesn't have any chemicals on it that could harm your cat.) Use a long thick piece of wood for the actual scratching post. Make the post taller than your cat when he's standing on his hind legs so he can stretch while he's scratching. Also be sure the scratching post is sturdy enough so it won't tip over. One tip is likely to turn your cat off to that post forever. For extra support, you can attach the post to a floor or wall.

If you want to get fancier, you can add shelves to the post for the cat to sleep on. Wrap old carpet or sisal rope around the post for the cat to scratch on. Old bluejeans also work well. In about an hour, you'll have a good sturdy scratching post that will last for years. It won't tip over like the discount-store models that most cats disdain anyway, and it won't break your bank account like most luxury models since it's basically free.

Happiness is Vacationing With Your Pet

If you consider your pet a part of the family, you probably don't want to leave him behind when you go on vacation. For tips on providing your animal with a safe and happy travel experience, send for the free brochure, *Traveling with your Pet,* from the American Veterinary Medical

Association, 930 North Meachum Road, Shaumburg, IL 60196. Include a self-addressed stamped envelope.

When the Fur Flies

If you sneeze every time you're around your cat, you may be in trouble — it could be an allergy. The American Academy of Allergy, Asthma, and Immunology offers a free pamphlet, *Allergies to Animals,* explaining the causes and treatments of these types of problems. Write to the Academy at 611 E. Wells St., Milwaukee, WI 53202; 414-272-6071. Include a business-sized self-addressed stamped envelope.

Lost: One Small Brown Dog

Pets who spend time outdoors should have an identification tag in case they get lost. But many of those fancy tags may cost more than you want to spend. For only $1, you can outfit your furry friend with a colorful plastic I.D. tag personalized with his name, address and telephone number. Just write to PALS, PO Box 1271, San Luis Obispo, CA 93406. Ask for a pet I.D. tag, and include your pet's name as well as your address and phone number. Enclose a long self-addressed stamped envelope and $1. You won't ever have to worry about losing your pet again!

Get a Horse and Ride'em Cowboy

You don't have to go to the Wild West to re-enact the movie City Slickers. Horses roaming on government land can be adopted, possibly for as little as $125. If you want something smaller, you might get a burro for $75. You must go through a bidding process, and those prices are the lowest bids accepted.

For details, call 800-417-9647. Or write to the Bureau of Land Management, U.S. Department of the Interior, PO Box 12000, Reno, NV 89520. You'll also find information at the website <www.adoptahorse.blm.gov/>.

Help With Diet and Exercise

You've heard it many times before, but there's no denying its truth: a healthy diet and regular exercise routine can not only improve your health but your overall quality of life. Of course it's impossible to dictate one eating plan and one exercise method for everybody — we are all too individual — but there are guidelines everyone should follow that can mean less risk of illness or disease and more enjoyment out of life.

Although you can't put a price tag on good health, eating right and exercising properly shouldn't cost an arm and a leg. Here are some ways to make healthy choices and save money doing it.

From Food Pyramids to Nutritious Snacks

Did you know it takes five servings of fruit and vegetables a day to stay healthy? Or that low-fat on a canned food label really means 3 grams or less of fat per serving?

The Food and Drug Administration (FDA) is the agency that comes up with the latest scientific evidence to support findings like these. They have lots of information, publications, and brochures you can request, including:
- *Nutrition and the Elderly*
- *An FDA Guide to Dieting*
- *Food and Drug Interactions*
- *Keep Your Food Safe*
- *Facts About Weight Loss: Products & Programs*

All these and more are free by contacting the Office of Consumer Affairs, Food and Drug Administration, 5600 Fishers Lane, HFE88, Rockville, MD 20857; 888-463-6332, 800-532-4440; or visit their Internet site at <www.fda.gov>.

You can also get information on nutrition, Recommended Daily Allowances, food labels, and hundreds of other topics through the Consumer Information Center, Pueblo, CO 81009. Write to them for a complete catalog of their informational brochures. (Some cost a nominal fee).

A Cookbook for Diabetics

As a diabetic you may be challenged by planning meals that meet your dietary requirements yet are still fun and tasty. Well, the National Diabetes Information Clearinghouse has news for you. They have a whole listing of mouth-watering recipes that are healthy and easy to prepare. Also, if you are wondering how some diabetics are able to keep their condition in check without taking insulin, they can provide you with information on that, as well.

This Clearinghouse is probably the world's best source for anything you need to know about the causes, cures, and treatment for diabetics.

For more information or a complete list of publications, contact National Diabetes Information Clearinghouse, 1 Information Way, Bethesda, MD 20892-3560; 301-654-3327; or online at <www.niddk.nih.gov>.

The American Diabetes Association also can help you make the proper eating choices. They publish a brochure entitled, "Exchange Lists for Meal Planning." It is designed to be used under the guidance of a registered dietician. There is a charge for this publication, $1.75 per copy plus $4.99 for shipping and handling. Contact the ADA by calling 800-ADA-ORDER (232-6733).

Slim Down for Free

If you don't want to take out a second mortgage for a gym membership and if your basement can't hold one more piece of dusty exercise equipment, take notice. Grab a free booklet that will tell you how to exercise in water and save your joints from developing arthritis, how to develop a walking routine as the only exercise program you will ever need, or how you can get more energy with an easy-to-do fitness program. They are all available from the President's Council on Physical Fitness and Sports.

For information, contact them at 200 Independence Ave., SW, Humphrey Building, Room 738H, Washington, DC 20201; 202-690-9000; or online at <www.os.dhhs.gov>.

Free First-rate Facts on Fabulous Fiber

You may have grown up calling it "roughage." And perhaps you associate it with all those vegetables you loved to hate. Today nutritionists use the term fiber, and hopefully, now that you're older, you're more willing to make room for high-fiber foods on your plate. That's because fiber may do more good things for your body than any other single nutrient.

In the battle against cancer, fiber-rich foods have no equal. They are not only full of powerful cancer-fighting antioxidants, but they move harmful substances through your digestive system before they can be absorbed by your body.

The American Institute for Cancer Research has a free brochure, *The Facts About Fiber*, that discusses the link between fiber and cancer and how you can get more of this important element in your daily menu. Send a SASE to: The American Institute for Cancer Research, Dept. FI, Box 97167, Washington, DC 20069-7167; or call 800-843-8114.

Easy Answers to Age-Old Problems

As you age, your body changes. You need different types of food in different amounts. It can be a confusing process, full of trial and error. But why do things the hard way? The Aging Information Center has dozens of free fact sheets and publications that can help you with your food and nutrition concerns, including a 50-page book, *Food Facts For Older Adults*.

Contact the National Institute on Aging Information Center, PO Box 8057, Gaithersburg, MD 20898-8057; 800-222-2225; or online at <www.nih.gov/nia>.

Step, Walk, or Run for Your Life

Looking for a fun way to bring exercise into your life? Here are some tips and ideas that just might make it easier to get off the couch and on your way to a healthier, happier you.

Sports Music Inc. has a workout music catalog full of audiotapes you can walk, run, skate, cycle, or climb to. They come in all fitness levels and geared to every music taste. Call them at 800-878-4764 or write and request your free copy at: Sports Music Inc., Box 769689, Roswell, GA 30076.

If mall-walking or marching out with the dog are more your thing, send for a free walking tip sheet from *The Walking Magazine.* They'll tell you how to pick the right shoes, do the proper stretches, and plan a walking program. Send a SASE to Walking Tip Sheet, 45 Bromfield St., 8th Floor, Boston, MA 02108.

The National Institute on Aging has articles and other general information on how exercise can help you live a longer, healthier life. Contact the National Institute on Aging Information Center, PO Box 8057, Gaithersburg, MD 20898-8057; 800-222-2225; or online at <www.nih.gov/nia>.

Good Food, Better Choices

Many of the foods you eat are part of your menu simply out of habit. You've always bought this kind of cheese or used that kind of cooking oil. But with better information, you could be making healthier choices without sacrificing ease or taste.

The American Institute for Cancer Research has a free brochure, *Sensational Ingredient Substitutions,* that gives you alternatives for many not-so-healthy foods, like chocolate, cream, oils, and nuts. By following their simple suggestions you could be lowering your risk of heart disease, high blood pressure, and other dangerous conditions. Call 800-843-8114, or write to them at 1759 R Street NW, Washington, DC 20009.

If salt is on your list of no-no's but you just can't get by without it, hold that shaker! There are several salt substitutes on the market that can satisfy your craving without hurting your blood pressure. Nu-Salt, a 100 percent natural substitute, even offers free samples and recipes. Call them at 800-206-9454.

Milk and You

If you are a woman over 50, calcium is more important to your health now than ever before. In order to ward off the tragic effects of osteoporosis, you need at least 1200 mg of calcium every day. That's not always easy, especially if you don't like or can't digest milk.

But now it's easier than ever to discover how to get the calcium you need in different ways. The WHY MILK campaign offers seven informational brochures covering topics like: *High Blood Pressure Recipes, Celebrities Best Milk Recipes,* and *Lactose Intolerance - Enjoy Milk.* You can order any of their brochures by calling 800-WHY-MILK (949-6455) or visiting their website at <www.whymilk.com>.

If digesting milk continues to be a problem for you, there are many products that supply the enzymes your body lacks. Lactaid Ultra even offers free samples so you can try it out, risk-free. Call them at 888-858-7266 for yours today.

☆☆☆

Save the Right Way With Rite Aid

Rite Aid stores and pharmacies offer several programs designed to save you money on your day-to-day necessities. First there is the Vitamin Club which offers a 10 percent discount on vitamins purchased on Tuesdays. See your pharmacist about getting a club card then simply have it scanned along with your purchase. What could be easier?

Then there is the Single Check Rebates Program. Buy any of the products listed in the store directory between the dates listed on the Rebate Submission Form found at their website (<www.riteaid.com>). Save the original cash register receipts from your purchases. Circle the rebated items and write the rebate offer number next to each one. Complete the submission form and tally sheet. Mail it in according to the directions and Rite Aid will send you a single check back for all of your completed rebates. No more hassling with dozens of different manufacturers.

And finally, Rite Aid is testing a new program called the Rite Reward Program. Rite Reward customers will receive a discount card for all Rite Aid brand products and certain name-brand sale items. As you shop, you'll receive 10 percent off these items. In addition, your purchase amount will be tracked each month and qualify you for various gift certificates. The more you spend, the larger your monthly gift certificate. The Rite Reward Program is not available in all areas yet, but be on the lookout for it.

These are three easy ways to save hundreds of dollars on items you purchase anyway. Call their toll-free number, 800-RITEAID (748-3243) for the store nearest you, to speak to a pharmacist about medications, or to talk to a customer service representative.

Busy Lives Need Better Health Care

Just because you've got things to do and places to go doesn't mean you should neglect your health. In fact, just such a lifestyle needs even more attention placed on eating right and exercising regularly. But if you feel too overwhelmed to do the job properly, take heart. The American College of Sports Medicine, in conjunction with other associations, has free information you're going to love.

Eating Smart Even When You're Pressed for Time and *Fitting Fitness In Even When You're Pressed for Time* address the importance of good nutrition for people on the go and give advice on including fitness in even the busiest of days. Send a SASE to the American College of Sports Medicine, Box 1440, Indianapolis, IN 46206-1440. Be sure to explain which booklet you want. For other information visit their website (<www.acsm.org>) or call them at 317-637-9200. They have several brochures, publications, audio and videotapes either free or available for a nominal fee from their Public Information Department.

The government has good information about healthy diets, too. Consumer information publications are available from the Center for Nutrition Policy and Promotion. They conduct research on the nutritive value of foods and the nutritional adequacy of diets and food supplies. Two good publications, *Check It Out! The Food Label, the Pyramid and You*, and *Dietary Guidelines and Your Diet*, can be ordered by contacting the Government Printing Office. Call 202-512-1800, or write to Superintendent of Documents, Washington, DC 20402.

For more information, contact the Center for Nutrition Policy and Promotion, USDA, 1120 20th St. NW, Suite 200N, Washington, DC 20036; 202-418-2312; or online at <www.usda.gov/fcs/cnpp. htm>.

Penny-pinching the Smart and Easy Way

Where's the one place in your budget you can save the most without giving up a thing? Your monthly food allowance. It's true. You can save hundreds of dollars at the grocery store check-out and still eat all your favorite foods simply by learning how to get the most from your money.

The first step is to compare stores. Some offer special pricing or discount programs. For instance, if you have a Kroger in your neighborhood, start shopping on Wednesdays — when seniors receive a 5 percent discount. That can add up every week. Call around or stop at other area grocers and ask about senior discounts.

Some grocery stores offer frequent shopper programs. Most often you simply sign up and get a discount card. Others require a membership fee or minimum purchases. Again, check out your local store's policy. For example, Food Lion and Kash n' Karry customers who are part of their MVP/Preferred Customer program can get discounts of about 20 percent on over a thousand items each week. That's in addition to regular specials available to all customers.

And then, of course, there are coupons. The first coupons were hand-written tickets back in 1894 for a free sample of a new product called Coca-Cola. Since then, coupons have become a huge industry in themselves. If you're willing to clip, collect, and sort, many claim you can save as much as $2,000 a year on groceries. Just think, even if you only spend $100 a week on groceries, it's possible to save 15 percent off your yearly grocery bill simply by clipping coupons.

To really get the benefits, however, you must be organized. Keep coupons handy, search out all sources, follow the coupon requirements, and buy items at their maximum savings. That means sometimes buying in quantity, and looking for supermarkets that double — even triple — coupon values. There are all kinds of newsletters and refund magazines that can lead you through the maze of couponing. So get an envelope, some scissors, and start clipping.

Another money-saving option is to join a food co-op. Neighborhood food cooperatives or buying clubs work like supermarkets except that as a member, you help run the store. There can be a fee for joining a co-op as well as a commitment to help out occasionally. But the savings on food items can be substantial. In addition, some offer senior citizen discounts on certain days. For a listing of food co-ops nationwide, look in the National Green Pages. For a copy, send $6.95 to Co-Op America Catalog, 1612 K Street NW, #600, Washington, DC 20006-2802; 202-872-5307; 800-58-GREEN (47336). If you have access to the Internet, you can look up co-op listings in your area at <www.coopamerica.org>.

And how can owning a computer save you hundreds of dollars on your grocery bill? It's easier than you think. A service called ValuPage is a free collection of coupons and rebates for brand-name products available through the World Wide Web. You first sign on to <www.supermarkets.com>. Then you enter your zip code. This will bring up a screen listing all the supermarkets in your area that participate in the ValuPage program. Select a store and a ValuPage will appear, listing all the items at that store on special. Print the page and take it with you when you go shopping. Purchase any of the items you want off the list and present the ValuPage to the cashier when you check out. Once she scans the page, special coupons called Web Bucks will print out. You can use these Web Bucks on any items during your next trip to that supermarket — just like money. They are usually worth more than the coupons you find in the newspaper or in mailings.

If you still have questions about this program, go ahead and access the web address above and click on to the FAQ (Frequently Asked Questions) link. Here you'll find detailed explanations about the ValuPage program.

Government Help With Your Food Budget

If your budget is so stretched that you are having trouble keeping food on the table, you may be eligible for Food Stamps. Call your local social service agency listed in the blue pages of your telephone book and ask about the Food Stamp Program. There are strict eligibility requirements, such as limits on monthly income, different benefit levels that are based on household size and household income, and restrictions on what items can be purchased, but if you are truly in need, the Food Stamp Program is there to help. The average yearly benefit is more than $800 per person.

Senior citizens are given special consideration. For example, seniors unable to go to the food stamp office to be interviewed may request a phone or home interview instead. Seniors can be living with others and still qualify as a separate household in order to receive this assistance. You can even go to school and still receive food stamps.

Contact the U.S. Department of Agriculture, Food and Consumer Service, Public Information Office, 3101 Park Ctr. Dr., Room 819, Park Office Center Bldg., Alexandria, VA 22302; 703-305-2276; or online at <www.usda.gov/fcs>.

Kitchen Magic: Free Recipes You'll Love to Cook

Everyone gets tired of meat loaf Mondays and tuna fish Tuesdays. If this sounds like your same old routine, try adding some spice in your kitchen. Look on the labels of your favorite baking, cereal, snack, and sauce products. Many times the manufacturers will have toll-free numbers you can call to get recipes and cooking ideas. Here are just a few ways to get free recipes and cooking ideas from major food manufacturers and organizations.

A1 Steak Sauce (free recipes)
888-A1-STEAK (217-8385)

Bertolli Olive Oil (25 recipes & coupons for $2 shipping & handling)
Bertolli, PO Box 2001, Grand Rapids, MN 55745

Betty Crocker Making a Home Catalog (48-page catalog and recipes)
800-328-8360 (only available in the U.S.)

Borden Eagle Brand Sweetened Condensed Milk (free recipes)
800-426-7336

California Pear Advisory Board (free recipes with a SASE)
1521 I St., Sacramento, CA 95814; 916-441-0432

Catfish Institute (free recipe booklet or free Nationwide Guide to Catfish-serving Restaurants)
The Catfish Institute, Box 327, Belzoni, MS 39038; 601-247-4913; <www.catfishinstitute.com>

Catfish Institute (free All-American Restaurant & Recipe Guide or catfish cooking guide)
The Catfish Institute, Box 1030, Belzoni, MS 39038; 601-247-4913; <www.catfishinstitute.com>

Comstock (recipe book for $2 shipping & handling)
Makin' it Easy, PO Box 10659, Dept. MIE, Rochester, NY 14610; 800-270-2743; <www.agrilinkfoods.com>

DelMonte Vegetable Refund (expires 12/31/00)
DelMonte Consumer Affairs, PO Box 8009, St. Cloud MN 56398-8009; 800-543-3090

Fundcraft-Personalized Cookbooks (free recipes & information on fundraising)
800-853-1364 ext. 508; <www.cookbooks.com>

Good Seasons (free recipe ideas)
800-431-1003; <www.kraftfoods.com/goodseasons>

Grandma Rena's Cajun Seasonings (free sample & catalog)
318-826-9424; <www.grandmarena.com

Grey Poupon (free recipe booklets)
888-G-POUPON (476-8766) or 800-GP-DIJON (473-4566); <www.nabisco.com>

Hidden Valley (free recipes)
800-723-2343

Hormel Foods (48-page recipe book & coupons for $1.50 postage and handling)
Pep it Up Recipe Book, PO Box 5000, Austin, MN 55912; 507-437-5611

Idaho Potatoes (free microwave cookbook with SASE & 2 first-class stamps)
Microwave Cookbook, Idaho Potato Commission, PO Box 1068, Boise, ID 83701; 208-334-2350; <www.idahopotato.com>

Jello (sugar-free recipes & information)
800-432-3101; <www.jell-o.com>

Kellogg's Rice Krispies (80 recipes for $2.99 & 2 proofs of purchase)
Kellogg's Rice Krispie Cereal Cookbook Offer, PO Box 185327, Battle Creek, MI 49018-5327; 800-237-1132; <www.treatsrecipes.com>

Knorr (free recipes)
800-338-8831

Milk (free recipes)
800-WHY-MILK (949-6455); <www.whymilk.com>

Morton Salt Household Hints (free brochure)
Morton Salt Tips, Chicago, IL 60606-1597; 312-807-2000

National Cattlemen's Beef Association (free beef recipes with a SASE)
NCBA Ad Dept., 444 N. Michigan Ave., Chicago, IL 60611; 312-467-5520

National Pork Producers Council (free recipes with a SASE)
Recipes, PO Box 10383, Des Moines, IA 50306; 505-223-2600; <www.nppc.org>

Ore-Ida Cookbook ($2)
Young America Corp., PO Box 6841, Young America, MN 55558-6841; 800-892-2401

Reynolds Kitchen (free recipes & cooking ideas)
800-745-4000; <www.rmc.com/wrap>

Rhodes Recipes (set of 24 bread recipe cards for $3)
Rhodes, Inc., PO Box 25487, Salt Lake City, UT 84125; <www.rhodesbread.com>

Shady Brook Farms (turkey tips & recipes with SASE)
Shady Brook Farms, PO Box 549, Harrisonburg, VA 22801;

Dial-A-Chef Holiday Hotline (10/31-12/31) 888-723-4468;
<www.shadybrookfarms.com>

Swanson Chicken Broth (free recipes)
800-44-BROTH (27684) (M-F 12-3:30 pm EST)

Tex Mex Salsa (free sample with a SASE)
Salsa San Antonio, 518E Houston St., San Antonio, TX 78205

Whole Fruit Sorbet (free recipes)
800-693-5286

Healthy Living for Less

Living Longer, Living Better

You rely on doctors and other health professionals to help diagnose and treat disease during times of crisis. But for improving and maintaining your health on a daily basis, the choices you make are really completely within your control. And taking charge of your health is absolutely free! The small decisions, made many times a day, may be as important in the long run as any doctor visit you ever make.

So what can you do to keep yourself as healthy as possible? Here are some choices that can improve your life and your health.

THINK POSITIVE. It may sound silly and simplistic, but try to believe that each day of your life is a gift and choose to use it the best way possible. Medical science already has evidence that stress may cause or aggravate heart disease, high blood pressure, cancer, depression, and a number of other serious conditions. More knowledge of the link between your emotions and your physical health is emerging every day. If you deal with stress by keeping a positive focus in your life, you can protect yourself from physical and emotional ills and gain a happier life in the bargain.

KEEP MOVING. You don't need to be a marathon runner to reap the benefits of regular exercise. The latest research says that just 30 minutes of exercise on most days, even broken up into 10-minute segments, can boost your health and lower your risk of many serious diseases, including heart disease and diabetes. A daily 20-minute walk, plus a few minutes of gardening or housework, can go a long way toward keeping you in good physical condition. Add a little weight training to strengthen your muscles and bones, and you have a winning formula. There is virtually no part of your body that isn't made stronger and healthier by regular, moderate exercise. And it will not only help you physically, but can ward off depression and emotional problems, too. If you haven't exercised in a while, don't be afraid to start. It's never too late.

EAT HEALTHY. Just like the smoothly running engine of an expensive sports car, your body needs the right kind of fuel to perform well. A healthy diet gives your body the nutrients it needs and gives you the energy you want. Aim for at least five servings of fresh fruits and vegetables each day. Keep your intake of fats, especially saturated fats (meat, dairy, hydrogenated, and coconut), low. Instead, use monounsaturated fats such as those found in nuts and olive oil. Eat sufficient protein, but not too much. Five or six ounces of lean meat and two glasses of skim milk a day will give you all the protein you need. Learn to like whole grains instead of refined ones. Whole wheat bread, brown rice, and rolled oats should become your preferred forms of carbohydrate, and they'll give you the fiber and minerals you can't get with gluey white flour products. Stay away from junk foods containing too much sugar and salt. They add calories that will boost your weight but not your health.

GET REGULAR CHECKUPS from your doctor to be sure no health problems sneak up on you. Watch your local newspaper for "health fairs," which give you the opportunity to have free health screenings and checkups to supplement your doctor's care. Then follow these basic guidelines for good health to give yourself the gift of a long and healthy life.

The Best Information for Aging Well

The National Institute on Aging (NIA) researches all kinds of subjects on aging, as well as the diseases and special problems of older people. They are also conducting the longest-running scientific examination of human aging ever undertaken, the Baltimore Longitudinal Study of Aging.

The NIA's "Age Pages" provide a quick, practical look at many of the health topics that interest older people. The NIA can answer your questions and provide you with all kinds of free publications on a wide variety of topics. Just tell them the subject you are interested in.

Contact the National Institute on Aging, Public Information Office, 9000 Rockville Pike, Building 31, Room 5C27, Bethesda, MD 20892; 800-222-2225; or online at <www.nih.gov/nia>.

☆☆☆

Alternative Treatments for Natural Relief

Given the choice, most people would prefer to treat their aches and illnesses naturally, with gentle, healthy ingredients and methods, like herbal remedies, aromatherapy, hypnosis, biofeedback, and acupuncture. In one form or another, these kinds of treatments have been around for thousands of years. However, modern science places a great deal of importance on chemical and manufactured remedies. It is a difficult dilemma because the bottom line is, you just want to feel better. Today it's important to realize there's nothing wrong with exploring all your medical options, and even combining therapies, old and new.

There is a wealth of information available on natural health products, and much of it is free. If you need just some basic information on which herbs do what, the free quarterly herb newsletter from Nature's Resource Premium Herbs may be for you. It's packed full of timely facts and helpful tips on everything from echinacea to St. John's wort. To order, simply call 800-227-9527 and leave your mailing information. If you have other questions or concerns, you can talk to a real live person by calling Nature's Resource herb hotline at 800-314-HERB (4372). They'll give you specific information on herb use, possible side effects, and drug interactions.

A handful of leaves in boiling water was probably mankind's first medicine. Today, even modern health experts recognize the value of herbal teas. That is why you'll find your grocery and health food stores stocked with a wide selection. One manufacturer, Traditional Medicinals, is so convinced you'll like their natural plant remedies that they're offering free samples. Blends to treat colds, sore throats, insomnia, and other common health problems are just a cup away. Call 800-FREE-TEA (373-3832) to get a free taste of Traditional Medicinals (while supplies last).

Quantum Natural Health Products, <www.quantumhealth.com>, offers various free samples of their merchandise including natural relief from colds, flu, cold sores, allergies, and migraines. They also carry a line of natural insect repellents and itch and bite relief. You can call them at 800-448-1448 or e-mail a request for free samples to: <freesamples@quantumhealth.com>.

To browse through more than 500 natural herb remedies, vitamins, supplements, and alternative care products, order Botanic Health's free color catalog. Write them at Botanic Health, Indiana Botanic Gardens, P.O. Box 5, Hammond, IN 46325, or call 800-644-8327.

A Healthy Heart

When it comes to your health, having a good, strong, pumping mechanism that gets oxygen and nutrients to all parts of your body is really the heart of the matter. A healthy heart makes all your body's systems run more efficiently, but if you have high blood pressure or high cholesterol, your heart is probably not doing its best. So what can you do to improve your heart if it's not in peak condition? Here are some pointers.

EXERCISE. Using your muscles makes them stronger. Your heart is a muscle, too — pump it up by getting moderate, regular exercise. Walking for 30 minutes five days a week should be enough to make a big improvement.

LOSE YOUR EXTRA WEIGHT. Excess pounds put a bigger burden on your heart. Losing even five to 10 pounds can help lower high blood pressure and high cholesterol.

EAT MORE FIBER. Raising your level of fiber intake to 25 to 30 grams a day can help lower your blood pressure and your cholesterol level. Oat bran and buckwheat are winners at lowering your cholesterol, along with psyllium and other high-fiber grains. A big bowl of whole-grain cereal each morning is a delicious way to help your heart.

FLEE FROM SATURATED FAT. You don't need to cut all the fat out of your diet, just cut down on the fats that seem most harmful: those found in meat and dairy products; partially hydrogenated fats, often found in crackers and cookies; and coconut and palm oils, also found in many snack foods. The fats found in olive oil and nuts are much healthier choices. Substitute cold-water fish, such as salmon, mackerel, and sardines, for some of the meat in your diet and you'll also get the protective effects of fish oil for your heart.

GO EASY ON THE SALT. For people who are salt-sensitive, a high intake can keep your blood pressure high. Instead, try seasoning foods with lemon juice, spices, fresh herbs, and balsamic vinegar, which contains no sodium.

MIND YOUR MINERALS. Potassium, calcium, and magnesium are heart-healthy minerals that help keep high blood pressure in check. Get enough potassium in your diet by eating lots of fresh fruits and vegetables. Get plenty of calcium from skim milk, nonfat yogurt, and sardines. Magnify your magnesium by eating spinach, baked potatoes, and black-eyed peas.

The National Heart, Lung, and Blood Institute (NHLBI) conducts research and responds to questions on cholesterol, high blood pressure, blood resources, sleep disorders, obesity, and asthma. They can conduct database searches to locate materials, and they distribute a wide variety of educational publications for both the consumer and professional. Some of the publications available include:

- *Controlling High Blood Pressure*
- *Take Steps — Prevent High Blood Pressure*
- *Facts About Heart Disease and Women*

- *So You Have High Blood Pressure*
- *Step by Step: Eating To Lower Your High Blood Cholesterol*
- *Check Your Healthy Heart IQ*

Many other publications are also available. Request a free catalog. Contact National Heart, Lung, and Blood Institute Information Center, PO Box 30105, Bethesda, MD 20824-0105; 301-251-1222; 800-575-WELL (recorded message line); or online at <www.nhlbi.nih.gov/nhlbi/ nhlbi.htm>.

Quit Lighting Up

You can lower your risk of developing osteoporosis, having a heart attack, getting pneumonia, and setting your bed on fire. And earn $750 in savings to take a trip to the Bahamas. All you have to do is stop smoking for a year.

But you're probably wondering if it's really worth it after smoking for so long. It is, according to the Office on Smoking and Health. They collect and distribute information on the health risks associated with smoking and secondhand smoke, as well as material on smoking cessation methods. Here are some of the pamphlets available:

- *Don't Let Another Year Go Up In Smoke: Quit Tips*
- *Good News For Smokers 50 and Older: It's Never too Late to Quit!*
- *Out of the Ashes: Choosing a Method to Quit Smoking*
- *Office on Smoking and Health's Information Resources*
- *Significant Developments Related to Smoking and Health*

The Office also has a fax service where they will fax you these and other articles. For a publications list or more information, contact Office on Smoking and Health, Centers for Disease Control, 4770 Buford Hwy., NE, Mail Stop K-12, Atlanta, GA 30341; 770-488-5705; 800-CDC-1311 (publications and fax service); or online at <www.cdc.gov/tobacco>.

Taking the Scare Out of Cancer

No one likes to think about the "C" word. But think about this: the earlier cancer is found, the better your chances of beating it. Your odds of surviving cancer are excellent if you watch for early warning signs and get regular cancer screenings. Here are some of the symptoms to watch for.

BREAST CANCER: a lump, thickening, swelling, or dimpling of the breast; a tender, painful, or distorted nipple; discharge.

PROSTATE CANCER: painful, frequent, or difficult urination; blood in the urine; constant pain in the lower back, pelvis, or upper thighs.

COLORECTAL CANCER: unexplained changes in bowel habits; blood in the stool.

LUNG CANCER: chronic coughing; chest pain; blood in the sputum; repeated bouts of pneumonia and bronchitis; an unpleasant sweet taste to your food.

UTERINE CANCER: abnormal bleeding or spotting; abnormal vaginal discharge.

OVARIAN CANCER: unexplained stomachaches, gas, and bloating; abnormal vaginal bleeding; an enlarged belly, caused by fluids.

The toll-free Cancer Information Service (CIS) can provide accurate, up-to-date information about cancer and cancer-related resources near you. Information is also available about treatment studies currently accepting patients and is available to doctors through a database known as PDQ (Physician Data Query). You can ask your doctor if you might be a candidate for one of these studies.

The National Cancer Institute also distributes free publications on specific types of cancer, treatment methods, coping with cancer, and other cancer-related subjects. Just a few of the publications available include:

- *Cancer Tests You Should Know About: A Guide For People 65 And Over*
- *Anticancer Drug Information Sheets*
- *Advanced Cancer: Living Each Day*
- *Chemotherapy and You: A Guide To Self Help During Treatment*
- *Questions and Answers About Pain Control*
- *What Are Clinical Trials All About?*
- *Radiation Therapy And You*
- *Facing Forward: A Guide for Cancer Survivors*
- *Eating Hints: Recipes and Tips*

Contact the National Cancer Institute, Office of Cancer Communications, Building 31, Room 10A16, 31 Center Dr., NSC2580, Bethesda, MD 20892-2580; Cancer Information Service, 800-4-CANCER (422-6237); or online at <www.nic.nih.gov>.

You can also get some helpful information about different types of cancer treatment by visiting the web site of Cancer Treatment Centers of America, a group of medical hospitals that specialize in treating all types of cancer. The Internet address is <www.cancercenter.com>.

☆☆☆

New Cancer Cure?

Ever seen a shark with cancer? You probably never wanted to get close enough to find out. Well, it's so rare that researchers have begun looking into what sharks have that we don't, and they think they may have found it — in the sharks' cartilage. In a Cuban study, a number of cancer patients who received shark cartilage treatments showed significant improvement.

But before you spend $115 on a bottle of shark cartilage pills, contact the National Cancer Institute. They'll send you a series of articles on this controversial treatment to help you better decide if it's for you. Contact: National Cancer Institute, Bldg. 31, Room 10A16, 31 Center Dr., NSC 2580, Bethesda, MD 20892; 1-800-4-CANCER; or online at <www.nci.nih. gov>.

Breast Cancer Information for Every Woman

It may be every woman's worst nightmare — finding a lump during your monthly breast exam. But changes in your breast tissue don't always mean cancer. That's why the National Cancer Institute has published a free 52-page guide, *Understanding Breast Changes*. In it there's information on mammographies and a list of questions to ask your doctor either during your routine physical or if you think something may be wrong.

Order this booklet by calling 1-800-4-CANCER (226237) or writing to NCI, Bldg. 31, Rm. 10A16, Bethesda, MD 20892.

In addition, the National Cancer Institute has publications on many other topics related to cancer, including nutrition, detection, prevention, types, smoking, supporting people with cancer, and surviving cancer. A full listing is available at their web site: <www.nci.nih.gov>.

☆☆☆

Making Sense of Menopause

Menopause can be a difficult time for many women. Not only do you have to deal with the physical changes going on in your body, but there are also emotional issues and medical decisions to deal with. You may find it helpful to have information that you can settle down with in your living room and read over at your leisure. Then, if all your questions aren't answered or if you want to discuss new options with your doctor, you can do so.

The North American Menopause Society (NAMS) offers what they call a MenoPak. It contains a 50-page menopause guidebook full of educational information, a list of menopause doctors by geographic area, a list of menopause support groups by geographic area, and a suggested reading list. Send a check or money order for $5 to cover shipping and handling to: NAMS, P.O. Box 94527, Cleveland, OH 44101-4527. You can also visit them on the Internet at <www.menopause.org> or call their toll-free number 800-774-5342.

The National Menopause Foundation also has educational material and information on support groups. Simply call 800-MENO-ASK (636-6275).

For help with some of those difficult decisions, send for the free brochure *What's Right For Me?* published by the Wellness Councils of America (WELCOA). It covers such topics as osteoporosis, heart disease, estrogen replacement therapy, and other medical choices. This national nonprofit organization can be reached by calling 800-561-2781.

If you're looking for natural alternatives, you might want to consider one of the many plant estrogens for women experiencing midlife changes. Novogen, Inc. markets a dietary supplement called Promensil, an estrogen from red clover. Request information by calling 888-NOVOGEN (668-6436), visiting their web site at <www.novogen.com>, or by writing to Novogen, Inc., 6 Landmark Square, 4th Floor, Stamford, CT 06901.

Menopause marks an enormous change in a woman's life. Physical appearance, feelings of well-being, mood, and sexual function can all be affected. Don't forget there are places to turn to for information, ways to cope, and help finding local support groups.

When Aspirin Isn't Enough

If you suffer from chronic headaches, sometimes even several doses of aspirin may not do the trick. New treatment options have greatly improved our lives. Drug therapy, biofeedback training, and elimination of certain foods from the diet are just a few of the most common methods of preventing and controlling migraines and other types of headaches. These tips can also help you deal with chronic headaches.

KEEP A HEADACHE DIARY. In it, write down the circumstances surrounding each headache and what you have been eating that day. This should help identify the foods or situations that may be triggering your headaches.

LEARN TECHNIQUES TO REDUCE YOUR STRESS LEVEL. Many headaches are brought on by tension from stress.

DON'T GO FOR LONG PERIODS OF TIME WITHOUT EATING. Eating at regular intervals will keep your blood sugar level stable and head off some headaches.

DON'T SLEEP MORE THAN YOU NEED TO. Although you may need sleep to get relief from a pounding head, too much sleep can bring on headaches in some people.

PUT A COLD COMPRESS ON YOUR HEAD AND TAKE A HOT BATH. This should direct the flow of blood away from the swollen blood vessels in your head and toward the rest of your body.

The National Institute of Neurological Disorders and Stroke has put together a publication entitled *Headache: Hope Through Research* that provides journal articles, research reports, and other resources for headache sufferers. For your free copy, contact the National Institute of Neurological Disorders and Stroke, Information Office, Building 31, Room 8A06, 31 Center Dr., MSC 2540, Bethesda, MD 20892-2540; 800-352-9424; or online at <www.ninds.nih.gov>.

To get more free information, you can call the Excedrin Headache Resource Center at 1-800-580-4455. They will send you free materials, including a newsletter called *The Headache Relief Update*, and product samples. To contact Excedrin online, go to <www.excedrin.com/>.

Dealing With Diabetes

Having diabetes can be a challenge, but it doesn't have to keep you from enjoying life to the fullest. With the proper diet and exercise program, you can remain healthy and active. Keeping your insulin level as even as possible is the way you control your diabetes. This, in turn, is controlled mostly by the food and lifestyle choices you make. But your best tool for dealing with diabetes is information. In addition to the information your doctor gives you, here are a few tips you might not know.

GO FAR ON FIBER. Eating foods high in natural fiber, such as fresh fruits and vegetables and whole grains, can help regulate your insulin level. Highly refined and processed foods, such as white bread, white rice, and french fries, can't do this.

GIVE SUGAR THE SLIP. The medical stance on diabetic people eating sugar has softened over the years, but it is still basically not a good idea. Sugary junk foods are low in fiber and nutrients, and they raise your insulin too high and too fast.

MAINTAIN YOUR VIM WITH VITAMINS. Vitamins A, C, and E are nutrients you need, especially if you have diabetes. You should get them naturally from food, however, instead of from supplements. You'll find vitamin A in milk, liver, and deep orange and dark green fruits and vegetables such as sweet potatoes, carrots, and spinach. Vitamin C abounds in strawberries, citrus fruits, sweet red peppers, and broccoli. Look for vitamin E in vegetable oils such as safflower, canola, and corn oils. It's also in wheat germ, sunflower seeds, and sweet potatoes.

SHY AWAY FROM RAW SEAFOOD. Sushi and oysters on the half-shell can be home to deadly bacteria, and as a diabetic, you are especially vulnerable. Don't take the risk.

COUNT ON CAFFEINE. If you have diabetes, a few cups of tea or coffee can play a special role in helping you ward off low blood sugar (hypoglycemia). The stimulating effect of caffeine seems to help heighten sensation and intensify the early warning symptoms of low blood sugar. If you know hypoglycemia is coming on, you can have a little snack to level off your blood sugar before it dips too low.

To get more information on living well with diabetes, contact the National Diabetes Information Clearinghouse. They can answer any of your questions regarding diabetes and will send you the *Diabetes Dateline* newsletter and a calendar of meetings and educational programs. They also have a wonderful collection of free publications on diabetes and how it can be controlled. Here are some of the titles:

- *Diabetes Dictionary*
- *Insulin Dependent Diabetes*
- *Questions to Ask Your Doctor About Blood Sugar Control*
- *Non-insulin Dependent Diabetes*
- *Do Your Level Best: Start Controlling Your Blood Sugar*

A complete list of publications is available by contacting the Clearinghouse at National Diabetes Information Clearinghouse, 1 Information Way, Bethesda, MD 20892-3560; 301-654-3327; or online at <www.niddk.nih.gov>.

Relieve Your Aches and Pains

For some people, aching joints are a fact of life. More than 50% of people over 65 suffer from some form of arthritis, whether it is a mild stiffness in your joints when it rains or full-blown osteoarthritis. But for many, a simple change in diet and exercise could improve their condition. Here are a few tips to put you on the right path.

OPT FOR SOME EXERCISE. It may be tough to work out when your joints are aching, but exercise helps keep your joints mobile and strengthens the muscles around them. Swimming and water aerobics are often good exercise choices for people with arthritis, since they are gentle on joints. If your knees are strong enough, walking and bicycling are healthy ways to get your regular exercise, too.

KEEP MOVING. Standing or sitting in one position for too long can aggravate your joint pain. Get up, move around, or change your position at least every hour to give your body a break.

TRY FOR PERFECT POSTURE. Adjust your body so your back is straight and your neck is at a natural angle when you stand or sit. Putting your joints in stressful positions will strain them and aggravate your arthritis.

SLIM DOWN FOR LESS STRESS ON YOUR JOINTS. Extra pounds on your frame put more pressure on your joints, especially knees and feet. Choose a healthy, well-balanced weight loss program to peel off a few pounds.

INCREASE YOUR FRUITS AND VEGGIES. Everyone should eat at least five servings of fresh fruits and vegetables a day, but it may be even more important if you have arthritis. Eating more fruits and vegetables and less meat helps some people with arthritis pain. Healthy food choices will also give you more vitamins C, E, and beta-carotene, antioxidant vitamins that some researchers have found may keep osteoarthritis in your knees from getting worse.

The National Institute of Arthritis and Musculoskeletal and Skin Diseases (NIAMS) conducts research on a number of chronic, disabling diseases, including osteoarthritis, rheumatoid arthritis, muscle diseases, osteoporosis, Paget's disease, back disorders, gout, and more.

The Clearinghouse can answer questions, provide you with publications, and search the Combined Health Information Database (CHID) for other references on specific topics. Some of the free publications include:
- *Lupus* (AR-96) 6/95
- *Osteoarthritis* (AR-73) 9/94

- *Behcet's Syndrome* (AR69) 12/89
- *Back Pain* (AR-78)
- *Arthritis* (AR-27)

For more information, contact National Arthritis and Musculoskeletal and Skin Diseases Information Clearinghouse, 1 AMS Circle, Bethesda, MD 20892-3675; 301-495-4484; or online at <www. nih.gov/niams>.

Better Back Care

Back pain is such a — well, pain in the back. It strikes at millions of people, and can affect every part of your daily routine, from carrying groceries to picking up your grandson. The American Physical Therapy Association has a job: helping your body function better on a day-to-day basis. And they believe information on the proper way to stand, sit, lift, and exercise will keep your back in tip-top shape.

Their brochure, *Taking Care of Your Back*, is available for free. To receive one, you can call their public relations department at 703-706-3248, or write: American Physical Therapy Association, P.O. Box 37257, Washington, D.C. 20013.

Other public information they offer includes *You Can Do Something About Incontinence* and *For the Young at Heart - Exercise Tips for Seniors*.

Visit their web site at <www.apta.org>.

Keep Active and Safe

One organization that really wants you to keep an active and functional life is the American Academy of Orthopaedic Surgeons. These very specialized doctors work with the parts of your body that allow you to move, work, and play — your bones, joints, muscles, nerves, and everything that holds them together. If you twist it, sprain it, break it, or pull it, chances are you'll wind up seeing an orthopedist. He may treat you with medical counseling, medications, casts, splints, or therapies such as exercise or surgery.

The AAOS has produced a series of brochures designed to give you information on common orthopedic injuries or conditions, like *Arthritis, Carpal Tunnel, Back Pain, Osteoporosis, Scoliosis*, and *Joint Replacements*.

They also have a number of brochures on prevention such as:

- *Climb It Safe!*
- *Don't Let a Fall Be Your Last Trip*
- *Keep Moving for Life*
- *Live it Safe*
- *If the Shoe Fits Wear It*
- *Keep Active - Safe at Any Age*
- *Play It Safe - Sports*
- *Drive it Safe*

To order one of these free brochures, or one from their Health Care Issues series, send a self-addressed, stamped envelope to AAOS, PO Box 2058, Des Plaines, IL 60017. Visit their web site at <www.aaos.org> for a complete listing.

Prostate Solutions

Research shows that if a man lives long enough, he's almost certain to have some kind of non-cancerous problem with his prostate. Fortunately, there are also many effective treatments.

Herbal treatments have become popular recently, and three of these may actually help with the symptoms of an enlarged prostate, also called Benign Prostatic Hyperplasia (BPH). Saw palmetto, pygeum, and stinging nettle have been found to help relieve urine flow problems and treat prostate inflammation. Check first with your doctor and then with your local health food store to see if one of these herbs might be right for you.

You can also get excellent help in the form of a brochure on treating your enlarged prostate. It discusses symptoms of BPH, how a diagnosis is made, and pros and cons of various treatments. The information is free if you send a self-addressed, stamped, business-size envelope to the Agency for Health Care Policy and Research Publications Clearinghouse, Box 8547, Silver Spring, MD 20907. Ask for publication #94-0584.

To learn more about prostate problems and treatment options (for conditions other than prostate cancer), you can also contact the National Kidney and Urologic Diseases Information Clearinghouse. They can answer questions, provide publications, and conduct a search on the Combined Health Information Database (CHID) for more information.

Some of the free publications include:

- *Prostate Enlargement: Benign Prostatic Hyperplasia*
- *Age Page: Prostate Problems*

For more information, contact the National Kidney and Urologic Diseases Information Clearinghouse, 3 Information Way, Bethesda, MD 20892-3580; 301-654-4415; or online at <www.niddk.nih.gov>.

Special Benefit for Vietnam Vets

You slogged through the jungles of South Vietnam and lived to tell about it. Or you were stationed on a crowded warship off the coast. In either case, you were most probably exposed to the infamous Agent Orange. Scientists think this poisonous herbicide not only affected people on land, but was even carried through the air to ships in the area.

If you have been diagnosed with prostate cancer and you served in Vietnam between January 9, 1962 and May 7, 1975, you may apply to the VA (Department of Veterans Affairs) for disability compensation. You may also qualify for this benefit if you have one of several other conditions associated with Agent Orange. To get help with a claim, veterans or survivors of veterans should call the nearest county Veterans Service Office. To get more information or advice, call the VA claims or counseling offices at 800-827-1000.

Everything You Should Know About Thyroid Disease

If you are suffering from fatigue, hair loss, depression, nervousness, weight changes, or muscle weakness, you could be one of the 20 million Americans who have thyroid disease. Unfortunately, most people with this disease either don't know they have it or are misdiagnosed.

The thyroid is a small gland in your neck that helps control how fast your body uses energy. Sometimes the thyroid produces too much of its regulating hormone, resulting in hyperthyroidism, and sometimes it produces too little, a condition known as hypothyroidism. Other conditions involving your thyroid are thyroiditis, Graves' disease, developing nodules, or goiter.

The Thyroid Society is a national, not-for-profit organization searching for treatment and cures of thyroid disease. They publish several education brochures including:
- *What is Thyroid Disease?*
- *What is Hyperthyroidism?*
- *What is Hypothyroidism?*

- *What is Thyroiditis?*
- *Are all Nodules Cancerous?*
- *What about Thyroid Disease and Pregnancy?*
- *What about Tests and Treatment?*

You can obtain these free brochures by calling 1-800-THYROID (849-7643) or by sending a self-addressed, stamped envelope to The Thyroid Society, 7515 S. Main St., Suite 54, Houston, TX 77030.

Sleep Tight, Sleep Right Tonight

Getting a good night's sleep can mean the difference between a wonderful, productive day and one where you just feel out of sorts. If you've had a few too many of the grumpy days, you need to get in touch with the National Heart, Lung, and Blood Institute.

They offer good, clear information on all kinds of sleep disorders, from restless legs syndrome (RLS) to sleep apnea to insomnia. Their brochures talk about causes, symptoms, and treatment options, and also tell you where to go for further help.

So if you're tired of waking up tired, call the NHLBI at 301-251-1222. Many of their publications are free, but some have a small charge (50 cents to 75 cents each). If you'd like a full catalog of their brochures, write to: National Heart, Lung, and Blood Institute, Information Center, Box 30105, Bethesda, MD 20824-0105.

Should You Get Your Flu Shot?

Each winter, millions of people suffer from the unpleasant effects of the flu. For most people, a few days in bed, a few more days of rest, aspirin, and fluids will be the best treatment. For older people though, the flu can be life-threatening.

A flu shot can give your body time to build the proper immunity, but you must have it several weeks before you are exposed to the flu in order for it to work. Check with your doctor's office in early fall to see when you should get your flu shot. And watch your local newspaper for information on getting your flu shot in a public location such as a grocery store for free or for a small fee. Some places even offer free "drive-through" flu shots that you can receive without getting out of your car.

To better understand infectious diseases and the immune system, the National Institute of Allergy and Infectious Diseases conducts research and clinical trials. They have a free publication entitled *Flu* that can give you some great tips for the flu season.

For more information, contact National Institute of Allergy and Infectious Diseases, Office of Communications Building 31, Room 7A50, 31 Center Dr. MSC2520, Bethesda, MD 20892-2520; 301-496-5717; or online at <www.niaid.nih.gov>.

Learn Lyme Disease Self-Defense

Lyme disease is an infection caused by bacteria carried by deer ticks. Untreated, it can travel throughout your body and cause a number of symptoms, some of them quite severe. The infection begins with a skin rash, headache and fever, and can later turn into arthritis and heart damage. If Lyme disease is diagnosed and treated early enough with antibiotics, you will almost always fully recover. Even with treatment, however, the symptoms can still linger for months or even years.

Since 1982, more than 100,000 cases have been reported to the Centers for Disease Control and Prevention (CDC) in the U.S. alone. The best way to protect yourself is to be informed about this modern malady. For informational brochures on Lyme disease, its symptoms, treatment, and prevention, contact the American Lyme Disease Foundation, Inc., Mill Pond Offices, 293 Route 100, Somers, NY 10589; 914-277-6910 or 1-800-889-LYME (5963). If you have access to a computer, you can order from a larger selection of brochures for a small fee at their web site, <www.aldf.com>.

Defend Yourself From the Senseless Killer

Carbon monoxide is a poisonous gas that you can't see, smell, or taste. It sometimes creeps into people's homes and does terrible damage — not to the homes, but to the people who live there. Carbon monoxide can be the result of exhaust from a car, a fireplace, or a faulty heater. Children, seniors, and people with heart or lung problems are the most vulnerable to the poison of carbon monoxide.

The symptoms of carbon monoxide poisoning are similar to the flu: headache, fatigue, nausea, dizziness, confusion, and irritability. If you have these symptoms and have reason to believe they might be from carbon monoxide, get out of your house and get help.

The best way to defend yourself from the danger of carbon monoxide is to be informed about the precautions you should take. To get a free brochure about carbon monoxide, send a postcard with your name and address to *The Senseless Killer* #4464, Consumer Product Safety Commission, Washington, D.C. 20207. You can also get free, helpful information from the web site of First Alert, a company that makes carbon monoxide detectors for homes. The Internet address is <www.firstalert.com>.

Eat Your Calcium and Build Your Bones

Getting enough calcium and maintaining a good exercise program are two important steps you can take to help prevent or delay the onset of osteoporosis. Some excellent sources of calcium are plain low-fat yogurt, sardines, low-fat milk, cheddar cheese, turnip greens, canned salmon, refried beans, and peanuts. To strengthen your bones, exercise should be the weight-bearing kind, such as walking, aerobics, running, and weight lifting.

To learn more about the causes, risk factors, and treatment of osteoporosis, contact the National Resource Center on Osteoporosis and Related Disease, National Osteoporosis Foundation, 1150 17th St. NW, Suite 500, Washington, DC 20036-4603; 202-223-0344; or online at <www.osteo.org>.

More About Osteoporosis
and Related Bone Diseases

Information ranging from slip and fall prevention to fibrous dysplasia is available from the Osteoporosis and Related Bone Diseases National Resource Center (ORBD-NRC). ORBD-NRC's resource database provides current information on subjects such as:
- Osteoporosis
- Paget's disease of bone
- Osteogenesis imperfecta

• Primary hyperparathyroidism

Contact the ORBD-NRC to receive free publications or facts sheets from: Osteoporosis and Related Bone Diseases National Resource Center, 1150 17th St. NW, Suite 500, Washington, DC 20036-4603; 800-624-BONE; or online at <www.osteo.org>.

You can also get free information on preventing and treating osteoporosis from the Merck Healthy Bone Center. Call them at 800-290-4123. Give them your mailing address and they will send you the literature.

Rehab Assistance

If you or someone you love has had a stroke or has some other physical disability, you can get free information that may really help. The National Rehabilitation Information Center provides information covering all types of physical and mental disabilities.

For example, do you need to find a special kind of wheelchair or communication board? What about handrails for the bathroom? The Center can conduct a search of their database to learn about research, journal articles, and more dealing with your topic of interest.

To learn more about the information and assistance this Center can provide, contact National Rehabilitation Information Center, Suite 935, 8455 Colesville Rd., Silver Spring, MD 20910; 301-588-9284; 800-346-2742.

Keep Your Brain Healthy

Here's some great news: strokes can be prevented today. In fact, the death rate from strokes has fallen as much as 50 percent since 1970. This decline has come about, in part, because of new tests and treatments. In addition, many people are adopting sensible health habits such as controlling their high blood pressure and taking a daily aspirin. Here are some other steps you can take to prevent stroke.

STOP SMOKING. This habit greatly increases your risk of stroke.

KEEP UP YOUR INTAKE OF VITAMIN C. People who do are much less likely to suffer a stroke. You can take a supplement, but it's better to get your C from fresh fruits and veggies such as sweet red peppers, orange juice, green peppers, and strawberries. Just eating more fresh fruits and veggies of any kind may lower your risk by as much as 22 percent.

MAKE MUCH OF MILK. A recent long-running study found that men who drank no milk had twice as many strokes as men who drank two glasses of milk a day. A couple of glasses of skim or low-fat milk could add to your nutrition and possibly protect you from stroke as well.

SAY NUTS TO STROKE. Vegetable oils such as canola, olive, and soy contain alpha-linoleic acid, a substance also found in nuts. Researchers have found that even a small increase in the amount of alpha-linoleic acid in the blood cuts down on the risk of stroke. Cooking with these oils or substituting nuts for some of the meat in your diet could be good strategies to protect yourself.

The National Institute of Neurological Disorders and Stroke (NINDS) supports and conducts research and research training on the cause, prevention, diagnosis, and treatment of hundreds of neurological disorders in addition to stroke. Some of their other studies involve Alzheimer's disease, Parkinson's disease, Huntington's disease, multiple sclerosis, and amyotrophic lateral sclerosis (ALS). Some of the free publications available include:

- *Stroke: Hope Through Research*
- *Dizziness: Hope Through Research*
- *Multiple Sclerosis: Hope Through Research*
- *Parkinson's Disease: Hope Through Research*
- *Shingles: Hope Through Research*

Contact the National Institute of Neurological Disorders and Stroke, Information Office, Building 31, Room 8A06, 31 Center Dr. MSC 2540, Bethesda, MD 20892-2540; 800-352-9424; or online at <www.ninds.nih.gov>.

If you or a loved one need an electric wheelchair to move around, you may be able to get one, with 80 percent of the cost paid by Medicare. Diane Davis, a Registered Nurse who works for Davis Medical Supply, can help you determine whether you qualify and make all the arrangements to get you a chair. To get in touch with Diane, the toll-free number is 888-579-8658. If you would like to check out this offer on the Internet, the address is <http://seniors-site.com/ads/wheelchr/index.htm>.

Incontinence Is Not Inevitable

Incontinence is nothing to be ashamed of. It's actually a lot more common than you may think. But it's not an inevitable part of aging. About one person in 10 suffers from it, but in most cases it can be treated and controlled, if not cured.

Believe it or not, incontinence often results from the use of medications or certain common medical conditions. Some of the types of drugs that can cause incontinence are antihistamines, decongestants, antidepressants, diuretics, antihypertensives, antipsychotic agents, and sedative-hypnotics. Surgeries, weight gain, childbirth, weak bladder muscles, nerve disorders, prostate problems, and urinary tract infections are some of the other problems that can cause incontinence. Once your doctor finds out the cause, there may be simple steps you can take to help correct this frustrating problem.

The National Kidney and Urologic Diseases Information Clearinghouse can answer questions and provide information about all kidney and urologic diseases. They have free publications and can conduct a search on the Combined Health Information Database (CHID) for more information on a specific subject. Some of the free publications include:

- *Urinary Tract Infections In Adults*
- *Kidney Stones in Adults*
- *End-Stage Renal Disease*
- *Age Page: Urinary Incontinence*

For more information, contact National Kidney and Urologic Diseases Information Clearinghouse, 3 Information Way, Bethesda, MD 20892-3580; 301-654-4415; or online at <www.niddk.nih.gov>. You can also get free information from the National Association for Continence at 800-252-3337. Or you can write to Help for Incontinent People (HIP), PO Box 544, Union, SC 29379.

If treatments for incontinence simply don't work for you, don't feel hopeless. There are products today that can keep this problem private and allow you to live a normal, active life. One manufacturer that will send you a free sample is A & D Personal Care Products. Their toll-free number is 877-232-2737.

Conquer Kidney Disease
With Crucial Information

Do you, or someone you know, suffer from diabetes mellitus, high blood pressure, kidney stones, benign prostatic hyperplasia (BPH), urinary incontinence, kidney cancer, or testicular cancer? Diseases of the kidney and urinary tract are a major cause of illness throughout the world, killing more than 50,000 Americans each year. For this reason, the National Kidney Foundation is dedicated to educating the public on kidney and urologic diseases.

For free information on kidney diseases, research, transplants, and much more, contact you local Kidney Foundation or call 800-622-9010.

Help for Heartburn

No need to spend the rest of your life chugging antacids for that upset stomach; there are some simple home remedies for heartburn. Just by avoiding certain foods such as fatty and spicy dishes, grapefruit juice, orange juice, tomato juice, peppermint, spearmint, and chocolate, you can help control your heartburn. Eating small, frequent meals instead of large ones, chewing your food well, cutting down on coffee and tea, sitting up straight when you eat, and avoiding tight clothes around your middle can all help with heartburn.

You can even try elevating the head of your bed six inches, in case your heartburn is caused by acid reflux. A couple of bricks or wooden blocks should do the trick. If you can't raise the bed, putting a foam wedge under your upper body when you sleep might work as well.

Although they can't cure your heartburn or ulcer, the National Digestive Diseases Information Clearinghouse does offer helpful information about digestive diseases. They have free publications, and can conduct a search on the Combined Health Information Database (CHID) to provide you with references for further reading. Some of the fact sheets they have include:

- *Heartburn*
- *Constipation*
- *Hemorrhoids*
- *Pancreatitis*
- *Cirrhosis of the Liver*
- *Gallstones*

They also have information packets on many digestive diseases. For more information, contact National Digestive Diseases Information Clearinghouse, 2 Information Way, Bethesda, MD 20892-3570; 301-654-3810; or online at <www.niddk.nih.gov>.

Don't Be Galled by Gallstones

This year, approximately 500,000 people will have their gallbladders removed because of gallstones. This procedure, cholecystectomy, is the most common surgery performed in the United States.

If you're one of the millions of people who have gallstones, you may be curious about how they are formed and how they are treated. The American Liver Foundation has the information you need. They publish brochures and fact sheets on gallstones and other diseases like cirrhosis, sarcoidosis, and liver cancer.

If you have access to the Internet, you can get this information for free by visiting their web site: <www.liverfoundation.org>. If not, call 800-GO-LIVER (465-4837) or send a self-addressed, stamped envelope to: American Liver Foundation, 1425 Pompton Ave., Cedar Grove, New Jersey 07009. The brochures are available for 50 cents to 75 cents.

Turn Down the Volume

Now you have the government backing you up when you tell the kids to turn down the rock 'n' roll. Over one-third of all people who have hearing impairments can trace the damage back to exposure to loud sounds.

You can learn more about the causes of hearing loss, hearing aid information, and the latest research on the topic from the National Institute on Deafness and Other Communication Disorders. They conduct research on the diseases and disorders of hearing, balance, smell, taste, voice, speech, and language.

They can answer your questions and send out publications which explain common problems and inform you of the latest research being undertaken. For a publications list or more information, contact National Institute on Deafness and other Communication Disorders Clearinghouse, 1 Communication Ave., Bethesda, MD 20892-3456; 800-241-1044; or online at <www.nih.gov/nidcd>.

If you already have hearing loss and are shopping around for a hearing aid, you know that the choices are as varied as their price tags. Miracle Ear, a company that makes internal and external hearing aids, will send you a free video and information booklet on hearing loss if you call them at 800-896-6400. You can also visit their web site at <www.miracle-ear.com>.

Help for Hearing Aids

If your hearing needs help but your budget can't stretch enough to include a hearing aid, don't shut out the sounds of the world. In Rhode Island and New Jersey, the state may assist you in purchasing a hearing aid, if you are in need, through the Office of Rehabilitation Services. Other states may have similar programs. Check with your local Department of Public Health or Department of Social Services to see if there is a similar program in your area. You might also try your State Office on Deafness.

A charitable organization called HEAR NOW may be able to help you obtain a free hearing aid for yourself or a loved one. Their address is HEAR NOW, Elaine Hansen, 9745 East Hampden Avenue, Suite 300, Denver, CO 80231-4923. The phone number is 303-695-7797.

The Lion's Club, a well-known civic organization, collects and recycles hearing aids in many of its chapters across the country. The Lions Hearing Foundation Program finds hearing aids for financially needy people who don't qualify for other state-funded programs. Contact your local Lion's Club, or contact Lion Jon Oswald, 1906 Bunker Hill Ct., DePere, WI 54115, or on the Internet at <joswald@online.dct.com>.

If you are interested in simply getting a break on the price of a new hearing aid, there are two companies you might want to check with. Hearing Aids Online promises a 50 percent discount off the suggested retail price of name-brand, behind-the-ear hearing aids. Their toll-free number is 877-768-6399. Their mailing address is 14 Fieldstone, Upton, MA 01568-1597, or contact them online at <www.hearingaidsonline.com>. The other company, A Hearing Aid.Com, sells major brands of hearing aids "at wholesale prices." Their toll-free number is 800-468-9298, and their mailing address is 2334 Saturn Circle, Las Cruces, NM 88012. Their online address is <www.ahearingaid.com>.

Aid for Allergies

If you are plagued by the sneezing, sniffling, and itchy eyes of allergies, there are some simple but effective steps you can take to improve your daily life. For example, it's a good idea to get rid of any shag carpeting. Give the kid next door five bucks to mow your lawn. And get someone else to give the cat a bath when she needs it. Be sure to wear a dust mask when you work in the yard or even dust furniture in the house. Use your air conditioner when it's hot instead of opening the windows which lets in pollen and dust from the yard. And wash your bed linens weekly in hot water and vacuum your carpets frequently.

To learn about the different types of allergies and their treatment options, contact the National Institute of Allergy and Infectious Diseases. They will send you free publications and information to help you survive the sniffle season.
- *Allergic Disease: Medicine for the Public*
- *Something in the Air: Airborne Allergens*
- *Food Allergy and Intolerances*
- *Allergies: Living With Allergies*
- *How to Create a Dust-Free Bedroom*

For more information, contact National Institute of Allergy and Infectious Diseases, Office of Communications Building 31, Room 7A50, 31 Center Dr. MSC2520, Bethesda, MD 20892-2520; 301-496-5717; or online at <www.niaid.nih.gov>.

You can get a list of asthma and allergy doctors in your area, as well as a list of allergy support groups near you by calling the American Academy of Allergy, Asthma, and Immunology. They will send you helpful information on how weather affects pollen and mold allergies or other allergy-related subjects that you request. The number is 800-822-2762, and the information is free.

For a free catalog of products to help you with your allergy problems, such as air cleaners, special pillows, and items other than medicine, you can call National Allergy Supply at 800-522-1448.

If you use the prescription drug Claritin to treat your allergies, or think you might want to consider it, you can get additional information and a coupon for a $5.00 rebate by calling 800-252-7484.

Look Into the Future

Good vision is a priority for most people. Some tips to help you keep seeing clearly include having regular health checkups to detect diseases that could cause eye problems; having a complete eye exam at least every 2 or 3 years; and seeking eye health care more often if you have diabetes or a family history of eye problems.

The National Eye Institute (NEI) conducts research on the prevention, diagnosis, treatment, and pathology of diseases and disorders of the eye, and has free publications including:

- *Cataracts*
- *Don't Lose Sight of Glaucoma*
- *Don't Lose Sight of Diabetic Eye Disease*
- *Don't Lose Sight of Cataracts*
- *Don't Lose Sight of Age-Related Macular Degeneration*
- *Diabetic Retinopathy*

For more information, contact National Eye Institute, Information Office, Building 31, Room 6A32, 31 Center Dr. MSC 2510, Bethesda, MD 20892-2510; 301-496-5248; or online at <www.nei.nih.gov>.

To get a free information kit on degenerative diseases of the retina, write the Foundation Fighting Blindness, Executive Plaza I, Suite 800, 11350 McCormick Road, Hunt Valley, MD 21021, or call 800-610-4558.

The Glaucoma Foundation provides a wealth of helpful, free information just for the asking. They believe the best way to prevent blindness, especially from glaucoma, is through education and public awareness. To reach The Glaucoma Foundation, call toll free at 800-452-8266, visit their web site at <www.glaucoma-foundation.org>, or write to them at 33 Maiden Lane, New York, NY 10038. When you join their mailing list, the foundation will send you a packet of free information about glaucoma. They will also send you their free quarterly newsletter, *Eye to Eye*.

Vision Information That's Easy on the Eyes

Many people consider their eyesight to be the most valuable of their five senses. That's why even the smallest changes in vision seem so important. If you are experiencing flashes of light or floating spots, don't panic. These are common developments for many people.

Send away for a free brochure from Opticare Eye Health Center entitled *Floaters and Flashes: Small Specks and Flashes of Light in the Field of Vision*. This will explain what is happening and what you can do about it. Opticare's address is: 87 Grandview Ave., Waterbury, CT 06708. Include a self-addressed, stamped business-sized envelope. Or you can call them at 203-574-2020.

Beat the Blues

It's part of life. Being down in the dumps for a short period of time is a problem for many people, but it doesn't have to be a permanent part of normal aging. For most people, depression can be treated successfully. While some depression may require drug treatment, many other cases require simple changes in behavior or activities. Here are a few tricks you can try to chase away the blues.

EXERCISE. This is one of the most effective ways to treat depression. It actually releases "feel good" hormones into your bloodstream to improve your mood. People who exercise regularly are less likely to get depressed in the first place. The exercise you choose doesn't have to be intense — moderate movement will work just as well.

CALL A FRIEND. Sometimes just hearing another human being's voice at the other end of the line can help make you feel better. Ask your friend about her problems; maybe you can help.

CLEAN SOMETHING OR FIX SOMETHING. Getting involved in a specific task with a beginning and an end can give you a needed distraction from your problems for a while. It can also give you a sense of accomplishment when it's done.

EAT HEALTHY. Medical studies have shown that dieting can lead to feeling blue, and that people who get all the nutrients they need may be less prone to stress and depression. It's best to get good nutrition from a healthy diet, but if you have any doubts about yours, consider taking a multi-vitamin supplement as insurance.

DON'T KEEP IT TO YOURSELF. If you are suffering from depression and can't seem to shake it, don't suffer in silence. Tell your doctor, a relative, a friend, or someone so you can get some help. There is no shame in being depressed. It's simply a situation that calls for some action.

The National Institute of Mental Health conducts research to learn more about the causes, prevention, and treatment of mental and emotional illnesses. They can answer your questions and have publications on a wide variety of topics, including:
- *Depressive Illness: Treatments Bring New Hope*
- *Plain Talk About Depression*
- *Plain Talk About Handling Stress*
- *If You're Over 65 and Feeling Depressed ... Treatment Brings New Hope*

For more information, contact National Institute of Mental Health, Information Resources and Inquiries Branch, Room 7C02, 5600 Fishers Lane, MSC 8030, Bethesda, MD 20892; 301-443-4513; or online at <www.nimh.nih.gov>.

Proof Positive: Your Attitude Affects Your Life

You've heard the old saying, "you are what you eat." But what about, "you are how you think?" The late Dr. Norman Vincent Peale believed the mind has great influence over the body. His best-selling book, *The Power of Positive Thinking*, is a classic for those looking to improve their lives simply by changing the way they perceive the world.

If you want information on techniques for achieving peace of mind, happiness, and improved health, send for a free, condensed version of Dr. Peale's book today. You can mail your request with a self-addressed, stamped envelope to: The Peale Center for Positive Thinking, Attn: Jerie, 66 E. Main Street, Pawling, NY 12564. Or call 800-935-0158.

The Sunny Side of Life

You're tired of shoveling snow, so you're moving to Arizona or Florida to enjoy the sunshine. But you'd better think twice about enjoying that warm sun too much. No matter what age you are, the sun can do all kinds of harmful things to your skin, so you need to know how to protect yourself. The basics are: stay out of the sun between 10 a.m. and 2 p.m.; wear sunglasses and a hat when you go out; and protect as much of your skin as possible by wearing clothing made of tightly woven fabric. Of course, you also need to use sunscreen.

Read up on tanning and sunscreen products through two free publications from the Federal Trade Commission, titled *Indoor Tanning and Sunscreens*. These will help you keep your skin beautiful and healthy.

To receive your copies, contact Public Reference, Room 130, Federal Trade Commission, 6th St. & Pennsylvania Ave. NW, Washington, DC 20580; 202-326-2222; or online at <www.ftc.gov>.

Ease Your Wart Worries

From athlete's foot to warts, if it's a skin disorder, the American Academy of Dermatology can help you out. Whether you need information on eczema, rosacea, poison ivy, or skin cancer you'll find it through the AAD. Their brochures cover causes, types, symptoms, and treatment.

Call them toll free at 888-462-DERM (3376), visit their Internet site at <www.aad.org>, or send a self-addressed, stamped envelope to: American Academy of Dermatology, PO Box 681069, Schaumburg, IL 60168-1069.

A Super Skin-Saver

Have you tried expensive products promising smoother, younger-looking skin only to find they failed to live up to their bold advertising? Now you can get free information and a no-risk $10 coupon for an FDA-approved anti-aging product.

The cream, Renova, contains retinoic acid, known commercially as Retin-A. The Food and Drug Administration has approved it for the treatment of sun-damaged skin. It has worked for many people to lighten brown sunspots and help remove fine wrinkles.

Call 800-64-RENOVA, (736682) 24 hours a day, seven days a week to order.

Quack Alert

Ignore those seductive ads in the supermarket tabloid newspapers. No pill will automatically melt the fat off your body. And there's no such thing as an instant face-lift.

There are all kinds of miracle cure scams in the marketplace. The Federal Trade Commission has several pamphlets to help educate you about health fraud. Some of the free titles include *Health Claims: Separating Fact From Fiction*, and *Healthy Questions (To Ask Health Care Specialists)*.

To receive your copies, contact Public Reference, Room 130, Federal Trade Commission, 6th St. and Pennsylvania Ave. NW, Washington, DC

20580; 202-326-2222; or online at <www.ftc.gov>.

Which Treatment Is Best for You?

Seems like everybody's got an opinion about how you should treat a condition or disease. Even doctors disagree with one another. That's when it gets really confusing. All you want to know is "What's best for me?"

To help both you and your doctor make the best treatment choices, the Agency for Health Care Policy and Research (AHCPR) has developed some practical guidelines that you can use to help you with your health care choices.

In addition, they also look at research on health services, health care, and home health care. Some of the publications they have available include:

- *Pain Control After Surgery: A Patient's Guide* (AHCPR 92-0021)
- *Cataract in Adults: A Patient's Guide* (AHCPR 93-0544)
- *Depression is a Treatable Illness: A Patient's Guide* (ANCPR 93-2553)
- *Preventing Pressure Ulcers: A Patient's Guide* (AHCPR 92-0048)
- *Urinary Incontinence in Adults: A Patient's Guide* (AHCPR 92-0041)
- *Early Alzheimer's Disease*
- *You Can Quit Smoking*
- *Treating Your Enlarged Prostate*
- *Be Informed: Questions to Ask Your Doctor Before You Have Surgery*
- *Choosing and Using a Health Plan*
- *Prescription Medicines and You*
- *What You Should Know About Stroke Prevention*

For your free copies or more information, contact the Agency for Health Care Policy and Research, PO Box 8547, Silver Spring, MD 20907; 800-358-9295; or online at <www.ahcpr.gov>.

Secrets to No-Sweat Surgery

Going to the hospital for surgery doesn't have to be frightening — especially if you've got as much information as possible and are aware of all your choices. The American College of Surgeons is a scientific and educational association of surgeons whose main goal is to improve surgical care. They publish a series of brochures on specific surgical procedures, such as appendectomies, prostatectomies, and cataract surgeries. So no matter what you're going in for, you can get clear, easy-to-understand information on what will be done and what to expect. Their *Patient Choice* brochure will give you options that maybe even your doctor failed to mention.

To receive these publications, send a self-addressed, stamped envelope to: American College of Surgeons, 633 N. St. Clair Street, Chicago, IL 60611. Or call them at 312-202-5000 and ask for their Publications department. If you'd like to visit them on the world-wide web, their Internet address is <www.facs.org>.

☆☆☆

The Inside Story on Insurance Coverage

Many people worry that they don't have enough health coverage, so they spend billions on additional, and often unnecessary, insurance. A recent government study looked into this issue, and what they found out might save you thousands of dollars on your insurance premiums. This free report from the General Accounting Office (GAO) looks at typical insurance coverage that older Americans carry and the potential problems.

The GAO publishes results of research into issues that face seniors, including:

- *Health Insurance for the Elderly: Owning Duplicate Policies Is Costly and Unnecessary* (HEHS 94-185)
- *Medicare: Beneficiary Liability for Certain Paramedic Services May Be Substantial* (HEHS 94-122BR)
- *Mammography Services: Impact of Federal Legislation on Quality, Access, and Health Outcomes* (HEHS-98-11)
- *Housing for the Elderly: Information on HUD's Section 202 and Home PartnershipPrograms* (RCED-98-11)
- *Medicare Home Health: Success of Balanced Budget Act Cost Controls Depends on Effective and Timely Implementation* (T-HEHS-98-41)
- *Health Care Services: How Continuing Care Retirement Communities Manage Services for the Elderly* (HEHS-97-36)
- *Retiree Health Insurance: Erosion in Employer-Based Health Benefits for Early Retirees* (HEHS-97-150)

All reports are free and can be requested by contacting U.S. General Accounting Office, PO Box 6015, Gaithersburg, MD 20884-6015;

202-512-6000; or online at <www.gao.gov>.

Find High-Ranking Health Insurance

Choosing a health plan may be one of the most important decisions of your life, but without good information it's easy to make a mistake that could cost you money, time, and peace of mind. Fortunately, there are places you can go for help. One is the National Committee for Quality Assurance (NCQA). This nonprofit organization is dedicated to evaluating and reporting on the quality of managed care plans.

For their free brochure, *Choosing Quality: Finding the Health Plan That's Right For You*, call their toll-free number, 800-839-6487. If you need more specific information, they also offer a national listing by state of all the health plans they have reviewed and their findings. You can get this list by mailing $10 to: The National Committee for Quality Assurance, Publications Center, PO Box 533, Annapolis Junction, MD 20701-0533.

Visit their web site at <www.ncqa.org> for answers to frequently asked questions about managed care.

Making the Most of Medicare

For those who are covered by Medicare, the maze of questions about insurance coverage is confusing and frustrating. But there is help from the toll-free Medicare hotline which can answer your questions and refer you to local offices if necessary. They also distribute free information booklets including:

- *Guide to Health Insurance for People with Medicare* (518B)
- *Medicare: Coverage for Second Surgical Opinion* (521B)
- *Medicare: Hospice Benefits* (591B)
- *Medicare and Managed Care Plans* (592B)
- *Medicare and Other Health Benefits* (593B)
- *Medicare Coverage of Kidney Dialysis and Kidney Transplant Services* (594B)
- *Manual De Medicare* (595B) Spanish Edition
- *Medicare: Savings for Qualified Beneficiaries* (596B)
- *Medicare and Your Physician's Bill* (520B)

For more information, contact the Medicare Hotline, Health Care Financing Administration, 6325 Security Blvd., Baltimore, MD 21207; 800-638-6833; or online at <www.hcfa.gov>.

More Health Insurance for Those in Need

Being poor doesn't get you much in this country, but one of the things it may get you is free health insurance under the Medicaid program.

Medicaid is funded by the federal and state governments to provide medical assistance for certain low-income persons. Each state designs and administers its own Medicaid program, setting eligibility and coverage standards.

Although originally intended to provide basic medical services to the poor and disabled, Medicaid has also become the primary source of public funds for nursing home care. Many middle-income people turn to Medicaid when their financial resources are exhausted by the expense of living in a nursing home. To get more information and find out if you might qualify for Medicaid, look in the blue pages of your phone book for your local Medicaid office.

Help for Alzheimer's Patients and Families

Caring for a person with Alzheimer's can be emotionally, physically, and financially draining. But help is nearby. The Alzheimer's Disease Education and Referral (ADEAR) Center is a national resource that provides information on all aspects of Alzheimer's disease. They also maintain a database which includes references to patient and professional materials. The ADEAR Center distributes a quarterly newsletter and other publications such as:

- *Alzheimer's Disease Fact Sheet*
- *Forgetfulness in Old Age: It's Not What You Think*
- *Progress Report on Alzheimer's Disease*
- *Alzheimer's Disease Centers Program Directory*
- *Differential Diagnosis of Dementing Diseases*
- *Alzheimer's Disease: A Guide to Federal Programs*
- *Caring and Sharing: A Catalog of Training Materials from Alzheimer's Disease Centers*
- *Talking With Your Doctor: A Guide for Older People*

For more information, contact Alzheimer's Disease Education and Referral Center, PO Box 8250, Silver Spring, MD 20907; 301-495-3311, 800-438-4380; or online at <www.alzheimers.org>.

In addition, Journeyworks Publishing offers a 32-page book that deals with many of the issues concerning people who take care of Alzheimer's patients. The subjects of communication, anger, restlessness, sleep, hygiene, mealtime, and safety are discussed. To get your copy of *Caring for a Person with Memory Loss and Confusion*, send a check for $5.00 to cover shipping and handling, plus your name and address, to Journeyworks Publishing, Box 8466, Santa Cruz, California 95061. Or you can call them at 800-775-1998.

To find out more about the special problem that women with Alzheimer's disease might encounter, call for the free brochure *Women and Alzheimer's Disease* at 800-272-3900.

Free Treatment ... Taking Part in Finding a Cure

Although there is currently no way to prevent or cure Alzheimer's disease, the research continues. In fact, a recent study has located a possible genetic marker for Alzheimer's. Other areas of investigation range from the basic mechanisms of Alzheimer's disease to managing the symptoms and helping families cope with the effects of AD.

The National Institute on Aging currently funds 28 Alzheimer's Disease Centers (ADC's) at major medical institutions across the nation. These centers offer free diagnosis and treatment for those who volunteer for the research. There are also support groups and other special programs for volunteers and their families.

Contact the medical college, university, or medical center nearest you and ask for information about services they may provide for Alzheimer's patients, or research they may be doing. Perhaps your loved one might take part in a study or drug trial researching this disease.

Free Hospital Care

Your husband needs an operation. You know it will be expensive, but you don't know how you can possibly pay for it. Don't panic. Help may be just a phone call away, at the Hill-Burton Hotline.

Under the Hill-Burton Uncompensated Services Program, certain hospitals and other health care facilities provide free or low-cost medical care to patients who cannot afford to pay. You may qualify even if your income is up to double the Poverty Income Guidelines, which are $8,050 for a single person, $10,850 for two people in a family, $13,650 for three people in a family, and $16,450 for four people in a family (Figures are higher in Alaska and Hawaii.). You can apply before or after you receive care, and even after the bill has been sent to a collection agency.

Call the Hill-Burton Hotline to find out if you meet the eligibility requirements and to request a list of local hospitals who are participating. The number is 800-638-0742 for callers outside Maryland and 800-492-0359 for callers in Maryland. The Internet address is <www.hrsa.dhhs.gov>.

If you prefer to write for information, contact the Office of the Director, Division of Facilities Compliance and Recovery, Health Resources and Services Administration, Health and Human Services, Twinbrook Metro Plaza, 12300 Twinbrook Parkway, Suite 520, Rockville, MD 20852.

☆☆☆

Get Free Medical Care

Each year over 150,000 patients receive free medical care by some of the best doctors in the world. Many are older patients suffering from common conditions, like Alzheimer's, cataracts, and heart disease. This is possible because medical researchers get millions of dollars each year to study the latest causes, cures, and treatments for these diseases. If your condition is being studied somewhere, you might qualify for a clinical trial and get treatment for free.

There are several ways to find out about ongoing clinical trials across the nation. Your first call should be to the National Institutes of Health (NIH) Clinical Center. NIH is the federal government's focal point for health research and is the largest biomedical research organization in the world. The 300-acre NIH campus houses research laboratories, offices, and the Warren Grant Magnuson Clinical Center.

Approximately 9,000 patients are admitted each year to the Clinical Center. Another 85,000 outpatients visit the ambulatory care 13-story clinic adjacent to the hospital. Your own doctor can call the Patient Referral Line to find out if your disease is being studied. Then he'll be put in contact with the primary investigator who can determine if you meet the requirements for the study.

An information brochure is available describing the Clinical Center programs. Contact Clinical Center, National Institutes of Health, Building 10, Room 1C255, 10 Center Dr., MSC 1170, Bethesda, MD 20892-1170; 301-496-4891.

Your Medical Library

Want the latest medical research for your condition? What about doing a search of medical literature? The National Library of Medicine is the world's largest medical research library, containing more than 4.5 million journals, technical reports, books, photographs, and audiovisual materials covering hundreds of biomedical areas and related subjects.

References to journal articles can be retrieved quickly through MEDLINE. This computerized database includes hospital and health care literature, toxicology information, medical ethics information, cancer literature, and more.

You can learn about accessing MEDLINE, and receive a listing of regional medical libraries by contacting National Library of Medicine, 8600 Rockville Pike, Bethesda, MD 20894; 800-272-4787; or you can access it online at <www.nlm.nih.gov>.

If you don't have a personal computer to reach the Internet, you can get connected at your local library. A university library would also be a good place to go if you have one nearby. Feel free to ask a librarian for help if you need it.

When you get access to the MEDLINE web site, you might want to have a medical dictionary nearby, unless you already have some knowledge or experience in the medical field. Some of the terms used in the articles are fairly technical. But the information is taken directly from medical journals and the people doing the actual research, so it's usually worth the extra effort to understand it. The articles are also fascinating, and give you a glimpse into current medical research all over the world.

Find Research Grants and Experts

You can learn who's being awarded research grants to study your health condition, simply by requesting a CRISP (Computer Retrieval for

Information on Scientific Projects) search to be done by the Division of Research Grants.

The search can provide you with information on grants awarded by the National Institutes of Health, Food and Drug Administration, and other government research institutions, universities, or hospitals that deal with the topic in which you are interested. In some cases, the researchers may be looking for people willing to take part in clinical trials.

To learn how to request a search, contact Office of Extramural Research (NIH), 6701 Rockledge Dr., Rockledge Bldg. #2, MSC 7772, Bethesda, MD 20814-7772; 301-435-0656; or go online at <www.nih. gov>.

When you get to the web site, go to "Grants and Contracts," then to "Research Details" for a given year. This will take you to a database you can search by the disease or condition you are looking for. A list of institutions and researchers will appear and you can see whether any research is being done that applies to you. Then, if you wish, you can find a phone number for the institution and possibly contact the researcher. This would certainly be getting your information "straight from the horse's mouth."

Insurance Coverage Denied?

Did your insurance company claim a medical treatment was experimental or unnecessary, so they denied your claim? Have you been denied coverage, but you feel you qualify?

Contact your state's Insurance Commissioner. They handle complaints involving insurance policies, including premiums, deductibles, claims, or anything else related to your insurance coverage. They will review your complaint, and if they find that your insurance company has acted in an unlawful or unethical way, they have the power to force the insurance dealer to compensate you or correct whatever mistake they have made.

To locate your state Insurance Commissioner, look in your telephone book's blue pages or in the Directory of State Information at the end of this book.

★ ★ ★

Are You Caught in the Middle?

For many seniors, Medicare takes care of a majority of health care bills, but there is still the deductible and the Medicare Part B premium.

Many states have developed programs to provide coverage for older people with low incomes. Usually called Qualified Medicare Beneficiary Program, these programs provide benefits to individuals who do not qualify for Medicaid, but cannot afford some of the expenses of Medicare.

Most programs cover the premiums and annual deductibles for Medicare Part B, plus the payment of co-insurance and deductible amounts for the services of Medicare. To learn if your state has such a program, contact your state Department on Aging, located in the Directory of State Information at the end of this book.

Sex for Seniors

Sex can be lots of fun, and it can keep you young, too — both physically and mentally. Here are just five healthy reasons to have sex: It banishes pain, relieves stress, improves incontinence, helps insomnia, and boosts self-esteem. Most older people want — and are able to lead — an active, satisfying sex life. There are some normal changes in your body that may affect your desire and ability, but as long as you're aware of what is happening and why, your sex life can continue to be great!

Sexy Seniors

A recent poll found that many Americans are enjoying each other's charms well into their seventies. Many of them even swear that sex, like wine, gets better with age.

With age, women do not ordinarily lose their physical capacity for orgasm nor men their capacity for erection and ejaculation. There is, however, a gradual slowing of response, especially in men. This slowing down is currently considered part of normal aging, but may be eventually treatable or even reversible.

A pattern of regular sexual activity helps to preserve sexual ability. When problems occur, they should not be viewed as inevitable. They could be the result of disease, disability, drug reactions, or emotional upset, and may require medical care. Illness, disabilities, and even some medicines can affect sex or sexual desire.

The National Institute on Aging has a free publication titled *Age Page: Sexuality in Later Life* that provides information on normal physical changes, effects of illness or disability, and other factors that may affect sex for older adults. For your free copy, contact National Institute on Aging, Information Center, PO Box 8057, Gaithersburg, MD 20898; 800-222-2225; or online at <www.nih.gov/nia>.

Is Estrogen Really the Fountain of Youth?

It will make you young, beautiful, and sexy. No, we are not talking about the latest hair care product. Estrogen is getting a lot of hype these days as a cure-all for aging women who wish to remain youthful and sexually active through menopause and beyond.

Estrogen is taken by millions of women and does help relieve symptoms of menopause, such as hot flashes and vaginal changes that cause problems during sex. Some vaginal changes can be treated with local applications of creams that contain estrogen, which may lower the risk to the rest of the body from estrogens that are taken orally.

The Food and Drug Administration (FDA) has information on estrogen to help women understand the benefits and risks of this drug when deciding the best course of therapy. Contact the Center for Drug Evaluation and Research, Food and Drug Administration, 5600 Fishers Lane, HFD-8, Rockville, MD 20857; 301-827-4573, 800-532-4440; or online at <www.fda.gov/cder>.

☆☆☆

Impotence ... When Love Is a Letdown

It is not exactly an easy subject to talk to your doctor about, but many elderly men suffer from impotence. You don't have to forgo sex in your remaining years because of this problem. Many types of sexual dysfunction can now be treated successfully.

Close to 10 million men suffer from impotence, and Uncle Sam can give you the latest on medical therapies, from penile implants to encounter sessions. There are 15 different models of penile implants, and they all have a 90 percent success rate.

The National Kidney and Urologic Diseases Information Clearinghouse can answer questions and provide information about impotence and penile implants. It has free publications and can conduct a search on the Combined Health Information Database (CHID) for more information on a specific subject.

Contact National Kidney and Urologic Diseases Information Clearinghouse, 3 Information Way, Bethesda, MD 20892-3580; 301-654-4415; or online at <www.niddk.nih.gov>.

The Impotence Information Center offers free information on the causes and treatments of impotence. It also provides names of urologists and support groups in your area. Write to the Impotence Information Center, PO Box 9, Minneapolis, MN 55440, or call 800-843-4315.

The Latest Love Potion

The new wonder drug, Viagra, has been a blessing for many men who suffer from impotence. If you're having this problem, it just may be the answer for you, too. However, the drug does have side effects, including potentially fatal interactions with certain medications such as nitroglycerin. Other problems include headaches, flushing, upset stomach, stuffy nose, urinary tract infections, diarrhea, and visual changes.

You need to thoroughly investigate this drug and discuss it with your doctor before deciding if it's the "love potion" you need to spice up your sex life. The FDA's Center for Drug Evaluation and Research has a multitude of information online at <www.fda.gov/cder/consumerinfo/viagra>. Or contact the center at 5600 Fishers Lane, HFD-8, Rockville, MD 20857; 301-827-4573; 800-532-4440.

The manufacturer of the drug, Pfizer Inc., also offers consumer information on its web site <www.viagra.com> or you can call the company at 888-4VIAGRA (484-2472).

Bald Is Sexy

Many women think bald heads are sexy, but if you're happier with hair, you do have some options. For the most part, over-the-counter hair restorers won't solve your problem. But one medication can help, according to the Food and Drug Administration. The FDA has approved the lotion Minoxidil (sold as Rogaine) for treating hair loss. It's the only over-the-counter product medically proven to regrow hair and can be used by both men and women.

If you want a more permanent solution, you might consider a hair transplant. However, this type of surgery is only for people with hereditary hair loss that follows a predictable pattern.

The American Hair Loss Council can give you more information about medical and cosmetic treatments for hair loss. You'll find its web site at <www.ahlc.org>. The National Alopecia Areata Foundation offers support groups throughout the country. For a free information packet, write to 710

C St., San Rafael, CA 94901.

For free information on the causes and treatments of hair loss, call the American Academy of Dermatology at 888-462-3376.

AIDS: Changing Sex in the Nineties

AIDS is not something that affects only the young but is found in every age group. In fact, more than 40,000 people have received their AIDS diagnosis when they were 50 years or older.

The disease is not only contracted from unprotected sex, but that is the biggest danger for sexually active people of any age. Even if you don't need them for birth control, condoms should be a part of any sexual rendezvous. Don't risk your life over this very serious matter — you need to get the facts.

You may feel overwhelmed by all the information out there regarding AIDS. How do you know what's true and what's not? The National AIDS Hotline can answer questions about HIV transmission and prevention, HIV testing, and HIV/AIDS treatments. Callers can receive referrals to national, state, and local HIV/AIDS service organizations. There is a catalogue of brochures, pamphlets, reports, posters, and audiovisuals that are available free or at a very low cost.

For more information, contact National AIDS Hotline, PO Box 13827, Research Triangle Park, NC 27709; 800-342-AIDS; 800-458-5231 (publications); or online at <www.cdcnac.org>.

Free and Low-Cost Dental Care

Don't suffer through a sore tooth or bleeding gums just because you can't afford to go to a dentist. There are hundreds of programs across the country that offer free or low-cost dental care for seniors and practically anyone else who needs it, often regardless of your income level. You just need to know where to look.

Most health insurance plans don't include dental coverage. This means people often go without regular dental care simply because they think they can't afford it. But many programs actually require that you don't have dental insurance to qualify for free or largely discounted dental care. Be sure and ask.

★★★

Money-Saving Help for Happier Teeth

Here are some general examples of the kinds of programs funded all across the country.

SPECIAL TREATMENT FOR SENIORS. You'll find that most states have special programs just for senior citizens, especially those on a limited income who have trouble paying for dental care. Some give automatic senior discounts of 15 to 80 percent. Call your state's Department of Public Health for more information.

DENTAL SOCIETIES ARE THERE FOR YOU. Each state's dental society keeps track of its own free and low-cost dental programs, so it's a good idea to call if you have any questions or if you're interested in learning about any new dental programs. You'll find their addresses in the state-by-state listing at the end of this chapter.

Some dental societies also act as a clearinghouse to identify dentists who volunteer their services to those with emergencies or other special problems.

SMILE ALL THE WAY BACK TO SCHOOL. The best-kept secrets about low-cost dental care are the 53 dental schools across the country. They offer quality dental care at a fraction of the cost of private dentists. Many will even set up a repayment plan for you if you can't afford to pay the bill.

Also, researchers at many dental schools receive big money from the federal government to do cutting-edge dental research, and these researchers often need patients to work on for free. Be sure to ask about any clinical research underway at the dental school nearest you.

FREE AND LOW-COST DENTAL CLINICS. Many state and local health departments support dental clinics that offer their services for free or on a sliding-fee basis. Services are usually restricted to those with limited income or those with special needs.

DENTAL CARE FOR SPECIAL NEEDS. There are special programs just for those with mental or physical disabilities, including those with mental retardation, cerebral palsy, multiple sclerosis, and much more. Many states also offer free dental care for children born with cleft palates.

FREE DENTURES FOR SENIORS. Don't endure false teeth that hurt or don't fit properly. Many states have discount denture programs where you can receive big savings on false teeth no matter what your age. Your state health department or dental society can point you in the right direction and help get you smiling again.

DENTISTS ON WHEELS. If you have trouble getting around because of a handicap or other infirmity, some states, like Illinois, Arizona, and Missouri, have mobile dental vans that will actually come to your home or nursing home and provide you with dental care right there on the spot. Check with your state dental society for more information.

You Can Benefit From Dental Research

Tooth implants and impacted molar removal are just two of the many subjects top dental researchers are studying at the National Institute of Dental Research, part of the National Institutes of Health in Bethesda, Maryland. Also underway are studies on facial pain, taste disorders, herpes simplex, and dry mouth conditions.

Patients who participate in these clinical trials receive their dental care free of charge. For information about the clinical studies program at the National Institutes of Health, you or your doctor can contact: Patient Recruitment and Referral Center, The Warren Grant Magnuson Clinical Center, National Institutes of Health, Bethesda, MD 20892-2655; 800-411-1222.

Maryland is not the only place where doctors receive government grants to conduct dental research and treat patients for free. Each year hundreds of dental schools and other dental research facilities around the country receive money to work on everything from gum disease to fitting dentures.

You can contact the following office to receive information about on-going or up-coming dental research in your area: National Institute of Dental and Craniofacial Research, 31 Center Dr., MSC 2190, Bldg. 31 Room 5B49, Bethesda, MD 20892-2190; 301-496-4261. You can also find these doctors by contacting the dental schools in the state-by-state listing.

Dental Care Resources Listed by State

ALABAMA

Dental Programs
Department of Public Health, Dental Health Division, PO Box 303017, Montgomery, AL 36130; 334-206-5675

Dental School
School of Dentistry, University of Alabama, 1919 Seventh Ave. South, Birmingham, AL 35394; 205-934-3000, 205-934-4546 (children)

Dental Society
Alabama Dental Association, 836 Washington Ave., Montgomery, AL 36104-3893; 334-265-1684

ALASKA

Dental Programs
Social Services, Department of Public Health, PO Box 110610, Juneau, AK 99811-0610; 907-465-3090

Dental Society
Alaska Dental Society, 3305 Arctic Blvd. #102, Anchorage, AK 99503; 907-563-3003

ARIZONA

Dental Programs
Department of Health Services, Office of Oral Health, 1740 West Adams St., Phoenix, AZ 85007; 602-542-1866

Dental Society
Arizona State Dental Association, 131 N. 36th St., Phoenix, AZ 85018-4761; 602-957-4777

ARKANSAS

Dental Programs
Department of Health, Dental Division, 5800 West 10th St., Little Rock, AR 72204; 501-661-2279

Dental Society
Arkansas State Dental Association, 2501 Crestwood Rd., Suite 205, North Little Rock, AR 72116; 501-771-7650

CALIFORNIA

Dental Schools

School of Dentistry, University of California San Francisco, 707 Parnassus Ave., San Francisco, CA 94143; 415-476-1891

University of California Los Angeles, School of Dentistry, Box 951668, 10833 LeConte Ave., Los Angeles, CA 90095-1668; 310-206-3904

School of Dentistry, University of Southern California, 925 W. 34th St., Los Angeles, CA 90007; 213-740-2800

School of Dentistry, Loma Linda University, 11092 Anderson St., Loma Linda, CA 92350; 909-824-4675

Dental Society

California Dental Association, PO Box 13749, Sacramento, CA 95853-4749; 916-443-0505

COLORADO

Dental Programs

Department of Health, Family and Community Health Services-Dentistry, 4300 Cherry Creek Dr., South A4, Denver, CO 80246; 303-692-2360

Dental Society

Colorado Dental Association, 3690 S. Yosemite Ave. Suite 100, Denver, CO 80237-1808; 303-740-6900

CONNECTICUT

Dental Programs

Department of Public Health, Bureau of Community Health, MS 11 DNT, PO Box 340308, 410 Capitol Ave., Hartford, CT 06134-0308; 860-509-7807

Dental Schools

Connecticut Childrens Medical Center, 282 Washington St., Hartford, CT 06106; 860-545-9030 (children)

UConn Dental Clinic, 131 Coventry St., Hartford, CT 06112; 860-714-2140 (children)

UConn Dental Clinic, 263 Farmington Ave., Hartford, CT 06112; 860-679-2325 (adults)

Dental Society

Connecticut Dental Association, 62 Russ St., Hartford, CT 06106-1589; 860-278-5550

DELAWARE

Dental Programs

Division of Public Health, William Center Dental Clinic, 805 River Rd., Dover, DE 19901; 302-739-4755

Dental Society

Delaware Dental Society, 1925 Lovering Ave., Wilmington, DE 19806; 302-654-4335

DISTRICT OF COLUMBIA

Dental Programs

Department of Public Health, Dental Health Division, 4130 Hunt Place, Washington, DC 20019; 202-727-0530

Dental School

College of Dentistry, Howard University, 600 W St. NW, Washington, DC 20059; 202-806-0007 or 0008 (adults), 202-806-0307 (children)

Dental Society
District of Columbia Dental Society, 502 C St. NE, Washington, DC 20002-5810; 202-547-7613

FLORIDA

Dental Programs
Department of Health and Rehabilitative Services, Public Health Dental Program. 2020 Capital Circle SE, Bin #A14, Tallahassee, FL 32399-1724; 904-487-1845

Dental School
College of Dentistry, University of Florida, 1600 Archer Rd., Gainesville, FL 32610; 352-392-4261, 352-392-9820 (geriatric clinic)

Dental Society
Florida Dental Association, 1111 E. Tennessee St., Suite 102, Tallahassee, FL 32308; 800-877-9922, 352-681-3629

GEORGIA

Dental Programs
Department of Human Resources, Oral Health Section, Two Peachtree St., 6th floor, Atlanta, GA 30303; 404-657-2574

Dental School
School of Dentistry, Medical College of Georgia, 1459 Laney Walker Blvd., Augusta, GA 30912; 706-721-2696

Dental Society
Georgia Dental Association, 7000 Peachtree Dunwoody Road NE, Bldg. 17 Suite 200, Atlanta, GA 30328; 404-636-7553

HAWAII

Dental Programs
Department of Health, Dental Health Division, 1700 Lanakila Ave., Room 203, Honolulu, HI 96817; 808-832-5710

Dental Society
Hawaii Dental Association, 1000 Bishop St., Suite 805, Honolulu, HI 96813-4281

IDAHO

Dental Programs
Department of Health and Welfare, Dental Program, PO Box 83720, 450 West State St., 1st Floor, Boise, ID 83720-0036; 208-334-5966; 800-926-2588

Dental Society
Idaho Dental Association, 1220 W. Hays St., Boise, ID 83702-5315; 208-343-7543

ILLINOIS

Dental Programs
Illinois Dental Society, PO Box 376, Springfield, IL 62705; 217-525-1406

Dental Schools
Northwestern University Dental School, 240 E. Huron, 1st Floor, Chicago, IL 60611; 312-503-6837.

School of Dental Medicine, Southern Illinois University, 2800 College Ave., Building 263, Alton, IL 62002; 618-474-7000

College of Dentistry, University of Illinois, 801 S. Paulina St., Chicago, IL 60612; 312-996-7558

Dental Society
Illinois Dental Society, PO Box 376, Springfield, IL 62705-0376; 217-525-1406

INDIANA

Dental Programs
Department of Public Health, Dental Health Division, 2 N. Meridan St., Indianapolis, IN 46204-3003; 317-233-7417. The Indiana Counsel on Aging (317-254-5465) also has information on reduced-fee dental care for seniors.

Dental School
School of Dentistry, Indiana University, 1121 West Michigan St., Indianapolis, IN 46202; 317-274-7957; Clinic: 317-274-8111 (children); 317-274-3547 (adults)

Dental Society
Indiana Dental Association, 401 West Michigan St., Suite 1000, Indianapolis, IN 46202; 317-634-2610

IOWA

Dental Programs
Dental Bureau, Iowa Department of Public Health, 321 East 12th St., Des Moines, IA 50319-0075; 515-281-3733

Dental School
College of Dentistry, University of Iowa, 322 Dental Science Bldg., Elliot Ave., Iowa City, IA 52242-1001; 319-335-7499; special-care clinic for geriatrics and handicapped, 319-335-7373

Dental Society
Iowa Dental Association, 505 Fifth Ave., Suite 333, Des Moines, IA 50309-2379; 515-282-7250

KANSAS

Dental Programs
Department of Health and Environment, Dental Program, Attn: Dr. Corinne Miller, Landon State Office Bldg., 900 SW Jackson, Room 1051 South, Topeka, KS 66612-1290; 913-296-6215

Dental Society
Kansas Dental Association, 5200 SW Huntoon St., Topeka, KS 66604-2398; 785-272-7360

KENTUCKY

Dental Programs
Department of Health, Dental Health Division, 275 East Main St., Frankfort, KY 40621; 502-564-3246

Dental Schools
College of Dentistry, University of Kentucky, 800 Rose St., Lexington, KY 40536; 606-323-6525

University of Louisville, School of Dentistry, Louisville, KY 40292; 502-852-5096 (adult), 502-852-5642 (children)

Dental Society
Kentucky Dental Association, 1940 Princeton Dr., Louisville, KY 40205-1873; 502-459-5373

LOUISIANA

Dental Programs
Department of Public Health, Dental Health Division, 200 Henry Clay Ave., New Orleans, LA 70118; 504-896-1337, emergency dental service information, 504-897-8250

Dental School
School of Dentistry, Louisiana State University, 1100 Florida Ave., New Orleans, LA 70119; 504-619-8700

Dental Society
Louisiana Dental Association, 7833 Office Park Blvd., Baton Rouge, LA 70809; 504-926-1986

MAINE

Dental Programs
Department of Human Services, Bureau of Health, Division of Community and Family Health, Oral Health Program, 11 State House Station, 151 Capitol St., Augusta, Maine 04333; 207-287-3121

Dental Society
Maine Dental Association, PO Box 215, Association Dr., Manchester, ME 04351-0215; 207-622-7900

MARYLAND

Dental Programs
Maryland State Health Department, Dental Health Division-Baltimore, 201 West Preston St., Baltimore, MD 21201-3046; 800-492-5231

Dental School
Baltimore College of Dental Surgery, University of Maryland, 666 W. Baltimore St., Baltimore, MD 21201; 410-706-5603

Dental Society
Maryland Dental Association, 6450 Dobbin Road, Suite F, Columbia, MD 21045-5824; 410-964-2880

MASSACHUSETTS

Dental Programs
Department of Health and Hospitals, Community Dental Programs, 1010 Massachusetts Ave., Boston, MA 02118; 617-534-4717

Dental Schools
Harvard School of Dental Medicine, 188 Longwood Ave., Boston, MA 02115; 617-432-1423

School of Graduate Dentistry, Boston University, 100 E. Newton St., Boston, MA 02118; 617-638-4671

School of Dental Medicine, Tufts University, One Kneeland St., Boston, MA 02111; 617-636-6547

Dental Society
Massachusetts Dental Society, 83 Speen St., Natick, MA 01760-4144; 508-651-7511

MICHIGAN

Dental Programs
Department of Public Health, Dental Health Division, 3423 N. Martin Luther King Jr. Blvd., PO Box 30195, Lansing, MI 48909; 517-335-8898

Dental Schools

School of Dentistry, University of Detroit-Mercy, 2985 E. Jefferson Ave., Detroit, MI 48207; 313-494-6600

School of Dentistry, University of Michigan, 1011 North University, Ann Arbor, MI 8109-1078; 313-763-6933

Dental Society

Michigan Dental Association, 230 North Washington Square, Suite 208, Lansing, MI 48933-1392; 517-372-9070

MINNESOTA

Dental Programs

State Health Department, Dental Division, 717 Delaware Street SE, Minneapolis, MN 55440; 612-676-5529

Dental School

School of Dentistry, University of Minnesota, 515 SE Delaware St., Minneapolis, MN 55455; 612-625-2495

Dental Society

Minnesota Dental Association, 2236 Marshall Ave., St. Paul, MN 55104-5792; 612-646-7454

MISSISSIPPI

Dental School

School of Dentistry, University of Mississippi, 2500 North State St., Jackson, MS 39216; 601-984-6155

Dental Society

Mississippi Dental Association, 2630 Ridgewood Rd., Jackson, MS 39216-4920; 601-982-0442

MISSOURI

Dental Programs

Department of Public Health, Dental Health Division, 930 Wildwood, PO Box 570, Jefferson City, MO 65109; 573-751-6247

Dental School

School of Dentistry, University of Missouri, 650 E. 25th St., Kansas City, MO 64108-2795; 816-235-2100

Dental Society

Missouri Dental Association, 230 W. McCarty, PO Box 1707, Jefferson City, MO 65102-1707; 573-634-3436

MONTANA

Dental Programs

Health Services Division, Dental Department, Health and Environment Sciences, Cogswell Building, 1400 Broadway, Helena, Montana 59620; 406-444-0276

Dental Society

Montana Dental Association, PO Box 1154, Helena, MT 59624-1154; 406-443-2061

NEBRASKA

Dental Programs

Health Department, Dental Health Division, 3140 N. St., Lincoln, NE 68510; 402-441-8015

Dental Schools

School of Dentistry, Creighton University, 2802 Webster St., Omaha, NE 68178; 402-280-2865

College of Dentistry, University of Nebraska Medical Center,

40th and Holdrege Sts., Lincoln, NE 68583; 402-472-1333 (adult), 402-472-1305 (children)

Dental Society
Nebraska Dental Association, 3120 O St., Lincoln, NE 68510-1599; 402-476-1704

NEVADA

Dental Programs
Nevada State Board of Dental Examiners, 2225 Renaissance Drive, Suite E, Las Vegas, NV 89119; 702-486-7044

Dental Society
Nevada Dental Association, 6889 W. Charleston #B, Las Vegas, NV 89117; 702-255-4211

NEW HAMPSHIRE

Dental Programs
Department of Health and Human Services, Dental Division, 6 Hazen Dr., Concord, NH 03301; 603-271-4685

Dental Society
New Hampshire Dental Society, 23 South State St., PO Box 2229, Concord, NH 03302-2229; 603-225-5961

NEW JERSEY

Dental Programs
Department of Health, Dental Health Division, PO Box 364, 50 E. State St., 5th Floor, Trenton, NJ 08625-0364; 609-292-1723

Dental School
New Jersey Dental School, University of Medicine and Dentistry, 150 Bergen St., Newark, NJ 07103; 973-972-4300

Dental Society
New Jersey Dental Association, One Dental Plaza, PO Box 6020, North Brunswick, NJ 08902-6020; 732-821-9400

NEW MEXICO

Dental Programs
Department of Health, Dental Division, 1190 Saint Francis Dr., Santa Fe, NM 87502-6110; 505-827-2389

Dental Society
New Mexico Dental Association, 3736 Eubank Blvd. NE, #C1, Albuquerque, NM 87111-3556; 505-294-1368

NEW YORK

Dental Programs
Oral Health Programs and Policies, Health and Hospital Corp., 299 Broadway, Suite 500, New York, NY 10013; 212-978-5540

Dental Schools
School of Dental and Oral Surgery, Columbia University, 630 W. 168th St., New York, NY 10032; 212-305-6726

College of Dentistry, New York University, 345 E. 24th St., New York, NY 10010; 212-998-9800, 212-998-9767 (geriatric clinic)

School of Dental Medicine, State University of New York at Stony Brook, Rockland Hall

Health Science Center, Stony Brook, NY 11794; 516-632-8989, 516-632-8967 (children), 516-632-8974 (adults), 516-632-9245 (geriatric clinic)

School of Dental Medicine, State University of New York at Buffalo, 325 Squire, 3435 Main St., Buffalo, NY 14212-3008; 716-829-2821, 716-829-2723 (children), 716-829-2720 (adults)

Dental Society
Dental Society of New York, 7 Elk St., Albany, NY 12207; 518-465-0044

NORTH CAROLINA

Dental Programs
Health and Natural Resources Environment, Dental Health Department, PO Box 29598, Raleigh, NC 27626-0598; 919-733-3853

Dental School
School of Dentistry, University of North Carolina, 211 H Brauer Hall, Chapel Hill, NC 27514; 919-966-1161

Dental Society
North Carolina Dental Society, PO Box 4099, Cary, NC 27519; 919-677-1396

NORTH DAKOTA

Dental Programs
North Dakota Department of Health, Maternal and Child Health Division, 600 E. Blvd. Ave., Dept. 301, Bismarck, ND 58505-0200; 701-328-2493

Dental Society
North Dakota Dental Association, PO Box 1332, Bismarck, ND 58502-1332; 701-223-8870

OHIO

Dental Programs
State Health Department, Dental Health Division, 246 North High, Columbus, OH 43266-0588; 614-466-4180

Dental Schools
College of Dentistry, The Ohio State University, 305 W. 12th Ave., Columbus, OH 43210; 614-292-2751

School of Dentistry, Case Western Reserve University, 2123 Abington Rd., Cleveland, OH 44106; 216-368-3200

Dental Society
Ohio Dental Association, 1370 Dublin Rd., Columbus, OH 43215-1098; 614-486-2700

OKLAHOMA

Dental Programs
State Department of Health, Dental Health Services, 1000 Northeast Tenth St., Oklahoma City, OK 73117-1299; 405-271-5502

Dental School
College of Dentistry, University of Oklahoma, 1001 Stanton L. Young Blvd., PO Box 26901, Oklahoma City, OK 73190-3044; 405-271-6056

Dental Society
Oklahoma Dental Association, 629 W. Interstate 44 Service Rd., Oklahoma City, OK 73118-6032; 405-848-8873

OREGON

Dental Programs
Department of Health, Dental Health Division, 800 NE Oregon St., Portland, OR 97232; 503-731-4098

Dental School
School of Dentistry, Sam Jackson Park, Oregon Health Sciences University, 611 SW Campus Dr., Portland, OR 97201; 503-494-8867

Dental Society
Oregon Dental Association, 17898 SW McEwan Rd., Portland, OR 97224-7798; 503-620-3230

PENNSYLVANIA

Dental Programs
Department of Public Health, Dental Health Division, 500 South Broad Street, Philadelphia, PA 19146; 215-875-5666

Dental Schools
School of Dentistry, Temple University, 3223 N. Broad St., Philadelphia, PA 19140; 215-707-2900

School of Dental Medicine, University of Pennsylvania, 4001 Spruce St., Philadelphia, PA 19104; 215-898-8961

School of Dental Medicine, University of Pittsburgh, 3501 Terrace St., Salk Hall, Pittsburgh, PA 15261; 412-648-8760

Dental Society
Pennsylvania Dental Association, 3501 N. Front St., PO Box 3341,

Harrisburg, PA 17110; 717-234-5941

RHODE ISLAND

Dental Programs
Department of Public Health, Oral Health Division, 3 Capital Hill, Providence, RI 02908-5097; 401-222-2588

Dental Society
Rhode Island Dental Association, 200 Centerville Rd., Warwick, RI 02886-4339; 401-732-6833

SOUTH CAROLINA

Dental Programs
Department of Health and Environmental Control, 2600 Bull St., Columbia, SC 29201; 803-734-4972

Dental School
College of Dental Medicine, Medical University of South Carolina, 171 Ashley Ave., Charleston, SC 29425; 803-792-2611

Dental Society
South Carolina Dental Association, 120 Stonemark Ln., Columbia, SC 29210-3841; 803-750-2277

SOUTH DAKOTA

Dental Programs
Department of Health, Dental Division, Anderson Building, 445 E. Capitol Ave., Pierre, SD 57501; 605-773-3361

Dental Society
South Dakota Dental Association, PO Box 1194, Pierre, SD 57501-1194; 605-224-9133

TENNESSEE

Dental Programs
Department of Health, Oral Health Services, Cordell Hull Bldg. 5th Floor, 426 5th Ave. North, Nashville, TN 37247; 615-741-7213

Dental Schools
School of Dentistry, Meharry Medical College, 1005 D.B. Todd Blvd., Nashville, TN 37208; 615-327-6669

College of Dentistry, University of Tennessee, 875 Union Ave., Memphis, TN 38163; 901-448-6257

Dental Society
Tennessee Dental Association, PO Box 120188, Nashville, TN 37212-0188; 615-383-8962

TEXAS

Dental Programs
Contact the closest regional office:

Texas Public Health, 1109 Kemper St., Lubbock, TX 79403; 806-744-3577

Texas Public Health, 2561 Matlock Road, Arlington, TX 76015-1621; 817-792-7224

Texas Public Health, 1517 West Front St., Tyler, TX 75702; 903-595-3585

Texas Public Health, 10500 Forum Place Drive, Suite 123, Houston, TX 77036-8599; 713-995-1112

Texas Public Health, 2408 South 37th St., Temple, TX 76504; 817-778-6744

Texas Public Health, 1021 Garnerfield Rd., Uvalde, TX 78801; 210-278-7173

Texas Public Health, 601 West Sesame Drive, Harlingen, TX 78550; 210-423-0130

Dental Schools
Baylor College of Dentistry, 3302 Gaston Ave., Dallas, TX 75246; 214-828-8100

Health Science Center, Dental Branch, University of Texas, 6516 John Freeman Ave., Houston, TX 77030; 713-792-4056

Health Science Center, Dental School, University of Texas, 7703 Floyd Curl Dr., San Antonio, TX 78284; 210-567-3222

Dental Society
Texas Dental Association, PO Box 3358, Austin, TX 78764-3358; 512-443-3675

UTAH

Dental Society
Utah Dental Association, 1151 E. 3900 South, #B160, Salt Lake City, UT 84124-1216; 801-261-5315

VERMONT

Dental Programs
Island Pond Health Center, PO Box 425, Island Pond, VT 05846; 802-723-4300

Dental Society
Vermont Dental Society, 132 Church St., Burlington, VT 05401-8401; 802-864-0115

VIRGINIA

Dental Programs
Health Department, Dental Division, 1500 E. Main, Room 239, Richmond, VA 23219; 804-786-3556

Dental School
School of Dentistry, Virginia Commonwealth University, Box 980566, Richmond, VA 23298; 804-828-9095

Dental Society
Virginia Dental Association, PO Box 6906, Richmond, VA 23230-0906; 804-358-4927

WASHINGTON

Dental Programs
Health Care Authority, Dental Services, PO Box 42710, Olympia, WA 98504-2710; 360-923-2753

Dental School
School of Dentistry, University of Washington, Health Science Building, Northeast Pacific St., Seattle, WA 98195; 206-543-5830

Dental Society
Washington Dental Association, 2033 6th Ave., Suite 333, Seattle, WA 98121-2514; 206-448-1914

WEST VIRGINIA

Dental Programs
Department of Health and Human Resources, Dental Information State Capital Complex, Bldg. 6, Charleston, WV 25305; 304-926-1700

Dental School
School of Dentistry, West Virginia University, The Medical Center, Morgantown, WV 26505; 304-598-4810

Dental Society
West Virginia Dental Association, 1002 Kanawha Valley Building, 300 Capitol St., Charleston, WV 25301-1794; 304-344-5246

WISCONSIN

Dental Programs
Bureau of Public Health, 1414 E. Washington Ave., Madison, WI 53703; 608-266-5152

Dental School
School of Dentistry, Marquette University, 604 N. 16th St., Milwaukee, WI 53233; 414-288-6500

Dental Society
Wisconsin Dental Association, 111 E. Wisconsin Ave., Suite 1300, Milwaukee, WI 53202-4811; 414-276-4520

WYOMING

Dental Programs
State Health Department, Dental Division, Hathaway Building, 4th Floor, Cheyenne, WY 82002; 307-777-7945

Dental Society
Wyoming Dental Association, 330 S. Center St., Suite 322, Casper, WY 82601-2875

Prescription Drug Savings

Years ago, when a doctor prescribed a drug for a medical problem, you would take it without question. Today, things are different. You know more about the dangers and side effects of prescription drugs, and you know that being informed is one of the best ways to stay healthy. You know, too, that prescription drugs are expensive. If you get the right one for your ailment in the first place, and take it correctly, you won't be wasting a penny of the costly stuff. Following are some things you need to know about prescription drugs, how to take them, and how to save money — even get them for free.

7 Questions to Ask About Your Prescription

When your doctor writes you a prescription for any kind of medicine, here are some basic questions you should ask. Take pen and paper with you and write down the answers to the questions, so you'll have them to refer to.

- What is the name of this medicine, and how exactly does it work?
- Is this something I need for my present condition? How much improvement can I expect?
- How and when should I take this medicine, how much should I take, and for how long?
- What are the possible side effects of this medicine, and what should I do if they occur?
- Is this drug compatible with other medicines I am taking?
- Are there any specific foods, drugs, or activities I should avoid while taking this medicine?
- Do you have any written information, such as a pamphlet, about this drug that you can give me?

If your doctor is not willing to answer these questions for you, perhaps it would be wise to find another doctor who is. You are the one who has the greatest stake in this situation — your body and your health.

Take Your Medications Safely

Once you are ready to have your prescription filled, there are a few more ways to check that you are getting the right medicine. First, read the label and make sure it is the same drug that your doctor ordered. You might want to repeat back to the pharmacist the name of the drug, the dosage, and what it is for.

Be sure to take your medicine exactly the way your doctor prescribed it. Never take more than the recommended amount. Does it really matter if a tablet isn't taken at precisely the right time? What if you miss a dose? Don't just assume that you can double the dosage the next time to make up for it. Swallow capsules whole. Don't chew tablets. Drink plenty of fluids. Remember that results may take a while, so be patient. If you have any questions or problems, call your doctor.

The Food and Drug Administration's (FDA) Office of Consumer Affairs has good information on these issues. They can also refer you to other offices within the FDA for more information and free publications that deal with drugs, medical devices, and health concerns. *Buying Medicine? Stop, Look, Look Again!* and *When Medicines Don't Mix* are two helpful brochures you can send for. You can also ask for pamphlets from the "How to Take Your Medicines" series. You can get them on acetaminophen, antihistamines, beta blockers, cephalosporin, codeine, diuretics, erythromycin, estrogen, NSAIDs, and penicillin.

For these publications and more information, contact the Drug Information Branch, Food And Drug Administration, 5600 Fishers Lane, HFD-210, Rockville, MD 20857; 800-532-4440; or online at <www.fda.gov>.

Check Out Your Prescription Drugs

Since you started taking estrogen, you've been getting sudden headaches and gaining some weight. Is it just a coincidence? The Center for Drug Evaluation and Research does all kinds of studies on side effects of prescription drugs, and can answer a variety of drug-related questions.

They are also the ones who make sure drug companies follow guidelines for warning labels. They can provide you with information on types of medications as well as send you the package insert for specific medications.

For more information, contact the Center for Drug Evaluation and Research, Food and Drug Administration, 5600 Fishers Lane, HFD210,

Rockville, MD 20857; 800-532-4440; or online at <www.fda.gov>.

How to Save $ on Your Next Prescription

- Drug companies are always giving doctors free samples of medicines. Why not ask if your physician will pass some of these freebies on to you?

- In many cases you can save up to 50 percent on a prescription by asking the pharmacist for a generic equivalent.

- Many larger-dose pills come already scored so they can be split for a smaller dosage. If your doctor prescribes a smaller-dose pill, many times you can save money on the prescription by buying the larger-dose pill, splitting it, and taking only half of it at a time. Check with your pharmacist to see if this will work with your prescription, and if it will save you money. Of course you'll have to invest in an inexpensive pill splitter (available at most drug stores) to cut the tablet in two. Just remember not to try this with capsules or pills with shiny coatings.

- Comparison shopping shouldn't just apply to a loaf of bread or a pair of tennis shoes. Some larger chain stores offer lower pharmacy prices than the small local drug stores.

- Make sure you have read all the fine print on your health insurance policy and any coverage offered by your employer. Many benefits are not claimed simply because people don't know they are entitled to them.

- Before you leave your doctor's office, ask if there's an over-the-counter medication that can do nearly the same thing as the prescription drug; they're usually cheaper. Or simply ask your pharmacist — they are there to help. However, if your insurance plan will cover the cost of prescriptions, an over-the-counter alternative wouldn't save you any money.

Read on to discover other ways to really cut down on your prescription bills.

Discount Drug Programs

If you need help beating the high price of prescription drugs, simply pick up the phone. Ten states have special drug programs that give huge discounts to seniors who are not eligible for Medicaid and who don't have private insurance.

Often, all it takes to participate in one of these programs is a phone call and filling out a simple form. You will have to meet income eligibility, though, which can vary from state to state. If your state is not listed below, contact your state Department of Aging listed in the Directory of State Information in the back of this book to see if you may be eligible to get your prescription drugs at a special discount.

CONNECTICUT

Conn PACE, PO Box 5011, Hartford, CT 06102; 800-423-5026 (in CT); 860-832-9265.

Eligibility: You must be 65 years old or older; or receive Social Security disability. You must have lived in Connecticut for six months. Your income cannot exceed $13,800 if you are single, or $16,600 if you are married. You may not have an insurance plan that pays for all or a portion of each prescription, a deductible insurance plan that includes prescriptions, or Medicaid.

Cost: You pay a $25 one-time registration fee, and you pay $12 for each prescription. You must get generic drugs whenever possible, unless the doctor writes on the prescription "brand drug only."

DELAWARE

Nemours Health Clinic, 915 N. Dupont Blvd., Milford, DE 19963-1092; 302-424-5420; 800-763-9326.

Eligibility: You must be a Delaware resident and a U.S. citizen. You must be 65 or older. Your income cannot exceed $11,900 if you are single, or $16,300 if you are married.

Cost: You must pay 20 percent of the prescription drug cost.

ILLINOIS

Pharmaceutical Assistance Program, Illinois Department of Revenue, PO Box 19021, Springfield, IL 62794; 800-624-2459; 217-785-7100.

Eligibility: You must be 65 years of age or older; or over 16 and total-ly disabled; or a widow or widower who turned 63 before your spouse's death. You must be a resident of Illinois. Your income must be less than $14,000. You must file a Circuit Breaker claim form.

Cost: Pharmaceutical Assistance card will cost either $40 or $80, depending on your income. Your monthly deductible will be $15 if the cost of your card is $40, and $25 if the cost of your card is $80. You must choose the generic brand when available, unless you are willing to pay the difference in price.

MAINE

Elderly Low-Cost Drug Program, Bureau of Taxation, State Office Building, Augusta, ME 04333-0024; 207-626-8475.
Eligibility: You must be a Maine resident. You may not be receiving SSI payments. You must be at least 62 years old or part of a household where one person is 62 years old. Your income may not exceed $10,300 if you live alone, or $12,700 if you are married or have dependents.
Cost: Each drug will cost $2 or 20 percent of the price allowed by the Department of Human Services, whichever is greater.

MARYLAND

Maryland Pharmacy Assistance Program, PO Box 386, Baltimore, MD 21203-0386; 410-767-5397; 800-492-1974.
Eligibility: For anyone in the state who cannot afford their medications. Income requirements vary, so it is best to call. You must be a permanent resident of Maryland.

NEW JERSEY

Pharmaceutical Assistance to the Aged and Disabled (PAAD), Special Benefit Programs, CN 715, Trenton, NJ 08625; 800-792-9745; 609-588-7049.
Eligibility: You must be a New Jersey resident. Your income must be less than $17,500 if you are single, or less than $21,519 if you are married. You must be at least 65 years of age. Drugs purchased outside the state of New Jersey are not covered, nor is any pharmaceutical product whose manufacturer has not agreed to provide rebates to the state of New Jersey.
Cost: You pay $5 for each covered prescription. PAAD collects payments made on your behalf from any other assistance program, insurance, or retirement benefits which may cover prescription drugs.

NEW YORK

Elderly Pharmaceutical Insurance Coverage EPIC, PO Box 15018, Albany, NY 12212; 800-332-EPIC (3742) in N.Y. only; 518-452-6828 outside N.Y. Eligibility: You must be 65 or older. You must reside in New York

State. Your income must not exceed $18,000 if you are single, or $23,700 if you are married. You are not eligible if you receive Medicaid benefits.

Cost: You pay between $3 and $23 per prescription depending upon the prescription cost. There are two plans for EPIC. To qualify right away, you can pay an annual fee (from $20 to over $75) depending upon your income. But this can be paid in installments. With the EPIC Deductible plan, you pay no fee, but you pay full price for your prescriptions until you spend the deductible, which varies by income and starts at $468.

PENNSYLVANIA

PACE Card, (Pennsylvania Pharmaceutical Assistance Contract For The Elderly), Pennsylvania Department of Aging, PO Box 8806, 400 Market St., 6th Floor, Harrisburg, PA 17101-2301; 717-787-7313; 800-225-7223.

Eligibility: You must be 65 or older. Your income cannot exceed $14,000 if you are single, or $17,200 if you are married. You must have lived in the state for at least 90 days. PACE NET program has higher income eligibility requirements than other state programs and you must also meet the $500 prescription deductible.

Cost: You pay an $8 co-payment for each prescription. You may not purchase drugs out of state. PACE limits drug amounts to no more than a 30-day supply or 100 pills. There are no vacation supplies allowed.

RHODE ISLAND

Rhode Island Pharmaceutical Assistance to the Elderly (RIPAE), Rhode Island Department of Elderly Affairs, 160 Pine St, Providence, RI 02903; 401-277-3330.

Eligibility: You must be a Rhode Island resident. You must be 65 years old. Your income must not exceed $15,042 if you are single, or $18,804 if you are married. You cannot have any other prescription drug coverage.

Cost: Members pay 40 percent of the cost of prescription drugs used to treat certain illnesses.

VERMONT

VScript program, Department of Social Welfare, Medicaid Division, 103 South Main St., Waterbury, VT 05671; 802-241-3971; 800-529-4060.

Eligibility: You must be a resident of Vermont. You must be at least 65. You may not have income in excess of 175 percent of the federal poverty guidelines. You may not be in a health insurance plan that pays for all or a portion of your prescription drugs.

Cost: There will be a co-payment requirement. The amount will be a percentage of the charge for a drug, with the percentage amount determined at the beginning of each fiscal year.

Drug Companies That Give It Away

Valium, Prozac, Dilantin, Insulin — these are just a few of the medications you can get free, directly from the drug companies themselves. Drug companies will give their drugs free of charge to certain people who need them but can't afford the medications.

To participate in these "indigent patient programs," the pharmaceutical companies require that your doctor call or write them, stating that you cannot afford the drugs you need. You cannot get this help without a doctor. Once the forms are filled out, you will be able to pick up your prescription drugs directly from your doctor's office, without charge.

There are two ways to apply for assistance. First you will need the directory that lists the drug companies participating in the program. You can get this directory either through the government or from the Pharmaceutical Research and Manufacturers of America (PhRMA).

Call or write the Special Committee on Aging, U.S. Senate, SD-G31, Washington, DC 20510; 202-224-5364. Tell them you need the *Guide to Low Income Medication Assistance Programs* (publication #105-DRG) and give them your mailing address. They will send you a listing of the pharmaceutical companies participating in the program, a list of the drugs they manufacture, and a letter of explanation to your doctor.

If you have access to the Internet (remember you can go to the library for this), you can visit the web site of the U.S. Senate Special Committee on Aging at <www.senate.gov/~aging>. Go to "Committee Publications," then to "Publications List." At the bottom of the page, click on *Guide to Low Income Medication Assistance Programs*, and it will give you the same information that would be mailed to you.

Or you can contact PhRMA at 1100 Fifteenth St. NW, Washington, D.C. 20005; 800-762-4636. The directory is also online at: <www.phrma.org/>.

You need to make a list of the prescription drugs you are taking, check them with the drug list, then take this to your doctor so he can qualify you and make the call to the drug companies. If you need this assistance, don't hesitate to ask for it.

Free Medicine With the Right Insurance

Do you have the kind of health insurance that pays about 80 percent of the cost of drugs while you pay the other 20 percent? If so, a company called Drugs By Mail has a deal for you — free prescription drugs!

Drugs By Mail is willing to "absorb" the 20 percent co-payment you would ordinarily have to make. Your insurance company pays the 80 percent directly to Drugs By Mail. The company will even file the insurance claim for you.

This only applies to people who carry "indemnity" medical insurance (the kind where you make a co-payment for your prescriptions) and it applies after you have met your insurance deductible for the year. But if you have any kind of chronic condition that requires you to regularly fork over your hard-earned money to your local pharmacist, this program could be a real help.

You can reach Drugs By Mail at 5007 N. Central, Phoenix, AZ 85012. The toll-free number nationwide is 800-775-6888. If you live in Arizona, the number to call is 602-274-9956. Your doctor can call in your prescription to Drugs By Mail, or you can send it by fax at 602-241-0104. Delivery is free, and is usually by "UPS Next Day." In the Phoenix area, free delivery can be arranged on the same day as your order. Or you can even call, go by, and pick it up.

You can also contact Drugs By Mail through e-mail at <sales@ drugsbymail.com>, or you can visit the company's web site at <www. drugsbymail.com/ #nocost>.

Deep Prescription Discounts
Through Mail-Order Pharmacies

Most mail-order pharmacies play by the same rules: They carry prescription and generic drugs, sometimes over-the-counter products. Many even offer catalogs for you to look through at home. Your prescription must either be phoned in by a doctor, faxed in, or sent through the mail. You can usually receive price quotes over the phone.

Most will take credit cards but only some will allow billing after shipment. There are usually no membership fees and most have no shipping or handling fees. Your prescriptions will arrive in about a week. Insurance issues should be addressed directly with the company you choose to deal with.

If you need the same medicine over a long period of time, mail-order pharmacies are a great way to save money. Plan on knocking at least 30 percent off your regular prescription bills.

American Association of Retired Persons (AARP): 800-456-2277; <www.aarp.org/benefits/msms.html>. To receive prescriptions through the AARP, you don't even have to be a member of this organization. They have a special department that exclusively markets diabetic products.

Merck-Medco Managed Care, LLC: 800-247-1003; <www.merck-medco.com>. In order to take advantage of the drug savings offered through Merck-Medco, your insurance company must have a contract with them. Call to find out if you qualify.

Medi-Mail: 800-331-1458; 800-922-3444. There is a handling fee for items that require shipping on ice, like insulin, in which case it is sent next-day air. Medi-Mail requires payment at the time of service (no billing).

Preferred Prescription Plan: call 800-881-6325.

Express RX: 501-963-6400; <www.expressrx.com>. This company does not have a toll-free number, but they will accept collect calls.

Ordering anything through the mail can be a case of "consumer beware!" Make sure you are dealing with a reputable company before you give out any credit card information. Large, established companies like these are usually safe and reputable. However, the Better Business Bureau wants you to know that ordering prescription drugs through foreign mail-order houses is illegal and potentially dangerous.

A dead give-away is if the company does not require a doctor's prescription to place the order. In addition, drugs purchased abroad are not subject to the same FDA restrictions and qualifications that U.S.-patented drugs are.

If you have any questions or concerns about a particular mail-order pharmacy, contact your Better Business Bureau for more information.

Retirement Options and Answers

You finally made it to retirement — congratulations! Time to kick back and relax, see a bit of the country, spend some time with your grand-kids. You've earned a break from the daily grind of the workaday world, but retirement is not all fun and games.

A lot of people sort of stumble into retirement without having prepared themselves for this new lifestyle. Retirement brings many changes that you'll need to be aware of in order to enjoy your reward in comfort and security. Most of the questions you'll face will deal with your new financial situation. How can I check on my pension? What should I expect from Social Security? Are there any new tax concerns I should be aware of?

You can get answers to these and many other questions about retirement by taking advantage of government resources. There are entire departments whose sole purpose is to provide information on planning for and enjoying your retirement. Other groups also provide free information and materials that can help you get settled and stay on top of your retirement. In most cases, all you have to do is pick up the phone.

Even if retirement is not in your near future, it's never too early to start planning for it. The faster you learn what you need to do to prepare for a comfortable retirement, the easier your task will be down the road. So stop worrying about retirement and get the information you need. You'll be glad you did, and Uncle Sam will be glad to help.

The First Day of the Rest of Your Life

Most folks look forward to retirement as a well-earned reward. But this reward can lose a good deal of its shine if you haven't prepared for it. Fortunately, there are experts out there to help you every step of the way, and often for free. The AFL-CIO, for example, puts out a brochure called *Aging & The Community,* which offers lots of information on how to enjoy your retirement to its fullest. Send for this free resource by writing to their Department of Community Services, 815 16th Street NW, Washington, DC 20006.

Are You Ready to Take the Retirement Plunge?

It's tough saving for retirement. With all the expenses involved in day-to-day living, money to put away for later can be hard to come by. Many people rely on the promise of Social Security payments, but before you base a retirement decision on this source of income, be certain that it is going to be enough. It might not be.

Social Security was designed to replace a portion of the income a person loses when they retire, have a death in the family, or become disabled, with monthly benefits based upon a worker's earnings. Over 92 percent of American seniors receive monthly payments from Social Security, but most find that they need another source of income to continue to live comfortably.

Get in touch with the Social Security people today to find out where this benefit will fit into your post-retirement financial picture. The Administration has established a hotline to provide answers to all your questions. You can learn how to get a duplicate Social Security card, change your address, and most importantly, learn how much you would earn each month if you retired today.

It is important to get a copy of your Personal Earnings and Benefits statement each year. The statement is free and will show you what you have earned year by year, so that you can figure out what future benefits you can expect from Social Security. To request yours, contact the Social Security Hotline at 800-772-1213; or online at <www.ssa.gov>.

For the Ladies Only

Women's roles in the workplace have varied a great deal over the past 50 years. Many women are self-employed, or have taken time off to raise families, and some women (and men) have never been employed at all. Because of this, many women face certain issues that men do not when planning for retirement. The government knows this, and wants to help.

Request your free copy of *Social Security: What Every Woman Should Know* by calling the Social Security Administration at 800-772-1213.

Keep an Eye on the Piggy Bank

Financial planners have many different theories on how to invest for retirement, but they all agree on one thing: The sooner you start to save, the better off you'll be. It's also a good idea to keep track of what you have put away, and to check back periodically to make sure you're on the right track to have a secure retirement. But how do you know if it will be enough?

Put the pros at Scudder Investor Services to work for you. Give them a call at 800-728-3337, extension 3220, and they'll send you a free Retirement Money Calculator. This cardboard display is a handy tool for calculating your probable retirement income by matching your nest egg amount with your years of saving to show how this money will grow between now and retirement. If you're thinking about hanging up the old work boots, this is some valuable insight you cannot afford to be without.

Is This Going to Be Enough?

A 1998 investigation by the Employee Benefit Research Institute revealed that nearly one-third of Americans are not saving for their retirement. If you are one of them, it's time to change your ways.

The Department of Labor can help you do that with such free workbooks as *Top 10 Ways to Beat the Clock and Prepare for Retirement,* and *Women and Pensions: What Women Need to Know and Do.* These and many other helpful worksheets and checklists are available by calling the Department of Labor's Publication Hotline at 800-998-7542. They can also be viewed online at <dol.gov/dol/pwba>, and most are available in Spanish.

A Small Investment in Big Savings

Even with careful financial planning, new retirees often experience a mild shock when dealing with a smaller income. If you don't adjust to this change quickly, you can sink into a debt situation that can be hard to pull out of.

Advice on how to deal with this transition is available for an investment of $2.75. Call 800-876-8636 to request the 16-page workbook titled *Adjusting to Suddenly Reduced Income*. This resource is aimed at helping families to cut costs and learn how to manage their new financial situation without sacrificing quality of life.

For an even smaller investment, you can receive a sample copy of a newsletter that gives great ideas on living well for less. Send $2 to *Creative Downscaling*, Dept FC, PO Box 1884, Jonesboro, GA 30237-1884.

Give Your Medical Insurance a Checkup

Do you know how retirement will affect your medical insurance? As we get older, most of us tend to need health insurance more, not less, so any reductions in your coverage can be very costly. If you're on Medicare, be sure there are no gaps in coverage because you are no longer working.

For a free, 35-page book to help you make sure your coverage is complete without paying for duplicate benefits, order the *Guide to Health Insurance for People with Medicare* (Code #528E), by calling the Consumer Information Center at 888-878-3265, or write CIC-8D, PO Box 100, Pueblo, CO 81002.

While you're on the phone, ask them to send you another free booklet, *Medicare Managed Care* (Code #530E). This resource will help you decide between managed care options and fee-for-service plans.

Now Versus Later: When Is the Right Time?

Of course the traditional retirement age is 65, but in recent years, many people are opting for early retirement. If this is your plan, you should be fully aware of how cutting out early will affect the Social Security benefits you will receive.

Currently, if you retire before 65, you can expect to take a .555 percent reduction in your monthly payment for each month you collect before reaching 65. If you retire a few years early, that cut can really add up. The increase in your benefit for retiring later is a bit trickier to figure out, as it is based on a number of factors.

In any event, before deciding when to call it quits, you should do a little math and figure out how an early or late retirement will impact your financial picture. Your friends at the Social Security Administration will help you do that. Request their free booklet called *Retirement* by calling 800-772-1213.

Your Pension Watchdogs

The main sources of income for over 50 million retirees are their employer-sponsored pension plans. Most private plan participants are covered under a defined-benefit plan, which generally bases the benefits paid during retirement on the employee's salary and length of service. But like any financial fund, pension programs can gain or lose value, and the results can have a dramatic effect on the retirees who rely on them.

The Pension Benefit Guaranty Corporation (PBGC) keeps an eye on the many different benefit plans and takes over those that are underfunded. They have several free publications concerning this issue to help you look out for your best interests and make sure your pension income is secure.

The Employer's Pension Guide provides a general overview of the responsibilities under federal law of employers who sponsor "single-employer defined benefit pension plans." If your business has such a plan, learn what benefits you are entitled to.

Your Guaranteed Pension answers some of the most frequently asked questions about your rights and security as laid out in your particular pension.

Your Pension: Things You Should Know About Your Pension Plan serves as an explanation of pension plans: what they are, how they operate, and the rights and options of participants

To request these and more free sources of information, write or call Public Affairs, Pension Benefit Guaranty Corporation, 1200 K St. NW, Washington, DC 20005; phone 202-326-4000, or look online at <www.pbgc.gov>.

How to Check Up on Your Pension

For many of us, our pension income is the lifeblood of our financial security. So every now and then, it's a good idea to check its pulse, pressure, and heart rate. You want to make sure your pension is around as long as you need it.

The Pension and Welfare Benefits Administration can help you do that. They require administrators of private pension and welfare plans to provide plan participants with easily understandable summaries of plans, to file those summaries with the agency, and to report annually on the financial operation of the plans.

They also provide free publications to help participants understand some of the finer points of how pensions work. Two of the most helpful of these publications are: *What You Should Know About The Pension Law,* which gives a summary of what is required of pension plans, and *How To File A Claim For Your Benefit,* which explains what you need to do to receive your benefit.

Contact Public Information, Pension and Welfare Benefits Administration, U.S. Department of Labor, 200 Constitution Ave. NW, Room N5656, Washington, DC 20210; phone 202-219-8921, or do your homework online at <www.dol.gov/dol/pwba>.

Keeping an Eye on Your Pension Money

The Pension Benefit Guaranty Corporation (PBGC) says they will cover the pension plans that are underfunded, but what if several of the big ones collapse at the same time? Would they all be protected?

Scary possibilities like this one can make you lose faith in the pension process — that's why you need all the facts. Are other options any safer? What if your company offers you a lump-sum retirement instead? Another GAO report looks at several of these offers and examines the pros and cons. Other titles of the GAO reports focusing on income security issues include:

- *Lump-Sum Retirements* (GAO/GGD 93-2R)
- *Pension Plans: Hidden Liabilities Increase Claims Against Government Insurance Program* (GAO/HRD 93-7)
- *Pension Plans: Labor Should Not Ignore Some Small Plans That Report Violations* (GAO/HRD 93-45)
- *Pension Restoration Act* (GAO/HRD 93-7R)
- *Private Pensions: Protections for Retirees' Insurance Annuities Can Be Strengthened* (GAO/HRD 93-29)
- *Underfunded State and Local Pension Plans* (GAO/HRD 93-9R)

All reports are free and can be requested by contacting the U.S. General Accounting Office, PO Box 6015, Gaithersburg, MD 20884; phone

202-512-6000; or go online at <www.gao.gov>.

For Those Who Served Our Country

The U.S. Military has a very good pension plan, with veterans entitled to retirement pay after 20 years of service. In 1990, there were 1.6 million retirees and survivors receiving three main types of benefits from Uncle Sam, with the specific payments depending on factors such as length of service, ending pay, and age at retirement.

Generally speaking, military benefits continue until the death of the participant. There is also a special program available, called the Military Survivor Benefit Plan, which allows a military retiree to have a portion of his or her retired pay withheld to provide a benefit to his or her survivors.

Veterans with limited incomes may also be eligible for a different kind of support if they have 90 days or more of active military service under their belt. However, they must be permanently and totally disabled for reasons not due to the military.

Every veteran should take a careful look at his pension options, because there are many programs and there may be benefits available that you don't know about. To learn more about the retirement plans, contact the U.S. Department of Veterans Affairs, 810 Vermont Ave., NW, Washington, DC 20420; phone 800-827-1000; or look online at <www.va.gov>.

Have You Been Working on the Railroad?

To protect the retirement of all those engineers, conductors, linesmen, and caboose riders out there, the Railroad Retirement System regulates railroad retirement programs. It covers all railroad firms and distributes retirement and disability benefits to employees, their spouses, and survivors.

Workers must amass 120 months of employment to qualify for a pension. In some cases, military service may be counted as railroad service. The Board has several fact sheets including a booklet titled *Railroad Retirement and Survivor Benefits*, which explains who qualifies and how to apply. For more information, contact Railroad Retirement Board, 844 North Rush St., Chicago, IL 60611; phone 312-751-4500; or look online at <www.rrb.gov>.

For Those of Us Who Served in the 'Family Business'

Uncle Sam tries to look after all his nieces and nephews, but he takes special care of those dutiful bureaucrats who did his work through the Federal Employees Retirement System (FERS). FERS is comprised of three parts: a defined-benefit plan, Social Security, and a Thrift Savings Plan. If you have served as a government employee, check into the retirement options available to you.

Under the defined-benefit plan, you earn 1 percent of the average of your highest three consecutive years of wages for each year of service completed. You also contribute to Social Security. The Thrift Savings Plan (TSP) is similar to the 401(k) plans used by private employers. Sound complicated? It's not, once you do your required reading.

To learn more specific details about the plan and retirement information, contact Federal Employees Retirement System, Office of Personnel Management, 1900 E St., NW, Washington, DC 20415; phone 202-606-0490, or go online at <www.opm.gov>.

Up to $5000 to Help You Pay Your Bills

If your check is too small to live on and you can't seem to make ends meet, don't be discouraged. If you don't qualify for Social Security, or if your benefits are very low, you may qualify for Supplement Security Income (SSI).

This program was established to help low-income people over 65, as well as the blind and disabled, meet basic living needs. Those who meet SSI's standards can usually also receive Medicaid coverage and Food Stamps benefits. To qualify, neither your monthly income nor the total value of your assets may exceed a certain fixed level. Your eligibility is based on many factors, and can vary from state to state.

Studies have found that between 40 percent and 60 percent of seniors with incomes low enough to qualify for SSI actually receive benefits under the program. That's a lot of people, but it also means there are thousands of seniors out there not taking advantage of this valuable program. To find out if you qualify, contact your local Social Security office or call the Social Security Hotline at 800-772-1213; or go online at <www.ssa.gov>.

Little Known Tax Tidbits

Did you know that the IRS considers you 65 on the day before your 65th birthday? Why? Who knows? The important question is: How does this affect your taxes? Sixty-five is a magic number to the IRS, and when you hit it (or the day before you do), you instantly qualify for some extra tax bonuses that could be some of the nicest birthday presents you'll ever get.

It's important to get the scoop on what tax breaks you've got coming. The IRS is there to provide this information free of charge, and give you the latest updates about which forms you'll need, what to figure in for church donations, and how to determine what qualifies as a deduction. The Information Line provides answers to all your tax questions, and is willing to assist you in completing your tax return. They can even refer your call to tax specialists for answers to more detailed tax questions. Or, if you just need a quick answer, you can listen to pre-recorded answers to over 140 frequently asked tax questions on the Tele-Tax Line.

For more information on your taxes, contact Internal Revenue Service, U.S. Department of the Treasury, 1111 Constitution Ave. NW, Washington, DC 20224. Information Line: 800-829-1040. Forms Line: 800-829-3676. Tele-Tax Line: 800-829-4477. You can also visit the web site at <www.irs. gov>.

Showing Good Form(s)
for the IRS

Those thoughtful crusaders at the IRS were thinking only of you when they wrote their retirement-oriented Publication #554. It's called *Tax Information For Older Americans*, and it answers all your specific tax questions about the right forms, your filing status, retirement benefits, life insurance proceeds, and more. It even shows you how to keep most of what you made (up to a point anyway) on the sale of your house if you meet certain requirements.

The IRS Forms Line distributes all of the IRS tax forms and many more free publications like the one above. Some of those dealing with typical retiree concerns include:

- *Tax Information on Selling Your Home* (pub. 523)
- *Credit for the Elderly or Disabled* (pub. 524)
- *Comprehensive Tax Guide to U.S. Service Retirement Benefit* (pub. 721)
- *Pension and Annuity Income* (pub. 575)
- *Tax Information for Handicapped and Disabled Individuals* (pub. 907)
- *Social Security Benefits and Equivalent Railroad Retirement Benefits* (pub. 915)
- *Medical and Dental Expenses* (pub. 502).

To get your free copies, contact the IRS Forms Line at 800-829-3676, or go online at <www.irs.gov>.

Angels With Dirty Erasers

Ever sat there with your pencil and your practice sheet, making mistake after mistake until the whole form was an ugly smear of shredded grey pulp? If so, you're like most Americans. But unlike most Americans, you, as a senior, have an ace in the hole that they don't. You can get the IRS to do the dirty work for you.

Through a program called Tax Counseling for the Elderly, the IRS brings free tax help right to the door of people who are 60 years and older. Their staff of helpful volunteers will go wherever they are needed: nursing homes, community centers, even your own home. A nice advantage to this program is that most of the volunteers are retirees just like you, so they're likely to be very knowledgeable about how to best prepare a fellow retiree's return. If you're having trouble figuring your taxes, let these angels show you the light.

The IRS Information Line can refer you to the closest program, so call 800-829-1040; or online at <www.irs.gov>.

The Seniors' Secret Tax Strategy:
Foolproof and Free

Sometimes it feels like all we do is pay and pay and pay, even after we're retired. If we claim too many deductions, the taxman gets angry, but if we don't claim enough, he doesn't seem to care. Now there's someone who does care. If you're a senior citizen, make sure you get your hands on a copy of a free publication titled *Protecting Older Americans Against Overpayment of Income Taxes.*

This manual was designed to ensure that older Americans claim every legitimate income tax deduction, exemption, and tax credit they have coming. It is well written and easy to understand, and it provides examples and checklists to help you figure out what you owe and what you don't. This publication is updated annually in January and includes a section that points out those income tax items which will change in the following year.

For your free copy, contact the Special Committee on Aging, U.S. Senate, SDG 31, Washington, DC 20410; phone 202-224-5364; or look online at <www.senate.gov/committee/ aging.html>.

Free Help With Money Matters

Your money and how it's invested should not be keeping you awake at night. But very few people are financially savvy enough to maneuver through all the investment and banking options by themselves and come out ahead. If you want a sound and lucrative financial portfolio, you need to make use of every government and commercial source available before you make your next big deal.

Quick and Easy Access to Your Money

Rather than worry each month whether or not your check will arrive in time, many programs will directly deposit your check into a bank account. You can even have this done with your tax return in some places. It allows you to access your funds on the same day each month without the fear of your check being stolen or misplaced.

And don't let your bank tell you there is a long waiting period. Electronic payments, money orders, and certain checks, such as cashier's certified or teller's checks, must be available on the next banking day after they were deposited.

If you are interested in having your Social Security checks deposited directly, contact your local Social Security office or call their hotline at 800-772-1213; or contact them online at <www.ssa.gov>.

When Your Bank Takes You to the Cleaners

What if you have good credit and a good job, but your bank won't give you a car loan because you're divorced? What if your bank makes unusual deductions from your bank account each month for maintenance charges you don't understand? What if you are having trouble with your bank-issued credit card or mortgage?

Your State Banking Commissioner handles complaints about state-chartered banks doing business in your state. If you cannot resolve your problem with your bank, contact the Banking Commissioner's office and they will investigate for you. To locate your State Banking Commissioner, you can look in the Directory of State Information at the back of this book. Or you can look in the blue pages (the municipal listings) of your local phone book. The title of this department may vary from state to state. Look for the key words "banking" or "finance."

Credit Unions Win Big in Customer Benefits Battle

A credit union is a not-for-profit cooperative financial institution that is owned and controlled by its members — people just like you. Usually members share something in common, like an employer, a community, or a church. Since credit unions do not operate for profit, they are less likely to charge fees for certain services, and more likely to offer attractive loan and investment rates.

Are you eligible to join a credit union?

- Ask your boss if your company sponsors a credit union.

- Call the Credit Union National Association (CUNA) at 800-358-5710. They will direct you to the credit union league in your state which can help you find one to join.

- Talk to your family members. Some credit unions allow extended family members, like cousins, nephews, etc. to join.

- Ask your neighbors if there is a community-based credit union (serving a specific geographic area).

- Check your phone book for local listings. Call them up and ask if you can join. You'll never know unless you ask.

In order to offer credit union customers even more advantages, CUNA and CO-OP Network publish a directory of no surcharge ATMs in twenty-two states (at this time). Avoiding even small fees can add up to big savings over time. Get your directory by calling CUNA at 800-356-9140 or CO-OP Network at 800-782-9042.

If you have access to the Internet, you can view this directory at <www.cuna.org> or <www.THECO-OP.org>.

The Independent Bankers Association of American also has a list of free ATMs at their web site <www.ibaa.org>.

How to Get the Most Bang
for Your Banking Bucks

- If you use direct deposit, see if your bank will offer free checking.

- Write fewer checks each month; it could mean free checking at a lower minimum balance.

- Consolidate your banking and your brokering — you could earn higher interest on all your cash.

- Keep the minimum amount you need in your account to avoid fees and put the rest in a money-market fund.

- Look into "ATM-only" or "express" checking accounts. You may never pay a fee for using an ATM machine — only if you see a bank teller.

- If you are charged for each check you write, pay for utilities and insurance via credit card. Then you'll only be paying for one check — to pay off your credit card company. Or have these routine bills automatically debited from your account.

- Join a credit union if possible. You'll save service fees and monthly maintenance charges.

- See if your bank offers free online banking.

- Order checks through a mail-order printer, not your bank. Two companies that provide this service are Current at 800-426-0822 and Checks in the Mail at 800-733-4443.

- Apply for overdraft protection on your checking account. No one plans on it happening, but even the occasional bounced check fee can be financially painful.

- Ask if your bank offers special services for senior citizens, such as free checking with a low minimum balance and no fees on ATM transactions or special check services.

Insurance for Your Bank

Ever wonder how secure your savings are? For example, many people have set up separate accounts to safeguard their money against bank failure, but unless they are under different types of ownership categories, such as single or joint ownership, the maximum limit per institution is $100,000. And you might not know that Treasury bonds or notes purchased through a particular institution are not covered by insurance.

The Federal Deposit Insurance Corporation's Division of Compliance and Consumer Affairs answers questions and addresses complaints regarding FDIC regulated institutions and your FDIC insured deposit. A computerized system helps to track complaints from their initial filing to their resolution.

You can request information on financial reports and compliance of different institutions, as well as free brochures such as *Deposit Insurance and Consumer Protection.* The FDIC even publishes a quarterly newsletter which answers common questions, and informs you about what to do in the event of a problem.

Banking questions may be directed to your nearest regional FDIC office, or Division of Compliance and Consumer Affairs, Federal Deposit Insurance Corporation, 550 17th St., NW, Washington, DC 20429; 800-934-FDIC (3342); or online at <www.fdic.gov>.

★★★

Make Sure You Have Credit Credibility

Securing credit is as important for older adults as it is for anyone else. Yet older consumers, and particularly older women, may find they have special problems establishing credit.

For example, if you've paid for everything with cash all of your life, you may find it difficult to open a credit account, because you have "no credit history." If you now are living on a lower salary or pension, you may find it harder to obtain a loan because you have "insufficient income." Or, if your spouse dies, you may find that creditors try to close credit accounts that you and your spouse once shared.

To learn what legal rights and recourses you have, request the publication *Equal Credit Opportunity,* which explains the credit process, gives tips on establishing credit, and tells you what to do if you are denied credit.

216

To receive your free copy, contact the Consumer Response Center, Federal Trade Commission, 6th and Pennsylvania Avenues NW, Room H-130, Washington, DC 20580; 202-326-2222; or online at <www.ftc.gov>.

Have you ever seen your own credit report? You should look at it before you make any major financial changes. That way you can correct any errors you find before they become a problem. You can request a report from one of the three major credit bureaus, Equifax (800-997-2493), Experian (formerly TRW) (888-397-3742), or Trans Union (800-888-4213). In most cases the fee ranges from $2 to $10, however Experian offers one report a year for free. You can get a free credit report from any of the bureaus if:

- you live in Colorado, Georgia, Massachusetts, Maryland, New Jersey, or Vermont. In these states you are entitled to one free credit report every twelve months.
- you are unemployed.
- you are on welfare.
- you are a victim of credit fraud.
- you have been denied credit within the last 60 days because of information in your credit report.

The ABCs of Finance

Teaching the grandkids about the value of money? Want to learn more about how bonds work? What about international economics? Or even consumer protection issues? The Federal Reserve has a free list of public information materials available from their various district offices. You can learn about inflation, public debt, and macroeconomic data.

To receive this information, contact the Publications Service, Board of Governors of the Federal Reserve System, Mail Stop-127, Federal Reserve Board, Washington, DC 20551; 202-452-3244 (for a listing of publications); 202-728-5886 (to order with a credit card over the phone); or online at <www.bog.frb.fed.us>.

For information on the stock market, go to the best source around, the American Stock Exchange. Call them at 212-306-1000 for a copy of their publication *Journey Through a Stock Exchange*. Or write to their publications department at 86 Trinity Place, New York, NY 10006-1872.

Free Advice on Money-Managing Your Life

Trying to live on a limited budget is never easy. And with so many financial options available, it's not surprising that many people get confused trying to sort out the best financial plan.

Your County Cooperative Extension Offices frequently have pamphlets or classes which can help you examine your situation and come up with a financial plan you can live with. For example, free publications in Ohio include *Estate Planning Considerations for Ohio Families; Evaluating Nursing Home Insurance; Financial Planning For Retirement;* and *Personal Property Inventory.*

To learn what your local office has to offer, look in the blue pages of your phone book for the office nearest you, or call 202-720-3029.

For more information, contact the Cooperative State Research Education and Extension Service, U.S. Department of Agriculture, Room 3328, Washington, DC 20250; or online at <www.reeusda.gov>.

And of course, the federal government's Consumer Information Center has more information than you probably have time to read. With over 30 brochures, either free or available for a small charge, you're sure to find one covering a financial topic you're interested in. You can write them at Pueblo, CO 81002 for a complete catalog; call in an order to the Consumer Information Center at 888-878-3256; or view and order brochures online at <www.gsa.gov/staff/pa/cic/money.htm>.

Want to look over financial advice from a reputable business in the privacy and comfort of your own home? Then call MetLife at 800-638-5433. They offer over 85 free brochures in a series that deals with business, insurance, money, health, and family issues. They call the series "Life Advice." Brochure titles include:

- *Selling a Business*
- *Doing Your Taxes: Tax Tips*
- *Running a Small Business*
- *Making Charitable Contributions*
- *Enjoying Retirement*
- *Life Insurance*
- *Nursing Homes*
- *Lump Sum Retirement Distributions*
- *Dealing with Disability*

You can order up to three brochures at a time, but there's no limit on the number of times you can order. You can also write them at One Madison Avenue, New York, NY 10010, or visit them on the Internet at <www.lifeadvice.com>.

Other organizations offer free information as well. Here are some you might try:

- *How to Manage Your Financial Resources: Creating a Spending Plan You Can Control*, and *Selecting a Qualified Financial Planning Professional: Twelve Questions to Consider* (The Institute of Certified Financial Planners; 800-282-7526)

- *A Common Sense Guide to Taking Charge of Your Money* (Fidelity Investments; 800-544-4774)

- *Getting Your Financial House in Order* and *Finding a Financial Adviser Who's Right For You* (Oppenheimer Funds Inc.; 800-525-7048)

- Brochures on financial planning and retirement (American Express Financial Advisors; 800-386-2042)

- *Financial Facts Tool Kit* (Securities and Exchange Commission; 800-732-0330)

Safe Investing — Everything You Need to Know to Protect Yourself and Your Money

Shady telemarketers and investment brokers have duped more than one unsuspecting consumer out of their life savings. At last count, the number of victims climbed into the millions. If you don't want to be one of these, all it takes is a call to the Federal Trade Commission. Several of their free publications can help you become a more informed investor. Ask for the brochures *Multilevel Marketing Plans*, *Costly Coupon Scams*, and *Wealth Building Scams*.

For more information, contact the Consumer Response Center, Federal Trade Commission, 6th and Pennsylvania Avenues NW, Room H-130, Washington, DC 20580; 202-326-2222; or online at <www.ftc.gov>.

The National Futures Association at 800-621-3570, also offers two brochures that can help you avoid costly mistakes: *Investors' Bill of Rights* and *Investment Swindles: How They Work and How to Avoid Them*.

Do Your Homework — Getting Help
Making Your Financial Decisions

Before making a securities investment, you must first make several important decisions. Which brokerage firm or stockbroker will you use and where will you invest? Unfortunately we do live in a world where it is "Buyer Beware!" But there are places you can go for helpful information.

Talk with several brokerage firms, preferably in person (which is an especially important step in avoiding telecommunication fraud). Remember that they want to invest your money to earn their commission, so do not rush. Do the necessary background investigation on both the firm and the sales representative.

You can find out about the disciplinary history of any brokerage firm and sales representative by calling a toll-free hotline operated by NASD Regulation, the regulatory arm of the National Association of Securities Dealers, Inc. (NASD). The NASD Regulation will provide information on disciplinary actions, civil judgments, arbitration, indictments, criminal judgments, and other actions taken by securities regulators and criminal authorities.

Contact NASD Regulation, 1735 K St., NW, Washington, DC 20006, 800-289-9999; or online at <www.nasdr.com>.

The North American Securities Administrators Association can also run a background check on investment brokers. Call 202-737-0900 to find out who to talk to in your state.

For a full background check on any company that's offering public stock simply call the Securities and Exchange Commission. They can tell you if a broker or brokerage firm has been found guilty of wrongdoing, and can provide general information about the federal securities laws, as well as information on investor inquiries and complaints. They have many free publications available including *Invest Wisely: An Introduction To Mutual Funds, The Work of the SEC*, and *What Every Investor Should Know*. For an overall look at choosing and monitoring your broker, send for *Invest Wisely: Advice from Your Securities Industry Regulators*. This brochure gives good advice on all your investment decisions.

Contact the Securities and Exchange Commission, Office of Consumer Affairs, 450 Fifth St., NW, Washington, DC 20549; 202-942-4040, 800-SEC-0330 (publications only); or online at <www.sec.gov>.

The International Association for Financial Planning can help you select a financial adviser by giving you general information and tips on what to ask in an interview. They offer different series of free brochures, so call them at 888-806-7526, extension 7896, for your free information.

If you'd like a list of members of the National Association of Personal Financial Advisers in your area, call 800-366-2732. They will also send you questions you should ask any adviser before entrusting him with your finances.

☆☆☆

Foreign Investment Advice Straight From the Experts

Do you follow the rise and fall of the deutschemark and the pound? Are you fascinated by overseas markets? Do you have a yen for trading in yen? If so, international investing deserves a second look. It's important, though, to get sound advice before plunging into the world of foreign trade.

T. Rowe Price, the investment management company, can help you decide how much risk you're willing to take in the international market. By calling them at 800-638-5660, you can get a free guide to diversifying overseas which includes a worksheet to help you organize an investment portfolio and your investment strategies. You can also write to them at 100 E. Pratt St., Baltimore, MD 21202; or get help online at <www.troweprice.com>.

Scudder Investor Services, Inc. also offers a free 30-page book called *Investing Globally.* It will help you reorganize your investment portfolio and guide you through the ins and outs of multinational corporations. Call them at 800-SCUDDER (728-3337) or visit them online at <funds.scudder.com> for your copy today.

You should find out as much as you can about the country you are about to invest in. State Department Country Officers provide current political, economic, and background information on marketing and business practices for every country in the world. Although they can't tell you whether your computer deal is going to fly, they can give you enough information to help you better weigh your options.

Write to the SR Coordinator for Business Affairs, E-CBA, Room 2318, U.S. Dept. of State, Washington, DC 22204; or online at <www.state.gov/index.html>.

If you're a bit nervous about taking the international plunge, check out this brochure, *International Investment Fraud,* which tells you how to protect yourself from phony overseas investments. Published by the North American Securities Administrators, it will also give you information on legitimate markets, Contact them at 10 G St. NE, Suite 710, Washington, DC 20002; 202-737-0900; or at <www.nasaa.org>.

Silver and Gold

Investing in gold or silver seems like a solid idea. It's not as confusing as bonds or bills or funds. Or is it? Actually, investing in American Eagle Gold and Silver Bullion Coins produced by the U.S. Mint is not quite as foolproof as you might think.

Gold coins are available in a variety of weights, while silver coins are minted only in a one-ounce size. Check listings in your daily newspaper to find out the current market values.

Coins may be purchased from brokerage companies, participating banks, coin dealers, and precious metal dealers. For a listing of dealers and sales locations in your area, call 800-USA-GOLD (872-4653). For more general information, write Customer Service, U.S. Mint, U.S. Department of the Treasury, 10003 Derekwood Lane, Lanham, MD 20706; or call 202-283-COIN (2646); or visit the web site at <www.usmint.gov>.

Know the Difference Between
Junk Bonds and Junk Food?

If you think you might have a taste for trading in commodities, the Commodities Futures Trading Commission (CFTC) offers several free booklets explaining how the commodities market operates. Some of the titles they have include *Futures and Options: What You Should Know Before You Trade*, *The CFTC*, and *Economic Purposes of Futures Trading*.

You can find out that commodity prices are tied to the weather, strikes, foreign exchange rates, and even storage factors. A small amount of money (the initial margin) controls a commodity futures contract worth a large amount of money.

The risk is high because a small change in the price of the commodity can either bring a large return on your money, or it can wipe out your initial margin and require that you immediately make additional margin payments.

The CFTC will send you a free copy of their annual report which includes a handy glossary of trading terms. Contact the Commodities

Futures Trading Commission, Office of Public Affairs, 3 Lafayette Center, 1155 21st St. NW, 9th Floor, Washington, DC 20581; 202-418-5080; or visit online at <www.cftc.gov>.

Free Lesson on How to Buy a T-Bill

On the golf course, your investment adviser tells you that considering current interest rates, maybe it's time to consider T-Bills. And he's not talking golf tees. Treasury bills, notes, and bonds are a way to invest in this country's future, he claims.

The T-Bill hotline provides general information on buying treasury bills, notes, and bonds, and can tell you how they can be purchased and when they will be auctioned. You can also find out about buying directly from Federal Reserve Banks and branches throughout the country — even online. If you buy direct, you'll save the normal commission charge.

Contact the Bureau of the Public Debt, U.S. Department of the Treasury, 13th and C Streets SW, Washington, DC 20239-0001; 202-874-4000; or online at <www.publicdebt.treas.gov>.

☆☆☆

Free Legal Help With a Franchise

Tipsy McSwiggers Restaurants claim to be the hottest franchise to come down the pike since McDonald's, and they are letting you in on the ground floor.

Before you get too flattered and lose your shirt, you should find out everything you can about this new business from the Federal Trade Commission. They can tell you all the ins and outs of the franchise world and what you need to ask when you actually visit a couple of the franchises and talk to the owners.

You can learn about the Franchise and Business Opportunity Rule, state disclosure requirements, and more. For your packet of franchise information, contact the Consumer Response Center, Federal Trade Commission, 6th and Pennsylvania Avenues NW, Room H-130, Washington, DC 20580; or call 202-326-3128; or visit online at <www.ftc.gov>.

☆☆☆

Check Out Phony Charities

Everywhere you turn it seems there are worthy causes asking for donations. But are they worthy? It may be hard sometimes to decide when to give.

First, don't fall for appeals, especially the ones over the phone, that insist you send money right away.

Then, check them out. There are several different organizations like the National Charities Information Bureau or the Philanthropic Advisory Service at the Council of the Better Business Bureau, where you can learn more about a particular charity's activities, finances, and fundraising practices.

The free publication *Charitable Donation$: Give or Take*, outlines steps you can take to check out any organization and make sure your money is put into good hands. For your copy, contact the Consumer Response Center, Federal Trade Commission, 6th and Pennsylvania Avenues NW, Room H-130, Washington, DC 20580; 202-326-2222; or online at <www.ftc.gov>.

You can also find out just how your donation will be spent by sending for the National Charities Information Bureau's free *Wise Giving Guide*. It evaluates hundreds of charities and lets you know just how they use their funds. You can also order a detailed report on a specific charity. Call them at 212-929-6300.

The American Institute of Philanthropy publishes the *Charity Rating Guide* and *Watchdog Report*, a free account of what percentage of income charities spend on their stated purpose. Their number is 301-913-5200.

Take the Deduction

When you finally do find a good organization you'd like to donate money or gifts to, don't forget that you can take a tax deduction for that contribution. If you spend $50 to attend a special dinner for a cause, is the entire amount deductible? No, but part may be allowed.

What about if you pay $100 for a Golf for Gallstones benefit? Anything over and above the usual charge for golfing may be deductible.

Request the publication *Charitable Contributions* (Publication 526), that explains which contributions you may deduct and what qualifies as a contribution. For your copy, contact the Internal Revenue Forms Line at

800-829-3676; or online at <www.irs.gov>.

More Internet Tools to Fix Your Financial Woes

The number of financial institutions providing information and doing business on the World Wide Web seems to be increasing every day. If you have access to a computer with an Internet connection (don't forget your public library), you may want to check out some of these helpful financial web sites:

Microsoft Money Insider, <moneyinsider.msn.com>, provides personal finance information on banks, taxes, investing and brokers.

Charles Schwab at <www.schwab.com> has information on mutual funds and a searchable database of specific funds.

Bank Rate Monitor at <www.bankrate.com> has rate information on banks, certificates of deposit, credit cards, mortgages, and auto loans.

Credit.com, <www.credit.com>, is a complete financial services network.

Hoovers Company Capsules, <www.hoovers.com>, provides short company profiles with financial information and links to their home pages.

Standard & Poor's Personal Wealth at <www.personalwealth.com> gives you information on stocks along with recommendations from leading analysts.

Finding Hidden Gold

It's the biggest trend in easy money since television game shows — unclaimed billions lying around in federal, state, and private vaults. The bulk of this fortune comes from undeliverable pensions and benefits checks, but stocks, bonds, tax refunds, and death bequests account for millions as well.

If you think you have unclaimed money somewhere, you can pay for the services of a professional finder (someone who will do the legwork and keep a chunk of the findings), or you can hunt through the public records on your own. In either case, be prepared to produce all kinds of hard proof that you are entitled to whatever is found.

Here are the places to look for that "hidden gold":

- your state's agency responsible for unclaimed or abandoned property
- the federal Pension Benefit Guaranty Corporation (PBGC) (800-400-7242) for pension benefits from companies that are out of business
- the Social Security Administration (800-772-1213) for undeliverable benefit checks
- previous employers for disability, health, life insurance, pension and severance payments
- the IRS (800-829-1040) for unclaimed tax refunds
- <www.foundmoney.com> for a paid service to match you up with potential found money

Cut Your Legal Costs

Fire your lawyer! Sounds like fun, doesn't it? Well, the happy truth is, you probably don't need your lawyer as much as you think you do. Instead, you can use government resources to answer most of your legal questions for free. You can learn how to write a Living Will, take on big companies for age discrimination, and even resolve disputes with local stores, just by putting your tax dollars to work for you. For those special or sensitive cases when you really do need an attorney, you can even use the government to help you find one that you can afford.

So call up Mister Joe Esquire in the fancy suit and give him his walking papers. You've got *Free Stuff for Seniors*!

The Pension Tax Guys

No need to pay money to an attorney to interpret the tax issues surrounding retirement and pension plans. You can talk to the guys who wrote the law! The Internal Revenue Service operates a hotline service that allows you to speak to tax attorneys specializing in retirement and pension plan issues.

They are available Monday through Thursday, from 1:30 p.m. to 3:30 p.m. They can be reached at Employee Plans Technical and Actuarial Division, Internal Revenue Service, U.S. Department of the Treasury, Room 6550, CP:E:EP, 1111 Constitution Ave. NW, Washington, DC 20224; phone 202-622-6074 or 6076.

A Kinder, Gentler IRS

Whoever said that the IRS was out to get us? Whoever it was surely didn't know about all the free help they offer to taxpayers. Sure, maybe they take a lot of your money, but they can also show you ways to keep a lot of it.

The *Guide to Free Tax Services for the Tax Year* is just a phone call away. In this free publication, the IRS lists different ways that you can file, tips on how to do so most effectively, toll-free numbers for help in preparing your forms, and other services that are available free of charge. Call the IRS at 800-829-3676, and ask for Publication #910.

Number Crunchers at Crunch Time

Everybody knows that the IRS tax forms are self-explanatory, right? Then how come it often feels like you need to be an accountant, a lawyer, and an electrical engineer in order to make sense of them? If you've ever felt this way, take heart. You don't need an accountant, or a lawyer, or anybody else to get free tax help. You just need a computer.

There are many web sites dedicated to helping the little guy figure out his big tax problems. They can give you immediate help in everything from dealing with forms to understanding changes in the tax laws. So when it comes down to crunch time this spring, check out some of these free helpers.

IRS: <www.irs.ustreas.gov>. Believe it or not, the IRS wants you to file the right way, and their site shows you just how to do it. You can also get copies of almost any form you'll need.

LIFENET: <www.lifenet.com/taxes.html>. This site features a program that helps you figure out the benefits you'd get from changing your filing status.

H&R BLOCK: <www.hrblock.com>. Download software from H&R Block and make sure everything's in the right place on your return.

YAHOO! TAX CENTER: <dir.yahoo.com/government/taxes>. This site is a good starting point for finding tax help on the Internet. Yahoo! provides a directory of valuable tax sites and links to get you there.

CCH INTERNET TAX RESEARCH NETWORK: <www.cch.com>. CCH provides lots of helpful hints about preparing for tax season and filing your return.

Last-Minute Lifesavers

For those of us who wait until the last minute, there's still hope, and it's still free. Money Minds is a group that sells financial and tax advice over the phone, but once a year — usually around April 12th — they give it away for free. Certified public accountants and financial planners take calls answering tax problems for most of the day, but both the hours and the day itself vary from year to year. Give them a call a few days early at 800-275-2272 to find out what your options are this year.

Put the Power Back in 'Power of Attorney'

Sometimes you need to focus on the big picture of living your life and let someone else manage the details. There may come a day when you no longer have the time or the energy to handle all the responsibilities of managing your own finances.

In many cases, you can sign over a Power-of-Attorney form to a trusted relative or friend that will allow them to make financial decisions in your behalf. When it involves handling your Social Security check, you need to designate the person as a Representative Payee. This will allow the person to receive your Social Security check so they can pay your bills for you.

Bear this in mind, too: A person can petition the courts to be designated a Representative Payee if their loved one cannot do so himself due to a physical or mental condition. If someone has offered or is planning to take such an action on your behalf, be sure you know what responsibilities and what rights you are giving up. And before you willingly go along with this action, make sure you know the individual very well.

To learn more about Representative Payee guidelines, contact your local Social Security office or call the Social Security Hotline at 800-772-1213; or visit online at <www.ssa.gov>.

You Have the Right to a (Free) Attorney

You don't have to go to your neighbor's wife's cousin's kid who is an attorney, unless you want to pay for his legal advice. Uncle Sam has set up law offices all across the country to help those who cannot afford standard legal fees.

It is the Legal Services Corporation's job to give legal help to low-income individuals in civil matters. They are staffed by over 6,400 attorneys and paralegals, and have handled over 1.5 million cases. Each program follows certain guidelines as to what cases it accepts and what financial eligibility possible clients must meet.

To learn about the program nearest you, look in the blue pages of your phone book, or contact Legal Services Corporation, 750 First St. NE, 11th Fl., Washington, DC 20002; phone 202-336-8800; or online at <www.lsc.gov>.

Good Will Writing

Fill in the blanks, sign on the line. You've seen those How To Write A Will books in the bookstore. Why not save your money for your grandkids instead? Many County Cooperative Extension Offices give classes, pamphlets, and even general forms to help you along the way.

To learn what your local office has to offer, look in the blue pages of your phone book for the office nearest you. For help in locating your county office, contact the Cooperative State Research, Education and Extension Service, U.S. Dept. of Agriculture, 14th and Independence Ave. SW, Room 3328, South Bldg., Washington, DC 20250; or online at <reeusda.gov>.

Where There's a Way, There's a Will

There's a right way and a wrong way to go about writing your will. You don't need a lawyer to walk you through it, but you might like some advice. If you want some answers and you want them fast, talk to one of the advisers at the MetLife Consumer Education Center. They'll be able to walk you through the ABCs of writing this important document, and help you figure out the best way to meet your particular needs, and all for free. Call 800-638-5433.

Funeral-Home Funny Business

Planning a loved one's funeral is an emotional time. The last thing you want to worry about is whether or not you're being taken advantage of. But that's exactly what happens to hundreds of people each year.

You don't have to let grief get in the way of sound judgment. The Federal Trade Commission puts out publications entitled *Caskets and*

Burial Vaults and *Funerals: A Consumer Guide,* which point out the issues you need to address when planning a funeral, and questions you should ask any funeral home that you deal with.

To receive your free copy, contact the Consumer Response Center, Federal Trade Commission, 6th and Pennsylvania Avenues NW, Room H-130, Washington, DC 20580; phone 202-326-2222; or online at <www.ftc.gov>.

Make Your Plans Final

Planning your funeral in advance may sound like a morbid thought, but it is actually a great courtesy to your family. After a death in the family, many people are so caught up in the grieving process that they don't make the best choices, and often wind up wasting a lot of money. By taking care of things beforehand, you can save your loved ones much time and aggravation.

Memorial Societies are organizations that realize the truth in this and are there to help. For a small, one-time fee, usually about $25.00, you can join a memorial society. They will help you outline everything you want in great detail, from the casket to the flowers to the funeral service itself. This information is filed with a funeral home, and when you die, the details are already taken care of. The prices are all negotiated as well, so you know up front what the costs will be but you won't have to pay at that time. Financial planners agree that it's not a good idea to pay for your funeral or burial plot before you die. While you should make all the arrangements for your burial, there's no need to put money down. That's money that could be working for you while you're still alive. The funeral homes that work with Memorial Societies generally give very good prices for these arrangements, because such programs help bring in business.

To locate a Memorial Society near you, contact the Continental Association of Funeral & Memorial Societies, 6900 Lost Lake Road, Egg Harbor, WI 54209. You can also get all the necessary forms by leaving your name and address at 800-765-0107.

Lots More Legal Freebies

Don't waste too much of your time trying to learn the confusing ins and outs of Social Security or Medicare. Instead, talk directly to an attorney who is on a first name basis with the people who run these programs, and can help you deal with your problem or concern without spending time getting up to speed on the complicated statutes surrounding these programs.

The following is a list of hotlines designed specifically to serve the needs of senior citizens. Services may vary from organization to organization. Some will refer you to lawyers who will offer legal assistance on a sliding fee scale; some will handle your case for you. If your state is not listed below, contact your state Department of Aging listed in the Directory of State Information at the end of this book.

Another resource that's often overlooked is local law schools. Many offer legal clinics staffed by law students, although they are supervised closely by top-level lawyers who are also professors.

CALIFORNIA
Senior Legal Hotline
Legal Services of Northern California, 1004 18th St.
Sacramento, CA 95814
Phone 800-222-1753; or 916-442-1212

They will give legal advice and referrals. Some lawyers offer services on a reduced scale based on income. For seniors in northern California only.

DISTRICT OF COLUMBIA
Legal Council for the Elderly
601 E St., NW
Building A, Fourth Floor
Washington, DC 20049
Phone 202-434-2120

They give advice and referrals. Services are offered on a reduced fee scale based on age and income.

FLORIDA
Legal Hotline for Older Floridians
3000 Biscayne Blvd., 4th Floor
PO Box 370705
Miami, FL 33137

Phone 800-252-5997; or 305-576-5997

Lawyer Referral Service
Florida Bar Association
650 Apalachee Parkway
Tallahassee, FL 32399-2300
Phone 800-342-8011

This is strictly a referral service for attorneys willing to work for reduced fees.

MAINE
Legal Service for the Elderly
Maine Legal Services
PO Box 2723
Augusta, ME 04338-2723
Phone 800-750-5353; or 207-623-1797

They will give advice and referrals. Services offered to anyone 65 or older, regardless of income.

MICHIGAN
Senior Alliance Inc.
3850 Second St., Suite 160
Wayne, MI 48184
Phone 800-347-LAWS (MI only); or 313-722-2830

They give advice and referrals over

the telephone. They have a list of attorneys that will work pro bono for people 60 or older.

NEW MEXICO

Lawyer Referral Services for the Elderly, PO Box 25883 Albuquerque, NM 87125 Phone 800-876-6657; or 505-797-6005

They give advice and referrals. Some attorneys offer sliding fee scales based on income.

OHIO

ProSeniors Inc.
105 E. Fourth St., Suite 1715 Cincinnati, OH 45202-4008 Phone 800-488-6070; or 513-621-8721

They give advice and referrals over the telephone. Actual legal services can be done on a sliding scale based on income. ProSeniors also offers an ombudsman service if you are having any long-term health care problems. For example, if you are having trouble with the care given in a nursing home, this agency can investigate the problem.

PENNSYLVANIA

Legal Hotline for Older Americans
Legal Council for the Elderly PO Box 23180 Pittsburgh, PA 15222 Phone 800-262-5297; or 412-261-5297

They will give legal advice and referrals. Some lawyers offer services on a reduced scale based on income.

TEXAS

Legal Hotline for Older Texans State Bar of Texas PO Box 12487, Austin, TX 78711-2487; Phone 800-622-2520; or 512-463-1463

They will give legal advice and referrals. Some lawyers offer services on a reduced scale based on income.

☆☆☆

Free Legal Help With Age Discrimination

Age discrimination is a serious problem in our country, a problem only made worse by the fact that it is often very difficult to prove. Some companies often try to get rid of their older, more experienced workers so they can hire youngsters that they don't need to pay as much. Have you recently been let go from your job without a reasonable explanation? Do you feel that your age was a factor in not getting a job for which you were qualified? If so, there are people you should talk to.

Persons 40 years of age or older are protected by the Age Discrimination in Employment Act of 1967. The law prohibits age discrimination in hiring, discharge, pay, promotions, and other terms and conditions of employment. Retaliation against a person who files a charge of age discrimination, participates in an investigation, or opposes an unlawful practice also is illegal.

Last year, the Equal Employment Opportunity Commission (EEOC) received 17,425 complaints of age discrimination. For assistance, contact the Equal Employment Opportunity Commission, 1801 L St. NW, Washington, DC 20507; phone 800-669-4000; or 800-669-3362 (publications only); or online at <www.eeoc.gov>.

Bullies Beware

There's no need to take harassment or bullying on the job sitting down. Here is your chance to fight back. Remember, if your boss or another employee is discriminating against you because you are different in some way, they are probably doing it to others and will continue to do it until someone forces them to stop.

If you believe you have been discriminated against by an employer, labor union, or employment agency when applying for a job or while on the job because of race, color, sex, religion, national origin, age, or disability, you may file a charge with the Equal Employment Opportunity Commission (EEOC). The toll-free number will direct you to the appropriate EEOC number for more information and to file a complaint. The EEOC also distributes a variety of publications including:

- *The American Disability Act: Questions and Answers*
- *Fact Sheet: National Origin Discrimination*
- *Fact Sheet: Religious Discrimination*
- *Sexual Harassment Resource Kit*
- *Information For The Private Sector*

For more information, contact Equal Employment Opportunity Commission, 1801 L St. NW, Washington, DC 20507; phone 800-669-4000; or 800-669-3362 (publications only); or online at <www.eeoc.gov>.

Legal Help Locator

There's one phone number that can hook you up with more services for seniors than there are flavors of ice cream: the Eldercare Locator. This hotline provides access to an extensive network of organizations serving older people at state and local levels.

The service can connect you to a variety of services, including legal assistance and other advocates and ombudsmen. In some cases, the legal assistance services may actually come to your home or nursing home to help you complete paperwork.

To find out what's available near you, contact the Eldercare Locator, National Association of Area Agencies on Aging, 1112 16th St. NW, Suite 100, Washington, DC 20036; phone 800-677-1116; or online at <www.ageinfo.org/elderloc/elderloc.html>. The phone lines are open between 9 a.m. and 11 p.m. EST.

Be Your Own Consumer Expert

You'd never guess by watching all those slick ads on TV that one of the most frequent things people complain about is the sale and repair of new cars. Or what about the health club that gets you to sign up for a life-time membership only to close down the next day? Or even the store that advertises a great deal on a new television, only to claim to be "out of stock" when you try to buy one?

If you feel you have been deceived or taken advantage of in some way, contact your state Consumer Protection Offices. Depending on the circumstances, the office may contact the offending company and try to resolve the complaint on your behalf. If there are several complaints against a particular company, the Consumer Protection Office may even take legal action.

Look in the Directory of State Information at the back of this book to find the Consumer Protection Office for your state.

Mug the Muggers

Each year, millions of American families fall victim to every manner of crime. Hopefully, you will never become part of this unfortunate statistic, but if you do, there are people who can help you recover. Congress has passed a law to establish a Crime Victims Fund to compensate victims of violent crime.

One of the nice things about this program is that the money does not come out of the taxpayers' pockets. Instead, it is collected from the criminals themselves through criminal fines, forfeited bail bonds, penalty fees, and forfeited literary profits. Nothing can fully compensate a victim of violent crime, certainly, but sometimes a bit of financial assistance can help reduce some of the inconveniences caused by missed work, destruction of property, or psychological distress.

To learn who you need to talk to in your state, contact the Office of Congressional and Public Affairs, Office of Justice Programs, U.S. Department of Justice, 633 Indiana Ave. NW, Room 1244, Washington, DC 20531; phone 202-307-0781; or go online at <www.ojp.usdoj.gov>.

Better Living Through Better Information

Of course you always take your time when making a big purchase. A large investment like the car you drive deserves careful research, but some of the most critical information isn't going to be available at the auto dealer. For your safety's sake, and that of your family, you owe it to yourself to check out the facts on any car you purchase.

The Highway Loss Data Institute compiles safety statistics on which cars are involved in the most accidents, accidents involving injuries, and are most often stolen. This information can help you make a safe choice when buying a car, and can also save you a good bit of money when it comes time to pay your insurance premium. To get your hands on their most recent listings, send a self-addressed, stamped, business-size envelope to the Highway Loss Data Institute, Box 1420, Arlington, VA 22201.

The Kind of Trouble
No Lawyer Can Get You Out Of

Insurance is a fact of life, and no responsible homeowner should be without it. All the legal mumbo-jumbo in the world can't help you if your house goes up in flames and you are not insured. But just having a policy isn't enough. You need to have the right policy and know exactly what it covers in case disaster strikes.

Your insurance company has lawyers working for them whose job it is to make sure the company doesn't pay out too much. Your job is to make sure they don't pay out too little. Find out how to do this with a free brochure called *Make Homeowners Insurance Part of Your Home Security.* You'll get information on documenting your possessions, how to file a claim, and how to determine if you've got enough insurance. Send a self-addressed, stamped, business-size envelope to Chartered Property Casualty Underwriters, Box 3009, Malvern, PA 09355. You can also call them at 800-932-2728.

For further information on how to avoid the devastation of being inadequately or incorrectly insured, call the Federal Emergency Management Association (FEMA). Their *Never Say Never* brochure and other literature show you how to best safeguard against insurance disasters. Call FEMA at 888-225-5356, extension 190.

Insurance Made Easy

Nobody likes to plan for the worst, but the truth is your insurance is the glue that holds your financial security together. Without the right kind and right amount of life and health insurance, you and your family could get into a lot of financial and even legal trouble. So get the facts and protect yourself. Here are some good publications you'll want to send for.

GUIDE TO LONG-TERM-CARE INSURANCE: Seniors have unique needs when it comes to insurance. Depending on your health and situation, you might require long term care, which can get very expensive. Get answers to common questions on this insurance option and find out if it's right for you. Write to the Health Insurance Association of America, 555 13th Street NW, Suite 600E, Washington, DC 20004-1109. Send them a self-addressed, stamped envelope for this helpful brochure.

CHOOSING A HEALTH PLAN: Your health coverage gets trickier as you age, and sometimes a plan that covered all your needs before doesn't do so anymore. How do you fix this, and get the most out of the coverage you have? Contact the Arthritis Foundation for this free booklet by writing to Box 7669, Atlanta, GA 30357.

FREE CONSUMER'S GUIDE TO INSURANCE: Everything you need to know about insurance, from different types available to how much you should pay. The non-profit group called Life & Health Insurance Foundation for Education can help steer you through the insurance maze.

Call 888-LIFE-777 (888-543-3777); or visit <www.life-line.org> on the web.

☆☆☆

When You Get Caught in the Legal Runaround

Because of a slip-up by your lawyer, you went to jail for a parking ticket. Then there was that lawyer to whom you paid an expensive retainer, only to learn that she seems to have moved to Tahiti permanently. Don't think you have to put up with a bad lawyer just because they know more about the law than you do.

Often affiliated with State Bar Associations, Attorney Grievances offices can help you resolve ethical, billing, and theft complaints against lawyers in your state. They can also tell you if an attorney has been sanctioned in any way before you even start to do business with him.

The Attorney Grievance programs deal with ethical complaints; the Fee Arbitration programs will help resolve billing complaints; and the Client Security Trust Funds provides money to clients who have had money stolen from them by their lawyers.

Look in the Directory of State Information at the back of this book to find the program nearest you.

☆☆☆

When All Else Fails

You have done your best, written letters, documented phone calls, yet you still feel as if you haven't been helped. Use the power of the voting booth, and call your Senator or Representative. Each one has a support staff set up to solve the problems of the people who voted them into office and keep them happy so that they'll keep voting for them. Offices are located in both Washington, DC, and in their home districts.

Remember, these are the people who vote to renew an agency's budget, so they usually have a very strong arm in getting government agencies to act. Businesses also know laws and regulations can help them or hurt them, so they won't want to bite the hand that feeds them.

To locate your U.S. Senator or Representative, look in the blue pages of your phone book, or contact The Capitol, Washington, DC 20510; phone 202-224-3121; or online at <www.house.gov> or <www.senate.gov>.

Jump Back Into the Job Market

Once upon a time, a typical American went to work for a big company at a young age, worked hard for that company for 30 years, then retired and received a gold watch. While this career path still exists for some, it can no longer be called typical.

Today, the American work force is more diverse and confusing than ever before. For many reasons, older Americans are working longer, taking limited retirements, or re-entering the job market. In fact, according to a report from the United States General Accounting Office (GAO), the 55 and older age group will soon be the fastest growing group in the labor force.

Capable seniors are out there working and working well. Whether you need a job as an enjoyable diversion or a means of support, there are plenty of opportunities for you to find work. These opportunities are often no more than a phone call, a letter, or a little bit of research away. And more often than not, they're free.

Getting the best deal is usually a simple matter of knowing where to look for it. Job-hunting is no exception. This chapter is designed to show you just where to look — right down to a state-by-state agency listing — and what you can expect to find there.

Free Help to Get a Job

America's population is aging. In fact, the number of Americans over the age of 65 is about the same as the entire population of Canada. For many seniors, however, 65 doesn't automatically mean retirement anymore. Too often, Social Security and pension income just isn't enough to make ends meet.

For this reason, thousands of seniors are working longer, or embarking on new "post-retirement" careers. This can be exciting and interesting, but it can also be intimidating. Finding the right job can be tough if you haven't worked in a long time, or if you've never had a job outside your home. You might have a physical challenge that makes it hard to do certain jobs, live far away from employers, or have less education than other job-seekers. Another common concern is that a Social Security income will prevent employers from hiring you.

The good news is, you don't have to go it alone. If you find that you do need a job but don't know where to look, there's plenty of free information out there to help get you started. All across the country there are free job training programs set up just for seniors who need help getting the job skills they need.

How $2 Can Change Your Life

So you're thinking about getting a new job — where do you begin? Whether you're looking for a second career or just something to help you put away a few bucks, the Consumer Information Center (CIC) can help you get started.

Since 1970, the CIC has worked with the U.S. government to get useful information into the hands of citizens. Located in Pueblo, Colorado, this organization distributes numerous pamphlets and brochures that can help you decide what kind of work you are suited for, where to find good jobs, and how to get started on your own. Many of their publications are totally free, while others cost between 50 cents and a couple of bucks.

You can order from the CIC over the phone or by mailing them a check. (Note: For the free pamphlets, you can order up to 25 copies for a $2.00 postage charge. For the ones with specific prices, this extra fee does not apply.) Order by calling toll free 888-878-3256, or sending your check or money order to: R. Woods, CIC-8D, PO Box 100, Pueblo, CO 81002.

The following sources are among those available from the CIC to help in your quest for new employment. When requesting materials, be sure to include the number and letter code for each item to help them process your order.

Code 103E: ($1.25) *Resumes, Application Forms, Cover Letters, and Interviews.* This booklet helps with organizing your credentials, getting in touch with employers, and winning the job once you have an interview.

Code 104E: ($1.75) *Tips for Finding the Right Job.* This offers advice on figuring out what kind of work you'd be happiest with, and how to land such work.

Code 105E: ($1.75) *Tomorrow's Jobs.* This pamphlet takes a look at how the job market is changing, and how you can prepare yourself for the kinds of jobs that will be available in the near future.

Code 519E: (Free) *The GED Diploma*. This teaches you what you need to know about the GED high school equivalency test, how to prepare for the test, and where to look for more details.

Code 101E: ($1.00) *High Earning Workers Who Don't Have A Bachelor's Degree*. If you didn't go to college, this will provide you with a list of more than 100 good jobs that don't require a degree.

Code 102E: ($1.50) *Nontraditional Education: Alternative Ways to Earn Your Credentials*. This shows you how to get your diploma or college credit without actually going back to school.

How $2 Can Change Your Job

If you think the Consumer Information Center only helps those who are looking for work, think again. The CIC is also a great source of information for working people who need help with certain problems. You can order the following brochures using the same address and phone number listed above. Again, remember to include the code number for any information you order.

Code 315E: (50 cents) *Health Benefits Under COBRA*. COBRA is a program that allows you to keep your health benefits after you've lost your job, for a certain period of time. This brochure explains this important program.

Code 316E: (50 cents) *How To File A Claim For Your Benefits*. If your company's insurance won't pay for a claim, this will show you what to do about it.

Code 314E: (50 cents) *Handy Reference Guide to the Fair Labor Standards Act*. This pamphlet walks you through federal laws that regulate your rights in the workplace, such as minimum wage standards and working conditions.

Get a Job Through the Forest Service

If you are over 55 years of age and meet certain income eligibility guidelines, you may be a candidate for the Senior Community Service

Employment Program (SCSEP).

This program provides education, retraining and employment opportunities to persons 55 and above. SCSEP's goal is to place seniors in productive, unsubsidized employment in the regular working community.

To learn about the program, contact your local Forest Service office or U.S. Forest Service, U.S. Department of Agriculture, SCSEP, Senior, Youth, Volunteer Programs, PO Box 96090, Washington, DC 20090; 703-235-8860.

☆☆☆

Make $15 an Hour With the EPA

The Environmental Protection Agency (EPA) has a special program for hiring senior citizens 55 years and over. When an EPA regional office has a shortage of workers, they notify one of the organizations listed below, which in turn recruits workers.

Senior citizens get involved in all kinds of activities from conducting national surveys to fulfilling general administrative tasks. These jobs carry many regular benefits, including unemployment, workmen's compensation, Social Security, and health plans.
There are 4 levels of pay:

Level 1 — Copy machine operators, messengers, telephone assistants; $6-$8 an hour

Level 2 — secretaries, administrative assistants; $7.25-$10 an hour

Level 3 — writers and editors; $8.50-$11.50 an hour

Level 4 — professionals with relevant degrees; $10.50-$15 an hour

To find our more about the program, contact the Senior Environmental Employment Program (SEE), U.S. Environmental Protection Agency, National Center for Environmental Research and Quality Assurance, 401 M St. SW, Mail Stop 3641, Washington, DC 20460. The phone number is 202-260-2574.

These are organizations that regularly participate in the SEE Program. You can contact them directly for recruitment information.

National Council on the Aging, 409 Third St., SW, Suite 200, Washington, DC 20024; 202-479-1200.

National Older Worker Career Center, 1615 L St., NW, Suite 750, Washington, DC 20036; 202-331-5017.

National Association for Hispanic Elderly, 1452 W. Temple St.,

Suite 100, Los Angeles, CA 90026; 213-487-1922.

National Caucus and Center on Black Aged, Suite 500, 1424 K St., NW, Washington, DC 20005; 202-637-8400.

National Pacific/Asian Resource Center on Aging, Suite 410, 2033 6th Ave., Seattle, WA 98101; 206-624-1221.

Clock In at Your Kitchen Table

Maybe you need a job, but don't feel much like going back to a frantic workplace environment. If so, home employment might be the right choice for you. Finding the right situation, however, can be tricky.

There are lots of opportunities for seniors to work out of their homes, but there are also a lot of scams. Some newspaper and magazine ads make very tempting claims, but then demand that you order expensive "training materials" or pay for "start up costs." Be very careful with outfits like these — it's hard to tell the difference between a legitimate company and someone who just wants to take your money.

As usual, the best way to be safe is to be informed. Information from the Home Employment Project may be able to help you sort through the bogus claims and find legitimate home employment opportunities. For their free newsletter that can start you in the right direction, call 800-574-6184. Ask for extension 111.

The Best Boss You'll Ever Have ... Is You

America might be "the Land of the Free," but it's also the land of free enterprise. Millions of Americans from all walks of life — and of all ages — have started their own businesses, and you can too.

Think of it: No boss to report to, no regular hours to keep, just your idea and your passion and your hard work. If that sort of work environment sounds good to you, perhaps starting a home-based business is your best option.

An important first step is to get the facts on just what goes into making a small business successful. A good source of this information is U.S. Small Business Administration (SBA), which provides numerous free brochures that can answer many of your questions. Give them a call, and they'll send you information about writing a business plan, marketing your goods or services, keeping accurate records, and expanding your business. Your packet will also include a description of the many programs offered by the SBA to help people just starting out in their own businesses, as well a listing of their offices throughout the United States where you can go for extra assistance.

If you're serious about starting a small business, or you're just curious about your options, give the SBA a call at 800-827-5722.

How the Best Boss You'll Ever Have
Takes Care of Business

If you choose to strike out on your own with a small business, there's a lot you'll need to know. Parts of doing business that you might not have thought about can cause problems if you're not ready for them. Your success depends on your ability to deal with such matters as employee rights, customer service, and effective advertising. You can do it, but you'll want some help. Here's where to get it, boss.

Code 589E: (Free) *Starting a Business.* This short booklet reviews the four basic business types and helps you organize your plans.

Code 362E: (50 cents) *Resource Directory for Small Business Management.* This one gives you a list of informative materials, such as videos and books, that are particularly useful when going it on your own.

Code 361E: (50 cents) *Guide to Business Credit for Women, Minorities, and Small Businesses.* How do you apply for and get credit as a business? Your questions are answered here.

Code 586E: (Free) *Americans with Disabilities Act: Guide for Small Business.* Here's what you'll need to know as an employer to stay in line with certain government standards and rules.

All of the above brochures are available from the Consumer Information Center by calling toll free 888-878-3256, or sending your check or money order to: R. Woods, CIC-8D, PO Box 100, Pueblo, CO 81002.

They Can't Pay You
If They Don't Know Who You Are

You've got your business all planned out. You know what goods or services you will offer, how you will provide them, and how long it should take you to get rich. Just one problem: you know you're in business, but nobody else does.

For a mere $1.50, you can get some help in solving this critical problem. The booklet is called *101 Publicity Tips: How to Publicize Yourself or Your Business*. To get your hands on this valuable information, send a check or money order, along with a self-addressed, stamped envelope to: 2nd Mile Productions, Box 12280, Mill Creek, Washington 98082.

The Customer Is Still Always Right

Years ago in Chicago, a sales clerk was having trouble with some difficult requests from a customer. When the owner of the store heard what was going on, he quickly went over and asked what the problem was. No one remembers what the clerk's reply was, because it made no difference to the owner. The owner's immediate response: "Give the lady what she wants!"

That store owner's name was Marshall Field, and his department stores across the country have made millions because of their commitment to keeping customers happy. After all these years, the golden rule of customer service remains the same, but do you know how to follow it?

For some free help, contact the Quill Corporation, Public Relations Department 67187, 100 Schelter Road, Lincolnshire, Illinois, 60069. They'll send you their brochure called *How to Win Through Great Customer Service,* and your new business can start giving everybody what they want!

Smart Savers for the Savvy Self-Employed

You might be worried that you don't have the money to start your own home business, but don't let that stop you. Really all you need is a work area, a phone, and some business cards. Depending on what type of business you start, you'll need other equipment, too, but you can save up for most of these as you become more successful. When you're just starting out, though, cutting a few dollars off your capital investment can really make things a lot easier.

For example, don't go overboard in setting up your office. Used office furniture sells for a fraction of the price of new furniture, and works just as well. Call the Business Products Industry Association at 800-542-6672 to find a used dealer near you.

Same goes for carpeting. Why spend hundreds on sprucing up your home office, when a remnant would cover your floor just as well? Remember, every dollar you don't spend on your office is a dollar that can go toward making your business grow.

You're probably going to need a computer eventually, and when you get it, don't throw out your old one. Instead, donate it to a church or other group and write its value off as a charitable deduction from your taxes. Whenever you've got something to throw away, remember: Don't toss it until you're sure nobody else is willing to take it off your hands, either by sale or by charity. The nonprofit group Gifts in Kind America can help you find new homes (and tax relief) for your old stuff. Call them at 703-836-2121.

The Truth About Age Discrimination

Age discrimination is a very real, and very unfair problem in America. According to the government's General Accounting Office (GAO), 28 percent of all cases filed with the Equal Employment Opportunity Commission (EEOC) deal with age discrimination. If you feel you have been discriminated against by an employer because of your age, your first step is to get more information.

The GAO is the department of Congress that investigates and reports on government programs and activities. They offer many free reports that can help you learn how to best go about filing a complaint, and what sort of results you should expect.

The following reports dealing with employment issues are available from the GAO:
- *Multiple Employment Training Programs: Overlap Among Programs Raises Questions About Efficiency* (HEHS 94-193)
- *Federal Personnel: Employment Policy Challenges Created by an Aging Workforce* (GAO/GGD 93-138)
- *The Changing Workforce: Demographic Issues Facing Employers* (GAO/T-GGD 92-61)

- *Age Employment Discrimination: EEOC's Investigation of Charges Under 1967 Law* (HRD 92-82)
- *EEOC: An Overview* (GAO/T-HRD 93-30)

To request any of these reports, contact the U.S. General Accounting Office, PO Box 6015, Gaithersburg, MD 20884; 202-512-6000.

Comfortable Retirement — A "Wealth" of Information

Retiring isn't as simple as it once was. Retirement plans are becoming more complex and varied in order to meet the needs of both workers and employers. A little help from Uncle Sam can help you sort through your options, decide on the best time to retire, and make the transition from work to retirement a bit smoother.

The Congressional Research Service (CRS) writes reports that provide a general overview of retirement topics and provide relevant newspaper articles and bibliographies. These reports are free but must be requested through your Congressman. CRS reports dealing with employment include:

- *Jobs: Job Training and Labor Market Issues* (IP246J)
- *Age Discrimination in Employment Act: Recent Enforcement Actions by the EEOC* (87-783A)
- *Early Retirement Incentive Plans under the Age Discrimination in Employment Act of 1967* (88-608A)
- *A Demographic Portrait of Older Workers* (88-636E)
- *Lists of Federal Job Openings* (CRS-1)
- *Older Workers: The Transition to Retirement* (89-28E)
- *Age Discrimination in Employee Benefit Plans* (89-478A)

You can get these and other CRS reports by writing to your Senator or Representative, The Capitol, Washington, DC 20510; 202-224-3121.

Your Job & Your Health — Know Your Rights

As the American workforce continues to age, many workers are finding that they need extra time to take care of a parent or spouse. Caregiving for elderly dependents can involve such time-consuming activities as arranging doctors' appointments, paying bills, and helping with daily needs such as bathing, dressing, and meal preparation.

Eldercare is a concern to both employers and employees because the time and stress involved in caregiving can be enormous. In the past, workers were often denied the freedom of taking off time to fulfill their roles as caregivers. Fortunately, the government now requires that employers give more flexibility to caregivers.

The Family and Medical Leave Act allows employees to take up to 12 weeks of unpaid leave in any 12 month period for the birth or adoption of a child; the serious illness of a child, spouse, or parent; or the serious illness of the employee. Workers must have been employed for one year, and have worked at least 1,250 hours to qualify.

These regulations do not apply to all employment situations, however. To find out what benefits you are entitled to, contact the Work and Family Clearinghouse, U.S. Department of Labor, Women's Bureau, 200 Constitution Ave., NW, Washington, DC 20210; 800-827-5335. You can also look online for more information and publications available at < www.dol. gov/dol/wb>.

Care for Your Employees — It's the Law

The Work and Family Clearinghouse has a free Work and Family Resource Kit which provides an overview and options for eldercare. The Clearinghouse can show you how companies similar to yours have established resources and programs to help out this population.

AT&T, Stride-Rite, and Travelers have begun to design innovative programs to decrease employee caregiver problems; your company can too. The Clearinghouse can also answer your Family and Medical Leave questions.

For more information, contact Work and Family Clearinghouse, U.S. Department of Labor, Women's Bureau, 200 Constitution Ave., NW, Washington, DC 20210; 800-827-5335; or contact them online for information and publications available at <www.dol.gov/dol/wb>.

☆☆☆

Free Job Training and Part-Time Jobs

Looking for a job to supplement a small retirement income? The Senior Community Service Employment program offers part-time training and employment opportunities for eligible low-income persons 55 years of age and older in a variety of public and private nonprofit community service settings. These include jobs working with senior centers, nutrition programs, social service agencies, libraries, environmental projects, and many others.

The program provides seniors with income and the opportunity to learn new skills or improve the ones they already have. The program also helps you make the transition to the private job market through training, job search support and counseling. Typical program participants work at such jobs as: activities coordinator, bookkeeper, cashier, clerk typist, custodian, data entry clerk, day care worker, driver, food service worker, grounds keeper, mechanic, receptionist, salesperson, security guard, and teacher's aide.

The Job Training Partnership Act program (JTPA) trains and places older workers in full- and part-time jobs with private businesses. Program participants not only receive on-the-job experience, but also have an opportunity to develop job skills and good work habits.

Other services available to seniors in this program include job counseling, help with polishing up your resume, job searches, and classroom training. Participating businesses who hire JTPA graduates receive financial and tax incentives for doing so. The offices listed below will help direct you to job training programs for older workers in your area, including the JTPA and Senior Community Service Employment Program (Title V). In addition, many states offer their own special assistance programs for the elderly. Be sure to ask them for any and all information they have available.

State Job Programs

ALABAMA: Commission on Aging, 770 Washington Ave., RSA Plaza, Suite 470, Montgomery, AL 36130; 334-242-5743. National Caucus on Black Aging; 334-265-1451. Offers specialized, regional assistance in nine counties, including Montgomery. Department of Economic and Community Affairs, 401 Adams Ave., PO Box 5690, Montgomery, AL 36103-5690; 334-242-5300.

ALASKA: Older Alaskans Commissions, PO Box 110209, 333 Willoughby Ave., Juneau, AK 99801; 907-465-3250. Department of Community and Regional Affairs, 150 Third St., PO Box 112100, Juneau, AK 99811-2100; 907-465-4814, 907-465-5545.

ARIZONA: Department of Economic Security, Aging and Adult Administration, 950A, 1789 W. Jefferson, Phoenix, AZ 85007; 602-542-4446.

ARKANSAS: Arkansas Division of Aging and Adult Services, PO Box 1437, Slot 1412, Little Rock, AR 72201; 501-682-2441. Arkansas Able program, 501-660-4110. More information on senior employment opportunities. JTPA Department of Labor, 500 West Markham, Suite 220, West Wing, Little Rock, AR 72201; 501-371-4487.

CALIFORNIA: California Department of Aging, Administrative Services Branch, Senior Employment (Title V) Section, 1600 K St., Sacramento, CA 95814; 916-323-0217, 916-323-7515. Private Industry Council, 800-FOR-A-JOB. Further employment information. JTPA, State of California, Employment Development Department, PO Box 826880, MIC 69, Sacramento, CA 94280-0001; 916-654-7110.

COLORADO: Colorado Department of Labor and Employment, 1515 Arapahoa St., T2-400, Denver, CO 80202; 303-620-4200.

CONNECTICUT: Department of Social Services, Elderly Services Division, 25 Sigourney St., Hartford, CT 06106; 860-424-5274.

DELAWARE: Services for Aging and Adults With Physical Disabilities, Health and Social Services Department, 1901 North DuPont Hwy., Main Building, 2nd Floor Annex, New Castle, DE 19720; 302-577-4660. Career Exploration Program, Prime Time, 302-573-2474. Training & placement program for workers 55 and older.

DISTRICT OF COLUMBIA: DC Office on Aging, 441 4th St. NW, Suite 900 South, Washington, DC 20001; 202-724-5622, 202-724-3662. Department of Employment Service, 500 C St. NW, Room 327, Washington, DC 20001; 202-724-7073.

FLORIDA: Department of Elder Affairs, 4040 Esplanade Way, Tallahassee, FL 32399-7000; 850-414-2108, Elder Helpline: 800-96-ELDER (in FL only). Internet: <www.state.fl.us/doea/doea.html>.

GEORGIA: Department of Human Services, Division of Aging Services, 2 Peachtree St., NW, 36th Floor, Atlanta, GA 30303; 404-657-5258, 404-657-5330.

HAWAII: Executive Office on Aging, Office of the Governor, 250 S. Hotel St., Suite 109, Honolulu, HI 96813-2831; 808-586-0100. Honolulu Community Action Program, Department of Labor, 830 Punchbowl St., Room 316, Honolulu, HI 96813; 808-586-8813/8828.

IDAHO: Commission on Aging, PO Box 83720, Boise, ID 83720-0007; 208-334-3833. ElderCare Locator, 800-677-1116. Provides local employment contacts and an Older Worker Employment Program staff listing.

ILLINOIS: Department on Aging, 421 East Capitol Ave., Springfield, IL 62701; 217-785-0117, 800-252-8966 (IL only). Department of Commerce and Community Affairs, 620 East Adams St., Springfield, IL 62701; 217-782-7500, 217-785-6006.

INDIANA: Disability, Rehabilitation and Aging Services, Family and Social Services Administration, 402 West Washington St., Indianapolis, IN 46207; 317-232-7000, 317-232-7459.

IOWA: Department of Elder Affairs, 200 10th St., 3rd Floor, Des Moines, IA 50309; 512-281-5187.

KANSAS: Department of Aging, Docking State Office Building, 1st Floor, Room 150 South, 915 SW Harrison, Topeka, KS 66612; 913-296-4986. Three other Kansas programs receive local or private funds for job referral and training: New Directions Program, Services for Seniors, Inc., and Project EARN. Ask for the free booklet, *Employment Services for Workers 55 and Over.*

KENTUCKY: Aging Services Division, Department for Social Services, 275 East Main St., 5th Floor W., Frankfort, KY 40621; 502-564-6930. JTPA Coordinator, Office of Training and Reemployment, 209 St. Clair St., 4th Floor, Frankfort, KY 40601; 502-564-5360.

LOUISIANA: Office of Elderly Affairs, Office of the Governor, PO Box 80374, Baton Rouge, LA 70898-0374; 504-342-7100. Ask for the free fact sheet on employment programs.

MAINE: Bureau of Elder and Adult Services, Department of Human Services, State House Station #11, 35 Anthony Ave., Augusta, ME 04333-0011; 207-624-5335. Bureau of Employment Services, Department of Labor, 55 State House Station, Augusta, ME 04333-0055; 207-624-6390.

MARYLAND: Maryland Office on Aging, 301 Preston St., Room 1004, Baltimore, MD 21201; 410-767-1102, 800-AGE-DIAL. Ask for the free booklet, *Senior Information and Assistance on Benefits and Services for Older Persons.*

MASSACHUSETTS: Executive Office of Elder Affairs, One Ashburton Place, Boston, MA 02108; 617-727-7750, 800-882-2003.

MICHIGAN: Office of Services to the Aging, PO Box 30676, Lansing, MI 48909-8176; 517-373-8230. Michigan Job Commission, 201 N. Washington Square, Victor Office Center, 4th Floor, Lansing, MI 48913; 517-373-9808.

MINNESOTA: Minnesota Board on Aging, Human Service Building, 4th Floor, 444 Lafayette Rd., St. Paul, MN 55155; 612-296-2770, 800-882-6262 (MN only). Program Specialist, Community Based Services, Department of Jobs and Training, 390 N. Robert St., Room 125, St. Paul, MN 55101; 612-297-1054.

MISSOURI: Division of Aging, Department of Social Services, PO Box 1337, Jefferson City, MO 65102; 573-751-3082. Division of Job Development and Training, PO Box 1087, Jefferson City, MO 65102; 573-751-7896, 800-877-8698.

MONTANA: Green Thumb, Box 2587, Great Falls, MT 59403; 406-761-4821. Montana JTP, Inc., 302 N. Last Chance Gulch, Suite 409, Helena, MT 59601; 406-444-1309.

NEBRASKA: Department on Aging, 301 Centennial Mall S., PO Box 95044, Lincoln, NE 68509-5044; 402-471-2307.

NEVADA: AARP, PO Box 4395, Bonanza Station, Las Vegas, NV 89127; 702-648-3356. Nevada Business Services, 930 W. Owens, Las Vegas, NV 89106; 702-647-4929. Division for Aging Services, 340 N. 11th St., Suite 203, Las Vegas, NV 89101; 702-486-3545.

NEW HAMPSHIRE: AARP, PO Box 398, Main and Grove Sts., North Conway, NH 03860; 603-356-3117, 800-652-8808 (NH only). Job Training Council, 64 Old Suncook Rd., Concord, NH 03301-5134; 800-772-7001 (NH only), 603-228-9500. Division of Elderly and Adult Services, Department of Health and Human Services, 115 Pleasant St., Annex Bldg., #1, State Office Park South, Concord, NH 03301-3843; 603-271-4680.

NEW JERSEY: Department of Health and Senior Services, Division of Senior Affairs, PO Box 807, 101 South Broad St., CN 807, Trenton, NJ 08625-807; 609-292-4833. This office also has information on ACTION programs that offer volunteer opportunities through the Foster Grandparent Program (FGP) and the Senior Companion Program (SCP). Ask for the free guide *Federal Programs for Older Persons.* Senior Citizens Information and Referral Service, 800-792-8820. Department of Environmental Protection and Energy, Division of Personnel, Recruitment Unit, 440 East State St., CN 408, Trenton, NJ 08625-0408; 609-984-3701. New Jersey Department of Labor, Division of Employment and Training, John Fitz Plaza, Room 407, PO Box 055, Trenton, NJ 08625-0055; 609-292-5005.

NEW MEXICO: State Agency on Aging, 228 East Palace Ave., Santa Fe, NM 87501; 505-827-7640, 800-432-2080 (only in New Mexico).

State Department of Labor, Job Training Division, 1596 Pacheco St., Santa Fe, NM 87502; 505-827-6827.

NEW YORK: State Office For the Aging, 2 Empire State Plaza, Albany, NY 12223-1251; 518-474-4425, 518-474-1946, 800-342-9871.

NORTH CAROLINA: Department of Human Resources, Division of Aging, 693 Palmer Dr., Raleigh, NC 27626-0531; 919-733-3983. Department of Commerce, Division of Employment and Training, 441 N. Harrington St., Raleigh, NC 27603; 919-733-6383.

NORTH DAKOTA: Department of Human Services, Aging Services Division, 600 S. 2nd St., Suite 1C, Bismarck, ND 58504-5729; 701-328-8910, 701-328-2825. Green Thumb, 2206 E. Broadway, Bismarck, ND 58501-4930; 701-258-8879.

OHIO: Department of Aging, 50 West Broad St., 9th Floor, Columbus, OH 43215-5928; 614-466-5500, 614-466-1242. JTPA Division, Ohio Employment Service Division, 145 S. Front St., PO Box 1618, Columbus, OH 43215; 614-466-3817.

OKLAHOMA: O.E.S.C. - JTPA, 2401 N. Lincoln, Oklahoma City, OK 73532; 405-557-5323. Department of Human Services, Aging Services, 312 NE 28th St., Oklahoma City, OK 73105; 405-521-2327.

OREGON: Department of Human Resources, Senior and Disabled Services Division, 500 Summer St., NE, Salem, OR 97310-1015; 503-945-6413. JTPA, State Economic Development, 775 Summer St., NE, Salem, OR 97310; 503-373-1995.

PENNSYLVANIA: Department of Aging, 555 Walnut St., 5th Floor, Forum Place, Harrisburg, PA 17101-1919; 717-783-1550, 717-783-6007. Department of Labor and Industry, Bureau of Employment Services and Training, 7th and Forster Sts., 12th Floor, Harrisburg, PA 17120; 717-783-0142.

RHODE ISLAND: Department of Elderly Affairs, 160 Pine St., Providence, RI 02903; 401-222-2858.

SOUTH CAROLINA: Department of Health and Human Services, Office on Aging, PO Box 8206, Columbia, SC 29202-8206; 803-253-6177. Ask for information on Operation Able, a worker/job match service. JTPA SAU, Employment Security Commission, 1550 Gadsden St., PO Box 1406, Columbia, SC 29202; 803-737-2660.

SOUTH DAKOTA: Adult Services and Aging Division, 120 S. Indiana Ave., Sioux Falls, SD 57103; 605-332-7991. JTPA, Department of Labor, 700 Governors Dr., Pierre, SD 57501; 605-773-5017.

TENNESSEE: Commission on Aging, 500 Deaderick St., Andrew Jackson Bldg., 9th Floor, Nashville, TN 37243-0860; 615-741-2056. JTPA, Department of Labor, 4th Floor, Andrew Johnson Bldg., 710 James Robertson Pkwy., Nashville, TN 37243-0658; 615-741-1031.

TEXAS: Senior Texans Employment Program, 5400 Bosque Blvd., Waco, TX 76710; 254-776-7002. Texas Workforce Commission, 101 E. 15th St., Room 112T, Austin, TX 78778-0001; 512-936-0345.

UTAH: Department of Human Services, Division of Aging and Adult Services, 120 North 200 West, Room 325, Salt Lake City, UT 84103; 801-538-3910. Senior Employment Office, 801-468-2785. Ask for a free copy of the Senior Resource Directory, which includes referral numbers for numerous older worker programs. JTPA, Economic Development and Training Division, 2001 South State, S2600, Salt Lake City, UT 84115; 801-468-3246.

VERMONT: Department of Aging and Disabilities, 103 S. Main St., Waterbury, VT 05671-2301; 802-241-2400. Vermont Associates for Training and Development, Senior Community Service Employment Program, 132 N. Main St., St. Aldans, VT 05478; 802-524-3200.

VIRGINIA: Department For the Aging, 1600 Forest Ave., Suite 102, Richmond, VA 23229; 804-662-9333. Ask for a Title V and JTPA directory with complete list of local contacts.

WASHINGTON: Job Development and Training, 701 Sleater-Kinney Rd., SE, Suite 99A, Lacey, WA 98503; 360-786-5586.

WEST VIRGINIA: Bureau of Senior Services, 1900 Kanawha Blvd. E., Capitol Complex/Holly Grove, Bldg. 10, Charleston, WV 25305; 304-558-3317. JTPA Employment Services, States College University System, 1018 Kanawha Blvd. E., Suite 700, Charleston, WV 25301; 304-558-2664.

WISCONSIN: Division of Workforce Excellence, Department of Workforce Development, Labor and Human Relations, PO Box 7972, Madison, WI 53707; 608-266-6886.

WYOMING: Wyoming Senior Citizens, Inc., 413 West 18th St., Cheyenne, WY 82001; 307-635-1245. Department of Health, Division on Aging, 139 Hathaway Building, Cheyenne, WY 82002; 307-777-7986.

College Tuition
for Golden Agers

Did your college career get interrupted or postponed by marriage or military service? Maybe when you were younger a higher education seemed so out of reach you didn't even allow yourself to dream of it. Chances are, you worked hard helping your kids get a good education. Perhaps you made it possible for your grandchildren to get a college degree. As the years went by, you may have thought of starting or returning to school yourself. But the time never seemed right for you.

Well, it's not too late to follow your dream. And the really good news is, you may be able to attend college for free. Believe it or not, more than 350 colleges and universities all across the country have special programs for senior citizens who are interested in going back to school.

In addition to free or low-cost tuition, seniors may find discounts on fees and books, and even special deals on housing. So why not join the growing number of older Americans who are returning to the classroom?

If the idea of keeping up with the younger folks seems a little frightening, put your mind at ease. Research shows that the brain doesn't necessarily slow down with age. And the more you use it to learn new and different things, the better it works. Don't forget the value of your life experience. You lived through things that younger students may be learning about for the first time, so you are miles ahead of them. If you are still a little hesitant, these guidelines might help you ease into your studies.

CONSIDER AUDITING THE FIRST CLASS. You won't have to take tests and you aren't graded. This takes away some of the pressure. And in some cases where there are fees, the cost is lower for auditing classes. You don't get credit toward a degree, however, in audited classes.

CHOOSE CLASSES THAT REALLY INTEREST YOU. One kind of memory seems to slow down with age: remembering meaningless information. There should be little or no slowdown, however, in remembering stimulating material. So look for the most fascinating topics, and you'll hold your own with fellow classmates.

STUDY WHEN YOU ARE MOST ALERT. While younger college students may prefer late-night study sessions, research indicates that with age our biological cycles change. We tend to be sharper earlier in the day rather than in the evening. But each person is different, so pay attention to your own cycles. Notice especially when you get the sleepiest. If you like an afternoon siesta, don't sign up for a class that meets right after lunch.

ASK YOUR PROFESSORS QUESTIONS. By raising questions, you'll add to your own knowledge. And you'll also be adding to the quality of classroom discussions by bringing a different, more mature perspective.

So relax and enjoy being a college student again, or at long last. Whether you earn a diploma, graduate magna cum laude, or just learn for the sake of learning, you'll probably have loads of fun. And you'll definitely give your brain some healthy exercise.

Eligibility requirements, fees, and tuition vary from one school to another. This list will give you an idea of what to expect from some of the schools in your state. Special fees may apply to some classes. Generally, labs, books, and materials are additional expenses. And there may be other fees to cover parking, student activities, and health services.

Whether it's listed here or not, contact the school that interests you to find out about their current policies. They'll tell you about their programs for seniors and how to apply.

☆☆☆

College Programs for Seniors, Listed by State

ALABAMA

Gadsden State Community College
Admissions
PO Box 227
Gadsden, AL 35902-0227
205-549-8260
Minimum Age: 60
Tuition: free
Basic Fees: none
Credit: yes

Jefferson State Community College
Admissions
2601 Carson Rd.
Birmingham, AL 35215-3098
205-853-1200
Minimum Age: 60
Tuition: free
Basic Fees: $4 per credit hour
Credit: yes

Livingston University
Station 2
Livingston, AL 35470
205-652-3400
Minimum Age: 55
Tuition: free
Basic Fees: $15 one time application fee
Credit: no

University of Montevallo
Station 6065
Montevallo, AL 35115
205-665-6065
800-292-4349
Minimum Age: 65

Tuition: free
Basic Fees: $15 per class
Credit: no

ALASKA

**Prince William Sound
Community College**
PO Box 97
Valdez, AK 99686
907-835-2678
Minimum Age: 60
Tuition: free
Basic Fees: $2.50 for one to
three credit hours; $5 for four to
five credit hours; $25 for seven
or more credit hours
Credit: yes

University of Alaska Anchorage
Enrollment Services
3211 Providence Dr.
Anchorage, AK 99508
907-786-1525
Minimum Age: 60
Tuition: free
Basic Fees: $45 for three credit
hours; $57 for six credit hours
Credit: yes

University of Alaska Fairbanks
Admissions and Records
PO Box 757640
Fairbanks, AK 99775-0060
907-474-7821
Minimum Age: 60
Tuition: free
Basic Fees: $25 for three credit
hours; $155 for 12 credit hours;
parking and health insurance
can be waived if not needed
Credit: yes

University of Alaska Southeast
11120 Glacier Hwy.
Juneau, AK 99801

907-465-6457
Minimum Age: 60
Tuition: free
Basic Fees: $5 for one credit
hour; $8 for two credit hours; $17
for three or more credit hours
Credit: yes

ARIZONA

Arizona Western College
PO Box 929
Yuma, AZ 85366-0929
520-726-1050
Minimum Age: 60
Tuition: $16 per credit hour
Basic Fees: none
Credit: yes

Central Arizona College
Student Records
8470 North Overfield Rd.
Coolidge, AZ 85228
602-426-4444
Minimum Age: 60
Tuition: $18 per credit hour with
the sixth, sixteenth, seventeenth
and eighteenth hours free
Basic Fees: none
Credit: yes

ARKANSAS

Arkansas State University
Admissions
PO Box 1630
State University
Jonesboro, AR 72467-1630
800-382-3030
Minimum Age: 60
Tuition: free
Basic Fees: $4 per credit hour
Credit: yes

**Arkansas State University,
Beebe Branch**
PO Drawer H

257

Beebe, AR 72012
501-882-6452
Minimum Age: 60
Tuition: free
Basic Fees: none (auto sticker $5)
Credit: yes

Arkansas Tech University
Admissions
Russelville, AR 72801-2222
501-968-0343
Minimum Age: 60
Tuition: free
Basic Fees: none
Credit: yes

East Arkansas Community College
1700 Newcastle Rd.
Forest City, AR 72335-9598
501-633-4480
Minimum Age: 62
Tuition: free
Basic Fees: $3 per credit hour
Credit: yes

Garland County Community College
101 College Dr.
Hot Springs, AR 71913
501-767-9371
Minimum Age: 60
Tuition: free
Basic Fees: $10 per session
Credit: yes

Henderson State University
Registrar
PO Box 7534
Arkadelphia, AR 71999-7534
501-203-5000
Minimum Age: 60
Tuition: free
Basic Fees: $36 for three credit hours
Credit: yes

Northern Arkansas Community College
Pioneer Ridge
Harrison, AR 72601
501-743-3000
Minimum Age: 60
Tuition: free
Basic Fees: none
Credit: yes

Phillips County Community College
Campus Dr.
PO Box 785
Helena, AR 72342
501-338-6474
Minimum Age: 60
Tuition: free
Basic Fees: none
Credit: yes

CALIFORNIA

California State University, Sacramento
Re-Entry Services
6000 J St.
Sacramento, CA 95819-6048
916-278-6750
Minimum Age: 60
Tuition: $3 per session
Basic Fees: none (students receive free public transportation in the Sacramento area)
Credit: yes

COLORADO

Adams State College
Alamosa, CO 81102
719-589-7712
Minimum Age: 65
Tuition: free
Basic Fees: none
Credit: no

Colorado Mountain College, Alpine Campus

1330 Bob Adams Dr.
Steamboat Springs, CO 80487
970-870-4444
Minimum Age: 62
Tuition: 50 percent off (regular tuition $32 per credit hour)
Basic Fees: $50 for up to nine credit hours; $65 for 12 or more credit hours
Credit: yes

Colorado State University

Admissions and Records
Administrative Annex Bldg.
Ft. Collins, CO 80523
970-491-6909
Minimum Age: 62
Tuition: free
Basic Fees: none
Credit: no

Metropolitan State College of Denver

Adult Learning Services
PO Box 173362
Denver, CO 80217
303-556-8342
Minimum Age: 62
Tuition: free
Basic Fees: none
Credit: no

University of Colorado, Boulder

Regent Administrative Center 125
Office of Admissions
Campus Box 6
Boulder, CO 80309
303-492-6301
Minimum Age: 55
Tuition: member of alumni $5 per session; non-alumni member $15 per session
Basic Fees: none
Credit: no

University of Colorado at Denver

PO Box 173364
Campus Box 146
Denver, CO 80217-3364
303-556-2400
Minimum Age: 60
Tuition: free
Basic Fees: none
Credit: no

University of Northern Colorado Admissions

Greeley, CO 80639
970-351-2881
Minimum Age: 60
Tuition: free
Basic Fees: none
Credit: no

CONNECTICUT

Asnuntuck Community College

Admissions
170 Elm St.
Enfield, CT 06082
203-253-3043
Minimum Age: 62
Tuition: free
Basic Fees: none (lab fee also waived)
Credit: yes

Central Connecticut State University

Admissions Office
1615 Stanley St.
New Britain, CT 06050
860-832-3200
Minimum Age: 62
Tuition: free
Basic Fees: $37 per semester
Credit: yes

Eastern Connecticut State University

Registrar
83 Windham St.
Willimantic, CT 06226
203-465-5389
Minimum Age: 62
Tuition: free
Basic Fees: $12 per credit hour for part-time
Credit: yes

University of Connecticut, Storrs

2131 Hillside Rd.
Storrs, CT 06269-3088
203-486-3137
Minimum Age: 62
Tuition: free
Basic Fees: $222 full-time per semester
Credit: yes

University of Hartford

Adult Services
200 Bloomfield Ave.
West Hartford, CT 06117-0395
203-768-4457
Minimum Age: 70
Tuition: free
Basic Fees: $30 per semester (one-class limit)
Credit: no

Western Connecticut State University

Office of Continuing Education
181 White St.
Danbury, CT 006810
203-837-8230
Minimum Age: 62
Tuition: $10 per semester (non-credit $10 per class)
Basic Fees: Part-time none (full-time varies)

Credit: yes

DELAWARE

Delaware State College

Admissions
1200 N. Dupont Hwy.
Dover, DE 19901
302-739-4917
Minimum Age: 62
Tuition: free
Basic Fees: $25 per semester
Credit: yes

Delaware Technical and Community College: Jack F. Owens Campus

PO Box 610
Georgetown, DE 19947
302-856-5400
Minimum Age: 60
Tuition: free
Basic Fees: none
Credit: yes

Delaware Technical and Community College, Stanton/Wilmington Campus

333 Shipley St.
Wilmington, DE 19801
302-571-5343
Minimum Age: 60
Tuition: free
Basic Fees: none
Credit: yes

Delaware Technical and Community College, Terry Campus

1832 N. Dupont Pkwy.
Dover, DE 19901
302-741-2700
Minimum Age: 60
Tuition: free
Basic Fees: none
Credit: yes

DISTRICT OF COLUMBIA

University of the District of Columbia
1100 Harvard St., Room 114
Washington, DC 20008
202-274-5010
Minimum Age: 65
Tuition: free (50 percent off if going for a degree)
Basic Fees: $20 per semester
Credit: yes

FLORIDA

Broward Community College, Ft. Lauderdale
Registration
225 E. Lasolas Blvd.
Ft. Lauderdale, FL 33301
305-761-7465
Minimum Age: 65
Tuition: free
Basic Fees: the school will cover up to $181.50 of basic fees
Credit: yes

Florida Atlantic University
500 Northwest 20th St.
Boca Raton, FL 33431-0991
407-367-3294
Minimum Age: 60
Tuition: free
Basic Fees: none
Credit: no

Florida International University
University Park
Miami, FL 33199
305-348-2363
Minimum Age: 60
Tuition: free
Basic Fees: none
Credit: no

Florida State University
2249 University Ct.
Tallahassee, FL 32306-1009
904-644-6200
Minimum Age: 62
Tuition: free
Basic Fees: none
Credit: no

Santa Fe Community College
PO Box 1530
3000 NW 83rd St.
Gainesville, FL 32602
352-395-5443
Minimum Age: 60
Tuition: free
Basic Fees: none
Credit: yes

University of Central Florida
PO Box 160111
Orlando, FL 32816-0111
407-823-3000
Minimum Age: 60
Tuition: free
Basic Fees: none
Credit: no

GEORGIA

Albany State College
504 College Dr.
Albany, GA 31705
912-430-4650
Minimum Age: 62
Tuition: free
Basic Fees: $10 per session
Credit: yes

Armstrong State College
11935 Abercorn St.
Savannah, GA 31419
800-633-2349
Minimum Age: 62
Tuition: free
Basic Fees: $10 per session
Credit: yes

Athens Area Technical Institute
US Highway 29 North
Athens, GA 30610-3099
706-542-8050
Minimum Age: 62
Tuition: free
Basic Fees: $12.50 per quarter
Credit: yes

Bainbridge College
2500 E. Shotwell St.
Bainbridge, GA 31717
912-248-2500
Minimum Age: 62
Tuition: free
Basic Fees: none
Credit: yes

Brunswick College
Admissions
3700 Altama Ave.
Brunswick, GA 31520-3644
912-264-7253
Minimum Age: 62
Tuition: free
Basic Fees: none
Credit: yes

Clayton State College
Admissions/Registrar
PO Box 285
Morrow, GA 30260
770-961-3400
Minimum Age: 62
Tuition: free
Basic Fees: none
Credit: yes

Columbus College
4225 University Ave.
Columbus, GA 31907-5645
706-568-2035
Minimum Age: 62
Tuition: free
Basic Fees: none
Credit: yes

Georgia College
Admissions and Records
Campus Box 023
Milledgeville, GA 31061
912-453-5004
Minimum Age: 62
Tuition: free
Basic Fees: none
Credit: yes

Georgia Southern University
Admissions
Landrum Box 8024
Statesboro, GA 30460-8024
912-681-5531
Minimum Age: 62
Tuition: free
Basic Fees: none
Credit: yes

Georgia Southwestern College
800 Wheatly St.
Americus, GA 31709-4693
912-928-1273
Minimum Age: 62
Tuition: free
Basic Fees: none
Credit: yes

Georgia State University
PO Box 4009
Atlanta, GA 30302-4009
404-651-2365
Minimum Age: 62
Tuition: free
Basic Fees: $82 per quarter
Credit: yes

HAWAII

University of Hawaii: Hawaii Community College
200 West Kawili St.
Hilo, HI 96720
808-933-3611
Minimum Age: 60

Tuition: free (no summer classes)
Basic Fees: none
Credit: yes

University of Hawaii:
Honolulu Community College
874 Dillingham Blvd.
Honolulu, HI 96817
808-845-9129
Minimum Age: 60
Tuition: free
Basic Fees: $10 per semester
Credit: yes

University of Hawaii:
Kapiolani Community College
4303 Diamond Head Rd.
Honolulu, HI 96816
808-734-9559
Minimum Age: 60
Tuition: free
Basic Fees: $10 per semester
Credit: yes

University of Hawaii:
Kauai Community College
3-1901 Kaomualii Hwy.
Lihue, HI 96766
808-245-8212
Minimum Age: 60
Tuition: free
Basic Fees: none
Credit: yes

University of Hawaii:
Leeward Community College
96-045 Ala Ike
Pearl City, HI 96782
808-455-0217
Minimum Age: 60
Tuition: free
Basic Fees: none
Credit: yes

University of Hawaii at Manoa
2600 Campus

Honolulu, HI 96822
808-956-8975
Minimum Age: 60
Tuition: free
Basic Fees: none
Credit: yes

University of Hawaii:
Maui Community College
310 Kaahumanu Ave.
Kahului, HI 96732
808-244-9181
Minimum Age: 60
Tuition: free
Basic Fees: $4 per session plus
50 cents per credit hour
Credit: yes

University of Hawaii:
Windward Community College
45-720 Keaahala Rd.
Kaneohe, HI 96744
808-235-7432
Minimum Age: 60
Tuition: free
Basic Fees: none
Credit: yes

IDAHO

Boise State University
1910 University Dr.
Boise, ID 83725
800-824-7017
Minimum Age: 60
Tuition: $5 per credit hour
Basic Fees: $20 per semester
Credit: yes

College of Southern Idaho
Admissions
PO Box 1238
Twin Falls, ID 83303-1238
208-733-9554
Minimum Age: 60
Tuition: free

Basic Fees: none
Credit: yes

Idaho State University
Enrollment Planning
Campus Box 8054
Pocatello, ID 83209
208-236-2123
Minimum Age: 60
Tuition: $5 per credit hour
Basic Fees: $20 per semester
Credit: yes

Lewis Clark State College
500 Eighth Ave.
Lewiston, ID 83501
208-799-5272
Minimum Age: 60
Tuition: $5 per credit hour
Basic Fees: $20 per semester
Credit: yes

North Idaho College
Business Office
1000 West Garden Ave.
Coeur d'Alene, ID 83814
208-769-3311
Minimum Age: 60
Tuition: 50 percent off (regular tuition $50 per credit hour)
Basic Fees: $130 full-time
Credit: yes

ILLINOIS

Belleville Area College
2500 Carlyle Rd.
Belleville, IL 62221
618-235-2700
Minimum Age: 60
Tuition: $35 per credit hour
Basic Fees: $10 one time application fee
Credit: yes

Chicago State University
95th St. and King Dr.

Chicago, IL 60628
312-995-2513
Minimum Age: 65
Tuition: free (income limitation of $12,000 annually)
Basic Fees: none (lab also waived)
Credit: yes

College of Du Page
22nd St. and Lambert Rd.
Glen Ellyn, IL 60137
708-858-2800, ext. 2482
Minimum Age: 65
Tuition: $3.45 per credit hour
Basic Fees: none
Credit: yes

Illinois State University
Adult Services
Campus Box 2200
Normal, IL 61790-2200
309-438-2181
Minimum Age: 65
Tuition: free
Basic Fees: none
Credit: no

Northern Illinois University
Office of Admissions
101 Williston Hall
Dekalb, IL 60115-2857
815-753-0446
Minimum Age: 65
Tuition: free (income limitation of $14,000 annually)
Basic Fees: $20-$40 per session
Credit: yes

INDIANA

Ball State University
Office of Admission
Lucina Hall
Muncie, IN 47306
317-285-8300
Minimum Age: 60

Tuition: 50 percent off (regular tuition $478 for up to three credit hours; $638 for four to five credit hours; $1008 for six to eight credit hours)
Basic Fees: none
Credit: yes

Indiana University at Kokomo
PO Box 9003
Kokomo, IN 46904-9003
317-453-2000
Minimum Age: 60
Tuition: 50 percent off up to 9 hours (regular tuition $83.30-$87.05 per credit hour)
Basic Fees: $15 maximum activity fee plus $2 per credit hour
Credit: yes

Indiana University-Purdue University at Fort Wayne
Financial Aid
2101 Coliseum Blvd., East
Fort Wayne, IN 46805
219-481-6820
Minimum Age: 60
Tuition: 50 percent off (regular tuition $80.25 per credit hour)
Basic Fees: none
Credit: yes

Indiana University Southeast
4201 Grant Line Rd.
New Albany, IN 47150
812-941-2212 ext. 2335
Minimum Age: 60
Tuition: 50 percent off, up to nine hours (regular tuition $87.05 per credit hour)
Basic Fees: none
Credit: yes

University of Southern Indiana
8600 University Blvd.
Evansville, IN 47712

812-464-1765
Minimum Age: 60
Tuition: $5 per class
Basic Fees: $10 ID fee per session
Credit: yes

IOWA

Clinton Community College
Enrollment Services
1000 Lincoln Blvd.
Clinton, IA 52732-6299
319-242-6841
Minimum Age: 62
Tuition: $3.65 per semester hour
Basic Fees: $5.50 per hour
Credit: yes

Des Moines Area Community College
Records and Services
2006 South Ankeny Blvd.
Ankeny, IA 50021
515-964-6241
Minimum Age: 65
Tuition: free
Basic Fees: none
Credit: yes

Indian Hills Community College
Admissions
525 Grandview St.
Ottumwa, IA 52501
515-683-5111
Minimum Age: 62
Tuition: 50 percent off (regular tuition $40 per credit hour)
Basic Fees: $4.50 per credit hour
Credit: yes

Iowa Western Community College
Business
923 East Washington St.
Clarinda, IA 51632

712-542-5117
Minimum Age: 55
Tuition: $22 per credit hour (3 credit hour limit per semester)
Basic Fees: $15 one time application fee plus $6 per credit hour
Credit: yes

KANSAS

Allen County Community College
1801 North Cottonwood St.
Iola, KS 66749
316-365-5116
Minimum Age: 60
Tuition: $28 per credit hour (book rental and fees are free)
Basic Fees: none
Credit: yes

Barton County Community College
Registrar
Rt. 3, Box 1362
Great Bend, KS 67530-9283
316-792-2701 ext. 215
Minimum Age: 65 (must be resident of county)
Tuition: free
Basic Fees: $10 per credit hour
Credit: yes

Butler County Community College
901 South Haverhill Rd.
Eldorado, KS 67042
316-321-2222
Minimum Age: 60
Tuition: free
Basic Fees: $10 per credit hour
Credit: yes

Cloud County Community College
221 Campus Dr.

PO Box 1002
Concordia, KS 66901-1002
913-234-1435
Minimum Age: 55
Tuition: $24 per credit hour (fee will increase soon)
Basic Fees: none
Credit: yes

Coffeyville Community College
400 West 11th
Coffeyville, KS 67337
316-251-7700
Minimum Age: 60
Tuition: free
Basic Fees: $10 per credit hour
Credit: yes

Emporia State University
Admissions
1200 Commercial
Emporia, KS 66801-5087
316-341-5465
Minimum Age: 60
Tuition: free
Basic Fees: none
Credit: no

Fort Hays State University
600 Park St.
Hays, KS 67601-4099
913-628-4222
Minimum Age: 60
Tuition: free
Basic Fees: none
Credit: no

Garden City Community College
Dean of Admissions
801 Campus Dr.
Garden City, KS 67846
316-276-7611
Minimum Age: 65
Tuition: free

Basic Fees: $7 per credit hour
Credit: yes

Hutchinson Community College
1300 North Plum St.
Hutchinson, KS 67501
316-665-3535
Minimum Age: 60
Tuition: $21 per credit hour
Basic Fees: none
Credit: yes

KENTUCKY

Ashland Community College
1400 College Dr.
Ashland, KY 41101
606-329-2999
Minimum Age: 65
Tuition: free
Basic Fees: none
Credit: yes

Eastern Kentucky University
Coates Box 2A
203 Jones Building
Richmond, KY 40475-3101
606-622-2106
Minimum Age: 65
Tuition: free
Basic Fees: none
Credit: yes

Elizabethtown Community College
600 College Street Rd.
Elizabethtown, KY 42701
502-769-1632
Minimum Age: 65
Tuition: free
Basic Fees: none
Credit: yes

Lexington Community College
203 Oswald Bldg., Cooper Dr.
Lexington, KY 40506-0235
606-257-4872

Minimum Age: 65
Tuition: free
Basic Fees: none
Credit: yes

Madisonville Community College
2000 College Dr.
Madisonville, KY 42431
502-821-2250
Minimum Age: 65
Tuition: free
Basic Fees: none
Credit: yes

Maysville Community College
1755 US 68
Maysville, KY 41056
606-759-7141
Minimum Age: 65
Tuition: free
Basic Fees: none
Credit: yes

Morehead State University
306 Howell McDowell
Morehead, KY 40351
606-783-2000
Minimum Age: 65
Tuition: free
Basic Fees: none
Credit: yes

Murray State University
Bursars Office
PO Box 9
Murray, KY 42071-0009
502-762-3741
800-272-4678
Minimum Age: 65
Tuition: free
Basic Fees: none
Credit: yes

Northern Kentucky University
Office of Admissions

Highland Heights, KY 41099
606-572-5220
800-637-9948
Minimum Age: 65
Tuition: free
Basic Fees: none
Credit: yes

University of Kentucky
100 Funkhouser Bldg.
Lexington, KY 40506-0054
606-257-2000
Minimum Age: 65
Tuition: free
Basic Fees: none
Credit: yes

University of Louisville
Office of Admissions
University of Louisville
Louisville, KY 40292
502-852-6531
Minimum Age: 65
Tuition: free (10 percent off
non-academic)
Basic Fees: none
Credit: yes

LOUISIANA

Delgado Community College
615 City Park Ave.
New Orleans, LA 70119
504-483-4114
Minimum Age: 60
Tuition: three credit hours free
per semester
Basic Fees: $15 per semester
Credit: yes

Grambling State University
PO Box 864
Grambling, LA 71245
318-274-2435
Minimum Age: 65
Tuition: free

Basic Fees: $15 per semester
Credit: yes

Louisiana State University and Agricultural and Mechanical College
Records and Registration
112 Thomas Boyd Hall
Baton Rouge, LA 70803
504-388-1175
Minimum Age: 65
Tuition: free
Basic Fees: none
Credit: yes

Louisiana State University at Alexandria
Financial Aid
8100 Highway 71 South
Alexandria, LA 71302-9633
318-473-6423
Minimum Age: 65
Tuition: free
Basic Fees: none
Credit: yes

Louisiana State University, Baton Rouge
Office of Admissions
Room 110 Thomas Boyd Hall
Baton Rouge, LA 70803
504-388-1175
Minimum Age: 65
Tuition: free
Basic Fees: none
Credit: yes

Louisiana State University at Eunice
PO Box 1129
Eunice, LA 70535
318-457-7311
Minimum Age: 65
Tuition: free (must pay one time
application fee of $5)

Basic Fees: $10 per semester
Credit: yes

Louisiana State University in Shreveport

Admissions and Records
One University Place
Shreveport, LA 71115
318-797-5207
Minimum Age: 65
Tuition: free
Basic Fees: $50 for part-time;
$65 for full-time
Credit: yes

Louisiana Tech University

PO Box 3178
Tech Station
Ruston, LA 71272
318-257-3036
Minimum Age: 65
Tuition: one class per quarter free
Basic Fees: $35 per quarter
Credit: yes

McNeese State University

PO Box 92495
Lake Charles, LA 70609
318-475-5000
Minimum Age: 60
Tuition: three credit hours free
per semester
Basic Fees: $10 per semester
Credit: yes

Nicholls State University

PO Box 2004
College Station
Thibodaux, LA 70310
504-448-4139
Minimum Age: 62
Tuition: three credit hours free
per semester
Basic Fees: $10 per semester
Credit: yes

Northeast Louisiana University

Student Affairs
Office of the Registrar
Monroe, LA 71209-1110
318-342-5252
Minimum Age: 60
Tuition: three credit hours free
per semester
Basic Fees: $15 per semester
Credit: yes

Northwestern State University

Fiscal Affairs
Cashier Section
Natchitoches, LA 71497
318-357-4503
Minimum Age: 60
Tuition: three credit hours free
per semester
Basic Fees: $5 one time
application fee
Credit: yes

Southeastern Louisiana University

Enrollment Services
PO Drawer 752
Hammond, LA 70402-0752
504-549-2123
Minimum Age: 60
Tuition: three credit hours free
per semester
Basic Fees: $10 per semester
Credit: yes

MAINE

University of Maine

Admissions
7513 W. Chadbourne Hall
Orono, ME 04469
207-581-1561
Minimum Age: 65
Tuition: free
Basic Fees: $9 for three credit

hours; $246.50 for 12 credit hours
Credit: yes

University of Maine at Augusta

Admissions
46 University Dr.
Augusta, ME 04330
207-621-3000
Minimum Age: 65
Tuition: free
Basic Fees: $4.50 per credit hour
Credit: yes

University of Maine at Farmington

102 Main St.
Farmington, ME 04938
207-778-7052
Minimum Age: 65
Tuition: No reduced rate. Case-by-case basis
Basic Fees: case-by-case basis
Credit: yes

University of Maine at Fort Kent

Admissions
25 Pleasant St.
Fort Kent, ME 04743
207-834-7500
Minimum Age: 65
Tuition: free (2 course limit)
Basic Fees: $20 for six credit hours
Credit: yes

MARYLAND

Alleghany Community College

Continuing Education
Willow Brook Rd.
Cumberland, MD 21502
301-724-7700
Minimum Age: 60
Tuition: free (non-academic only)
Basic Fees: up to $3 per course
Credit: no

Baltimore City Community College

Registration
2901 Liberty Heights Ave.
Baltimore, MD 21215
410-462-8300
Minimum Age: 60
Tuition: free
Basic Fees: $20 per credit hour (non-credit $10 per course)
Credit: yes

Bowie State University

Human Resources
14000 Jericho Park Rd.
Bowie, MD 20715
301-464-6515
Minimum Age: 62
Tuition: free
Basic Fees: $83.50 for up to 11 credit hours; $369 for 12 or more credit hours
Credit: yes

Coppin State College

Human Resources
2500 W. North Ave.
Baltimore, MD 21216
410-383-5990
Minimum Age: 60
Tuition: free
Basic Fees: part-time $47 plus $8 per credit hour; $333 for 12 credit hours
Credit: yes

Frostburg State University

Admissions
Frostburg, MD 21532-1099
687-680-4201
Minimum Age: 60
Tuition: free (three-course limit)
Basic Fees: nine credit hours approximately $115
Credit: yes

270

Salisbury State University

Human Resources
Camden and College Avenues
Salisbury, MD 21801-6862
410-543-6035
Minimum Age: 60
Tuition: free (two-course limit)
Basic Fees: six credit hours
approximately $18
Credit: yes

St. Mary's College of Maryland

Admission
St. Mary's City, MD 20686
301-862-0292
Minimum Age: 65
Tuition: free; apply for waiver
Basic Fees: $230 for nine to 11
credit hours, if space is available
Credit: yes

University of Maryland, College Park

Golden ID Program
College Park, MD 20742
301-314-8237
Minimum Age: 65 (60 if
employed less than 20 hours per
week)
Tuition: $103.50 per semester
(three-class limit per semester)
Basic Fees: $30 one-time applica-
tion fee
Credit: yes

MASSACHUSETTS

Berkshire Community College

1350 West St.
Pittsfield, MA 01201
413-499-4660
Minimum Age: 60
Tuition: free
Basic Fees: $25 per credit hour
Credit: yes

Boston University

881 Commonwealth Ave.
6th Floor
Boston, MA 02215
617-353-2300
Minimum Age: 60
Tuition: $20 per course
Basic Fees: none
Credit: no

Bridgewater State College

Gates House
Bridgewater, MA 02325
508-697-1237
Minimum Age: 60
Tuition: 50 percent off regular fee
Basic Fees: $201.42 for three
credit hours; $491.25 for 12 cred-
it hours
Credit: yes

Briston Community College

777 Elsbree St.
Fall River, MA 02720
508-678-2811
Minimum Age: 60
Tuition: $42 for three credit
hours, $55 for four credit hours
Basic Fees: none
Credit: yes

Bunker Hill Community College

250 New Rutherford Ave.
Boston, MA 02129-2991
617-228-2000
Minimum Age: 60
Tuition: free
Basic Fees: $35 per credit hour
Credit: yes

Cape Cod Community College

Rt. 132
West Barnstable, MA 02668-1599
508-362-2131

Minimum Age: 60
Tuition: 50 percent off fees;
apply for waiver
Basic Fees: $138 for three credit
hours
Credit: yes

Salem State College
352 Lafayette St.
Salem, MA 01970
508-741-6200
Minimum Age: 60
Tuition: $41.50 per credit
Basic Fees: $61 per credit hour;
full-time $743.50
Credit: yes

North Adams State College
Admissions
Church St.
North Adams, MA 01247
413-662-5000
Minimum Age: 65
Tuition: free
Basic Fees: none
Credit: yes

MICHIGAN

Alpena Community College
666 Johnson St.
Alpena, MI 49707
517-356-9021
Minimum Age: 60
Basic Fees: $10 per session plus
$6 per credit hour
Tuition: free
Credit: yes

Central Michigan University
Admissions
105 Warriner Hall
Mount Pleasant, MI 48859
517-774-3076
Minimum Age: 60
Tuition: free

Basic Fees: none
Credit: no

Charles Stewart Mott Community College
4503 East Court St.
Flint, MI 48503
810-762-0200
Minimum Age: 60
Tuition: free (50 percent off non-academic)
Basic Fees: none
Credit: yes

Delta College
Admissions
University Center, MI 48710
517-686-9092
Minimum Age: 60
Tuition: 50 percent off (regular
tuition $65 per credit hour)
Basic Fees: $25 per session
Credit: yes

Glen Oaks Community College
62249 Shimmel Rd.
Centreville, MI 49032
616-467-9945
Minimum Age: 60
Tuition: based on context hours
Basic Fees: none
Credit: yes

Macomb Community College
2800 College Dr., SW
Sidney, MI 48885-0300
517-328-2111 ext. 215
Minimum Age: 60
Tuition: in-district 50 percent off
tuition; out-of-district $22 per
credit hour
Basic Fees: $1.50 per credit hour
Credit: yes

Oakland Community College
District Office

George AB
Administration Center
2480 Opdyke Rd.
Bloomfield Hills, MI 48304-2266
810-540-1567
Minimum Age: 60
Tuition: 20 percent off (regular
tuition $47 per credit hour)
Basic Fees: $35 per session
Credit: yes

Wayne State University

Office of Undergraduate
Admission
Detroit, MI 48202
313-577-3577
Minimum Age: 60
Tuition: 50 percent off (regular
tuition $98 per credit hour)
Basic Fees: $70 per semester
Credit: yes

Western Michigan University

Office of Admission and
Orientation
Kalamazoo, MI 49008-5120
616-387-2000
Minimum Age: 62
Tuition: free
Basic Fees: none
Credit: no

University of Michigan, Ann Arbor

515 East Jefferson
1220 Student Activities
Ann Arbor, MI 48109-1316
313-764-7433
Minimum Age: 65
Tuition: 50 percent off (regular
tuition full-time $2,500)
Basic Fees: $87 per term
Credit: yes

MINNESOTA

Anoka-Ramsey Community College

11200 Mississippi Blvd., NW
Coon Rapids, MN 55433
612-427-2600
Minimum Age: 62
Tuition: $10 per credit hour
Basic Fees: $15 per session plus
$1 per credit hour
Credit: yes

Austin Community College

1600 Eighth Ave., NW
Austin, MN 55912
507-433-0535
Minimum Age: 62
Tuition: $6 per credit hour
Basic Fees: up to seven credit
hours free; 8 or more credit
hours $15 plus $2 per credit hour
Credit: yes

Bemidji State University

1500 Birchmont Dr., NE
Bemidji, MN 56601
218-755-2040
Minimum Age: 62
Tuition: $6 per credit hour
Basic Fees: $15 per session
Credit: yes

Brainerd Community College

501 West College Dr.
Brainerd, MN 56401
218-828-2508
Minimum Age: 62
Tuition: $10 per credit hour
Basic Fees: $15 per session plus
$2 per credit hour
Credit: yes

Fergus Falls Community College

1414 College Way

Fergus Falls, MN 56537
218-739-7501
Minimum Age: 62
Tuition: $6 per credit hour
Basic Fees: up to seven credit
hours free; 8 or more credit
hours $15 plus $3 per credit hour
Credit: yes

Hibbing Community College
1515 East 25th St.
Hibbing, MN 55746
218-262-6700
Minimum Age: 62
Tuition: $6 per credit hour
Basic Fees: up to seven credit
hours free; 8 or more credit
hours $15 plus $2 per credit hour
Credit: yes

Minnesota Universities, Twin Cities
Room 240, Pillsbury Dr., SE
Minneapolis, MN 55455
800-752-1000
Minimum Age: 62
Tuition: $6 per credit hour
Basic Fees: none
Credit: yes

MISSISSIPPI

Copiah-Lincoln Community College
Financial Aid Office
PO Box 649
Wesson, MS 39191
601-643-8307
Minimum Age: 65
Tuition: free
Basic Fees: none
Credit: yes

Delta State University
Registrar
Cleveland, MS 38733

601-846-4656
Minimum Age: 60
Tuition: $10 for one course up to
three credit hours
Basic Fees: none
Credit: yes

East Central Community College
Admissions
Decatur, MS 39327
601-635-2111
Minimum Age: 65
Tuition: free
Basic Fees: none
Credit: yes

Holmes Community College
PO Box 369
Goodman, MS 39079
601-472-2312
Minimum Age: 65
Tuition: free
Basic Fees: none
Credit: yes

Itawamba Community College
Admissions
602 W. Hill St.
Fulton, MS 38843
601-862-3101
Minimum Age: 65
Tuition: free
Basic Fees: none
Credit: yes

Jones County Junior College
Guidance Office
900 South Court St.
Ellisville, MS 39437
601-477-4025
Minimum Age: 65
Tuition: free
Basic Fees: none
Credit: yes

Meridian Community College
910 Highway 19 North
Meridian, MS 39307
601-483-8241
Minimum Age: 65
Tuition: $2.50 per class
Basic Fees: none
Credit: yes

Mississippi Gulf Coast Community College, Jackson County Campus
Business Services
PO Box 100
Gautier, MS 39553
601-497-9602
Minimum Age: 65 (ages 62 to 64 also qualify if retired)
Tuition: free
Basic Fees: none
Credit: yes

MISSOURI

Crowder College
601 LaClede Ave.
Neosho, MO 64850
417-451-3223
Minimum Age: 60
Tuition: free
Basic Fees: $12 per credit hour
Credit: yes

East Central College
Registration
PO Box 529
Union, MO 63048
314-583-5193
Minimum Age: 60
Tuition: free
Basic Fees: none
Credit: yes

Jefferson College
Continuing Education
1000 Viking Dr.

Hillsboro, MO 63050
314-789-3951
Minimum Age: 60
Tuition: 50 per cent off (regular tuition $38 per credit hour)
Basic Fees: $1 for a Lifetime Card
Credit: no

Lincoln University
820 Chestnut St.
Jefferson City, MO 65102
314-681-5000
Minimum Age: 60
Tuition: $12 per course
Basic Fees: $17 per session
Credit: no

Longview Community College
500 Longview Rd. SW
Lee's Summit, MO 64081
816-672-2000
Minimum Age: 65
Tuition: free
Basic Fees: none
Credit: yes

Maple Woods Community College
Development Center
2601 Northeast Barry Rd.
Kansas City, MO 64156
816-437-3050
Minimum Age: 65
Tuition: free
Basic Fees: none
Credit: yes

Missouri Southern State College
Business Office
3950 East Newman Rd.
Joplin, MO 64801-1595
417-625-9300
Minimum Age: 60
Tuition: free
Basic Fees: none
Credit: yes

Missouri Western State College
4525 Downs Dr.
St. Joseph, MO 64507
816-271-4200
Minimum Age: 60
Tuition: free
Basic Fees: none
Credit: yes

Moberly Area Community College
Financial Aid Office
College Ave. and Rollins St.
Moberly, MO 65270
816-263-4110
Minimum Age: 60
Tuition: free
Basic Fees: none
Credit: yes

St. Louis Community College
Office of Admission
11333 Big Bend Blvd.
Kirkwood, MO 63122
314-984-7601
Minimum Age: 62
Tuition: 50 percent off (regular tuition $40 per credit hour)
Basic Fees: none
Credit: yes

MONTANA

Dawson Community College
Business Office
300 College Dr.
Glendive, MT 59330
406-365-3396
Minimum Age: 60
Tuition: free
Basic Fees: none (most books can be borrowed)
Credit: yes

Flathead Valley Community College
777 Grandview Dr.
Kalispell, MT 59901
406-756-3846
Minimum Age: 62
Tuition: $30.25 per credit hour
Basic Fees: none
Credit: yes

Fort Belknap College
PO Box 159
Harlem, MT 59526
406-353-2607
Minimum Age: 55 (must be a member of a federally recognized tribe)
Tuition: free
Basic Fees: none
Credit: yes

Fort Peck Community College
PO Box 398
Poplar, MT 59255
406-768-5551
Minimum Age: 60
Tuition: free
Basic Fees: $12 per credit hour
Credit: yes

Miles Community College
2715 Dickinson St.
Miles City, MT 59301
406-232-3031
Minimum Age: 62
Tuition: free
Basic Fees: none
Credit: yes

Montana College of Mineral Science and Technology
1300 West Park St.
Butte, MT 59701
406-496-4178
800-445-8324
Minimum Age: 62

Tuition: apply for waiver
Basic Fees: $26.25 for three credit hours; $171 for 12 credit hours
Credit: yes

Northern Montana College
PO Box 7751
Havre, MT 59501
406-265-3700
Minimum Age: 62
Tuition: free
Basic Fees: $80.25 for three credit hours
Credit: yes

Western Montana College at the University of Montana
Continuing Education
710 South Atlantic
Dillon, MT 59725
406-683-7537
Minimum Age: 62
Tuition: one credit hour $20; $3 for each additional credit hour
Basic Fees: $30
Credit: yes

University of Montana
Missoula, MT 59812
406-243-0211
Minimum Age: 62
Tuition: all state supported costs waived, no discount on tuition
Basic Fees: $30 one time fee
Credit: yes

NEBRASKA

Chadron State College
Admissions
1000 Main St.
Chadron, NE 69337
308-432-6263
Minimum Age: 62
Tuition: no discount on tuition
Basic Fees: $35 for three

credit hours
Credit: yes

McNook Community College
Registrar
1205 East Third St.
McNook, NE 69001
308-345-6303
800-348-5343
Minimum Age: 62
Tuition: free
Basic Fees: none
Credit: no

Metropolitan Community College
Student Accounts
PO Box 3777
Omaha, NE 68103
402-457-5231
Minimum Age: 62
Tuition: 50 percent off (regular tuition $23 per credit hour)
Basic Fees: none
Credit: yes

Mid-Plains Community College
Accounting
1101 Halligan Dr.
North Platte, NE 69101
308-532-8740
Minimum Age: 60
Tuition: free
Basic Fees: $1.50 per credit hour
Credit: yes

Nebraska Indian Community College
Financial Aid Office
Mayce, NE 42837
402-878-2414
Minimum Age: 55
Tuition: free
Basic Fees: $10 one time application fee
Credit: yes

277

Southeast Community College, Beatrice Campus

Adult Education
Rt. 2, Box 35A
Beatrice, NE 68310
402-228-3468
Minimum Age: 62
Tuition: no discount on tuition
(regular tuition $35.25 per credit
hour)
Basic Fees: none
Credit: no

Southeast Community College, Lincoln Campus

Cashier
8800 O St.
Lincoln, NE 68520
402-437-2600
Minimum Age: 62
Tuition: no discount on tuition
Cashier: 402-437-2558
Basic Fees: varies by class
Credit: no

Southeast Community College, Milford Campus

Student Accounts
Rt. 2, Box D
Milford, NE 68405
402-761-2131
800-999-7223
Minimum Age: 65
Tuition: no discount on tuition
Basic Fees: varies by class
Credit: no

NEVADA

Community College of Southern Nevada

3200 East Cheyenne Ave.
North Las Vegas, NV 89030
702-651-4060
Minimum Age: 62
Tuition: free

Basic Fees: none
Credit: yes

Northern Nevada Community College

1500 College Pkwy.
Elko, NV 89801
702-738-8493
Minimum Age: 62
Tuition: free
Basic Fees: none
Credit: yes

Truckee Meadows Community College

7000 Dandini Blvd.
Reno, NV 89512
702-673-7000
Minimum Age: 62
Tuition: free
Basic Fees: none
Credit: yes

University of Nevada, Las Vegas

4505 Maryland Pkwy.
Las Vegas, NV 89154-1021
702-895-3011
Minimum Age: 62
Tuition: free
Basic Fees: none
Credit: yes

University of Nevada, Reno

Records and Enrollment
Services
Reno, NV 89557
702-784-6865
Minimum Age: 62
Tuition: tuition waiver fall-spring,
50 percent off during summer
Basic Fees: none
Credit: yes

Western Nevada Community College

2201 West College Pkwy.

Carson City, NV 89703
702-887-3138
Minimum Age: 62
Tuition: free
Basic Fees: none
Credit: yes

NEW HAMPSHIRE

New Hampshire Technical College, Berlin
2020 Riverside Dr.
Berlin, NH 03570
603-752-1113
800-445-4525
Minimum Age: 65
Tuition: free
Basic Fees: $16 for three credit hours
Credit: yes

New Hampshire Technical College, Claremont
One College Dr.
Claremont, NH 03743
603-542-7744
Minimum Age: 65
Tuition: free
Basic Fees: $10 per course
Credit: yes

New Hampshire Technical College, Manchester
1066 Front St.
Manchester, NH 03102
603-668-6706
Minimum Age: 65
Tuition: free
Basic Fees: none
Credit: yes

New Hampshire Technical College, Nashua
505 Amherst St.
Nashua, NH 03063
603-882-6923

Minimum Age: 65
Tuition: free
Basic Fees: none
Credit: no

New Hampshire Technical College, Stratham
Tech Dr. and Rt. 101
277 Portsmouth Ave.
Stratham, NH 03885
603-772-1194
Minimum Age: 65
Tuition: free
Basic Fees: none
Credit: yes

New Hampshire Technical Institute
Institute Dr.
Concord, NH 03301-7412
603-225-1800
Minimum Age: 65
Tuition: free
Basic Fees: none
Credit: yes

Notre Dame College
2321 Elm St.
Manchester, NH 03104
603-669-4298
Minimum Age: 65
Tuition: free (two-course per semester limit; six courses per year)
Basic Fees: $60 per semester
Credit: yes

Plymouth State College of the University System of New Hampshire
Bursars Office
17 High St.
Plymouth, NH 03264-1600
603-535-2237
Minimum Age: 65

Tuition: free
Basic Fees: $35 per credit hour
Credit: yes

School for Lifelong Learning
Learner Services
NSNH
125 N. State St.
Concord, NH 03301
603-228-8300
Minimum Age: 65
Tuition: free
Basic Fees: $15 per session
Credit: yes

University of New Hampshire at Manchester
220 Hackett Hill Rd.
Manchester, NH 03102
603-668-0700
Minimum Age: 65
Tuition: free up to eight credit hours or two non-credit courses; no discount if courses are being taken for economic gain; space available basis
Basic Fees: none
Credit: yes

NEW JERSEY

Atlantic Community College
5100 Black Horse Pike
Mays Landing, NJ 08330
609-343-4922
Minimum Age: 62
Tuition: free
Basic Fees: $20 per session
Credit: yes

Bergen Community College
Admissions and Registration
400 Paramus Rd.
Paramus, NJ 07652
201-447-7857
Minimum Age: 65

Tuition: $9.50 per credit hour
Basic Fees: $8.60 per credit hour
Credit: yes

Brookdale Community College
765 Newman Springs Rd.
Lincroft, NJ 07738
908-842-1900
Minimum Age: 65
Tuition: free
Basic Fees: $28 for three credit hours
Credit: yes

Burlington County College
Admission
County Rt. 530
Pemberton, NJ 08068
609-894-9311
Minimum Age: 62
Tuition: $65 for three credit hours
Basic Fees: none
Credit: yes

Camden County College
PO Box 200
Blackwood, NJ 08012
609-227-7200
Minimum Age: 62 (55 if unemployed)
Tuition: free
Basic Fees: none
Credit: yes

County College of Morris
214 Center Grove Rd.
Randolf, NJ 07869
201-328-5000
Minimum Age: 65
Tuition: $5 per credit hour
Basic Fees: none
Credit: yes

Essex County College
303 University Ave.
Newark, NJ 07102

201-877-3100
Minimum Age: 60
Tuition: free
Basic Fees: none
Credit: yes

Rowan State College
Oak Hall
Glassboro, NJ 08028
609-256-4200
Minimum Age: 55
Tuition: no fee if space is available
Basic Fees: none
Credit: no

Gloucester County College
Business Office
Tanyard Rd.
Deptford Township
RR #4, Box 203
Sewell Post Office, NJ 08080
609-468-5000
Minimum Age: 60
Tuition: $5 per credit hour
Basic Fees: $10 per credit hour
Credit: yes

Jersey City State College
2039 Kennedy Blvd.
Bursars Office
Jersey City, NJ 07305
201-200-3234
Minimum Age: 62
Tuition: free
Basic Fees: $73.50 for three credit hours
Credit: yes

Kean College of New Jersey
1000 Morris Ave.
Union, NJ 07083
908-527-2195
Minimum Age: 62
Tuition: free if space is available
Basic Fees: $60 for three credit hours

Credit: yes

Mercer County Community College
1200 Old Trenton Rd.
Trenton, NJ 08690-1099
609-586-0505
Minimum Age: 65
Tuition: free, residents of Mercer Co.
Basic Fees: none
Credit: yes

Middlesex County College
155 Mill Rd.
PO Box 3050
Edison, NJ 08818
808-906-2510
Minimum Age: 65
Tuition: apply for waiver
Basic Fees: $20 per semester plus $6 per credit hour
Credit: yes

Montclair State College
Normal Ave. and Valley Rd.
Upper Montclair, NJ 07043
201-655-4136
Minimum Age: 65
Tuition: free
Basic Fees: $25 per session
Credit: yes

Ocean County College
College Dr.
PO Box 2001
Toms River, NJ 08754
908-255-0304
Minimum Age: 65
Tuition: $24 per credit hour
Basic Fees: $15 per semester
Credit: yes

Ramapo College of New Jersey
505 Ramapo Valley Rd.
Mahwah, NJ 07430

201-529-7700
Minimum Age: 65
Tuition: free
Basic Fees: none
Credit: no

State University of New Jersey, Rutgers

Office of University
Undergraduate Admissions
Administrative Services Bldg.
PO Box 2101
New Brunswick, NJ 08903-2101
908-445-3770
Minimum Age: 62
Tuition: free
Basic Fees: none
Credit: no

NEW MEXICO

Clovis Community College

417 Schepps Blvd.
Clovis, NM 88101
505-769-4025
Minimum Age: 65
Tuition: $13 first credit hour, $5
for each additional credit hour
Basic Fees: none
Credit: yes

New Mexico State College at Carlsbad

1500 University Dr.
Carlsbad, NM 88220
505-885-8831
Minimum Age: 65
Tuition: $6 per credit hour
Basic Fees: $10 one time admission fee
Credit: yes

New Mexico State University

Registrars Office
Las Cruces, NM 88003
505-646-3121

Minimum Age: 65
Tuition: $25 per hour (six credit
hour limit in the fall) NM residents only
Basic Fees: $15 per semester for
part-time (full-time free)
Credit: yes

New Mexico State University at Alamogordo

Admissions
PO Box 477
Alamogordo, NM 88311
505-439-3600
Minimum Age: 65
Tuition: $8 per credit hour for in-
district, $13 per credit hour out-
of-district
Basic Fees: $10 one time admission fee (six credit hour limit)
Credit: yes

New Mexico State University at Grants

1500 North Third St.
Grants, NM 87020
505-287-7981
Minimum Age: 65
Tuition: $8 per credit hour
Basic Fees: $10 one time application fee
Credit: yes

University of New Mexico

Cashier
Student Services Center
Room 140
Albuquerque, NM 87131
505-277-5363
800-225-5866
Minimum Age: 65
Tuition: $5 per credit hour (6
credit hour limit)
Basic Fees: none
Credit: yes

NEW YORK

Adirondack Community College
Registrar
Bay Rd.
Queensbury, NY 12804
518-743-2264
Minimum Age: 60
Tuition: free
Basic Fees: none
Credit: no

Broome Community College
Student Accounts
PO Box 1017
Binghamton, NY 13902
607-778-5000
Minimum Age: 60
Tuition: free
Basic Fees: none
Credit: no

Cayuga County Community College
Records Office
197 Franklin St.
Auburn, NY 13021
315-255-1743
Minimum Age: 60
Tuition: free if space is available
Basic Fees: none
Credit: no

City University of New York: Baruch College
PO Box 279
17 Lexington Ave.
New York, NY 10010
212-802-2222
Minimum Age: 62
Tuition: free
Basic Fees: $52 per session
Credit: yes

City University of New York: Bronx Community College
Bursars Office
W. 181st and University Ave.
New York, NY 10453
718-289-5100
Minimum Age: 65
Tuition: free
Basic Fees: $52 per session
Credit: yes

City University of New York: Brooklyn College
2900 Bedford Ave.
1602 William James Hall
Brooklyn, NY 11210
718-951-5000
Minimum Age: 65
Tuition: $50 per session
Basic Fees: $50 per session
Credit: yes

City University of New York: City College
Convent Ave. at 138th St.
New York, NY 10031
212-650-6977
Minimum Age: 65
Tuition: free
Basic Fees: $52 per session
Credit: yes

City University of New York: College of Staten Island
Registrar
2800 Victory Blvd.
Bldg. 2A-110
Staten Island, NY 10314
718-982-2000
Minimum Age: 65
Tuition: free
Basic Fees: $52 per session
Credit: yes

City University of New York: Hostos Community College
Admissions
500 Grand Concourse
Bronx, NY 10451

283

718-518-4444
Minimum Age: 65
Tuition: $75 per semester
Basic Fees: $52 per session
Credit: yes

City University of New York: Hunter College

Admissions
695 Park Ave.
Room 203, North Bldg.
New York, NY 10021
212-772-4490
Minimum Age: 65
Tuition: free
Basic Fees: $52 per session
Credit: yes

City University of New York: Kingsborough Community College

2001 Oriental Blvd.
Brooklyn, NY 11235
718-368-5079
Minimum Age: 65
Tuition: free
Basic Fees: $70 registration fee
Credit: yes

NORTH CAROLINA

Alamance Community College

Student Services
PO Box 8000
Graham, NC 27253
910-578-2002
Minimum Age: 65
Tuition: free
Basic Fees: none
Credit: yes

Anson Community College

PO Box 126
Polkton, NC 28135
704-272-7635
Minimum Age: 65

Tuition: free
Basic Fees: $2 per quarter plus
$5 per credit hour
Credit: yes

Appalachian State University

Cashier's Office
Administration Bldg.
Boone, NC 28608
704-262-2120
Minimum Age: 65
Tuition: free plus fees (lab etc.)
Basic Fees: $117.50 for three
credit hours; $235 for six credit
hours
Credit: yes

Beaufort County Community College

PO Box 1069
Washington, NC 27889
919-946-6194
Minimum Age: 65
Tuition: free
Basic Fees: maximum $6 activity
fee per semester
Credit: yes

Bladen Community College

PO Box 266
Dublin, NC 28332
910-862-2164
Minimum Age: 65
Tuition: free
Basic Fees: none
Credit: yes

Blue Ridge Community College

Rt. 2, Box 133A
Flat Rock, NC 28731-9624
704-692-3572
Minimum Age: 65
Tuition: free
Basic Fees: $1.25 per quarter
Credit: yes

Brunswick Community College
PO Box 30
Supply, NC 28462
910-754-6900
Minimum Age: 65
Tuition: free
Basic Fees: $1.05 per quarter
Credit: yes

Cape Fear Community College
411 North Front St.
Wilmington, NC 28401-3993
910-343-0481
Minimum Age: 65
Tuition: free
Basic Fees: $1 ID fee per semester, maximum $6 activity fee per semester
Credit: yes

Carteret Community College
3505 Arendell St.
Morehead City, NC 28557
919-247-4142
Minimum Age: 65
Tuition: free
Basic Fees: $3.25 for three credit hours
Credit: yes

Catawba Valley Community College
2550 Highway 70, SE
Hickory, NC 28602
704-327-7009
Minimum Age: 65
Tuition: free
Basic Fees: $1.75 per quarter
Credit: yes

North Carolina University, Raleigh
Adult Credit Program
Box 7401
Raleigh, NC 27695-7401
919-515-2434
Minimum Age: 65
Tuition: free
Basic Fees: none
Credit: yes

University of North Carolina, Chapel Hill
CB# 2200, Jackson Hall
Chapel Hill, NC 27599
919-966-3621
Minimum Age: 65
Tuition: free
Basic Fees: $10 per semester
Credit: yes

NORTH DAKOTA

North Dakota State University
PO Box 5454
Admissions
Fargo, ND 58105
701-231-8643
Minimum Age: 65
Tuition: free
Basic Fees: $20 per session
Credit: no

North Dakota State University, Bottineau and Institute of Forestry
First and Simrall Blvd.
Bottineau, ND 58318
Minimum Age: 65
701-228-2277
Minimum Age: 55
Tuition: free
Basic Fees: none
Credit: no

Standing Rock College
HCI Box 4
Fort Yates, ND 58538
701-854-3861
Tuition: free (tuition, books and fees all waived if you don't qualify for Pell Grant)

Basic Fees: none (see above)
Credit: yes

University of North Dakota: Lake Region

1801 College Dr., North
Devils Lake, ND 58301-1598
701-662-1600
Minimum Age: 65
Tuition: free
Basic Fees: none
Credit: no

University of North Dakota: Williston

1410 University Ave.
Williston, ND 58801
701-774-4210
Minimum Age: 65
Tuition: free
Basic Fees: $10 per credit hour
Credit: no

Valley City State University

101 College St., SE
Valley City, ND 58072
701-845-7990
Minimum Age: 65
Tuition: free
Basic Fees: none
Credit: no

OHIO

Belmont Technical College

120 Fox Shannon Pl.
St. Clarisville, OH 43950
614-695-9500
Minimum Age: 60
Tuition: free
Basic Fees: none
Credit: yes

Bowling Green State University

Department of Continuing
Education
McFall Center

40 College Park
Bowling Green, OH 43403
419-372-2086
Minimum Age: 60
Tuition: free if space is available
Basic Fees: none
Credit: no

Bowling Green State University: Firelands College

901 Rye Beach Rd.
Huron, OH 44839
419-433-5560
Minimum Age: 60
Tuition: free, $10 registry fee
Basic Fees: $5 per semester
Credit: no

Central Ohio Technical College

1179 University Dr.
Newark, OH 43055
614-366-9222
Minimum Age: 60
Tuition: free
Basic Fees: $5 per credit hour
Credit: no

Central State University

Registrar
1400 Brush Row Rd.
Wilberforce, OH 45384
513-376-6231
Minimum Age: 60
Tuition: free
Basic Fees: none
Credit: no

Cuyahoga Community College District

Downtown Campus
Office of Admissions
2900 Community College Ave.
Cleveland, OH 44115
216-987-4200
Minimum Age: 60
Tuition: free

Basic Fees: none
Credit: yes

Kent State University
PO Box 5190
Kent, OH 44242-0001
216-672-2444
Minimum Age: 5O and retired
or 60
Tuition: free
Basic Fees: none
Credit: no

Ohio State University
Continuing Education
152 Mount Hall
Columbus, OH 43210
614-292-8860
Minimum Age: 60
Tuition: free
Basic Fees: none
Credit: no

University of Akron
381 Buchtel Common
Akron, OH 44325-2001
216-972-7100
Minimum Age: 60
Tuition: free (three-course limit)
Basic Fees: none
Credit: no

University of Cincinnati
Office of Admission
PO Box 210091
Cincinnati, OH 45221-0091
513-556-1100
Minimum Age: 60
Tuition: free
Basic Fees: none
Credit: no

University of Toledo
Evening Session
University of Toledo

Toledo, OH 43606-3398
419-530-4137
Minimum Age: 60
Tuition: free (income limitation
of $50,000 annually)
Basic Fees: none
Credit: yes

OKLAHOMA

Cameron University
Business Office
2800 West Fore Blvd.
Lawton, OK 73505
405-581-2230
Minimum Age: 65
Tuition: free
Basic Fees: none
Credit: no

Carl Albert State College
PO Box 1507
South McLenna
Poteau, OK 74953-5208
918-647-1200
Minimum Age: 65
Tuition: free
Basic Fees: none
Credit: no

Connors State College
Business Office
Rt. 1, Box 1000
Warner, OK 74469
918-463-6250
Minimum Age: 65
Tuition: free
Basic Fees: none
Credit: no

**Oklahoma Panhandle
State University**
PO Box 430
Goodwell, OK 73939
405-349-2611

Minimum Age: 65
Tuition: free if space is available
Basic Fees: none
Credit: no

Oklahoma State University

104 Whitehurse
Stillwater, OK 74078
405-744-6858
Minimum Age: 65
Tuition: free
Basic Fees: none
Credit: no

University of Oklahoma

Office of Admissions
1000 Asp Ave., Room 127
Norman, OK 73019
405-325-2251
Minimum Age: 65
Tuition: free
Basic Fees: none
Credit: no

OREGON

Blue Mountain Community College

Continuing Education
PO Box 100
Pendleton, OR 97801
503-276-1260
Minimum Age: 60
Tuition: $10 per credit hour
Basic Fees: none
Credit: yes

Central Oregon Community College

Admissions
2600 Northwest College Way
Bend, OR 97701
541-382-6112
Minimum Age: 62
Tuition: 25 percent off (regular
tuition $32 per credit hour)

Basic Fees: $1.50 per credit hour
Credit: yes

Chemeketa Community College

Business Office
PO Box 14007
4000 Lancaster Dr., NE
Salem, OR 97305
503-399-5006
Minimum Age: 62
Tuition: 35 percent off (regular
tuition $32 per credit hour)
Basic Fees: none
Credit: yes

Clackamas Community College

19600 South Molalla Ave.
Oregon City, OR 97045
503-657-6958
Minimum Age: 62
Tuition: free
Basic Fees: none
Credit: yes

Clatsop Community College

Extended Learning
1653 Jerome Ave.
Astoria, OR 97103
503-325-0910
Minimum Age: 62
Tuition: 50 percent off (another
10 percent for early payment);
regular tuition $30 per credit hour
Basic Fees: none
Credit: yes

Lane Community College

Admissions
4000 East 30th Ave.
Eugene, OR 97405
541-726-2207
Minimum Age: 62
Tuition: 50 percent off (regular
tuition $30 per credit hour)
Basic Fees: none
Credit: yes

Linn-Benton Community College
Registration
6500 Pacific Blvd., SW
Albany, OR 97321-3779
541-917-4999
Minimum Age: 62
Tuition: 50 percent off (regular
tuition $32 per credit hour)
Basic Fees: none
Credit: yes

Mount Hood Community College
Business Office
26000 Southeast Stark St.
Gresham, OR 97030
503-667-6422
Minimum Age: 62
Tuition: free
Basic Fees: none (self-enrich-
ment classes are usually $5 each
plus materials)
Credit: yes

Oregon Institute of Technology
Registrar
3201 Campus Dr.
Klamath Falls, OR 97601-8801
541-885-1150
800-343-6653
Minimum Age: 65
Tuition: free
Basic Fees: none to audit
Credit: no

Oregon State University
Corvallis, OR 97331
503-737-4411
Minimum Age: 65
Tuition: free to audit
Basic Fees: none
Credit: no

Portland Community College
Admissions
PO Box 19000
Portland, OR 97280-0990

503-244-6111 ext. 4724
Minimum Age: 62
Tuition: 50 percent off (regular
tuition $30 per credit hour)
Basic Fees: $7 per quarter full-
time; $2 per quarter part-time
Credit: yes

Portland State University
Senior Adult Learning Center
PO Box 751
Portland, OR 97207-0751
503-725-3511
800-547-8887
Minimum Age: 65
Tuition: free to audit
Basic Fees: none
Credit: no

PENNSYLVANIA

**Bloomsburg University
of Pennsylvania**
Extended Learning
700 West Main St.
Bloomsburg, PA 17815
717-389-4420
Minimum Age: 60
Tuition: free, space available
Basic Fees: $42.50 for three cred-
it hours; $304 for 12 credit hours
Credit: yes

**Bucks County
Community College**
Swamp Rd.
Newtown, PA 18940
215-968-8100
Minimum Age: 65
Tuition: free
Basic Fees: $48-$57 per semester
Credit: yes

**Butler County
Community College**
Registrar

PO Box 1203
Butler, PA 16003-1203
412-287-8711
Minimum Age: 60
Tuition: free
Basic Fees: none
Credit: no

**California University
of Pennsylvania**
COPE Program
250 University Ave.
California, PA 15419
412-938-5930
Minimum Age: 60
Tuition: free
Basic Fees: $135 for three credit
hours; $408 for 12 credit hours
Credit: yes

**Clarion University
of Pennsylvania**
Admissions
B-16 Carrier Hall
Clarion, PA 16214
814-226-2306
Minimum Age: 65
Tuition: free
Basic Fees: none
Credit: no

**Community College of
Beaver County**
One Campus Dr.
Monaca, PA 15061
412-775-8561
Minimum Age: 65
Tuition: free
Basic Fees: $20 per session
Credit: yes

Pennsylvania State University
201 Shields
University Park, PA 16802
814-865-6528

Minimum Age: 60
Tuition: free
Basic Fees: none
Credit: yes (evening classes)

University of Pennsylvania
3440 Market St.
Suite 100
Philadelphia, PA 19104
215-898-7326
Minimum Age: 65
Tuition: $50 donation for 1 class;
$75 donation for 2 classes
Basic Fees: none
Credit: no

University of Pittsburgh
407 CL
Pittsburgh, PA 15260
412-624-7308
Minimum Age: 60
Tuition: $15 per class
Basic Fees: none
Credit: no

RHODE ISLAND

**Community College of
Rhode Island**
Admissions
400 East Ave.
Warwick, RI 02886
401-825-2285
Minimum Age: 62
Tuition: free, waiver
Basic Fees: $15 per session
Credit: yes

Rhode Island College
Records Office
600 Mt. Pleasant Ave.
Providence, RI 02908
401-456-8234
Minimum Age: 65
Tuition: free plus registration fee
Basic Fees: $135 full-time

per semester
Credit: yes

University of Rhode Island
Financial Aid
Kingston, RI 02881-0806
401-792-2314
Minimum Age: 60, waiver, space available
Tuition: free (income limitation)
Basic Fees: $96 for three credit hours; $619 for 12 credit hours plus $480 for insurance, which can be waived if you have comparable coverage
Credit: yes

SOUTH CAROLINA

Aiken Technical College
PO Drawer 696
Aiken, SC 29802-0696
803-593-9231
Minimum Age: 60
Tuition: free
Basic Fees: none
Credit: yes

Chesterfield-Marlboro Technical College
Student Development
PO Drawer 1007
Cheraw, SC 29520
803-921-6900
Minimum Age: 60
Tuition: free
Basic Fees: $14.50 per semester
Credit: yes

The Citadel
171 Moultri St.
Charleston, SC 29409
803-953-5000
Minimum Age: 60
Tuition: free, $15 registration fee
Basic Fees: $40 per semester

Credit: yes

Clemson University
Business Affairs
G-08 Sikes Hall
PO Box 345307
Clemson, SC 29634-5307
864-656-2287
Minimum Age: 65
Tuition: free
Basic Fees: none
Credit: yes

College of Charleston
Treasurers Office
Charleston, SC 29424
803-953-5592
Minimum Age: 60
Tuition: $25 per semester
Basic Fees: none
Credit: yes

Denmark Technical College
Business Office
PO Box 327
Solomon Blatt Blvd.
Denmark, SC 29042
803-793-3301
Minimum Age: 62
Tuition: free
Basic Fees: none
Credit: yes

Florence-Darlington Technical College
Admissions
PO Box 100548
Florence, SC 29501-0548
803-661-8151
Minimum Age: 60
Tuition: free
Basic Fees: none
Credit: yes

Francis Marion College
Financial Aid

PO Box 100547
Florence, SC 29501-0547
803-661-1231
Minimum Age: 65
Tuition: free
Basic Fees: none
Credit: yes

Greenville Technical College
Admissions
PO Box 5616, Station B
Greenville, SC 29606-5616
803-250-8109
Minimum Age: 60
Tuition: free
Basic Fees: $23 per semester
Credit: yes

Horry-Georgetown Technical College
Financial Aid
PO Box 1966
Conway, SC 29526
803-347-3186
Minimum Age: 60
Tuition: $10 per class; $45 for computer classes
Basic Fees: $15 per session
Credit: yes

Lander College
Admissions
PO Box 6007
320 Stanley Ave.
Greenwood, SC 29649
864-229-8307
800-768-3600
Minimum Age: 60
Tuition: free
Basic Fees: none
Credit: yes

Midlands Technical College
Admissions
PO Box 2408

Columbia, SC 29202
803-738-7764
Minimum Age: 60
Tuition: free
Basic Fees: none
Credit: yes

SOUTH DAKOTA

Black Hills State University
Records and Admissions
USB 9502
Spearfish, SD 57799-9502
605-642-6343
800-255-2478
Minimum Age: 65
Tuition: $12.86 per credit hour
Basic Fees: none
Credit: yes

Dakota State University
Cashier
Heston Hall
Madison, SD 57042
605-256-5139
Minimum Age: 65
Tuition: $12.86 per credit hour
Basic Fees: $147.33 for three credit hours
Credit: yes

Northern State University
Finance Office
1200 South Jay St.
Aberdeen, SD 57401
605-626-2544
Minimum Age: 65
Tuition: 75 percent off (regular tuition $45.78 per credit hour)
Basic Fees: $29.05 per credit hour
Credit: yes

South Dakota School of Mines and Technology
Registrars Office

501 East St. Joseph St.
Rapid City, SD 57701-3995
605-394-2400
Minimum Age: 65
Tuition: $13.25 per credit hour
Basic Fees: $15 per session
Credit: yes

University of South Dakota

Admissions
414 East Clark
Vermillion, SD 57069-2390
605-677-5434
Minimum Age: 65
Tuition: 75 percent off (regular
tuition $47.18 per credit hour)
Basic Fees: $15 per session
Credit: yes

TENNESSEE

Austin Peay State University

Admissions
PO Box 4548
Clarksville, TN 37044
615-648-7661
800-426-2604
Minimum Age: 65
Tuition: $33 per credit hour not
to exceed $75 per session
Basic Fees: none
Credit: yes

Chattanooga State Technical Community College

Records Office
4501 Amnicola Hwy.
Chattanooga, TN 37406
423-634-7702
Minimum Age: 65 (60 to audit
free)
Tuition: 50 percent off not to
exceed $45 per session
Basic Fees: $12 per session
Credit: yes

Cleveland State Community College

PO Box 3570
Cleveland, TN 37320
423-472-7141
Minimum Age: 65 (60 for audit)
Tuition: $16 per credit hour not to
exceed $45 per session; audit free
Basic Fees: $5 per semester
Credit: yes

Columbia State Community College

Admissions
PO Box 1315
Columbia, TN 38402-1315
615-540-2722
Minimum Age: 65 (60 for audit)
Tuition: $20 per session
Basic Fees: $5 one time applica-
tion fee and $5 per session
Credit: yes

Dyersburg State Community College

PO Box 648
Dyersburg, TN 38025-0648
901-286-3200
Minimum Age: 60
Tuition: 50 percent off not to
exceed $50 per session
Basic Fees: $10 - $28 per session
Credit: yes

East Tennessee State University

Admissions
PO Box 70731
Johnson City, TN 37614
423-929-4213
Minimum Age: 65 (60 for audit)
Tuition: free
Basic Fees: $75 per semester
Credit: yes

Jackson State Community College

Business Office
2046 North Pkwy.
Jackson, TN 38301
901-424-3520
Minimum Age: 65
Tuition: 50 percent off (regular tuition $43 per credit hour)
Basic Fees: $5 per session
Credit: yes

Memphis State University

Admissions Office, Room 167
Memphis, TN 38152
901-678-2101
800-669-9678
Minimum Age: 65 (60 audit)
Tuition: $75 per semester; audit free
Basic Fees: none
Credit: yes

Middle Tennessee State University

Accounting and Records
Murfreesboro, TN 37132
615-898-2111
Minimum Age: 65
Tuition: 50 percent off regular tuition
Basic Fees: $20 per session
Credit: yes

Motlow State Community College

PO Box 88100
Tullahoma, TN 37388-8100
615-393-1500
Minimum Age: 65 (60 to audit)
Tuition: $20 per credit hour not to exceed $45 per session
Basic Fees: $5 per session
Credit: yes

University of Tennessee

451 Communication Bldg.
Knoxville, TN 37996-0341
423-974-5361
Minimum Age: 65 (60 can audit free)
Tuition: $7 per credit hour not to exceed $75 per session
Basic Fees: $15 one time application fee
Credit: yes

TEXAS

Alvin Community College

Records
3110 Mustang Rd.
Alvin, TX 77511-4898
713-388-4636
Minimum Age: 65
Tuition: no discount
Basic Fees: none
Credit: no

Amarillo College

Business Office
PO Box 447
Amarillo, TX 79176
806-371-5000
Minimum Age: 65 or belong to senior citizen association
Tuition: free (some courses excluded)
Basic Fees: $3 per semester
Credit: yes

Angelina College

PO Box 1768
Lufkin, TX 75902
409-639-1301
Minimum Age: 65
Tuition: free
Basic Fees: none
Credit: no

Bee County College
Business Office
3800 Charco Rd.
Beeville, TX 78102
512-358-3130
Minimum Age: 65
Tuition: free
Basic Fees: none
Credit: yes

Southwest Texas State University
SWT General Accounting
601 University Dr.
San Marcos, TX 78666-4603
512-245-2541
Minimum Age: 65
Tuition: free, space available
Basic Fees: none
Credit: no

University of Houston, Central Campus
Bursars Office
Houston, TX 77204-2160
713-743-1096
Minimum Age: 65
Tuition: free
Basic Fees: none
Credit: no

University of North Texas
PO Box 13797
Denton, TX 76203
817-565-2681
Minimum Age: senior citizen
Tuition: free
Basic Fees: none
Credit: no

University of Texas, Austin
Office of the Registrar
Main Bldg., Room 1
Austin, TX 78712-1157
512-471-7701

Minimum Age: 65
Tuition: free
Basic Fees: none
Credit: no

UTAH

Brigham Young University
BYU Evening Classes
120 Harman Bldg.
Provo, UT 84602
801-378-2872
Minimum Age: 55
Tuition: $10 per class
Basic Fees: none
Credit: no

College of Eastern Utah
451 East 400 North
Price, UT 84501
801-637-2120
Minimum Age: 65
Tuition: $10 per class
Basic Fees: none
Credit: no

Dixie College
The Office of the Registrar
225 South 700 East
St. George, UT 84770
801-673-4811 ext. 348
Minimum Age: 62
Tuition: $10 per quarter (some classes are excluded)
Basic Fees: none
Credit: no

Salt Lake Community College
Admissions
4600 South Redwood Rd.
Salt Lake City, UT 84130
801-957-4297
Minimum Age: 63
Tuition: $10 per class
Basic Fees: none
Credit: yes

Snow College
150 East College Ave.
Ephraim, UT 84627
801-283-4021
Minimum Age: 62
Tuition: $10 per quarter
Basic Fees: none
Credit: no

Southern Utah University
Cashiers Office
351 West Center
Cedar City, UT 84720
801-586-7740
Minimum Age: 62
Tuition: $10 per quarter
Basic Fees: none
Credit: yes

University of Utah
DCE
1185 Annex
Salt Lake City, UT 84112
801-581-8113
Minimum Age: 60
Tuition: $10 per quarter
Basic Fees: none
Credit: no

Utah State University
Registrar
Logan, UT 84322-1600
801-797-1107
800-662-3950
Minimum Age: 62
Tuition: $10 per class to audit
Basic Fees: none
Credit: no

Utah Valley State College
Registrar
800 West 1200 South
Orem, UT 84058
801-222-8000
Minimum Age: 65
Tuition: $20 per class
Basic Fees: $20 one time admission fee
Credit: no

Weber State University
3750 Harrison
Ogden, UT 84408-1015
801-626-6050
Minimum Age: 62
Tuition: $10 per quarter
Basic Fees: none
Credit: no

VERMONT

Castleton State College
Admissions
Castleton, VT 05735
802-468-5611
Minimum Age: 62
Tuition: free
Basic Fees: $19 per credit hour
Credit: yes

Community College of Vermont
Registrar
PO Box 120
Waterbury, VT 05676
802-241-3535
Minimum Age: 62
Tuition: 50 percent off (regular tuition $88 per credit hour)
Basic Fees: $42 per semester
Credit: yes

Johnson State College
Student Accounts
Stowe Rd.
Johnson, VT 05656
802-635-2356
800-635-2356
Minimum Age: 62
Tuition: 50 percent off (regular tuition $138 per credit hour)
Basic Fees: $292 per semester

plus $125 in one time fees
Credit: yes

Lyndon State College
Business Office
Lyndonville, VT 05851
802-626-9371, ext. 163
800-225-1998
Minimum Age: 60
Tuition: 50 percent off (regular tuition $138 per credit hour)
Basic Fees: $58.50 for three credit hours ($19.50 per credit hour)
Credit: yes

University of Vermont
194 South Prospect
Burlington, VT 05401
802-656-3170
Minimum Age: 62
Tuition: free
Basic Fees: none
Credit: yes

VIRGINIA

In the State of Virginia the following rule applies: If your annual federal taxable income is less than $10,000, tuition and application fees are waived (audit only).

Blue Ridge Community College
PO Box 80
Weyers Cave, VA 24486-9989
540-234-9261
Minimum Age: 60
Tuition: free
Basic Fees: none
Credit: yes

**Central Virginia
Community College**
Student Services
3506 Wards Rd.
Lynchburg, VA 24502
804-386-4500

Minimum Age: 60
Tuition: free
Basic Fees: none
Credit: yes

**Clinch Valley College of the
University of Virginia**
Admissions
College Ave.
Wise, VA 24293
540-328-0116
Minimum Age: 60
Tuition: free
Basic Fees: none
Credit: yes

College of William and Mary
Bursars Office
PO Box 8795
Williamsburg, VA 23187-8795
804-221-4000
Minimum Age: 60
Tuition: free
Basic Fees: none
Credit: yes

**Dabney S. Lancaster
Community College**
Continuing Education
PO Box 1000
Clifton Forge, VA 24422
540-862-4246
Minimum Age: 60
Tuition: free
Basic Fees: none
Credit: yes

Danville Community College
1008 S. Main St.
Danville, VA 24541
804-797-3553
Minimum Age: 60
Tuition: free
Basic Fees: none
Credit: yes

Eastern Shore Community College

Student Services
Rt. 1, Box 6
Melfa, VA 23410-9755
804-787-5912
Minimum Age: 60
Tuition: free
Basic Fees: none
Credit: no

George Mason University

Office of Admissions
GMU
4400 University Dr.
Fairfax, VA 22030
703-993-2400
Minimum Age: 60
Tuition: free
Basic Fees: none
Credit: no

Germanna Community College

Admissions
PO Box 339
Locust Grove, VA 22508
540-423-1333
Minimum Age: 60
Tuition: free
Basic Fees: none
Credit: yes

James Madison University

Student Accounts
Harrisonburg, VA 22807
540-568-6147
Minimum Age: 60
Tuition: free
Basic Fees: none
Credit: yes

Northern Virginia Community College

Admissions Office
8333 Little River Turnpike
Annandale, VA 22003
703-323-3400
Minimum Age: 60
Tuition: free
Basic Fees: none
Credit: no

University of Virginia

Charlottesville Regional Programs
Div. of Continuing Education
PO Box 3697
Charlottesville, VA 22903
804-982-3200
Minimum Age: 60
Tuition: free
Basic Fees: none
Credit: no

WASHINGTON

Bellevue Community College

3000 Landerholm Circle, SE
Bellevue, WA 98007
206-641-2222
Minimum Age: 60
Tuition: free (2 class limit)
Basic Fees: $2.50 per class
Credit: yes

Big Bend Community College

7662 Chanute St.
Moses Lake, WA 98837
509-762-6226
Minimum Age: 60
Tuition: $10 per course (two-course limit)
Basic Fees: none
Credit: yes

Central Washington University

400 E. 8th Ave.
Ellensburg, WA 98926
509-963-1211
Minimum Age: 60
Tuition: $5 per credit hour up to 6 credit hours
Basic Fees: $25 per session
Credit: no

Centralia College
600 West Locust
Centralia, WA 98531
360-736-9391
Minimum Age: 60
Tuition: $20 (two-class limit)
Basic Fees: none
Credit: no

Clark College
1800 East McLaughlin Blvd.
Vancouver, WA 98663
360-992-2000
Minimum Age: 60
Tuition: $5 per class (two-class limit)
Basic Fees: none
Credit: no

University of Washington
Access Program
Undergraduate Extension Office
5001 25th Ave., NE
Seattle, WA 98195
206-543-2320
Minimum Age: 60
Tuition: free plus $5 registration fee per quarter
Basic Fees: $5 per session
Credit: no

WEST VIRGINIA

Apparently, legislation has been proposed several times to no avail. We were unable to find any schools that offered a discount to senior citizens.

WISCONSIN

Chippewa Valley Technical College
620 West Clairmont Ave.
Eau Claire, WI 54701
715-833-6244
Minimum Age: 62
Tuition: free
Basic Fees: none
Credit: no

Madison Area Technical College
3350 Anderson St.
Madison, WI 53704-2599
608-246-6205
Minimum Age: 62
Tuition: varies ($3.50 and up non-credit only) inquire about course number
Basic Fees: varies
Credit: no

Mid-State Technical College
500 - 32nd St., North
Wisconsin Rapids, WI 54494
715-422-5500
Minimum Age: 62
Tuition: free
Basic Fees: none
Credit: no

Milwaukee Area Technical College
Downtown Campus
700 West State St.
Milwaukee, WI 53233
414 297-6600
Minimum Age: 62
Tuition: free
Basic Fees: none
Credit: no

Northcentral Technical College
Registrar
1000 W. Campus Dr.
Wausau, WI 54401
715-675-3331
Minimum Age: 62
Tuition: varies, reduced rate
Basic Fees: none
Credit: no

Northeast Wisconsin Technical College

Registrar's Office
PO Box 19043
Green Bay, WI 54307-9042
414-498-5703
800-272-2740
Minimum Age: 62
Tuition: up to 50 percent off (non-credit only)
Basic Fees: none
Credit: no

WYOMING

Casper College
125 College Dr.
Casper, WY 82601
307-268-2110 ext. 2491
Minimum Age: 60
Tuition: free to residents of county
Basic Fees: none
Credit: yes, with Golden Age card

Central Wyoming College

Continuing Education
2660 Peck Ave.
Riverton, WY 82501
307-856-9291 ext. 181
Minimum Age: 60
Tuition: free
Basic Fees: $11.50 per credit hour
Credit: yes

Eastern Wyoming College

Records
3200 West C St.
Torrington, WY 82240
307-532-8334
800-658-3195
Minimum Age: 60
Tuition: free
Basic Fees: $9 per credit hour
Credit: yes

Laramie County Community College

Admissions
1400 East College Dr.
Cheyenne, WY 82007
307-778-1212
Minimum Age: 65
Tuition: $5 per credit hour
Basic Fees: $10 one time application fee
Credit: yes

University of Wyoming

Admissions
PO Box 3435
Laramie, WY 82071
307-766-5160
Minimum Age: 65
Tuition: free
Basic Fees: none
Credit: yes

Western Wyoming Community College

PO Box 428
Rock Springs, WY 82901
307-382-1600
Minimum Age: 60
Tuition: free
Basic Fees: none
Credit: yes

☆☆☆

Save Money on College Expenses

Maybe the college nearest you doesn't have a program for seniors. Or perhaps you are still too young for the free tuition. Don't give up your dream or even postpone it any longer. Free advice with budgeting is available from the non-profit organization Consolidated Credit Counseling. Call them for a free copy of "The College Student Budgeting Kit." It contains worksheets and a monthly budget analyzer. Their toll-free number is 800-728-3632.

From the Kitchen to the College Classroom

If you are an older woman who spent many years caring for your family and now you need to earn an income, the Displaced Homemakers Network can help you get the education you need. This organization also helps women who have been full-time homemakers to get a paying job. For more information, call 202-467-6346.

Organizations for People Over Fifty

The over-fifty crowd is growing by leaps and bounds, staying active, and giving new meaning to the expression "act your age." Wisely, you are recognizing the strength in numbers as more and more of you join together to exercise your consumer and political power. As members of groups like AARP (American Association of Retired Persons), for example, you are staying well informed and demanding better value for your dollar. Through the lobbying efforts of political action groups like the National Council of Senior Citizens, you are making your collective voice heard in Congress.

Representatives of government and business alike are listening to you. And based on what they hear, they are creating agencies, changing laws and policies, and taking other steps to meet the changing needs of the older adult population. The National Institute on Aging and each state's Department on Aging are leading the way in providing you with services, reliable information, and other resources to enhance this golden period of your life.

★★★

Life Enrichment Close to Home

The later years should be an adventurous time filled with the joy of friendship, meaningful work, self-expression, and service to others. Or at least that is the philosophy of the organizers of the nearly 100 Shepherd's Centers of America. This is a non-profit, interfaith organization that helps seniors stay active and independent.

Centers offer opportunities to keep your brain and body active— learning to speak a foreign language or use a computer, practicing tai chi or walking your way to fitness. You can take field trips or play bridge; learn tennis or ballroom dancing; assess your nutrition in a class called Rate Your Plate; or get self-help information for dealing with arthritis or fibromyalgia.

The Shepherd's Centers also provide opportunities for seniors to help seniors. Each center has different offerings, but here's a sampling of what you might find:

HANDYMAN SERVICES: Retirees with skills and experience in minor home repairs will perform fix-it services for other seniors for a small service charge.

TELEPHONE ASSURANCE: Seniors living alone get a sense of security when they know that if an emergency arises someone will check on them. They make a daily call to a telephone partner. If the call doesn't come, the partner knows to take action to find out if that person is okay.

TRANSPORTATION FOR MEDICAL SERVICES: Volunteer drivers are scheduled to take individuals to doctors appointments when relatives are unable to get them there.

GRIEF SUPPORT: Recently widowed persons meet for group support as they share their feelings of sorrow over the loss of their loved ones.

SHOPPING FOR SENIORS: The need for food, medications, and other items doesn't stop just because your car is in the shop. Or maybe you need long-term help due to an injury or illness. At times like this, having a volunteer to shop for you is an invaluable service.

REMINISCENCE VISITS: Volunteers visit those who are unable to get out for activities. They listen to stories from the person's earlier life experiences. This provides mental and emotional stimulation as well as an affirmation of the worth of the person telling the stories. And it enriches the life of the listener as well.

To learn more about these programs or to find out how to start one in your community, write Shepherd's Centers of America, One W. Armour Blvd., Suite 201, Kansas, MO 64111. Or call 816-960-1083 or visit the web site at <www.qni.com/~shepherd>.

Eldercare Locator at Your Service

Staying independent is sometimes a challenge as people get older. But a lot of services are available to help you manage on your own. Eldercare Locator is an organization devoted to helping you get your needs met while remaining in your own home. They'll help you sign up for Meals on Wheels, locate a qualified home health aide, or find other health services in your area. They'll answer questions about where to find transportation, legal assistance, and housing options. If you are looking for recreation and social activities, but you don't know who to call, they can tell you. They'll even help you find someone to do home repairs.

And if you are a caregiver, they'll tell you about support services you can use. You'll have peace of mind knowing who to call if you become ill or just need a break from the daily stress of caring for an older person..

No matter where you live in the United States, Eldercare Locator can connect you to services in your community. Phone them toll free at 800-677-1116 between 9 a.m. and 8 p.m. EST. Be prepared to give them your city and county or zip code when you call. That way they can quickly give you information about the services closest to you. You can also write to Eldercare Locator, National Association of Area Agencies on Aging, 1112 16th St. NW, Suite 100, Washington, DC 20036. Learn more online at <www.aoa.dhhs.gov/elderpage/locator.html>.

All This for Just $8?

Chances are, you already know about the many benefits of joining AARP (American Association of Retired Persons). This is the most popular and most powerful of the non-profit, non-partisan membership organizations of older people. And even though, as the name reflects, the original organization was for retired people, today a large portion of the membership is actively employed. You become eligible to join at age fifty.

Because of the power of numbers, AARP is able to negotiate good prices for its members on all kinds of goods and services. When you join for just $8 a year, you receive a membership card that saves you money at hundreds of locations. You can get 10 to 50 percent discounts at participating hotels and 5 to 30 percent discounts on car rentals. You can save 10 to 15 percent off the cost of flowers or gourmet gifts sent by FTD (by phone only, not in retail shops). Look for savings with airlines, cruise organizations, insurance companies, and other businesses. Here are a few more of the good deals that come your way when you join AARP.

DRUGS FOR LESS AT AARP'S PHARMACY: You'll get discounts on prescription medications as well as thousands of other drugstore items. Your order is usually shipped within 24 to 48 hours after receiving it. Call 800-456-2277 for a catalog. Expect to wait on line for a little while, since this is the same number you call to place an order.

BETTER DRIVING AND LOWER INSURANCE: Over six million people have completed AARP's 55 Alive Mature Driving course. It was designed back in 1979 to help mature drivers adjust to changing situations that were causing a lot of traffic accidents. It focuses on things like vision and hearing changes, effects of certain medications, and changes in reaction time.

It also teaches you how to adjust to changes in the way automobiles operate. For example, maybe you aren't sure how to use anti-lock brakes properly. This course can teach you. The instructor also informs you about new laws and how they might affect you.

You pay only $8 for two four-hour sessions held in two consecutive weeks. You'll use a workbook, but there aren't any tests. After completion, most companies will give a 10 percent discount on automobile insurance. (This discount is mandatory in some states.) Plan ahead, because in some places there is a waiting list of three to four months for this popular program. You'll find more information at the web site <www.aarp.org/55alive/about.html>

A GREAT MAGAZINE: *Modern Maturity* is a monthly magazine free to members of AARP. It contains articles that focus on concerns and lifestyles of active, involved, mature adults. AARP also publishes The Bulletin 11 times a year. It contains up-to-date information about taxes, Social Security, retirement, and other issues that affect your life, as they are being debated in congress. AARP issues a number of free publications on topics like health and fitness, finances, and retirement. You'll also find informative articles online at the AARP web site.

HELP FOR FULL-TIME GRANDPARENTS: Visits from your grandchildren can be delightful. But when they live with you, the responsibility can be overwhelming. More and more grandparents today find themselves raising their grandchildren. As a result, AARP established the Grandparent Information Center (GIC) to help them bear the emotional, social, and financial responsibility of raising children. GIC not only provides information, it also works with social service agencies to help find solutions to problems.

If you could use some help with parenting your grandchildren, write to the AARP Grandparenting Center at the address below. You may call them weekdays between 9 a.m. and 5 p.m. at 202-434-2296. You can also get GIC publications and assistance in Spanish if you call 202-434-2281.

If you want more information about these and other programs, write AARP at 601 E Street NW, Washington, DC 20049; call 800-424-3410; online go to <www.aarp.org>.

Support Senior Power

You don't have to carry signs and march on Washington, D.C., to be an activist. If you are interested in changing or supporting laws related to issues of concern to older Americans, consider joining The National Council of Senior Citizens. The NCSC was established in 1961 in an effort to bring about a health-care program for older citizens. The result was Medicare. Since that time it has led the fight to protect Medicare, Medicaid, and Social Security. It has been involved in issues of housing, social opportunities, and jobs for older people, especially those with low incomes.

Your membership fee of $13 a year ($33 for 3 years, $200 for life) helps support NCSC efforts and get your messages heard. It also entitles you to benefits like a direct-mail prescription drug service and discounts on dental and vision care. You'll get reduced rates on travel services, hotels, and car rental. And you'll receive the monthly magazine, *Seniority,* which features news from Capitol Hill and articles on health, finances, and other issues of concern to elders. A monthly newsletter is also available for $7 a year.

For more information, contact NCSC, 8403 Colesville Road, Suite 1200, Silver Springs, MD 20910; phone 301-578-8911; or online at <www.ncscinc.org>.

Benefits for Veterans

If you are a veteran, the Department of Veterans Affairs can assist you and your family with applications for educational assistance, vocational rehabilitation, life insurance, or home loans. They will also help you get comprehensive dental and medical care in outpatient clinics, medical centers, and nursing homes around the country. And they provide burial services, including cemeteries, markers, and flags, to veterans and others who are eligible.

For more information on benefits and eligibility requirements, contact Department of Veterans Affairs, Office of Public Affairs, 810 Vermont Ave. NW, Washington, DC 20420; phone 800-827-1000; or online at <www.va.gov>.

Longevity Bonuses for Older Americans

Until just a few years ago, all residents of Alaska who were 65 and older received a monthly check that the state called a "Longevity Bonus." Unfortunately, as more folks reached senior status (Alaska is second only to Nevada in the growth of their senior citizen population.), this program became too expensive and they began to phase it out.

But all states have government organizations, as well as many private enterprises, devoted to the needs of seniors. Here are some of the "longevity bonuses" a few of them are providing. To learn what's available in your state, call the State Department on Aging listed in the Directory of State Information at the end of this book.

NO CAR, NO LICENSE, NO PROBLEM. Getting around town without a set of wheels is difficult for some seniors. Fortunately, many transit systems offer free or reduced fares to those over 65. They even offer special pick-up services for those who have trouble making it to the nearest bus stop or who are in wheelchairs. New Jersey offers the Senior Citizen and Disabled Resident Transportation Assistance Program which provides door-to-door service, local fare subsidies, and other assistance to those over 60. Contact your local transit authority to see what it offers.

FREE DEADBOLT LOCKS FOR SECURITY. You can make breaking into your home a little harder by using a deadbolt lock. The Senior Lock Program provides locks and installation for Wilmington, Delaware homeowners, age 65 and over, whose income is under $14,000. If you live in Wilmington, call the Police Department's Crime Prevention Unit to learn more. Elsewhere, contact your local police or fire department to learn what similar services they provide for seniors.

STIR UP A BREEZE WITH A FREE FAN. Fan Care is a cool program sponsored by Virginia Power Company. If you are a resident of Virginia and 60 or older, you may be eligible for a free fan to help you make it safely through the hot summer. To learn about eligibility requirements, contact Fan Care, Department for the Aging, 1600 Forest Ave., Suite 102, Richmond, VA 23229; phone 804-662-9333; or online at <www.aging.state.va.us/>. If you live in another state with hot weather, call your Department of Aging to see if they have a similar program.

SHOW ME THE SAVINGS. In Missouri, the "show-me" state, you'll believe this bonus is worth having. Citizens over 60 get special discounts on goods and services when they present their Governor's Silver Club card. If you live in Missouri, call 800-235-5503 to request an application. Missouri also has a program called Circuit Breaker that gives extra tax breaks to seniors over 65 whose income is $15,000 or less.

HUNT FOR NATURAL PLEASURES. Seniors in Vermont pay a one-time fee of $2 for a Green Mountain Passport which gives them free admission to all state parks and fully state-sponsored concerts and museum programs. A number of merchants also offer discounts on goods and services to folks with these passes. Residents 62 or older can apply for one at their town or city clerk's office. And there's more. Vermont residents 65 and older can get a lifetime hunting and fishing license for just $12.

GET THE SCOOP ON AGING. What older citizens throughout the state of Florida seem to want most is good, dependable information. That's why the Department of Elder Affairs publishes a free monthly newspaper called Elder Update. It's filled with articles of interest to seniors. To subscribe, write Department of Elder Affairs, PO Box 10118, Tallahassee, FL 32302.

PRODUCE YOUR OWN KIND OF TELEVISION SHOW. Tired of those shoot-em-up TV programs every night? How would you like to change channels and find something that's more to your liking? Arizona's Office of Aging produces a weekly cable television show which airs on its public access station. (There's also one in Ohio.) Interview topics include employment and volunteer opportunities, as well as legislation of interest to senior adults.

AND THE PERKS KEEP COMING. You can save 1 percent on sales tax in South Carolina and get a discount on cable television in New Jersey. Other states and towns offer free or reduced admission to golf courses, parks, and beaches. In some places automobile tags are provided at a discount to those over 65.

These programs should get you thinking about what "longevity bonuses" your state has for you now or may offer in the future. Could this be just the push you needed to get started writing letters to your state and local government representatives? Be sure to contact your local merchants' associations as well. Remind them of the spending power of your growing age group. By offering special deals, they'll bring more seniors into their places of business.

Link Up for Less

If you are like most folks, you wouldn't know what to do without your telephone. After all, it connects you to your children and grandchildren, the drugstore, the bank, and a network of friends and neighbors. And if you need the police and fire departments, they can come quickly when you dial 911. But maybe you or someone you know just can't afford the expense of having a telephone.

Under the Federal Communication Commission's Link-Up America program, low-income households seeking telephone service are given a 50 percent discount for connection charges. And they may be able to pay the remaining installation fees on an installment plan.

All states, the District of Columbia, and Puerto Rico have federally approved connection assistance programs. If you are interested in signing up for this service, contact your state Public Service Commission or Public Utilities Commission.

If you have trouble locating this service, you can contact the Federal Communications Commission (FCC) at 888-CALL FCC (225-5322). This is an information line with a menu, but you also have the option of speaking to a live person. The FCC will send you printed information if you request it.

More Phone Facts

Once you have the phone installed, you may need some help with the monthly bill. The FCC's Federal Lifeline program helps low-income subscribers reduce their monthly telephone bill by waiving or reducing the line charge, up to about $7 per month.

To date, over 40 states and the District of Columbia have federally approved Lifeline programs. Eligibility varies from state to state, with some having income or age requirements. For more information on Lifeline assistance, call 202-418-0940. The following is a list of organizations that handle this program and a description of eligibility requirements for each state. You can reach them by calling the state government operator located in your state capital.

Federal Lifeline and Link-Up America State Programs

ALABAMA
Public Service Commission
Eligibility: Recipient of SSI, AFDC, or Food Stamps
Income Verification: Medicaid or Food Stamp Card

ALASKA
Anchorage Telephone
Eligibility: Recipient of SSI, AFDC, or Food Stamps
Income Verification: Alaska Department of Health and Human Services

ARIZONA
Corporation Commission
Eligibility: Lifeline — Income below 150 percent poverty. Link Up — Income at or below poverty and participant in Senior Telephone Discount Program
Income Verification: Arizona Department of Economic Security

ARKANSAS
Public Service Commission
Eligibility: Recipient of SSI,

AFDC, HEAP, Food Stamps,
Medicaid, or Subsidized housing
Income Verification: Dept. of
Human Services

CALIFORNIA
Public Utilities Commission
Eligibility: Income at or below
150 percent poverty
Income Verification: Self certified

COLORADO
Public Utilities Commission
Eligibility: Recipient of SSI, Old
Age Pension, Aid to the Blind, or
Aid to the Needy and Disabled
Income Verification:
Department of Social Services

CONNECTICUT
Department of Public Utility
Control
Eligibility: Eligible for any low-
income assistance or energy
assistance program administered
by the Connecticut Department
of Human Resources or
Connecticut Department of
Income Maintenance or SSI
Income Verification:
Applicable agency of those listed

DISTRICT OF COLUMBIA
Public Service Commission
Eligibility: LIHEAP Eligible
Over age 65 (Flat rate $1); Head
of Household ($3 measured + 6.5
cents over 120 calls)
Income Verification: DC
Energy Office

FLORIDA
Public Service Commission
Eligibility: Recipient of Food
Stamps or Medicaid
Income Verification:

Department of Health and
Rehabilitative Services

GEORGIA
Public Service Commission
Eligibility: Recipient of SSI,
AFDC, and/or Food Stamps
Income Verification:
Department of Human
Resources

HAWAII
Public Utilities Commission
Eligibility: Age 60 or older or
handicapped with annual house-
hold income $10,000 or less
Income Verification: Hawaiian
Telephone Co.

IDAHO
Public Utilities Commission
Eligibility: Recipient of AFDC,
Food Stamps, Aid to the Aged,
Blind and Disabled, or Medical
Assistance
Income Verification: Medical
Assistance or Food Stamp ID
card

ILLINOIS
Illinois Commerce Commission
Eligibility: Recipient of public
assistance in programs adminis-
tered by the Illinois Department
of Public Aid
Income Verification:
Department of Public Aid

INDIANA
Utility Regulatory Commission
Eligibility: Recipient of SSI,
AFDC, HEAP, Medicaid, or Food
Stamps
Income Verification: Local
Exchange Companies

IOWA
State Utilities Board

311

Eligibility: Recipient of SSI, AFDC, LIHEAP, or Food Stamps
Income Verification: Local Exchange Companies

KANSAS
Corporation Commission
Eligibility: Recipient of SSI, AFDC, Food Stamps, Medicaid, or General Assistance
Income Verification: Local Exchange Companies

KENTUCKY
Public Service Commission
Eligibility: Recipient of SSI, AFDC, Food Stamps, or Medical Assistance
Income Verification: Cabinet for Human Resources

LOUISIANA
Public Service Commission
Eligibility: Recipient of SSI, AFDC, or Food Stamps
Income Verification: Medicaid or Food Stamp card

MAINE
Public Utilities Commission
Eligibility: Recipient of SSI, AFDC, HEAP, Medicaid, or Food Stamps
Income Verification: Department of Human Services

MARYLAND
Public Service Commission
Eligibility: Recipient of General Assistance
Income Verification: Dept. of Human Resources

MASSACHUSETTS
Dept. of Public Utilities
Eligibility: Recipient of SSI, AFDC, General Public Welfare, Food Stamps, Medicaid, and

Fuel Assistance
Income Verification: Dept. of Public Welfare and/or Office of Fuel Assistance

MICHIGAN
Public Service Commission
Eligibility: Income at or below 130 percent poverty level
Income Verification: Department of Social Services or Office of Services to the Aging

MINNESOTA
Public Utilities Commission
Eligibility: Age 65 or older or income level which meets state poverty levels
Income Verification: Department of Human Services

MISSISSIPPI
Public Service Commission
Eligibility: Recipient of SSI, AFDC, or Food Stamps
Income Verification: Medicaid or Food Stamp card

MISSOURI
Public Service Commission
Eligibility: Recipient of Medicaid
Income Verification: Dept. of Social Services

MONTANA
Public Service Commission
Eligibility: Recipient of SSI, AFDC, or Medicaid
Income Verification: Medicaid card and Social and Rehabilitation Services

NEBRASKA
Public Service Commission
Eligibility: Recipient of SSI, AFDC, Energy Assistance, Food Stamps, Medicaid, or Aid to the

Aged, Blind or Disabled
Income Verification: Medicaid Agency, Department of Social Service, or Food Stamp program

NEVADA
Public Service Commission
Eligibility: Recipient of SSI, AFDC, Energy Assistance, Food Stamps, Indian General Assist., Commodity Foods, or VA Improved Pension
Income Verification: Proof of enrollment in listed programs

NEW HAMPSHIRE
Public Utilities Commission
Eligibility: Recipient of SSI, AFDC, Food Stamps, Fuel Assistance, Old Age Assistance, Weatherization Assist., Aid to Permanently or Totally Disabled, Women, Infants and Children Feeding Program, Welfare, Title XX, or Subsidized Housing
Income Verification: Respective donor agency

NEW JERSEY
Public Service Commission
Eligibility: Recipient of SSI, AFDC, HEAP, Pharmaceutical Assistance to the Aged, Welfare, or Lifeline Credit
Income Verification: Local Exchange Companies

NEW MEXICO
Mountain Bell Telephone
Eligibility: Recipient of SSI, AFDC, or LITAP
Income Verification: Human Services Department

Western New Mexico Telephone Co.
Eligibility: Recipient of SSI,

AFDC, or CCIC
Income Verification: Human Services Department

NEW YORK
Public Service Commission
Eligibility: Recipient of SSI, AFDC, Food Stamps, Medicaid, or Home Relief
Income Verification: Administering Agency

NORTH CAROLINA
Utilities Commission
Eligibility: Recipient of SSI or AFDC
Income Verification: Dept. of Human Resources

NORTH DAKOTA
Public Service Commission
Eligibility: Eligible for Food Stamps, Fuel Assistance, AFDC, Medical Assistance
Income Verification: County Social Service Board

OHIO
Public Utilities Commission
Eligibility: Recipient of HEAP, E-Heap, Ohio Energy Credits Program, SSI, AFDC, and Medicaid
Income Verification: Local Exchange Companies

OKLAHOMA
Corporate Commission
Eligibility: Recipient of aid from state low income programs
Income Verification: Dept. of Human Services

OREGON
Public Utilities Commission
Eligibility: Eligible for Food Stamps and assistance programs, 135 percent of poverty level

313

Income Verification: Dept. of Human Resources

PENNSYLVANIA
Public Utilities Commission
Eligibility: Recipient of SSI, AFDC, Food Stamps, General Assistance, or Blue Card Medical Assistance; medically needy only
Income Verification: Department of Public Welfare

PUERTO RICO
PR Tel. Co.
Eligibility: Recipient of Nutritional Assistance Program
Income Verification: Dept. of Social Services

RHODE ISLAND
Public Utilities Commission
Eligibility: Recipient of SSI, AFDC, General Assistance, or Medical Assistance
Income Verification: Dept. of Human Services

SOUTH CAROLINA
Public Utilities Commission
Eligibility: Recipient of AFDC, Food Stamps, Medicaid, or Temporary Emergency Food Assistance
Income Verification: Local Exchange Companies

SOUTH DAKOTA
Northwestern Bell
Eligibility: Recipient of HEAP or Food Stamps
Income Verification: Dept. of Social Services

TENNESSEE
Public Service Commission
Eligibility: Recipient of SSI, AFDC, Medicaid, or Food Stamps

Income Verification: Medicaid card or Food Stamp Notice of Disposition

TEXAS
Public Utilities Commission
Eligibility: Eligible for SSI, AFDC, LIHEAP, Food Stamps, Medicaid, Medical Assistance, or Maternal Health Program
Income Verification: Local Exchange Companies

UTAH
Public Service Commission
Eligibility: Eligible for SSI, AFDC, Food Stamps, General Assistance, Home Energy Assistance, Medical Assistance, Refugee Assistance, or Energy Work Programs
Income Verification: Local Exchange Companies

VERMONT
Public Service Board
Eligibility: Recipient of SSI, AFDC, Food Stamps, Medicaid, or Fuel Assistance
Income Verification: Department of Social Welfare

VIRGINIA
Corporation Commission
Eligibility: Recipient of Virginia Universal Service Plan
Income Verification: Department of Medical Assistance Services

WASHINGTON
Utilities and Transportation Commission
Eligibility: Recipient of SSI, AFDC, Food Stamps, Refugee Assistance, Chore Services, or Community Options Program

Entry System
Income Verification:
Department of Social and Health
Services

WEST VIRGINIA
Public Service Commission
Eligibility: Disabled or age 60
or older and receives SSI, AFDC,
or Food Stamps, or is eligible for
SSI
Income Verification:
Department of Human Services

WISCONSIN
Wisconsin Bell, GTE

Eligibility: Recipient of AFDC,
SSI, Food Stamps, Title 19
Medical and Energy Programs
Income Verification:
Department of Health and Social
Services

WYOMING
Public Services Commission
United US West
Eligibility: Recipient of SSI,
AFDC, LIHEAP, or Food Stamps
Income Verification: Dept. of
Health and Social Services

☆☆☆

Help From Your Local Post Office

Do you like watching for your mail carrier every day and going to your mail box to see what's there? Maybe you'll find the current issue of your favorite magazine, a delightful new catalog, or cards and letters from far-away friends and family members.

If you enjoy writing and receiving lots of mail, you may find it hard to keep enough postage stamps on hand. Did you know you can order stamps and other postal items and they will be delivered right to your door? There's no extra charge for this convenience. Request an order form from your mail carrier or local post office. Orders normally take two to three business days.

Perhaps you like shopping by mail. At home there's no rush or bother. You can browse through catalogues, take your time filling out the order forms, and double-check your math at your leisure. You just send it all off and wait for your purchases to arrive.

But the mail box can bring bad news as well. Some people tend to be more trusting than others, so they are attractive targets for mail-order swindles. Thieves sometimes steal social security and other checks from mail boxes. The U.S. Postal Service has put together a booklet of tips on how to avoid being victimized by mail fraud and theft. It's called *A Consumer's Guide to Postal Crime Prevention.*, and you can get it through your local post office. If you find yourself a victim of mail schemes or theft, contact your local Postmaster for an investigation.

Many communities offer a Carrier Alert Program to protect elderly people. Mail carriers watch mail boxes for any unusual accumulation of mail that might indicate a need for help. They will also bring your mail to your door if your mail box is located some distance from your home.

For more information, contact your local Post Office branch. You can also write Public Affairs Branch, U.S. Postal Service, 475 L'Enfant Plaza SW, Room 3018, Washington, DC 20260; call 202-268-4293; or search online at <www.usps.gov>.

Helping Seniors Stay Informed

Talk may be cheap, but good reliable information isn't. In this age of rapid communication, we get bombarded with a lot of worthless facts and opinions. You may pay a couple of bucks for your Sunday newspaper and find a lot of it inaccurate and useless. A magazine that costs $3 may give you somebody's ideas about how to save money on insurance or live with diabetes, but is it based on research or just one person's experience?

It's sometimes hard to sift through it all to find what is really useful. That's where organizations for seniors can really help. They do a lot of the leg work to find the facts that help you make wise choices in your personal life and at the ballot box. The government agencies publish a lot of reliable information that seniors can use to make better informed decisions.

WHAT IS UNCLE SAM DOING FOR YOU? The U.S. Senate's Special Committee on Aging puts out a free report that outlines what each government agency is doing for seniors. It covers everything from special arts programs at the National Endowment for the Arts to clinical trials on treatments for Alzheimer's at the National Institutes of Health. And you can get free copies of special reports on a variety of topics like prescription drug price increases or women's health issues. Here are a few recent titles:

- *Shortchanged: Pension Miscalculations*, #105-06
- *Preparing for the Retirement of the Baby Boom Generation*, #105-16
- *The Cash Crunch: The Financial Challenge*, #105-17
- *The Stock Market and Social Security*, #105-20
- *Elder Care Today and Tomorrow*, #105-21
- *Transforming Health Care Systems*, #105-23
- *Living Longer, Growing Stronger*, #105-24
- *Protecting Older Americans Against Overpayment of Income Taxes*, #105-TAX

For a current listing of all publications, or to obtain one of the free publications listed above, contact Special Committee on Aging, United States Senate, SD-G31, Washington, DC 20510; phone 202-224-5364; or online at <www.senate.gov/~aging>.

THE GAO INVESTIGATES FOR YOU. If you are thinking about buying long-term care insurance, look at what the General Accounting Office has learned about the policies. Before you schedule laser surgery for cataracts, check out their findings about which procedures might be appropriate and what outcomes you might expect.

Lump sum retirements, pension plan violators, and rental housing problems for seniors are a few of the other topics listed in the GAO report entitled *Aging Issues*. Each listing includes a short summary of the report or testimony.

All reports are free and can be requested by contacting the U.S. General Accounting Office, PO Box 6015, Gaithersburg, MD 20884; phone 202-512-6000; or online at <www.gao.gov>.

WATCH OUT FOR CON ARTISTS. Older people tend to be trustworthy and they are sometimes too willing to believe everyone else is as honest as they are. The Federal Trade Commission has free publications that provide tips and information to help you avoid getting cheated by unfair or deceptive business practices.

The FTC focuses on truth in advertising, fair packaging and labeling of products, warranty performance, fair credit reporting, direct mail advertising, door-to-door sales, and business practices of nursing homes.

To learn more, contact the State Attorney General's office listed in the Directory of State Information at the back of this book. Or contact the Federal Trade Commission, Public Reference, Room 130, Washington, DC 20580; phone 202-326-2222; or online at <www.ftc.gov>.

SENIORS HAVE CONSUMER POWER. There are over 200 publications available from the Consumer Information Center, and many of them apply to seniors. *Nine Ways To Lower Your Auto Insurance Costs*; *Medicare Pays For Flu Shots*; *Understanding Social Security*; *Food Facts For Older Adults*; and *Estrogens — How To Take Your Medicine* are just a few of them. Four times a year, the Center publishes the Consumer Information Catalog, which lists selected federal government publications of interest to consumers. Topics covered include automobiles, health, food, money management, nutrition, housing, employment, and education. Prices are minimal, and many publications are free. For your free catalog, write Consumer Information Center, PO Box 100, Pueblo, CO 81009.

317

THEY HAVE THE PRESIDENT'S EAR. The Federal Council on Aging is a special advisory group to the President of the United States. Its members are older American citizens and representatives of business, labor, and national organizations with an interest in aging. The council reviews and evaluates federal policies, programs, and activities that affect the lives of older Americans. It also investigates topics related to mental health and aging, health care reform and long-term care, income security, housing and living arrangements, and the problems faced by minority elders. The council collects and distributes this information and publishes it in an annual report to the President.

For more information on how to keep up-to-date on these issues, contact Federal Council on Aging, Room 4280 HHS-N, 330 Independence Ave., SW, Washington, DC 20201; phone 202-619-2451.

GET STATISTICS ABOUT SENIORS. Did you know that that a child born in 1997 has an average life expectancy of 76.5 years? That's about 29 years longer than what was expected for a child born in 1900. Do you know which states have the fastest growing populations of older adults? How many people over 65 do the experts believe there will be on the planet in 2030? If you enjoy statistics, you might like to write for *A Profile of Older Americans: 1998*, AARP Fulfillment, 601 E Street, NW, Washington, DC 20049.

What other facts and figures interest you? *Aging America: Trends and Projections.* is another free publication of statistics about aging issues. It is produced by the National Association of Area Agencies on Aging. They also publish a quarterly subscription magazine, *Aging*, with topics of interest to seniors. For more information, contact the Administration on Aging, 330 Independence Ave., SW, Washington, DC 20201; phone 202-619-0641; or online at <www.aoa.dhhs.gov>.

Freebies For Kids And Grandkids

You may be a senior, but when you spend time with your kids or grand-kids, you become a child at heart. Surrounding yourself with children is one sure-fire way to stay young and vibrant. And it's good to know there are freebies out there for those special children in your life, whether it's your grandchildren, your Sunday School class, or just the kids in your neighborhood.

Bike Stickers and Stuff

As a responsible, caring grandparent, you've equipped your grandchild properly for bicycling with a good helmet and all the appropriate pads.

Now, you can get him some fun, free bicycle stuff from the American Bicycle Association. You'll receive a BMX information packet that includes an introduction to bicycle motocross, a directory of BMX tracks, a coupon for a free race, and some colorful stickers. You can also get a free sample issue of *BMXer*, the official publication of the American Bicycle Association.

For the free stickers and information packet, call 800-886-1269. For the sample issue of *BMXer*, send $2.00 postage and handling to: American Bicycle Association, PO Box 718, FB Offer, Chandler, AZ 85244.

Share Some Sewing Fun

You've always loved to sew, and you enjoy making clothes for your grandchildren. There is a lot of satisfaction in giving them things you made with your own hands. But remember the old saying "Give a man a fish and he eats for a day, but teach a man to fish and he eats for the rest of his life"? If you help them learn to sew, you can spend quality time with them and soon they'll be able to make things for themselves ... or for you.

They'll also get the same sense of pride that you feel when you make something for them.

The Sewing Prose program is a progressive series of sewing lessons for children ages 7 and up. The directions are easy to read and follow, and slowly become more difficult as the child's skill level increases. The company will send you a free simple pattern and a catalog, so you can decide if you want to order more. Write to: Sewing Prose, 132 West Collins, Casper, WY 82601-2448; or call 800-729-7182, and ask for a free sample of *Sewing Adventures for Children*, or visit their web site at <www.sewingprose.com/order.html>.

Teach a Child About Money

Your parents taught you the value of a dollar, but today the value of a dollar is much lower, and managing money is much more confusing than it was when you were younger. Still, one of the best things you can do for the children in your life is to teach them about money. If they learn their lessons early, they won't make major financial mistakes later on.

If you're not sure how to begin, there's help available. You can send for a free brochure, *Teaching Your Kids the ABCs of Money,* which includes hands-on activities for young children, recommendations for teaching older kids how to budget, and practical pre-career suggestions for teens. Write to: Reliastar Financial Corp., 20 Washington Ave. South, Minneapolis, MN 55401; or call 888-757-5757.

You can also order another helpful brochure, *Kids, Cash, Plastic and You,* which contains information on teaching kids about responsible saving and spending. Write to the Consumer Information Center, Dept. 657D, Pueblo, CO 81009.

Get Some Girl Power

Girls aren't just sugar and spice anymore. They're growing up stronger and more independent than ever, and you want to encourage that. Let your favorite little girl show the world that she's proud to be a girl with Girl Power products.

Take advantage of this national campaign to promote the spirit of girl power, by ordering any of these free items. Just call 800-729-6686, and refer to the inventory number for the items of your choice listed below, or visit their web site at <www.health.org/gpower/catalog/index.htm>.

- Poster which reads "Girl Power! Have You Got It?" (Inventory # GPPOST)
- Poster of Dominique Dawes, Olympic gymnastic champion (Inventory # GPDDP)
- Girl Power Diary (Inventory # GPDIR)
- Girl Power Stickers (Inventory # GPSTIK)
- Girl Power Bookmarks (Inventory # GPBOOK)
- Girl Power Button (Inventory # GPPIN)
- Girl Power Bookcover (Inventory # GPBKCVG)
- Girl Power Bookcover with puzzles and games (Inventory # GPCUTE)

Grab Bag Goodies

Don't you just love a surprise? Kids do too, and you can give a youngster a pleasant surprise by ordering them a free grab bag full of goodies and toys. Just send a self-addressed, stamped envelope with a 55-cent stamp on it to The Kids Shopper, Grab Bag Offer, 5600 North Frwy #240, Houston, TX 77076; or visit their web site at <www.thekidsshopper.com>.

A Fountain for Free

Water is one of our most important nutrients, but sometimes it's hard to get kids to drink water instead of sugar-laden sodas. You can make drinking water more fun and save the mess of cleaning up dirty drinking glasses when you install a Faucet Fountain.

You might get a whale, bear, or dinosaur design, depending on what's available. Just slip it over your faucet, and you have an instant fun fountain. Send $2.00 postage and handling ($1.75 for each additional order) to Jayne Products, Inc., Dept. 34, Box 10726, Naples, FL 34101, and ask for the Faucet Fountain.

A Horse of Course

Most kids, particularly girls, are crazy about horses. Do you know a child who has read all the *Black Stallion* and *Saddle Club* books — someone who perks up in the back seat every time you pass a horse farm? If so, you can send away for some free information and goodies from different breed organizations that she can add to her collection of horse stuff. Here are some good sources.

INTERNATIONAL ARABIAN HORSE ASSOCIATION (IAHA). Learn the fascinating history of the beautiful Arabian, and get free stickers and tattoos (while supplies last). Send a postcard with your name and address to International Arabian Horse Association, 10805 E. Bethany Dr., Aurora, CA 80014-2605. Ask for your IAHA kid's kit.

AMERICAN QUARTER HORSE ASSOCIATION (AQHA). The association for the "cowboy's horse" will send your horse-lover a horse activity book, poster, or bumper sticker. Send a postcard with your name and address to AQHA, PO Box 22, Amarillo, TX 79168. Be sure to specify which free gift you want.

TENNESSEE WALKING HORSE BREEDERS AND EXHIBITORS ASSOCIATION (TWHBEA). This flashy, smooth-gaited horse was a favorite of plantation owners. Get a colorful postcard featuring the Tennessee Walking Horse, and brochures that tell you more about the breed. Send a long self-addressed stamped envelope to FSK Postcard, TWHBEA, PO Box 286, Lewisburg, TN 37091. Ask for your postcard and brochures.

AMERICAN MINIATURE HORSE ASSOCIATION (AMHA). Send for your free booklet that tells all about the tiniest horses. Write to AMHA, 5601 South Interstate 35 W., Alvarado, Texas 76009; 817-783-5600; <www.minihorses.com/amha/>.

Cooking With Kids

All kids love to eat, especially when Grandma's cooking. But Grandma shouldn't have to do all the work. You can help teach kids to cook, and have fun at the same time with these cookbooks written just for kids.

- *Goodness Grape-cious Cookbook for Kids.* California Table Grape Commission, PO Box 27320, Fresno, CA 93729-7320; 209-447-8350.

- *Honey Magic, A Cookbook for Kids.* Send a long SASE to Honey Magic, National Honey Board, "Honey Magic" Dept. FRBE, 390 Lashley St., Longmont, CO 80501-6045; 303-776-2337.

- *Hershey's Halloween Treats.* Halloween tips and recipes. Send a self-addressed, stamped envelope with 64 cents postage to Hershey's Halloween Booklet, 704 Metro Drive, Lebanon, PA 17042.

- *Jolly Time Popcorn Ball Maker.* You can order a two-piece plastic mold for neater and easier popcorn-ball making, and get recipes for making sugar, caramel, and honey balls. Send $1.50 postage and handling to Jolly Time, Dept. FB, Box 178, Sioux City, IA 51102; 712-239-1232.

May the Force Be With You

Your grandson wants a light saber for Christmas. Your granddaughter wants a Princess Leia action figure. If you've spent a small fortune on Star Wars toys in the past, you'll be pleased to know that you can now get a Star Wars poster for free. Just call 800-405-9800. The limit is one per household.

A Penny for His Thoughts

Do you know a child who makes good grades? Would you like a unique and inexpensive way to reward him for all his hard work? Koins for Kids will send him a free coin for every "A" on his report card. He could get a foreign coin (chosen by the company), and start collecting coins from around the world. Just send a copy of his report card, or a note from his teacher on school stationary stating how many "A"s he made, and a self-addressed, stamped envelope to K4Kids, Mr. Lucker, Room 18, 3025 Ellington St., Houston, TX 77088.

Help for a Handykid

Did your grandson saw the legs off your coffee table when he was only three? Or nail your favorite cookbook to the wall, so you could read it easier? Now you can encourage those precocious craftsmen by enrolling them in the Sears Craftsman Kids Club. They'll get an official membership card and a quarterly newsletter packed with projects, tips, advice, and more. Pick up an application at the nearest Sears store, or call 800-682-8691.

Child-Friendly Environmental Protection

If you just look out your window, chances are you can see the changes that have occurred since you were a child. Fewer trees, more pavement, more buildings, and more people have put a strain on our environment. The key to making sure your great-great-great-grandchildren will still be able to climb a tree or savor the scent of freshly cut grass is to teach children today to take care of our environment. The Environmental Protection Agency will send your child a free coloring book that teaches him about endangered species or the benefits of recycling. Write to the U.S. Environmental Protection Agency, National Center for Environmental Publications and Information (NCEPI), Cincinnati, OH 45242. Ask for *Endangered Species Coloring Book: Save Our Species* (Document number 21T-3048), and *Adventures of the Garbage Gremlin: Recycle and Combat a Life of Grime* (Document number 530SW90024).

You can also get a free subscription to a fun bimonthly newsletter written by kids, for kids, all about the environment. Send your name and address to: Kids F.A.C.E. Illustrated, PO Box 158254, Nashville, TN 37215.

Fire Up a Child's Imagination

Nothing excites a child more than the sight and sound of a bright red fire engine roaring toward a blaze. And no hero is more deserving in a child's eyes than the men and women who risk their lives to pull people to safety out of dangerous infernos day after day.

If a firefighter is your child's role model, encourage that by ordering a deputy fire marshal kit. He'll get stickers, a badge, a colorful certificate, and priceless information about the rules of fire safety. Write to the Consumer Information Center, Dept. 523A, Attn: S. James, Pueblo, CO 81009.

Directory Of State Information

ALABAMA

Federal Information Center
All locations; 800-688-9889

State Information Office
334-242-8000
http://www.state.al.us

Cooperative Extension Offices
Dr. W. Gaines Smith Interim
Director; Alabama
CooperativeExtension Service;
109 A Duncan Hall, Auburn
University, Auburn, AL 36849-
5612; 334-844-4444
http://www.acesag.auburn.edu

Chinelle Henderson,
Administrator; Alabama A&M
University, Cooperative
Extension Service; PO Box
222, Normal, AL 35762;
205-851-5710
http://www.saes.aamu.
edu/exten.htm

Dr. Moore, Director;
Cooperative Extension
Program, U.S. Dept. of
Agriculture; Tuskegee
University, 207 N. Main St.,
Suite 400, Tuskegee, AL 36083-
1731; 334-727-8806
http://www.tusk.edu

Attorney Grievances
Alabama State Bar, Center for
Professional Responsibility; PO
Box 671, Montgomery, AL
36101; 334-269-1515
http://www.alabar.org/

Client Security Trust Fund & Fee Arbitration
Alabama State Bar; PO Box
671, Montgomery, AL 36101;
334-269-1515
http://www.alabar.org/

State Consumer Protection Office
Consumer Protection Division
Office of Attorney General;
11 S. Union St., Montgomery,
AL 36130; 334-242-7334,
800-392-5658 - in AL only
http://e-pages.com/aag/
cuspro.html

HUD Field Office
600 Beacon Pkwy, West, Suite
300, Birmingham, AL 35209;
205-290-7617
http://www.hud.gov

State Insurance Commissioner
Insurance Commissioner;
201 Monroe St., Suite 1700,
Montgomery, AL 36104;
334-269-3550

Nursing Home Ombudsmen
Commission on Aging;
770 Washington Ave., R.F.A.

Plaza, #470, Montgomery, AL 36130; 334-242-5743, 800-243-5463 - (AL only)

State Government Banking Commissioner
Superintendent of Banks; 401 Adams Ave., Suite 680, Montgomery, AL 36130; 334-242-3452

State Office on Aging
Aging Commission; 770 Washington Ave., Suite 470, Montgomery, AL 36130; 334-242-5743

State Utility Commission
Public Service Commission; PO Box 991, Montgomery, AL 36101; 334-242-5207, 800-392-8050 (AL only)

ALASKA

Federal Information Center
All locations; 800-688-9889

State Information Office
907-465-2111
http://www.state.ak.us

Cooperative Extension Office
Hollis D. Hall, Director; Alaska Cooperative Extension; University of Alaska Fairbanks, PO Box 756180, Fairbanks, AK; 99775-6180, 907-474-7246
http://zorba.uafadm.alaska.edu/coop-ext/index.html

Attorney Grievances, Client Security Trust Fund, & Fee Arbitration
Alaska Bar Association; PO Box 100279, 510 L. St., Suite

602, Anchorage, AK 99501; 907-272-7469
http://www.alaskabar.org

State Consumer Protection Office
Attorney General; 1031 W. Fourth Ave., Suite 200, Anchorage, AK 99501; 907-269-5100

HUD Field Office
Federal Bldg.; 222 W. 8th Ave., #64, Anchorage, AK 99513; 907-271-4170
http://www.hud.gov

State Insurance Director
Director of Insurance; PO Box 110805, Juneau, AK; 99811-0805; 907-465-2515
http://www.state.ak.us/local/akpages/commerce/ins.htm

Nursing Home Ombudsmen
State of Alaska Long Term Care Ombudsman
3601 C St., Suite 260, Anchorage, AK 99503-5209; 907-563-6393; 800-730-6393

State Government Banking Commissioner
Director of Banking, Securities and Corporations; PO Box 110807, Juneau, AK 99811-0807; 907-465-2521
http://www.commerce.state.ak.us/bsc/bsc.htm

State Office on Aging
Division of Senior Services, Commission on Aging; PO Box 110209, Juneau, AK 99811-0209, 907-465-3250
http://www.state.ak.us/

local/akpages/ADMIN/dss/
homess.htm

State Utility Commission
Public Utilities Commission;
1016 W. 6th Ave., Suite 400,
Anchorage, AK 99501;
907-276-6222
http://www.state.ak.us/local/
akpages/COMMERCE/
apuc.htm

ARIZONA

Federal Information Center
All Locations; 800-688-9889

State Information Office
602-542-4900
http://www.state.az.us

Cooperative Extension Office
Jim Christenson, Director;
Cooperative Extension Office,
University of Arizona, Forbes
301, Tucson, AZ 85721;
520-621-7205
http://ag.arizona.edu/ext/
coopext.html

Attorney Grievances, Client Security Trust Fund, & Fee Arbitration
Chief Bar Counsel, State Bar of
Arizona; 111 West Monroe,
Suite 1800, Phoenix, AZ 85003-
1742; 602-252-4804
http://www.azbar.org

State Consumer Protection Office
Consumer Protection Division,
Office of Attorney General;
1275 W. Washington St., Room

259, Phoenix, AZ 85007;
602-542-3702, 800-352-8431 (AZ
only)

HUD Field Office
400 N. 5th St., Suite 1600
2 Arizona Center, Phoenix, AZ
85004; 602-379-4434
http://www.hud.gov

State Insurance Commissioner
Director of Insurance;
2910 N. 44th St., Suite 210,
Phoenix, AZ 85018; 602-912-
8400
http://www.state.az.us/id

Nursing Home Ombudsmen
Aging and Adult
Administration;
1789 W. Jefferson, Phoenix, AZ
85007; 602-542-4446

State Government Banking Commissioner
Superintendent of Banks;
2910 N. 44th St., Suite 310,
Phoenix, AZ 85018; 602-255-
4421, 800-544-0708
http://www.azbanking.com

State Office on Aging
Aging and Adult Administration,
Economic Security Department
1789 W. Jefferson, Phoenix, AZ
85007; 602-542-4446

State Utility Commission
Corporation Commission
1200 W. Washington St.,
Phoenix, AZ 85007; 602-542-
3935, 800-222-7000 (AZ only)
http://www.cc.state.az.us

ARKANSAS

Federal Information Center
All Locations; 800-688-9889

State Information Office
501-682-3000
http://www.state.ar.us

Cooperative Extension Offices
David Foster, Director;
Cooperative Extension Service
PO Box 391, Little Rock, AR
72203; 501-671-2000
http://www.uaex.edu

Attorney Grievances
Committee on Professional
Conduct; Justice Bldg., Room
205, 625 Marshall St., Little
Rock, AR 72201; 501-376-0313

Client Security Trust Fund
Clerk; Clerk Office, 625
Marshall St., Justice Bldg.,
Little Rock, AR 72201;
501-682-6849

State Consumer Protection Office
Consumer Protection Division,
Office of Attorney General; 200
Catlitt-Prien Bldg., 323 Center
St., Little Rock, AR 72201
501-682-2341; 800-482-8982
(AR only)
http://www.ag.state.ar.us

HUD Field Office
425 W. Capitol, Suite 900, Little
Rock, AR 72201; 501-324-5931
http://www.hud.gov

State Insurance Commissioner
Insurance Commissioner;
1200 W. 3rd St., Little Rock, AR
72201; 501-371-2600

Nursing Home Ombudsmen
Division of Aging and Adult
Services; 1417 Donaghey Plaza
South, PO Box 1437, Slot 1412,
Little Rock, AR 72203-1437;
501-682-2441

State Government Banking Commissioner
Bank Commissioner
Tower Bldg., 323 Center St.,
Suite 500, Little Rock, AR
72201; 501-324-9019
http://www.state.ar.us/
bank/banking.html

State Office on Aging
Aging and Adult Services
Division; Box 1437, Slot 1412,
Little Rock, AR 72203;
501-682-2441
http://www.state.ar.us/
dhs.index2.html

State Utility Commission
Public Service Commission;
1000 Center St., PO Box 400
Little Rock, AR 72203-0400;
501-682-1453, 800-482-1164
(AR only)

CALIFORNIA

Federal Information Center
All Locations; 800-688-9889

State Information Office
916-322-9900
http://www.state.ca.us

Cooperative Extension Office
Kenneth Farrell, VP;
University of California,
Division of Agriculture and

Natural Resources; 300 Lakeside Dr., 6th Floor, Oakland, CA 94612-3560; 510-987-0060 (programs are at county level)

Attorney Grievances
Southern California; Chief Trial Counsel, State Bar of California; 1149 S. Hill St., 4th Floor, Los Angeles, CA 90015; 213-765-1000, 800-843-9053 (CA only)
http://www.calbar.org

Northern California
Chief Trial Counsel, State Bar of California; 100 Van Ness Ave., 28th Floor, San Francisco, CA 94102; 415-561-8200 800-843-9053 (CA only)
http://www.calbar.org

Client Security Trust Fund
Southern California Grievance Committee, State Bar of California; 1149 S. Hill St., 9th Floor, Los Angeles, CA 90017; 213-765-1140
http://www.calbar.org

Fee Arbitration
Chief Trial Counsel; State Bar of California; 100 Van Ness Ave., 28th Floor, San Francisco, CA 94102; 415-241-2020 800-843-9053 (CA only)
http://www.calbar.org

State Consumer Protection Offices
Public Inquiry Unit, Office of Attorney General; 1515 K St., Suite 511, PO Box 944255 Sacramento, CA 94244; 916-322-3360, 800-952-5225

(CA only)
http://caag.state.ca.us/piu/

California Department of Consumer Affairs
400 R St., Sacramento, CA 95814; 916-445-0660, 800-344-4410 (CA only)

Bureau of Automotive Repair
California Department of Consumer Affairs; 400 R St., Sacramento, CA 95814; 916-366-5100, 800-952-5210 (CA only-auto repair only)
http://caag.state.ca.us/piu/bar.htm

HUD Field Offices
611 W. 6th St., Suite 800, Los Angeles, CA 90017; 213-894-8007
http://www.hud.gov

450 Golden Gate Ave., PO Box 36003, San Francisco, CA 94102-3448; 415-436-6550
http://www.hud.gov

777 12th St., Suite 200, Sacramento, CA 95814; 916-498-5220
http://www.hud.gov

State Insurance Commissioner
Commissioner of Insurance; 300 S. Spring St., Los Angeles, CA 90013; 916-322-3555 (Santa Monica), 213-897-8921 (Los Angeles), 800-927-HELP (complaints)
http://www.insurance.ca.gov

Nursing Home Ombudsmen
Department of Aging; 1600 K

St., Sacramento, CA 95814; 916-323-6681, 800-231-4024 (CA only)

State Government Banking Commissioner

Superintendent of Banks; 111 Pine St., Suite 1100, San Francisco, CA 94111; 415-557-3535, 800-622-0620
http://www.dfi.ca.gov

State Office on Aging

California Department of Aging; 1600 K St., Sacramento, CA 95814; 916-322-5290
http://www.aging.state.ca.us

State Utility Commission

Public Utilities Commission; 505 Van Ness Ave., San Francisco, CA 94102; 415-703-2782
http://www.cpuc.ca.gov

COLORADO

Federal Information Center

All Locations; 800-688-9889

State Information Office

303-866-5000
http://www.state.co.us

Cooperative Extension Office

Milan Rewets, Director; Colorado State University, Cooperative Extension; 1 Administrative Building, Fort Collins, CO 80523; 970-491-6281
http://www.colostate.edu

Attorney Grievances S.C.D.C

Disciplinary Counsel; Supreme Court of Colorado; Dominion Plaza Bldg., 600 17th St., Suite 510 S., Denver, CO 80202; 303-893-8121

Client Security Trust Fund

Colorado Bar Association; 1900 Grant St., Suite 950, Denver, CO 80203-4309; 303-860-1115, 800-332-6736 (CO only)
http://www.cobar.org

Fee Arbitration

Legal Fee Arbitration Committee, Colorado Bar Association; 1900 Grant St., Suite 950, Denver, CO 80203-4309; 303-860-1112, 800-332-6736 (CO only)
http://www.cobar.org

State Consumer Protection Office

Consumer Protection Unit, Office of Attorney General; 1525 Sherman St., 5th Floor, Denver, CO 80203; 303-866-5189, 800-332-2071 (CO only)
http://www.state.co.us/gov_dir/dol/consprot.htm

HUD Field Office

633 17th St., Denver, CO 80202; 303-672-5258
http://www.hud.gov

State Insurance Commissioner

Commissioner of Insurance; 1560 Broadway, Suite 850, Denver, CO 80202; 303-894-7490
http://www.dora.state.co.us/insurance

Nursing Home Ombudsmen

The Legal Center; 455

Sherman St., Suite 130, Denver, CO 80203; 303-722-0300; 800-288-1376 (CO only)

State Government Banking Commissioner
State Bank Commissioner, Division of Banking; 1560 Broadway, Suite 1175, Denver, CO 80202; 303-894-7575
http://www.aclin.org/other/government/dora/aclin

State Office on Aging
Commission For Aging and Adult Services, Social Services Dept.; 110 16th St., Suite 200, Denver, CO 80202; 303-620-4147
http://www.aclin.org/~sherlock/colodaas.htm

State Utility Commission
Public Utilities Commission; 1580 Logan St., Logan Tower, Office Level 2, Denver, CO 80203; 303-894-2000, 800-888-0170 (CO only)
http://www.puc.state.co.us

CONNECTICUT

Federal Information Center
All Locations; 800-688-9889

State Information Office
860-240-0222
http://www.state.ct.us

Cooperative Extension Office
Associate Director, Cooperative Extension System; University of Connecticut, 1376 Storrs Rd., Storrs, CT 06269-4036; 860-486-6271

Attorney Grievances
Statewide Grievance Committee; PO Box 260888, 287 Main St., 2nd Floor, Suite 3, East Hartford, CT 06118; 860-568-5157

Client Security Trust Fund
George Buckley, Jr.; State Bar Association; 101 Corporate Place, Rocky Hill, CT 06067-1894; 860-721-0025
http://www.ctbar.org

Committee on Arbitration of Fee Disputes
State Bar Association; 101 Corporate Place, Rocky Hill, CT 06067-1894; 860-721-0025
http://www.ctbar.org

State Consumer Protection Office
Department of Consumer Protection; State Office Building, 165 Capitol Ave., Hartford, CT 06106; 860-566-4999, 800-538-CARS(2277), 800-842-2649 (complaints line) government information (CT only)
http://www.state.ct.us/dcp/

HUD Field Office
330 Main St., 1st Floor, Hartford, CT 06106; 860-240-4800
http://www.hud.gov/local/har/harhome.html

State Insurance Commissioner
Insurance Commissioner; PO Box 816, Hartford, CT 06142-0816; 860-297-3800
http://www.state.ct.us/cid

Nursing Home Ombudsmen
Department of Social Services, Elderly Services Division; 25 Sigourney St., Hartford, CT 06106; 860-424-5242

State Government Banking Commissioner
Banking Commissioner; 260 Constitution Ave., Hartford, CT 06103; 860-240-8299
http://www.state.ct.us/dob/

State Office on Aging
Elderly Services, Division of Social Services; 25 Sigourney St., Hartford, CT 06106; 860-424-5277
http://www.dss.state.ct.us/

State Utility Commission
Department of Public Utility Control; 10 Franklin Square, New Britain, CT 06051; 860-827-1553, 800-382-4586 (CT only)
http://www.state.ct.us/dpuc/

DELAWARE

Federal Information Center
All Locations; 800-688-9889

State Information Office
302-739-4000
http://www.state.de.us

Cooperative Extension Offices
Dr. Richard E. Fowler, Director; Cooperative Extension; 131 Townsend Hall, University of Delaware, Newark, DE 19717-1303; 302-831-2504
http://www.bluehen.ags.udel.edu/

Dr. Starlene Taylor, Assistant Administrator; Delaware State College, Cooperative Extension Service; 1200 N. DuPont Hwy., Dover, DE 19901; 302-739-5157
http://www.dsc.edu

Attorney Grievances
Office of Disciplinary Counsel; PO Box 472, Wilmington, DE 19899; 302-577-7042

Lawyer's Fund for Client Protection
200 W. 9th St., Suite 300B, Wilmington, DE 19899; 302-577-7034

State Consumer Protection Office
Justice Dept., Attorney General; Consumer Protection Unit; 820 N. French St., 4th Floor, Wilmington, DE 19801; 302-577-8600

HUD Field Office
Liberty Square Bldg.; 105 S. 7th St., Philadelphia, PA 19106-3392; 215-597-2560
http://www.hud.gov

State Insurance Commissioner
Insurance Commissioner; PO Box 7007, 841 Silver Lake Blvd., Dover, DE 19903-1507; 302-739-4251; 800-282-8611

Nursing Home Ombudsmen
Division of Aging and Disabilities; Milford State Service Ctr.; 18 N. Walnut St., Milford, DE 19963; 302-422-1386; 800-292-1515 (DE only)

State Government Banking Commissioner
State Bank Commissioner; 555 E. Lockerman St., Suite 210, Dover, DE 19901; 302-739-4235
http://www.state.de.us/ bank

State Office on Aging
Aging Division, Health and Social Services Department; 1901 N. Dupont Hwy., New Castle, DE 19720; 302-577-4791, 800-223-9074
http://kidshealth.org/
nhc/divage/index.html

State Utility Commission
Public Service Commission; 861 Silver Lake Blvd., Suite 100, Cannon Bldg., Dover, DE 19904; 302-739-4247, 800-282-8574 (DE only)
http://www.state.de.us

DISTRICT OF COLUMBIA

Federal Information Center
All Locations; 800-688-9889

District of Columbia Information Office
202-727-6161
http://www.ci.washington.dc.us

Cooperative Extension Office
Reginald Taylor, Acting Director; Cooperative Extension Service; University of the District of Columbia, 901 Newton St., NE, Washington, DC 20017; 202-274-6900

Attorney Grievances
Office of Bar Counsel; 515 5th St., NW, Building A, Room 127, Washington, DC 20001;

202-638-1501

Client Security Trust Fund
District of Columbia Bar; 1250 H St., NW, 6th Floor, Washington, DC 20005; 202-737-4700 x237
http://www.dcbar.org

Fee Arbitration
Attorney-Client Arbitration Board, District of Columbia Bar; 1250 H St., NW, 6th Floor, Washington, DC 20005; 202-737-4700 x238
http://www.dcbar.org

State Consumer Protection Office
Department of Consumer and Regulatory Affairs; 614 H St., NW, Washington, DC 20001; 202-727-7080
http://www.ci.washington.
dc.us/dcra

HUD Field Office
820 First St., NE, Washington, DC 20002; 202-275-9200
http://www.hud.gov

State Insurance Commissioner
Commissioner of Insurance; 441 4th St., NW, 8th Floor N; Washington, DC 20001; 202-727-7424

Nursing Home Ombudsmen
Legal Counsel for the Elderly; 601 E. St., NW, Building A, 4th Floor, Washington, DC 20049; 202-662-4933

State Government Banking Commissioner
Superintendent of Banking and

335

Financial Institutions; 717 14th St., NW, 11th Floor, Washington, DC 20006; 202-727-1563 http://www.ci.washington.dc.us

State Office on Aging
Aging Office; 441 4th St., NW, Suite 900, Washington, DC 20001; 202-724-5622 http://www.ci.washington. dc.us/aging/aghome.htm

State Utility Commission
Public Service Commission; 717 14th St., NW, Suite 200, Washington, DC 20005; 202-626-5110

FLORIDA

Federal Information Center
All Locations; 800-688-9889

State Information Office
850-488-1234
http://www.state.fl.us

Cooperative Extension Offices
Christine Taylor-Stephens, Dean; Florida Cooperative Extension Service; PO Box 110220, University of Florida, Gainesville, FL 32611-0210; 352-392-1761 http://www.ifas.ufl.edu

Lawrence Carter, Director, Cooperative Extension Service; 215 Perry Paige Building S., Florida A&M University, Tallahassee, FL 32307; 850-599-3546 http://www.famu.edu

Attorney Grievances, Client Security Trust Fund, & Fee

Arbitration
Staff Counsel, Florida Bar; 650 Apalachee Parkway, Tallahassee, FL 32399-2300; 850-561-5839; 800-342-8060 (FL only) http://www.flabar.org

State Consumer Protection Office
Division of Consumer Services; Mayo Building, Tallahassee, FL 32399-0800; 850-488-2221, 800-HELP-FLA (FL only)

HUD Field Office
301 W. Bay St., Suite 2200, Jacksonville, FL 32202; 904-232-2626 http://www.hud.gov/local/ jkv/jkv_home.html

State Insurance Commissioner
Insurance Commissioner; 200 E. Gaines St., Tallahassee, FL 32399-0300; 850-922-3100, 800-342-2762 http://www.doi.state.fl.us

State Government Banking Commissioner
State Comptroller, Department of Banking and Finance; State Capitol Bldg., Tallahassee, FL 32399; 850-488-0286 http://www.dbf.state.fl.us

Nursing Home Ombudsmen
State Long-Term Care Ombudsman; 501 S. Calhoun St., Tallahassee, FL 32399; 850-488-6190

State Office on Aging
Department of Elder Affairs; 4040 Esplanade Way, Tallahassee, FL 32399-0700;

850-414-2108, Elder Helpline: 800-96-ELDER (in FL)
http://www.state.fl.us/doea/doea.html

State Utility Commission
Public Service Commission; 2540 Shumard-Oak Blvd., Tallahassee, FL 32399-0850; 850-413-6344; 800-342-3552 (FL only)
http://www.scri.net/psc

GEORGIA

Federal Information Center
All Locations; 800-688-9889

State Information Office
404-656-2000
http://www.state.ga.us

Cooperative Extension Offices
Bob Isaac, Interim Director; Cooperative Extension Service; University of Georgia, 1111 Conner Hall, Athens, GA 30602; 706-542-3824
http://www.ces.uga.edu

Dr. Fred Harrison, Jr., Dir.; Cooperative Extension Service; PO Box 4061, Fort Valley State College, Fort Valley, GA 31030; 912-825-6269
http://agschool.fvsc.peachnet.edu

Attorney Grievances & Committee on Arbitration of Fee Disputes
State Bar of Georgia, Office of General Counsel; 800 Hurt Bldg., 50 Hurt Plaza, Atlanta, GA 30303; 404-527-8720, 404-527-8752 for fee arbitration,

404-527-8771 for client security trust fund
http://www.gabar.org

State Consumer Protection Office
Office of Consumer Affairs; 2 Martin Luther King, Jr. Dr., Suite 356, Plaza Level, East Tower, Atlanta, GA 30334; 404-656-3790, 800-869-1123 (GA only)

HUD Field Office
Richard B. Russell Federal Bldg., 75 Spring St., SW, Atlanta, GA 30303; 404-331-5136
http://members.aol.com/hudfiles/georgia.html

State Insurance Commissioner
Insurance Commissioner; 2 Martin Luther King, Jr. Dr., Atlanta, GA 30334; 404-656-2070, 800-656-2298
http://www.state.ga.us/ga.ins.commission/

Nursing Home Ombudsmen
Office of Aging, Dept. of Human Resources; 2 Peachtree St., NW, 18th Floor, Atlanta, GA 30303; 404-657-5319

State Government Banking Commissioner
Commissioner of Banking and Finance; 2990 Brandywine Rd., Suite 200, Atlanta, GA 30341; 770-986-1633
http://www.georgianet.org/services/dbf/

State Office on Aging
Aging Services Office; 2
Peachtree St., NW, Atlanta, GA
30303; 404-657-5258
http://www.state.ga.us/
departments/dhr/aging/html

State Utility Commission
Public Service Commission; 47
Trinity Ave., Atlanta, GA 30334
404-656-4501; 800-282-5813
(GA only)
http://www.psc.state.ga.us

HAWAII

Federal Information Center
All Locations; 800-688-9889

State Information Office
808-548-6222
http://www.state.hi.us

Cooperative Extension Office
Dr. Po'Yung Lai, Assistant,
Director; Cooperative
Extension Service; 3050 Maile
Way, Honolulu, HI 96822;
808-956-8397
http://www.hawaii.edu

Attorney Grievances
Office of Disciplinary Counsel,
Supreme Court of the State of
Hawaii; 1164 Bishop St., Suite
600, Honolulu, HI 96813;
808-521-4591

Lawyers Fund for Client Protection of the Bar of Hawaii
1164 Bishop St., Suite 600,
Honolulu, HI 96813; 808-599-
2483

Fee Arbitration
Attorney-Client Coordination

Committee, Hawaii State Bar
Assoc.; 1136 Union Hall Pew
House L, Honolulu, HI 96813;
808-537-1868
http://hsba.org

State Consumer Protection Office
Office of Consumer Protection
Department of Commerce and
Consumer Affairs; 235 S.
Beretania, 9th Floor, PO Box
3767, Honolulu, HI 96813-3767;
808-587-1234
http://www.state.hi.us/
dcca/ocp

HUD Field Office
7 Waterfront Plaza, Suite 500
500 Ala Moana Blvd.,
Honolulu, HI 96813-4918;
808-522-8187
http://www.hud.gov

State Insurance Commissioner
Insurance Commissioner; PO
Box 3614, Honolulu, HI 96811;
808-586-2790
http://www.state.hi.us/
insurance

Nursing Home Ombudsmen
Executive Office on Aging; 250
S. Hotel St., Suite 107,
Honolulu, HI 96813-2831;
808-586-0100

State Government Banking Commissioner
Commissioner, Financial
Institutions; PO Box 2054,
Honolulu, HI 96805;
808-586-2820

State Office on Aging
Aging Office; 205 S. Hotel St.,

Suite 107, Honolulu, HI 96813-2831; 808-586-0100

State Utility Commission
Public Utilities Commission; 465 S. King St., Room 103, Honolulu, HI 96813; 808-586-2020

IDAHO

Federal Information Center
All Locations; 800-688-9889

State Information Office
208-334-2411
http://www.state.id.us

Cooperative Extension Office
Dr. LeRoy D. Luft, Director; Cooperative Extension System, College of Agriculture; University of Idaho, Moscow, ID 83844-2338; 208-885-6639
http://www.uidaho.edu/ag/extension/

Attorney Grievances, Client Security Trust Fund, & Fee Arbitration
Bar Counsel; Idaho State Bar; PO Box 895, Boise, ID 83701; 208-334-4500
http://www.state.id.us/isb

HUD Field Office
400 SW 6th Ave., Suite 700, Portland, OR 97204-1632; 503-326-2561
http://www.hud.gov

State Insurance Commissioner
Director of Insurance; PO Box 83720, Boise, ID 83720-0043; 208-334-4250, 800-721-3272

http://www.doi.state.id.us/homepage.htm

Nursing Home Ombudsmen
Office on Aging; State House, Room 108, 700 W. Jefferson, PO Box 83720, Boise, ID 83720-0007; 208-334-3822

State Government Banking Commissioner
Department of Finance; PO Box 83720, Boise, ID 83720-0031; 208-332-8000
http://www.state.id.us/finance/dof.htm

State Office on Aging
Aging Office; PO Box 83720, Boise, ID 83720-0007; 208-334-3833
http://www.state.id.us/icoa/

State Utility Commission
Public Utilities Commission, PO Box 83720, Boise, ID 83720-0074; 208-334-0300
http://www.puc.state.id.us

ILLINOIS

Federal Information Center
All Locations; 800-688-9889

State Information Office
217-782-2000
http://www.state.il.us

Cooperative Extension Office
Dennis Campion, Director; University of Illinois, Cooperative Extension Svc.; 122 Mumford Hall, 1301 W. Gregory Dr., Urbana, IL 61801; 217-333-2660
http://www.ag.uiuc.edu

Attorney Grievances
Attorney Registration and
Disciplinary Commission of
the Supreme Court of Illinois;
700 E. Adams St., Suite 201,
Springfield, IL 62701-1507;
217-522-6838, 800-252-8048
(IL only)

Client Protection Program
1 Prudential Plaza; 130 E.,
Randolph Dr., Suite 1500,
Chicago, IL 60601;
312-565-2600

**Illinois State Bar
Association**
424 S. Second St., Springfield,
IL 62701; 217-525-1760
http://www.illinoisbar.org

**State Consumer Protection
Office**
Consumer Division; Attorney
General's Office; 500 S. Second
St., Springfield, IL 62706;
217-782-9011, 217-782-9012,
800-252-2518 (IL only)
http://www.ag.state.il.us

HUD Field Office
77 W. Jackson Blvd., 26th
Floor, Chicago, IL 60604-3507;
312-353-5680
http://www.towercom.
com/chhud/

**State Insurance
Commissioner**
Director of Insurance; 320 W.
Washington St., Springfield, IL
62767; 217-782-4515
http://www.state.il.us/ins/

Nursing Home Ombudsmen
Department on Aging; 421 East

Capitol Ave., Springfield, IL
62701; 217-785-3140,
800-252-8966

**State Government Banking
Commissioner**
Commissioner of Banks and
Trust Companies; 500 E.
Monroe St., Springfield, IL
62701; 217-782-7966,
800-634-5452
http://www.state.il.us/obr/

State Office on Aging
Aging Department; 421 E.
Capitol Ave. #100, Springfield,
IL 62701-1789; 217-785-2870
http://www.state.il.us/aging/

State Utility Commission
Commerce Commission; 527 E.
Capitol Ave., PO Box 19280,
Springfield, IL 62794-9280;
217-782-7295
http://www.state.il.us/icc

INDIANA

Federal Information Center
All Locations; 800-688-9889

State Information Office
317-232-1000
http://www.state.in.us

**Cooperative Extension
Office**
Dr. Wadsworth, Director; 1140
AGAD, CES Administration;
Purdue University, West
Lafayette, IN 47907-1140;
317-494-8489
http://www.agcom.purdue.
edu/agcom/extension/
ces.htm

Attorney Grievances
Disciplinary Commission of
the Supreme Court of Indiana;
115 W. Washington St., South
Tower, Suite 1060, Indianapolis,
IN 46204; 317-232-1807
http://www.state.in.us/
judiciary/welcome.html

**Clients' Financial
Assistance Fund**
Attn: Tom Pyrz, Indiana State
Bar Assoc.; 230 E. Ohio St., 4th
Floor, Indianapolis, IN 46204;
317-639-5465, 800-266-2581
http://www.inbar.org

Fee Arbitration
Contact Clients' Financial
Assistance Fund for referral to
local programs.

**State Consumer Protection
Office**
Consumer Protection Division,
Office of Attorney General; 219
State House, 402 W.
Washington, 5th Floor,
Indianapolis, IN 46204; 317-232-
6330, 800-382-5516 (IN only)
http://www.state.in.us/
hoosieradvocate/html/
speaker.html

HUD Field Office
151 N. Delaware St.,
Indianapolis, IN 46204;
317-226-6303
http://www.hud.gov

State Insurance Commissioner
Commissioner of Insurance;
311 W. Washington St., Suite
300, Indianapolis, IN 46204;
317-232-2385, 800-622-4461
http://www.state.in.us/idoi/

index.html

Nursing Home Ombudsmen
Aging Division, Department of
Human Services; PO Box 7083,
Indianapolis, IN 46207-7083;
317-232-7134, 800-622-4484 (IN
only)

**State Government Banking
Commissioner**
Department of Financial
Institutions; 402 W.
Washington St., Room W066,
Indianapolis, IN 46204-2759;
317-232-3955, 800-382-4880
http://www.dfi.state.in.us

State Office on Aging
Aging and Rehabilitative
Services Division, Family and
Social Services Administration;
402 W. Washington St., Room
W454, Indianapolis, IN 46207;
317-232-7020

State Utility Commission
Utility Regulatory Commission;
302 W. Washington St., Suite
E306, Indianapolis, IN 46204;
317-232-2701
http://www.state.in.us/iurc/
index.html

IOWA

Federal Information Center
All Locations; 800-688-9889

State Information Office
515-281-5011
http://www.state.ia.us

Cooperative Extension Office
Nolan R. Hartwig, Interim
Director; Cooperative
Extension Service; 315

Beardshear Hall, Iowa State University, Ames, IA 50011; 515-294-9434
http://www.exnet.iastate.edu

Attorney Grievances and Fee Arbitration
Iowa State Bar Association; 521 E. Locust, Suite 300, Des Moines, IA 50309-1939; 515-243-3179
http://www.iowabar.org

Client Security Trust Fund
Client Security Trust Fund Commission, Iowa Supreme Court; Iowa State House State Capitol, Des Moines, IA 50319; 515-246-8076

State Consumer Protection Office
Iowa Citizens' Aide Ombudsman; 215 E. 7th St., Capitol Complex, Des Moines, IA 50319; 515-281-3592, 800-358-5510 (IA only)

HUD Field Office
Federal Bldg., 210 Walnut St., Room 239, Des Moines, IA 50309; 515-284-4512
http://www.hud.gov

State Insurance Commissioner
Insurance Commissioner; Lucas State Office Bldg., 6th Floor, Des Moines, IA 50319; 515-281-5705
http://www.state.ia.us/government/com/ins/ins.htm

Nursing Home Ombudsmen
Department of Elder Affairs; 200 W. 10th St., Clemens Bldg.,

3rd Floor, Des Moines, IA 50309; 515-281-4656, 800-532-3213 (IA only)

State Government Banking Commissioner
Superintendent of Banking; 200 E. Grand, Suite 300, Des Moines, IA 50309; 515-281-4014
http://www.state.ia.us/government/com/bank

State Office on Aging
Elder Affairs Department; Clemens Bldg., 3rd Floor, 200 W. 10th St., Des Moines, IA 50309; 515-281-5188
http://www.sos.state.ia.us/register/r4/r4eldaf.htm

State Utility Commission
Iowa Utilities Board; Lucas State Office Building, 5th Floor, Des Moines, IA 50319; 515-281-5979
http://www.state.ia.us/government/com/util/util.htm

KANSAS

Federal Information Center
All Locations; 800-688-9889

State Information Office
913-296-0111
http://www.state.ks.us

Cooperative Extension Office
Mark Johnson, Interim Director; Cooperative Extension Service; Kansas State University, 123 Umberger Hall, Manhattan, KS 66506; 913-532-5820
http://www.oznet.ksu.edu

Attorney Grievances, Client Security Trust Fund & Fee Arbitration
Disciplinary Administrator, Supreme Court of Kansas; 3706 S. Topeka Ave., Suite 100, Topeka, KS 66609; 913-296-2486

State Consumer Protection Office
Consumer Protection Division, Office of Attorney General; Kansas Judicial Center, 301 West 10th St., Topeka, KS 66612; 913-296-3751, 800-432-2310 (KS only)

HUD Field Office
Gateway Towers 2, 400 State Ave., Kansas City, KS 66101-2406; 913-551-6812
http://www.hud.gov

State Insurance Commissioner
Commissioner of Insurance; 420 SW 9th St., Topeka, KS 66612; 913-296-7801, 800-432-2484
http://www.state.ks.us/public/kid

Nursing Home Ombudsmen
Department on Aging; Docking State Office Building, 150 South, 915 Southwest Harrison St., Topeka, KS 66612-4986; 913-296-6539, 800-432-3535 (KS only)

State Government Banking Commissioner
State Bank Commissioner; 700 SW Jackson St., Suite 300, Topeka, KS 66603;

913-296-2266
http://www.state.ks.us/public/bank_dept

State Office on Aging
Aging Department; 915 SW Harrison St., Docking State Office Bldg., Room 150, Topeka, KS 66612-1500; 785-296-4986
http://www.k4s.org/kdoa/default.htm

State Utility Commission
State Corporation Commission; 1500 SW Arrowhead Rd., Topeka, KS 66604-4027; 913-271-3100, 800-662-0027 (KS only)
http://www.kcc.state.ks.us

KENTUCKY

Federal Information Center
All Locations; 800-688-9889

State Information Office
502-564-3130
http://www.state.ky.us

Cooperative Extension Offices
Dr. Absher, Director; Cooperative Extension Service; 310 W.P. Garrigus Building, University of Kentucky, Lexington, KY 40546; 606-257-1846
http://www.ca.uky.edu

Dr. Harold Benson, Director; Kentucky State University, Cooperative Extension Program, Frankfort, KY 40601; 502-227-5905
http://www.kysu.edu

Attorney Grievances, Client Security Trust Fund, Fee Arbitration
Kentucky Bar Association; 514 W. Main, Frankfort, KY 40601-1883; 502-564-3795
http://www.kybar.org

State Consumer Protection Office
Consumer Protection Division, Office of Attorney General; PO Box 2000, Frankfort, KY 40602-2000; 502-432-9257, 888-432-9257 (KY only)
http://www.law.state.ky.us/cp/default.htm

HUD Field Office
PO Box 1044, 601 W. Broadway, Louisville, KY 40201; 502-582-5251
http://www.hud.gov

State Insurance Commissioner
Insurance Commissioner; 215 W. Main St., PO Box 517, Frankfort, KY 40602; 502-564-3630, 800-595-6053
http://www.state.ky.us/agencies/insur/default.htm

Nursing Home Ombudsmen
Division for Aging Services, Department for Social Services; 275 East Main St., 5th Floor West, Frankfort, KY 40621; 502-564-6930, 800-372-2991 (KY only)

State Government Banking Commissioner
Commissioner, Department of Financial Institutions; 477 Versailles Rd., Frankfort, KY 40601; 502-573-3390,

800-223-2579
http://www.dfi.state.ky.us

State Office on Aging
Aging Services Division, Cabinet for Families and Children; 275 E. Main St., 5th Floor, Frankfort, KY 40621; 502-564-6930

State Utility Commission
Public Service Commission; 730 Schenkel Lane, PO Box 615, Frankfort, KY 40602; 502-564-3940, 800-772-4636
http://www.state.ky.us/agencies/psc/pschome.htm

LOUISIANA

Federal Information Center
All Locations; 800-688-9889

State Information Office
504-342-6600
http://www.state.la.us

Cooperative Extension Offices
Dr. Jack Bagent, Director; Cooperative Extension Svc.; Louisiana State University, PO Box 25100, Baton Rouge, LA 70894-5100; 504-388-4141
http://130.39.57.11/wwwac/kes.html

Dr. Leadrey Williams, Administrator; Cooperative Extension Program; Southern University and A&M College, PO Box 10010, Baton Rouge, LA 70813; 504-771-2242

Grievances Fund
Office of Disciplinary Counsel; 2800 Veterans, New Orleans, LA 70002; 504-828-1414

Client Security Trust Fund

Executive Counsel, Louisiana State Bar Association; 601 St. Charles Ave., New Orleans, LA 70130; 504-566-1600, 800-421-5722
http://www.lsba.org

State Consumer Protection Office

Consumer Protection Section, Office of Attorney General; State Capitol Building, PO Box 94005, Baton Rouge, LA 70804; 504-342-9638, 800-351-4889
http://www.laag.com

HUD Field Office

Fisk Federal Bldg.; 501 Magazine St., 9th Floor, New Orleans, LA 70130; 504-589-7200
http://www.hud.gov

State Insurance Commissioner

Commissioner of Insurance; PO Box 94214, Baton Rouge, LA 70804-9214; 504-342-5900, 800-259-5300
http://wwwldi.ldi.state.la.us

Nursing Home Ombudsmen

Governors Office of Elderly Affairs; 412 N. 4th St., Baton Rouge, LA 70802; 504-342-7100, 800-259-4990

State Government Banking Commissioner

Commissioner, Financial Institutions; PO Box 94095, Baton Rouge, LA 70804-9095; 504-925-4660
http://www.premier. netl~la_ofi

State Office on Aging

Elderly Affairs; 412 N. 4th St., Baton Rouge, LA 70802; 504-342-1700

State Utility Commission

Public Service Commission; One American Place, Suite 1630, PO Box 9115H, Baton Rouge, LA 70825; 504-342-4404, 800-228-9368 (LA only)

MAINE

Federal Information Center

All Locations; 800-688-9889

State Information Office

207-582-9500
http://www.state.maine.us

Cooperative Extension Office

Vaughn Holyoke, Director, Cooperative Extension Service; University of Maine, 5741 Libby Hall, Room 102, Orono, ME 04469-5741; 207-581-3188
http://www.umext. maine.edu

Attorney Grievances and Fee Arbitration

Maine Board of Overseers of the Bar; PO Box 1820, Augusta, ME 04332-1820 207-623-1121

State Consumer Protection Office

Consumer Assistance Svcs., Office of Attorney General; 6 State House Station, Augusta, ME 04333-0006; 207-626-8849
http://www.state.me.us/ ag/homepage.htm

HUD Field Office

Norris Cotton Federal Bldg;

275 Chestnut St., Manchester, NH 03101; 603-666-7681
http://www.hud.gov

State Insurance Commissioner

Superintendent of Insurance; 34 State House Station, Augusta, ME 04333-0034; 207-624-8475
http://www.state.me.us/ pfr/ins/inshome2.htm

State Nursing Home

State Long-Term Ombudsman; 21 Bangor St., PO Box 126, Augusta, ME 04332; 800-499-0229, 207-621-1079

State Government Banking Commissioner

Superintendent of Banking; 36 State House Station, Augusta, ME 04333-0036; 207-624-8570
http://www.state.me.us/ pfr/bkg/bkghome2.htm

State Office on Aging

Elder and Adult Services, Human Services Department; 11 State House Station, 35 Anthony Ave., Augusta, ME 04333-0011; 207-624-5335
http://www.state.me.us/ beas/dhs_beas.htm

State Utility Commission

Public Utilities Commission; 18 State House Station, Augusta, ME 04333-0018; 207-287-3831, 800-452-4699 (ME only)
http://www.state.me. us/mpuc

MARYLAND

Federal Information Center

All Locations; 800-688-9889

State Information Office

800-449-4347
http://www.state.md.us

Cooperative Extension Offices

Dr. Thomas Fretz, Regional Directors Office; Cooperative Extension Svc.; Room 1104, Simons Hall, University of Maryland, College Park, MD 20742; 301-405-2907
http://www.agnr.umd. edu/ces/

Dr. Henry Brookes, Administrator; Cooperative Extension Service, UMES; Princess Anne, MD 21853; 410-651-6206
http://www.umes.umd. edu/dept/rudept.html

Attorney Grievance Commission and the Committee on Resolution of Fee Disputes

100 Community Place, Suite 3301, Crownsville, MD 21032; 410-514-7051, 800-492-1660 (MD only)

Client Security Trust Fund

100 Community Place, Suite 3301, Crownsville, MD 21032; 410-514-7051

State Consumer Protection Office

Consumer Protection Div., Office of Attorney General; 200 St. Paul Pl., Baltimore, MD

21202; 410-528-8662
http://www.oag.state.md.us

HUD Field Office
Equitable Bldg., 3rd Floor; 10 N. Calvert St., Baltimore, MD 21202; 410-962-2520
http://www.hud.gov

State Insurance Commissioner
Insurance Commissioner; 501 St. Paul Place, 7th Floor S., Baltimore, MD 21202; 410-468-2090, 800-492-6116

Nursing Home Ombudsmen
Office on Aging; 301 W. Preston St., 10th Floor, Baltimore, MD 21201; 410-767-1100
http://www.inform.umd. edu:8080/umststate/ md_resources/ooa

State Government Banking Commissioner
Bank Commissioner; 501 St. Paul Place, 13th Floor, Baltimore, MD 21202-2272; 410-333-6808
http://www.dllr.state.md.us/dllr

State Office on Aging
Aging Office; 301 W. Preston St., Room 1004, Baltimore, MD 21201-2374; 410-767-1100
http://www.inform.umd. edu:8080/umststate/ md_resources/ooa

State Utility Commission
Public Service Commission; 6 St. Paul St., Baltimore, MD 21202; 410-767-8000; 800-492-0474 (MD only)
http://www.psc.state.md.us/psc

MASSACHUSETTS

Federal Information Center
All Locations; 800-688-9889

State Information Office
617-722-2000
http://www.state.ma.us

Cooperative Extension Office
Dr. John Gerber, Associate Director; 212C Stockbridge Hall, University of Massachusetts, Amherst, MA 01003; 413-545-4800
http://www.umass.edu/umext/

Attorney Grievances and Client Security Trust Fund
Massachusetts Board of Bar Overseers; 75 Federal St., Boston, MA 02110; 617-728-8700
http://www.state.ma.us/ obcbbo/obcbbo.htm

Fee Arbitration
Massachusetts Bar Association Fee Arbitration Board, Attn: Stacy Shunk; 20 West St., Boston, MA 02111-1218; 617-542-3602
http://www.massbar.org

State Consumer Protection Office
Consumer Protection Division, Department of Attorney General; 131 Tremont St., Boston, MA 02111; 617-727-8400
http://www.state.ma.us/ ag/ago8.htm

HUD Field Office
Thomas P. O'Neill Jr., Federal

Bldg.; 10 Cassoway St., Room 375, Boston, MA 02222; 617-565-5234 http://www.hud.gov

State Insurance Commissioner

Commissioner of Insurance; 470 Atlantic Ave., 6th Floor, Boston, MA 02210; 617-521-7777 http://www.state.ma.us/doi/

Nursing Home Ombudsmen

Executive Office of Elder Affairs; 1 Ashburton Pl., Room 506, Boston, MA 02101; 617-727-7750 800-882-2003 (MA only)

State Government Banking Commissioner

Commissioner of Banks; 100 Cambridge St., Boston, MA 02202; 617-727-3145; 800-495-2265 http://www.state.ma.us/dob/

State Office on Aging

Elder Affairs Department; 1 Ashburton Place, 5th Floor, Room 506, Boston, MA 02108; 617-727-7750

State Utility Commission

Department of Telecommunications and Energy; 100 Cambridge St., 12th Floor, Boston, MA 02202; 617-305-3500 http://www.magnet.state. ma.us/dpu

MICHIGAN

Federal Information Center

All Locations; 800-688-9889

State Information Office

517-373-1837 http://www.state.mi.us

Cooperative Extension Office

Arlen Leholm, Director; Michigan State University Extension, Room 108, Agriculture Hall, Michigan State University, East Lansing, MI 48824; 517-355-2308 http://www.msue.msu. edu/msue

Attorney Grievances

Michigan Attorney Grievance Commission; 243 W. Congress, Marquette Bldg., Suite 256, Detroit, MI 48226; 313-961-6585

Client Protection Fund and Fee Arbitration

State Bar of Michigan; 306 Townsend St., Lansing, MI 48933-2083; 517-372-9030 http://www.michbar.org

State Consumer Protection Office

Consumer Protection Division, Office of Attorney General; PO Box 30213, Lansing, MI 48909; 517-373-1140

HUD Field Offices

Patrick V. McNamara Federal Bldg., 477 Michigan Ave, Detroit, MI 48226; 313-226-7900 http://www.hud.gov

2922 Fuller Ave., NE, Grand Rapids, MI 49505; 616-456-2100 http://www.hud.gov

State Insurance Commissioner

Commissioner of Insurance,

Insurance Bureau; PO Box 30220, Lansing, MI 48909-7720; 517-373-9273 http://www.cis.state.mi. us/ins

Nursing Home Ombudsmen
Citizens for Better Care; 416 N. Homer, Suite 101, Lansing, MI 48912-4700; 517-336-6753; 800-292-7852 (MI only)

State Government Banking Commissioner
Commissioner
Financial Institutions Bureau; PO Box 48909, Lansing, MI 48933; 517-373-3460 http://www.cis.state.mi.us/fib/

State Office on Aging
Aging Office; PO Box 30026, Lansing, MI 48909; 517-373-8230 http://mass.iog.wayne.edu/ masshome.html

State Utility Commission
Public Service Commission; 6545 Mercantile Way, PO Box 30221, Lansing, MI 48909; 517-334-6445; 800-292-9555 (MI only) http://ermisweb.cis.state.mi.us

MINNESOTA

Federal Information Center
All Locations; 800-688-9889

State Information Office
612-296-6013
http://www.state.mn.us

Cooperative Extension Office
Catherine Fennely, Director; Minnesota Extension Service;

University of Minnesota, 240 Coffey Hall, 1420 Eckles Ave., St. Paul, MN 55108; 612-625-1915 http://www.mes.umn.edu

Attorney Grievances and Client Security Trust Fund
Office of Lawyers' Professional Responsibility; 25 Constitution Ave., Suite 105; St. Paul, MN 55155-1500; 612-296-3952, 800-657-3601 (MN only)

Fee Arbitration
Minnesota Bar Association; 514 Nicollet Mall, Suite 300, Minneapolis, MN 55402; 612-333-1183, 800-882-MSBA (MN only) http://www.mnbar.org

State Consumer Protection Office
Office of Consumer Services; Office of Attorney General; 1400 N.C.L. Tower, 445 Minnesota St., St. Paul, MN 55101; 612-296-3353, 800-657-3787 http://www.ag.state.mn.us/ consumer

HUD Field Office
220 2nd St., South, Minneapolis, MN 55401; 612-370-3000 http://www.hud.gov

State Insurance Commissioner
Minnesota Department of Commerce, Insurance Division; 133 E. 7th St., St. Paul, MN 55101; 612-297-7161 http://www.commerce. state.mn.us

Nursing Home Ombudsmen
Board on Aging, Office of Ombudsman for Older Minnesotans; 444 Lafayette Rd., St. Paul, MN 55155-3843; 612-296-0382, 800-657-3591

State Government Banking Commissioner
Minnesota Department of Commerce, Division of Financial Examinations; 133 E. 7th St., St. Paul, MN 55101; 612-296-2135
http://www.commerce.state.mn.us

State Office on Aging
Aging Program Division, Social Services Department; 444 LaFayette Rd., St. Paul, MN 55155-3843; 612-296-2770

State Utility Commission
Public Utilities Commission; 121 7th Place East, St. Paul, MN 55501-2147; 612-296-7124, 800-657-3782 (MN only)
http://www.puc.state.mn.us

MISSISSIPPI

Federal Information Center
All Locations; 800-688-9889

State Information Office
601-359-1000
http://www.state.ms.us

Cooperative Extension Offices
Ronald A. Brown, Director; Cooperative Extension Service; Mississippi State University, PO Box 9601, Mississippi State, MS 39762; 601-325-3034
http://www.ces.msstate.edu/ces.html

LeRoy Davis, Dean; Co-operative Ext. Service, 1000 ASU Dr. #479, Lorman, MS 39096; 601-877-6128
http://www.alcorn.edu

Attorney Grievances, Client Security Trust Fund, & Fee Arbitration
Mississippi State Bar; PO Box 2168, Jackson, MS 39225-2168; 601-948-4471, 800-682-6423 (MS only)
http://www.msbar.org

State Consumer Protection Office
Consumer Protection Division, Office of Attorney General; PO Box 22947, Jackson, MS 39225; 601-359-4230, 800-281-4418
http://www.ago.state.ms.us/consprot.htm

HUD Field Office
Dr. A.H. McCoy Federal Bldg.; 100 W. Capitol St., Room 910, Jackson, MS 39269; 601-965-5308
http://www.hud.gov

State Insurance Commissioner
Commissioner of Insurance; 1804 Walter Sillers Bldg., PO Box 79, Jackson, MS 39201-0079; 601-359-3569, 800-562-2957
http://www.doi.state.ms.us

Nursing Home Ombudsmen
Division of Aging and Adult Services; 750 N. State St., Jackson, MS 39202; 601-359-4927, 800-948-3090 (MS only)

State Government Banking Commissioner
Commissioner, Department of Banking and Consumer Finance; PO Box 23729, Jackson, MS 39225-3729; 601-359-1031, 800-844-2499
http://www.dbcf.state.ms.us

State Office on Aging
Aging and Adult Services Division, Human Services Department; PO Box 352, Jackson, MS 39205-0352; 601-359-4925
http://www.mdhs.state.ms.us/aas.html

State Utility Commission
Public Service Commission; PO Box 1174, Jackson, MS 39215; 601-961-5400
http://www.mslawyer.com

MISSOURI

Federal Information Center
All Locations; 800-688-9889

State Information Office
573-751-2000
http://www.state.mo.us

Cooperative Extension Offices
Ronald J. Turner, Interim Director; Cooperative Extension Service; University of Missouri, 309 University Hall, Columbia, MO 65211; 573-882-7754
http://outreach.missouri.edu

Dyremple Marsh, Director; Cooperative Extension Service; Lincoln University, 110A Allen Hall, PO Box 29, Jefferson City, MO 65102-0029; 573-681-5550

Attorney Grievances
Office of Chief Disciplinary Council; 3335 American Ave., Jefferson City, MO 65109; 573-635-7400

Client Security Trust Fund & Fee Arbitration
Missouri Bar Association, PO Box 119, Jefferson City, MO 65102; 573-635-4128
http://www.mobar.org

State Consumer Protection Office
Public Protection Division, Office of Attorney General; PO Box 899, Jefferson City, MO 65102; 314-751-3321, 800-392-8222 (MO only)
http://services.state.mo.us/ago/homepg.htm

HUD Field Offices
(Eastern); 1222 Spruce St., St. Louis, MO 63103; 314-539-6560
http://www.hud.gov

(Western); Gateway Towers 2, 400 State Ave., Kansas City, KS; 66101-2406, 913-551-6812
http://www.hud.gov

State Insurance Commissioner
Director of Insurance; 301 W. High St., Room 630, PO Box 690, Jefferson City, MO 65102; 573-751-4126
http://www.state.mo.us/insurance/

Nursing Home Ombudsmen
Division of Aging; PO Box

1337, Jefferson City, MO
65102; 573-526-0727

State Government Banking Commissioner
Commissioner of Finance; PO
Box 716, Jefferson City, MO
65102; 573-751-3242
http://www.ecodev.state.
mo.us/finance

State Office on Aging
Aging Division; PO Box 1337,
Jefferson City, MO 65102;
573-751-3082
http://www.state.mo.us/
dss/da/da.htm

State Utility Commission
Public Service Commission;
PO Box 360. Jefferson City,
MO 65102; 573-751-3234,
800-392-4211 (MO only)
http://www.ecodev.state.
mo.us/psc

MONTANA

Federal Information Center
All Locations; 800-688-9889

State Information Office
406-444-2511
http://www.state.mt.us

Cooperative Extension Office
Vice Provost for Outreach and
Director of Extension; 212
Montana Hall, Montana State
University, Bozeman, MT
59717; 406-994-4371
http://extn.msu. montana.edu

Attorney Grievances
Commission on Practice of the
Supreme Court of Montana;

Justice Bldg., Room 315, 215 N.
Sanders, Helena, MT 59620-
3002; 406-444-2634

Client Security Trust Fund & Fee Arbitration
State Bar of Montana; PO Box
577, Helena, MT 59624;
406-442-7660
http://www.montanabar.org

State Consumer Protection Office
Office of Consumer Affairs,
Department of Commerce;
1424 9th Ave., Helena, MT
59620; 406-444-4312

HUD Field Office
301 South Park, Drawer 10095,
Helena, MT 59626;
406-441-1300
http://www.hud.gov

State Insurance Commissioner
Commissioner of Insurance;
PO Box 4009, Helena, MT
59604-4009; 406-444-2040,
800-332-6148 (MT only)
http://www.mt.gov/sao

Nursing Home Ombudsmen
Senior and Long Term Care
Division; PO Box 8005, Helena,
MT 59604-4210; 406-444-5900

State Government Banking Commissioner
Commissioner, Division of
Banking and Financial
Institutions; 846 Front St.,
Helena, MT 59620-0546;
406-444-2091
http://commerce.mt.gov/
finance.index.htm

State Office on Aging

Senior and Long Term Care
Division, Department of Public
Health and Human Services;
Box 4210, Helena, MT 59604;
406-444-4077
http://www.dphhs.mt.gov/
whowhat/sltc.htm

State Utility Commission

Public Service Commission;
1701 Prospect Ave., PO Box
202601, Helena, MT 59620-
2601; 406-444-6199
http://www.psc.mt.gov

NEBRASKA

Federal Information Center

All Locations; 800-688-9889

State Information Office

402-471-2311
http://www.state.ne.us

Cooperative Extension Office

Randy Cantrell, Director;
University of Nebraska; S.E.
Research and Extension
Center, Room 211, Mussehl
Hall, East Campus, Lincoln, NE
68583-0714; 402-472-2966
http://ianrwww.unl.edu/
ianr/coopext/coopext.htm

Attorney Grievances & Client Security Fund

Counsel for Discipline,
Nebraska State Bar
Association; 635 S. 14th St.,
Lincoln, NE 68508,
402-475-7091
http://www.nebar.com

State Consumer Protection Office

Consumer Protection Division,
Office of Attorney General;
2115 State Capitol, Room 2115,
Lincoln, NE 68509; 402-471-
2682, 800-727-6432

HUD Field Office

Executive Tower Centre; 10909
Mill Valley Rd., Omaha, NE
68154-3955, 402-492-3100
http://www.hud.gov

State Insurance Commissioner

Director of Insurance; 941 O
St., Suite 400, Lincoln, NE
68508; 402-471-2201,
800-833-0920
http://www.nol.org/
home/ndoi/

Nursing Home Ombudsmen

Department on Aging, State
Office Building; PO Box 95044
Lincoln, NE 68509; 402-471-
2306, 402-471-2307,
800-942-7830 (NE only)
http://www.hhs.state.ne.us/
ags/agsindex.htm

State Government Banking Commissioner

Director of Banking and
Finance; PO Box 95006,
Lincoln, NE 68509;
402-471-2171
http://www.ndbf/org/

State Office on Aging

Aging Department; PO Box
95044, Lincoln, NE 68509-5044;
402-471-2308
http://www.hhs.state.ne.
us/ags/agsindex.htm

State Utility Commission
Public Service Commission;
1200 N St., PO Box 94927,
Lincoln, NE 68509-4925; 402-
471-3101, 800-526-0017
http://www.nol.org/home/npsc/

NEVADA

Federal Information Center
All Locations; 800-688-9889

State Information Office
702-687-5000
http://www.state.nv.us

Cooperative Extension Office
Janet Usinger, Director;
Nevada Cooperative Extension;
2345 Redrock, Las Vegas, NV
89102; 702-222-3130

**Attorney Grievances, Client
Security Trust Fund, & Fee
Arbitration**
State Bar of Nevada; 600 E.
Charleston, Las Vegas, NV
89104; 702-382-0502

**State Consumer Protection
Office**
Consumer Affairs Division,
Department of Business and
Industry; 4600 Kietezke Lane
Building B, Suite 113; Reno,
NV 89502; 702-688-1800,
800-326-5202 (NV only)
http://www.state.nv.us/
busi_industry/cad/index.htm

HUD Field Office
333 North Rancho Dr., Suite
700, Las Vegas, NV 89106-3714;
702-388-6500
http://www.hud.gov

**State Insurance
Commissioner**
Commissioner of Insurance;
1665 Hot Springs Rd., Capitol
Complex 152, Carson City, NV
89710; 702-687-4270,
800-992-0900 (NV only)
http://www.state.nv.us/
busi_industry/id/index.htm

Nursing Home Ombudsmen
Division for Aging Services,
Department of Human
Resources; 340 N. 11th St.,
Suite 203, Las Vegas, NV
89101; 702-486-3545

**State Government Banking
Commissioner**
Commissioner, Financial
Institutions; 406 E. Second St.,
Carson City, NV 89710; 702-
687-4259
http://www.state.nv.us/b&i/fi/

State Office on Aging
Aging Services Division,
Human Resources Dept.; 340
N. 11th St., Howard Cannon
Center, Las Vegas, NV 89101;
702-486-3545
http://www.state.nv.us/
hr/aging/

State Utility Commission
Public Service Commission;
727 Fairview Dr., Carson City,
NV 89710; 702-687-6007
http://www.state.nv.us/puc/

NEW HAMPSHIRE

Federal Information Center
All Locations; 800-688-9889

State Information Office
603-271-1110
http://www.state.nh.us

Cooperative Extension Office
Peter J. Horne, Dean and
Director; UNH Cooperative
Ext.; 59 College Rd., Taylor
Hall, Durham, NH 03824;
603-862-1520
http://www.ceinfo.unh.edu/

Attorney Grievances
New Hampshire Supreme
Court, Professional Conduct
Committee; 4 Park St., Suite
304, Concord, NH 03301;
603-224-5828

**Clients' Indemnity Fund &
Fee Resolution Committee**
New Hampshire Bar
Association; 112 Pleasant St.,
Concord, NH 03301;
603-224-6942

**State Consumer Protection
Office**
Consumer Protection and Anti-
trust Bureau, Office of
Attorney General; 33 Capitol
St., Concord, NH 03301-0397;
603-271-3641
http://www.state.nh.us/
oag/cpb.html

HUD Field Office
Norris Cotton Federal
Building; 275 Chestnut St.,
Manchester, NH 03101-2487;
603-666-7681
http://www.hud.gov

**State Insurance
Commissioner**
Insurance Commissioner; 169
Manchester St., Concord, NH
03301; 603-271-2261, 800-852-
3416 (NH complaints only)
http://www.state.nh.us/
insurance

Nursing Home Ombudsmen
Division of Elderly and Adult
Services, New Hampshire
Long-Term Care Ombudsman
Program; 6 Hazen Dr.,
Concord, NH 03301-3843;
603-271-4375
or toll free in-state:
800-443-5640 (Calls for long
term care ombudsman only)

**State Government Banking
Commissioner**
Bank Commissioner; 169
Manchester St., Concord, NH
03301; 603-271-3561
http://www.state.nh. us/banking

State Office on Aging
Elderly and Adult Services
Division; State Office Park
South, 115 Pleasant St., Annex
Bldg. 1, Concord, NH 03301-
3843; 603-271-4680
http://www.state.nh.us/
dhhs/ofs/ofscstlc.htm

State Utility Commission
Public Utilities Commission; 8
Old Suncook Rd., Bldg. #1,
Concord, NH 03301; 603-271-
2431, 800-852-3793 (NH only)
http://www.state.nh.us/
puc/puc.html

NEW JERSEY

Federal Information Center
All Locations; 800-688-9889

State Information Office
609-292-2121
http://www.state.nj.us

Cooperative Extension Office
Zane Helsel, Director; Rutgers
Cooperative Extension, PO
Box 231, New Brunswick, NJ
08903; 732-932-9306
http://www.rce.rutgers.edu

Attorney Grievances & Fee Arbitration
Supreme Court of New Jersey;
Justice Complex, CN-963,
Trenton, NJ 08625;
609-530-4008

Client Protection Trust Fund
Supreme Court of New Jersey;
Justice Complex, CN-961,
Trenton, NJ 08625;
609-984-7179

State Consumer Protection Office
Division of Consumer Affairs;
124 Halsey St., Newark, NJ
071021; 973-504-6200
http://www.state.nj.us/
lps/ca/home.htm

HUD Field Office
One Newark Center, 13th
Floor, Newark, NJ 07102;
973-622-7900
http://www.hud.gov

State Insurance Commissioner
Commissioner, Department of
Insurance; 20 W. State St., CN-
329, Trenton, NJ 08625;
609-292-5316
http://www.naic.org.nj/
div_ins.htm

Nursing Home Ombudsman
Ombudsman Office for
Institutionalized Elderly; 101 S.
Broad St., 6th Floor, Trenton,
NJ 08625; 609-984-7831

State Government Banking Commissioner
Commissioner of Banking; 20
W. State St., CN-040, Trenton,
NJ 08625; 609-984-2777
http://www.naic.org.nj/
consumer.htm

State Office on Aging
Aging Division, Community
Affairs Dept.; 101 S. Broad St.,
CN807, Trenton, NJ 08625;
609-588-3447
http://www.state.nj.us/
health/senior/sraffair.htm

State Utility Commission
Board of Public Utilities; Two
Gateway Center, Newark, NJ
07102; 973-648-2027, 800-624-
0241 (NJ only)
http://www.njin.net/njbpu/

NEW MEXICO

Federal Information Center
All Locations; 800-688-9889

State Information Office
505-827-4011
http://www.state.nm.us

Cooperative Extension Office
Dr. Jerry Schickenanz; New
Mexico State University, Box
3AE, Las Cruces, NM 88003;
505-646-3016
http://www.cahe.nmsu.
edu/cahe/ces

Attorney Grievances
Disciplinary Board of the
Supreme Court of New
Mexico; 400 Gold SW, Suite
800, Albuquerque, NM 87102;
505-842-5781

Fee Arbitration
State Bar of New Mexico, Fee
Arbitration Committee; PO Box
25883, Albuquerque, NM
87125; 505-797-6000; 800-876-
6227 (NM only)
http://www.nmbar.org

**State Consumer Protection
Office**
Consumer Protection Division,
Office of Attorney General; PO
Drawer 1508, Santa Fe, NM
87504-1508; 505-827-6060, 800-
678-1508 (NM only)

HUD Field Office
625 Truman St., NE,
Albuquerque, NM 87110; 505-
262-6463
http://www.hud.gov

**State Insurance
Commissioner**
Superintendent of Insurance;
PO Drawer 1269, Santa Fe, NM
87504-1269; 505-827-4500,
800-947-4722

Nursing Home Ombudsmen
Agency on Aging; 228 East
Palace Ave., Ground Floor,
Santa Fe, NM 87501; 505-827-
7663, 800-432-2080 (NM only)

**State Government Banking
Commissioner**
Director, Financial Institutions
Division; PO Box 25101, Santa
Fe, NM 87504; 505-827-7100

http://www.state.nm.us/
rld/rld_fid.html

State Office on Aging
State Agency on Aging; 224 E.
Palance Ave., Santa Fe, NM
87501; 505-827-7640

State Utility Commission
Public Utility Commission; 224
E. Palace Ave., Santa Fe, NM
87501-2013; 505-827-6940, 800-
663-9782
http://www.puc.state.nm.us/

NEW YORK

Federal Information Center
All Locations; 800-688-9889

State Information Office
518-474-2121
http://www.state.ny.us

Cooperative Extension Office
William Lacy, Director; Cornell
Cooperative Ext.; 276 Roberts
Hall, Ithaca, NY 14853;
607-255-2237
http://www.cce.cornell.edu/

Attorney Grievances
Departmental Disciplinary,
Committee for the First
Judicial Department; 41
Madison Ave., 39th Floor, New
York, NY 10010; 212-685-1000

New York State Grievance,
Committee for the 2nd and
11th Judicial Districts; 210
Joralemon St., Municipal Bldg.,
12th Floor, Brooklyn, NY
11201; 718-624-7851

Grievance Committee for the
9th Judicial District, Crosswest
Office Center; 399 Knollwood

Rd., #200, White Plains, NY 10603; 914-949-4540

New York State Grievance Committee for the 10th Judicial District; 6900 Jericho Turnpike LL 102, Syosset, NY 11719; 516-364-7344

3rd Department Committee on Professional Standards; Alfred E. Smith Bldg., 22nd Floor, PO Box 7013, Capitol Station Annex, Albany, NY 12225-0013; 518-474-8816

Appellate Division, Supreme Court; 4th Judicial Department Office of Grievance Committee; 295 Main St., 1036 Ellicott Square Bldg., Buffalo, NY 14203; 716-858-1190

Lawyers' Fund for Client Protection
119 Washington Ave., Albany, NY 12210; 518-474-8438, 800-442-3863 (NY only)

State Consumer Protection Office
Bureau of Consumer Frauds and Protection, Office of Attorney General; 120 Broadway, New York, NY 10271; 212-416-8000, 800-771-7755
http://www.oag.state.ny.us

HUD Field Offices
(Upstate); Lafayette Ct., 465 Main St., Buffalo, NY 14203; 716-551-5755
http://www.hud.gov

(Downstate); 26 Federal Plaza, New York, NY 10278;

212-264-6500
http://www.hud.gov

State Insurance Commissioner
Superintendent of Insurance, Consumer Services Bureau; 25 Beaver St., New York, NY 10004; 212-480-6400, 800-342-3736 (NY only)
http://www.ins.state.ny.us/nyins.htm#top

Nursing Home Ombudsmen
Office for the Aging; Agency Building 2, Empire State Plaza, Albany, NY 12223; 518-474-0108, 800-342-9871 (NY only)

State Government Banking Commissioner
Superintendent of Banks; Two Rector St., New York, NY 10006; 212-618-6642, 800-522-3330 (NY only)
http://www.banking.state.ny.us

State Office on Aging
Aging Office; Bldg. 2, Empire State Plaza, Albany, NY 12223-001; 518-474-5731, 800-342-9871 (NY only)
http://aging.state.ny.us/nysofa/

State Utility Commission
Public Service Commission; 3 Empire State Plaza, Albany, NY 12223; 518-474-7080, 800-342-3377 (NY only)
http://www.dps.state.ny.us

NORTH CAROLINA

Federal Information Center
All Locations; 800-688-9889

State Information Office
919-733-1110
http://www.state.nc.us

Cooperative Extension Offices
Dr. Jon F. Ort, Director;
Cooperative Extension Svc.;
North Carolina State
University,, Box 7602, Raleigh,
NC 27695-7602; 919-515-2811
http://www.ces.ncsu.edu/

Dr. Dalton McAfee, Director;
Cooperative Extension
Program; North Carolina A&T
State University, PO Box
21928, Greensboro, NC 27420-
1928; 910-334-7956
http://www.ncat.edu/~soa

Attorney Grievances, Client Security Trust Fund, & Fee Arbitration
North Carolina Bar
Association; PO Box 3688,
Cary, NC 27519; 919-677-0561,
800-662-7407
http://www.ncbar.org

State Consumer Protection Office
Consumer Protection Div.,
Office of Attorney General; PO
Box 629, Raleigh, NC 27602;
919-716-6000
http://www.jus.state.nc.us/
justice/cpsmain/

HUD Field Office
2306 W. Meadowview Rd.,
Greensboro, NC 27407; 910-
547-4000
http://www.hud.gov

State Insurance Commissioner
Commissioner of Insurance;
Dobbs Bldg., PO Box 26387,
Raleigh, NC 27611; 919-733-
7343, 800-662-7777 (NC only)
http://www.sips.state.nc.us/doi/

Nursing Home Ombudsmen
Division of Aging, Dept. of
Human Resources; 693 Palmer
Dr., Raleigh, NC 27626-0531;
919-733-3983, 800-662-7030
(NC only)
http://www.csc.state.nc.
us/dhr/doa/home.htm

State Government Banking Commissioner
Commissioner of Banks; PO
Box 10709, 702 Oberlin Rd.,
Raleigh, NC 27605;
919-733-3016
http://www.banking.
state.nc.us

State Office on Aging
Aging Division, Human
Resources Dept.; 693 Palmer
Dr., Raleigh, NC 27603; 919-
733-3983
http://www.state.nc.us/
dhr/doa/home.htm

State Utility Commission
Utilities Commission; PO Box
29510, Raleigh, NC 27626-0510;
919-733-4249
http://www.ncuc.commerce.
state.nc.us

NORTH DAKOTA

Federal Information Center
All Locations; 800-688-9889

State Information Office
701-224-2000
http://www.state.nd.us

Cooperative Extension Office
Dr. Sharon Anderson, Director; Cooperative Extension Service; North Dakota State University, Morrill Hall, Room 311, Box 5437, Fargo, ND 58105, 701-231-8944
http://www.ext.nodak.edu/

Attorney Grievances
Disciplinary Board of the Supreme Court; PO Box 2297, Bismarck, ND 58502, 701-328-3925

Client Security Trust Fund & Fee Arbitration
State Bar Association of North Dakota; PO Box 2136, Bismarck, ND 58502; 701-255-1404, 800-472-2685 (ND only)

State Consumer Protection Office
Consumer Fraud Division, Office of Attorney General; 600 E. Blvd., Bismarck, ND 58505, 701-328-3404, 800-472-2600 (ND only)
http://www.state.nd.us/ndag

HUD Field Office
653 2nd Ave. North, PO Box 2483, Fargo, ND 58108-2483; 701-239-5136
http://www.hud.gov

State Insurance Commissioner
Commissioner of Insurance; Capitol Bldg., 5th Floor, 600 E. Boulevard Ave., Bismarck, ND 58505; 701-328-2440, 800-247-0560

Nursing Home Ombudsmen
Aging Services, Department of Human Services; 600 S. 2nd St., Bismarck, ND 58505; 701-328-7577, 800-472-2622 (ND only)

State Government Banking Commissioner
Commissioner of Banking and Financial Institutions; 2000 Schafer St., Suite G, Bismarck, ND 58501; 701-328-9933
http://www.state.nd.us/bank/banking.htm

State Office on Aging
Aging Services Division, Human Services Dept.; 600 South 2nd St., Suite 1-C, Bismarck, ND 58504-5729; 701-328-8910

State Utility Commission
Public Service Commission; State Capitol Bldg., 12th Fl., Bismarck, ND 58505-0480; 701-328-2400
http://www.psc.state.nd.us/

OHIO

Federal Information Center
All Locations; 800-688-9889

State Information Office
614-466-2000
http://www.state.oh.us

Cooperative Extension Office
Keith Smith, Director; OSU Extension; 2120 Fiffe Rd., Agriculture Administration

Building, Columbus, OH 43210; 614-292-6181
http://www.ag.ohio-state.edu/

Attorney Grievances
Office of Disciplinary Counsel of the Supreme Court of Ohio; 175 S. 3rd St., Suite 280, Columbus, OH 43215-5196; 614-461-0256

Clients' Security Fund
175 S. 3rd St., Suite 285, Columbus, OH 43215; 614-221-0562, 800-231-1680 (OH only)

Fee Arbitration
Ohio State Bar Association; 1700 Lake Shore Dr., PO Box 16562, Columbus, OH 43216-6562; 614-487-2050; 800-282-6556 (OH only)
http://www.ohiobar.org

State Consumer Protection Office
Consumer Protection Division, Office of Attorney General; 30 E. Broad St., State Office Tower, 25th Floor, Columbus, OH 43215-3428; 614-466-4986, 800-282-0515 (OH only)
http://www.ag.ohio.gov/

HUD Field Offices
525 Vine St., 7th Floor, Cincinnati, OH 45202; 513-684-2884
http://www.hud.gov

One Playhouse Sq., 1350 Euclid Ave., 5th Floor, Cleveland, OH 44114; 216-522-4065
http://www.hud.gov

200 N. High St., Columbus, OH 43215; 614-469-5737

http://www.hud.gov

State Insurance Commissioner
Director of Insurance; 2100 Stella Court, Columbus, OH 43215-1067; 614-644-2651, 800-686-1526, 800-686-1527 (fraud)
http://www.state.oh.us/ins/

Nursing Home Ombudsmen
Department of Aging; 50 West Broad St., 9th Floor, Columbus, OH 43215-5928; 614-466-7922 toll free in-state: 800-282-1206 (long term complaint line only)

State Government Superintendent of Financial Institutions
Ohio Dept. of Commerce, Division of Financial Institutions, 77 S. High St., 21st Floor, Columbus, OH 43266-0121; 614-728-8400
http://www.state.oh.us/com/fin/index.htm

State Office on Aging
Aging Department; 50 W. Broad St., 9th Floor, Columbus, OH 43215-5928; 614-466-5500

State Utility Commission
Public Utilities Commission, 180 E. Broad St., Columbus, OH 43215-3793; 614-466-3016, 800-686-7826 (OH only)
http://www.puc.state.oh.us/

OKLAHOMA

Federal Information Center
All Locations; 800-688-9889

State Information Office
405-521-2011
http://www.state.ok.us

Cooperative Extension Offices

Dr. C.B. Browning, Director; Oklahoma Cooperative Extension Service; Oklahoma State University, 139 Agriculture Hall, Stillwater, OK 74078; 405-744-5398 http://www.okstate.edu/ osu_ag/oces

Dr. Ocleris Simpston, Director; Cooperative Research and Extension; PO Box 730, Langston University, Langston, OK 73050; 405-466-3836 http://www.lunet.edu/

Attorney Grievances, Client Security Trust Fund, & Fee Arbitration

General Counsel, Oklahoma Bar Center; 1901 N. Lincoln Blvd., PO Box 53036, Oklahoma City, OK 73152; 405-524-2365

State Consumer Protection Office

Consumer Protection Unit, Office of Attorney General; 4545 N. Lincoln, Room 260, Oklahoma City, OK 73105-4894; 405-521-4274

HUD Field Office

500 W. Main St., Suite 400, Oklahoma City, OK 73102; 405-553-7401 http://www.hud.gov

State Insurance Commissioner

Insurance Commissioner, PO Box 53408, Oklahoma City, OK 73152; 405-521-2828,

800-522-0071 (OK only) http://www.oid.state.ok.us

Nursing Home Ombudsmen

Special Unit on Aging; 312 NE 28th St., Oklahoma City, OK 73105; 405-521-6734

State Government Banking Commissioner

Bank Commissioner; 4545 N. Lincoln Blvd., Suite 164, Oklahoma City, OK 73105; 405-521-2782 http://www.oklaosf.state. ok.us/~sbd/

State Office on Aging

Aging Services Division, Human Services Dept.; PO Box 25352, Oklahoma City, OK 73125; 405-521-2327

State Utility Commission

Corporation Commission; Jim Thorpe Office Building, PO Box 52000-2000, Oklahoma City, OK 73152-2000; 405-521-2211 http://www.occ.state.ok.us

OREGON

Federal Information Center

All Locations; 800-688-9889

State Information Office

503-378-3111 http://www.state.or.us

Cooperative Extension Office

Dr. Lila Houghlum, Director; Oregon State Extension Service Administration; Oregon State University, Ballard Extension Hall #101, Corvallis, OR 97331-3606;

541-737-2711
http://wwwagcomm.ads.
orst.edu/agcomwebfile/
extser/index.html

**Attorney Grievances &
Client Security Trust Fund**
Oregon State Bar; PO Box
1689, Lake Oswego, OR 97035;
503-620-0222
http://www.osbar.org

**State Consumer Protection
Office**
Financial Fraud Section,
Consumer Complaints; 1162
Court St., NE, Department of
Justice, Justice Building,
Salem, OR 97310; 503-378-4320
http://www.doj.state.or.us/
FinFraud/welcome3.htm

HUD Field Office
400 SW 6th Ave., Suite 700,
Portland, OR 97201,
503-326-2561
http://www.hud.gov

**State Insurance
Commissioner**
Insurance Commissioner,
Labor and Industries Building;
350 Winter St. NE, Room 440-2,
Salem, OR 97310; 503-378-4271
http://www.cbs.state.or.
us/external/ins/index.html

Nursing Home Ombudsmen
Office of LTC Ombudsman;
2475 Lancaster Dr., Bldg. B, #9,
Salem, OR 97310; 503-378-6533,
800-522-2602 (OR only)

**State Government Banking
Commissioner**
Administrator, Division of
Finance and Corporate

Securities; Labor and
Industries Bldg., 350 Winter St.
NE, Rm. 21, Salem, OR 97310;
503-378-4140
http://www.cbs.state.or.
us/external/dfcs/index.html

State Office on Aging
Senior and Disabled Svcs.; 500
Summer St., NE, Salem, OR
97310-1015; 503-945-5811
http://www.sdsd.hr.
state.or.us/

State Utility Commission
Public Utility Commission; 550
Capital St., NE, 2nd Floor,
Salem, OR 97310; 503-378-6611,
800-522-2404 (OR only)
http://www.puc.state.or.us

PENNSYLVANIA

Federal Information Center
All Locations; 800-688-9889

State Information Office
717-787-2121
http://www.state.pa.us

Cooperative Extension Office
Dr. Ted Alter, Director;
Pennsylvania State University;
Room 210, A.G. Administration,
University Park, PA 16802;
814-863-3438
http://www.cas.psu.edu/
docs/coext/coopext.html

**Attorney Grievances & Fee
Arbitration**
District 1: Office of the
Disciplinary Counsel; 1635
Market, 16th Floor,
Philadelphia, PA 19103;
215-560-6296

District 2: Office of the Disciplinary Counsel; One Sentry Pkwy, Bluebell, PA 19422; 610-270-1896

District 3: Office of the Disciplinary Counsel; 2 Lemoyne Dr., 1st Floor, Lemoyne, PA 17043; 717-731-7073

District 4: Office of the Disciplinary Counsel; Suite 400 Union Trust Building, 501 Grant St., Pittsburgh, PA 15219; 412-565-3173

Pennsylvania Client Security Fund
5035 Ritter Rd., Suite 900, Mechanicsburg, PA 17055; 215-560-6335, 800-962-4618

State Consumer Protection Office
Bureau of Consumer Protection, Office of Attorney General; Strawberry Square, 14th Floor, Harrisburg, PA 17120; 717-783-5048; 800-441-2555 (PA only)
http://www.oca.state.pa.us

HUD Field Offices
Wanamaker Bldg.; 100 Penn Sq. East, Philadelphia, PA 19107; 215-656-0600
http://www.hud.gov

State Insurance Commissioner
Insurance Commissioner; 1326 Strawberry Square, Harrisburg, PA 17120; 717-787-2317
http://www.state.pa.us/pa_exec/insurance/overview.html

Nursing Home Ombudsmen
Department of Aging; 400 Market St., State Office Bldg., 7th Floor, Harrisburg, PA 17101-2301; 717-783-3126
http://www.state.pa.us/pa_exec/aging/overview. html

State Government Banking Commissioner
Secretary of Banking; 333 Market St., 16th Floor, Harrisburg, PA 17101-2290; 717-787-2665, 800-PA-BANKS (PA only)
http://www.state.pa.us/pa_exec/banking/

State Office on Aging
Aging Department; 400 Market St., State Office Bldg., 6th Floor, Harrisburg, PA 17101-2301; 717-783-1550
http://164.156.7.66/pa_exec/aging/overview. html

State Utility Commission
Public Utility Commission; PO Box 3265, Harrisburg, PA 17120; 717-783-1740, 800-782-1110 (PA only)
http://puc.paonline.com/

RHODE ISLAND

Federal Information Center
All Locations; 800-688-9889

State Information Office
401-222-2000
http://www.state.ri.us

Cooperative Extension Office
Marsha Morreira, Director; Cooperative Extension,

Education Center; University of Rhode Island, East Alumni Ave., Kingston, RI 02881-0804; 401-874-2900
http://www.edc.uri.edu/

Attorney Grievances & Fee Arbitration

Disciplinary Board of the Supreme Court of Rhode Island; David D. Curtin Judicial Annex, 24 Weybuffet St., 2nd Floor, Providence, RI 02903; 401-222-3270

Client Security Trust Fund

Rhode Island Bar Association; 115 Cedar St., Providence, RI 02903; 401-421-5740
http://www.ribar.com

State Consumer Protection Office

Consumer Protection Division, Department of Attorney General; 150 South Main St., Providence, RI 02903; 401-274-4400, 800-852-7776

HUD Field Office

10 Weybuffet St., Providence, RI 02903; 401-528-5351
http://www.hud.gov

State Insurance Commissioner

Insurance Commissioner; 233 Richmond St., Providence, RI 02903; 401-222-2246

Nursing Home Ombudsmen

Department of Elderly Affairs; 160 Pine St., Providence, RI 02903-3708; 401-222-2858, 800-322-2880 (RI only)

State Government Banking Commissioner

Director and Superintendent of Banking and Securities; 233 Richmond St., Suite 231, Providence, RI 02903-4231; 401-222-2405

State Office on Aging

Elderly Affairs Department; 160 Pine St., Providence, RI 02903; 401-222-2858
http://www.sec.state.ri. us/stdept/sd23.htm

State Utility Commission

Public Utilities Commission; 100 Orange St., Providence, RI 02903; 401-222-3500, 800-341-1000 (RI only)
http://www.state.ri.us/ stdept/sd14.htm

SOUTH CAROLINA

Federal Information Center

All Locations; 800-688-9889

State Information Office

803-734-1000
http://www.state.sc.us

Cooperative Extension Offices

Carroll Culvertson, Director; Clemson University, Cooperative Extension Service; PO Box 995 Pickens, SC 29671; 864-868-2810
http://www.clemson. edu/extension

Director, Cooperative Extension Service; PO Box 8103; South Carolina State

University, Orangeburg, SC
29117-8103; 803-536-8928
http://192.231.63.160/
scsu/state.htm

Attorney Grievances
Grievance Commission; South
Carolina Supreme Court; PO
Box 11330, Columbia, SC
29211; 803-734-2038

**Client Security Trust Fund
& Fee Arbitration**
South Carolina Bar; PO Box
608, Columbia, SC 29202-0608;
803-799-6653
http://www.scbar.org

**State Consumer Protection
Office**
Dept. of Consumer Affairs; PO
Box 5757, Columbia, SC 29250;
803-734-9452, 800-922-1594
(SC only)
http://www.state.sc.us/
consumer/

HUD Field Office
Strom Thurmond Federal
Bldg.; 1835 Assembly St.,
Columbia, SC 29201;
803-765-5592
http://www.hud.gov

**State Insurance
Commissioner**
Chief Insurance
Commissioner; PO Box
100105, Columbia, SC 29202-
3105; 803-737-6117,
800-768-3467
http://www.state.sc.us/doi/

Nursing Home Ombudsmen
State Long Term Care
Ombudsman, Division on
Aging; 202 Arbor Lake Dr.,

Suite 301
Columbia, SC 29223;
803-737-7500

**State Government Banking
Commissioner**
Commissioner of Banking; PO
Box 12549, Columbia, SC
20211; 803-734-2001

State Office on Aging
Office on Aging, South
Carolina Department of Health
and Human Services; PO Box
8206, Columbia, SC 29201
803-253-6177

State Utility Commission
Public Service Commission;
PO Drawer 11649, Columbia,
SC 29211; 803-737-5230, 800-
922-1531 (SC only)
http://www.psc.state.sc.us

SOUTH DAKOTA

Federal Information Center
All Locations; 800-688-9889

State Information Office
605-773-3011
http://www.state.sd.us

Cooperative Extension Office
Mylo Hellickson, Director,
SDSU; Box 2207D, AG Hall
154, Brookings, SD 57007;
605-688-4792
http://www.abs.sdstate.
edu/ces

Attorney Grievances
State Bar of South Dakota;
Attn: Tom Barnett; 222 East
Capitol
Pierre, SD 57501; 605-224-7554
http://www.sdbar.org

Client Security Trust Fund
State Bar of South Dakota; 222
E. Capitol, Pierre, SD 57501;
605-224-7554, 800-952-2333
(SD only)
http://www.sdbar.org

State Consumer Protection Office
Div. of Consumer Affairs,
Office of Attorney General; 500
East Capitol, Capitol Building,
Pierre, SD 57501; 605-773-4400,
800-300-1986 (SD only)
http://www.state.sd.us/
state/executive/attorney/
consumer.htm

HUD Field Office
2400 West 49th St., Suite 1-201,
Sioux Falls, SD 67106-5558;
605-330-4223
http://www.hud.gov

State Insurance Commissioner
Director of Insurance;
Insurance Bldg., 118 W.
Capitol, Pierre, SD 57501;
605-773-3563
http://www.state.sd.us/
insurance

Nursing Home Ombudsmen
Office of Adult Services and
Aging; 700 Governor Dr.,
Pierre, SD 57501; 605-773-3656
http://www.state.sd.us/state/
executive/social/asa/asa.htm

State Government Banking Commissioner
Director of Banking; State
Capitol Bldg., 500 E. Capitol
Ave., Pierre, SD 57501-5070;
605-773-3421

http://www.state.sd.us/state/
executive/dcr/bank/bank-
hom.htm

State Office on Aging
Adult Services on Aging Office,
Social Services Department;
700 Governors Dr., Pierre, SD
57501; 605-773-3656
http://www.state.sd.us/state/
executive/social/asa/asa.htm

State Utility Commission
Public Utilities Commission;
500 E. Capitol Ave., Pierre, SD
57501; 605-773-3201,
800-332-1782
http://www.state.sd.us/state/
executive/puc/puc.htm

TENNESSEE

Federal Information Center
All Locations; 800-688-9889

State Information Office
615-741-3011
http://www.state.tn.us

Cooperative Extension Offices
Dr. Billy G. Hicks, Dean;
Agricultural Extension Service;
University of Tennessee, PO
Box 1071, Knoxville, TN 37901-
1071; 423-974-7114
http://tunnelweb.utcc.
utk.edu/~utext/

Cherry Lane Zon Schmittou,
Extension Leader; Davidson
County Agricultural Service;
Tennessee State University,
800 Second Ave. N., Suite 3,
Nashville, TN 37201-1084; 615-
254-8734

Attorney Grievances & Fee Arbitration

Board of Professional Responsibility of the Supreme Court of Tennessee; 1101 Kermit Dr., Suite 730, Nashville, TN 37217; 615-361-7500

State Consumer Protection Office

Division of Consumer Affairs; 500 James Robertson Parkway, 5th Floor, Nashville, TN 37243-0600; 615-741-4737, 800-342-8385 (TN only) http://www.state.tn.us/consumer

HUD Field Offices

710 Locust St., 3rd Floor, Knoxville, TN 37902; 423-545-4384 http://www.hud.gov

251 Cumberland Bend Dr., Suite 200, Nashville, TN 37228; 615-736-5213 http://www.hud.gov

State Insurance Commissioner

Commissioner of Insurance; 500 James Robertson Pkwy., Nashville, TN 37243-0565; 615-741-2176, 800-342-4029 http://www.state.tn.us/commerce

Nursing Home Ombudsmen

Commission on Aging; 500 Deaderick St., 9th Floor, Nashville, TN 37243-0860; 615-741-2056

State Government Banking Commissioner

Commissioner, Financial Institutions; John Sevier Bldg.,

500 Charlotte Ave., 4th Fl., Nashville, TN 37243; 615-741-2236 http://www.state.tn.us/financialinst

State Office on Aging

Aging Commission; 500 Deaderick St., 9th Floor, Nashville, TN 37243-0860 615-741-2056

State Utility Commission

Tennessee Regulatory Authority; 460 James Robertson Parkway, Nashville, TN 37243; 615-741-2904; 800-342-8359 (TN only) http://www.state.tn.us/tra/tra.htm

TEXAS

Federal Information Center

All Locations; 800-688-9889

State Information Office

512-463-4630 http://www.state.tx.us

Cooperative Extension Offices

Dr. Zerle Carpenter, Director; Texas Agricultural Extension Service; Administration Bldg. 106-A, Texas A&M University, College Station, TX 77843; 409-845-7967 http://agcomwww.tamu.edu/agcom/taex/taex.htm

Dr. Linda Willis, Director; Cooperative Extension Program; PO Box 3059, Prairie View, TX 77446-3059; 409-857-2023 http://www.pvamu.edu/

Attorney Grievances, Client Security Trust Fund, & Fee Arbitration
State Bar of Texas; PO Box 12487, Capitol Station, Austin, TX 78711; 512-463-1463, 800-204-2222

State Consumer Protection Office
Consumer Protection Division, Office of Attorney General; Capitol Station, PO Box 12548, Austin, TX 78711; 512-463-2070, 800-621-0508 (TX only)
http://www.oag.state.tx.us

HUD Field Offices
1600 Throckmorton, PO Box 2905, Fort Worth, TX 76113-2905; 817-978-9000
http://www.hud.gov

Norfolk Tower; 2211 Norfolk, Suite 200, Houston, TX 77098; 713-313-2274
http://www.hud.gov

Washington Square; 800 Dolorosa, San Antonio, TX 78207; 210-472-6806
http://www.hud.gov

State Insurance Commissioner
Director, Claims and Compliance Division, State Board of Insurance; PO Box 149091, Austin, TX 78714-9091; 512-463-6169, 800-252-3439
http://www.tdi.state.tx.us/

Nursing Home Ombudsmen
Department on Aging; PO Box 12786, Capitol Station, Austin, TX 78711; 512-424-6840, 800-252-2412 (TX only)

State Government Banking Commissioner
Banking Commissioner; 2601 N. Lamar Blvd., Austin, TX 78705-4207; 512-475-1300
http://www.banking.
state.tx.us

State Office on Aging
Aging Department; Box 12786 Austin, TX 78711; 512-424-6840
http://www.texas.gov/
agency/340.html

State Utility Commission
Public Utility Commission; 1701 N. Congress Ave., Austin, TX 78701; 512-936-7000
http://www.puc.state.tx.us

UTAH

Federal Information Center
All Locations; 800-688-9889

State Information Office
801-538-3000
http://www.state.ut.us

Cooperative Extension Office
Dr. Robert Gilliland, Vice President for Extension and Continuing Education U.M.C. 4900; Utah State University, Logan, UT 84322-4900; 801-797-2200
http://ext.usu.edu/

Attorney Grievances & Fee Arbitration
Bar Counsel, Utah State Bar; 645 S. 200 East, Salt Lake City, UT 84111-3834; 801-531-9110
http://www.utahbar.org

Client Security Trust Fund
Bar Counsel, Utah State Bar;

645 S. 200 East, Salt Lake City, UT 84111-3834; 801-531-9077 http://www.utahbar.org

State Consumer Protection Office

Division of Consumer Protection, Department of Commerce; 160 E. 300 South, PO Box 146704, Salt Lake City, UT 84114-6704; 801-530-6601 http://www.commerce.state. ut.us/web/commerce/conpro/ consprot.htm

HUD Field Office

257 Tower, 257 East, 200 South, Suite 550, Salt Lake City, UT 84111-2048; 801-524-5241
http://www.hud.gov

State Insurance Commissioner

Commissioner of Insurance; Room 3110, State Office Bldg. Salt Lake City, UT 84114; 801-538-3805, 800-439-3805 http://www.ins-dept.state.ut. us/welcome.htm

Nursing Home Ombudsmen

Division of Aging and Adult Services; PO Box 45500, Salt Lake City, UT 84145; 801-538-3910

State Government Banking Commissioner

Commissioner, Financial Institutions; PO Box 89, Salt Lake City, UT 84110-0089; 801-538-8830

State Office on Aging

Aging and Adult Services

Division, Human Services Dept.; 120 North, 200 West, Salt Lake City, UT 84107; 801-538-3910
http://www.dhs.state.ut.us/ agency/daas/homeage.htm

State Utility Commission

Public Service Commission; 160 East, 300 South, PO Box 45585, Salt Lake City, UT 84145; 801-530-6716 http://web.state.ut.us/bbs/ psc/html/index.htm

VERMONT

Federal Information Center

All Locations; 800-688-9889

State Information Office

802-828-1110
http://www.state.vt.us

Cooperative Extension Office

Dr. Larry Forchier, Dean; Division of Agriculture, Natural Resources and Extension; University of Vermont, 601 Main, Burlington, VT 05401-3439; 802-656-2990 http://ctr.uvm.edu/ext/

Attorney Grievances

Professional Conduct Board, c/o Bar Counsel; 59 Elm St., Montpelier, VT 05602; 802-828-3368

Client Security Trust Fund & Fee Arbitration

Vermont Bar Association; PO Box 100, Montpelier, VT 05601; 802-223-2020
http://www.vtbar.org

State Consumer Protection Office

Consumer Assistance Program; 104 Morrill Hall, University of Vermont, Burlington, VT 05405; 802-656-3183, 800-649-2424

HUD Field Office

Federal Bldg.; 11 Elmwood Ave., Room 244, PO Box 879, Burlington, VT 05402-0879; 802-951-6290
http://www.hud.gov

State Insurance Commissioner

Commissioner of Banking and Insurance; 89 Main St., Drawer 20, Montpelier, VT 05620-3101; 802-828-3302
http://www.state.vt.us/bis/

Nursing Home Ombudsmen

Vermont Legal Aid; 264 N. Winooski, Burlington, VT 05402; 802-863-5620

State Government Banking Commissioner

Commissioner, Banking and Insurance; 89 Main St., Drawer 20, Montpelier, VT 05620-3101; 802-828-3307
http://www.state.vt.us/bis/

State Office on Aging

Vermont Department of Aging and Disabilities; 103 S. Main St., Waterbury, VT 05676; 802-241-2400
http://www.state.vt.us/dad/busdir.htm

State Utility Commission

Public Service Board; 112 State St., Chittenden Bank Bldg., 4th Floor, Drawer 20, Montpelier, VT 05620-2701; 802-828-2358, 800-622-4496 (VT only)
http://www.state.vt.us/psb

VIRGINIA

Federal Information Center

All Locations; 800-688-9889

State Information Office

804-786-0000
http://www.state.va.us

Cooperative Extension Offices

Dr. Clark Jones, Interim Director; Virginia Cooperative Extension; Virginia Tech, Blacksburg, VA 24061-0402; 540-231-5299
http://www.ext.vt.edu/

Lorenza Lyons, Administrator, Cooperative Extension; Virginia State University, Rox 9081, Petersburg, VA 23806-9081; 804-524-5961

Attorney Grievances

Virginia State Bar; 707 E. Main St., Suite 1500; Attn: June Fletcher, Esquire; Richmond, VA 23219-2900; 804-775-0500
http://www.vsb.org

Client Security Trust Fund

Virginia State Bar; 707 E. Main St., Suite 1500; Attn: Susan Busch; Richmond, VA 23219-2900; 804-775-0500
http://www.vsb.org

State Consumer Protection Office

Div. of Consumer Affairs; PO Box 1163, Richmond, VA

23218-1163; 804-786-2042,
800-552-9963 (VA only)
http://www.state.va.us/
~vdacs/vdacs.htm

HUD Field Office
3600 West Broad St., PO Box
90331, Richmond, VA 23230;
804-278-4507
http://www.hud.gov

State Insurance Commissioner
Commissioner of Insurance;
PO Box 1157, Richmond, VA
23218; 804-371-9741, 800-552-
7945 (VA only)

Nursing Home Ombudsmen
Virginia Association of Area
Agencies on Aging; 530 E.
Main St., Suite 428, Richmond,
VA 23219; 804-644-2804, 800-
552-3402 (VA only)

State Government Banking Commissioner
Commissioner, Financial
Institutions; PO Box 640,
Richmond, VA 23218-0640; 804-
371-9704, 800-552-7945 (VA
only)

State Office on Aging
Aging Department; 1600
Forest Ave., Suite 102,
Richmond, VA 23229; 804-662-
9333
http://www.aging.state.va.us/

State Utility Commission
State Corporation Commission;
PO Box 1197, Richmond, VA
23218-1197; 804-371-9967, 800-
552-7945 (VA only)
http://www.state.va.us/
scc/index.html

WASHINGTON

Federal Information Center
All Locations; 800-688-9889

State Information Office
360-753-5000
http://www.state.wa.us

Cooperative Extension Office
Dr. Harry Burcalow, Director
Cooperative Extension; 411
Hulbert, Washington State
University, Pullman, WA 99164-
6230; 509-335-2811
http://www.cahe.wsu.
edu/ce/html

Attorney Grievances, Client Security Program, & Fee Arbitration
Washington State Bar
Association; 2101 4th Ave., 4th
Floor, Seattle, WA 98121; 206-
727-8200
http://www.wsba.org

State Consumer Protection Office
Consumer and Business Fair
Practice Division, Office of
Attorney General; 900 4th Ave.,
Suite 2000, Seattle, WA 98164;
206-464-6684, 800-551-4636 (WA
only)
http://www.wa.gov/ago/
cpd/cphone.html

HUD Field Office
Seattle Federal Office Bldg.;
909 1st Ave., Suite 200, Seattle,
WA 98104; 206-220-5101
http://www.hud.gov

State Insurance Commissioner

Insurance Commissioner; Insurance Bldg. AQ21, PO Box 40255, Olympia, WA 98504-0255; 360-753-7301, 800-562-6900 (WA only)
http://www.wa.gov/ins/

Nursing Home Ombudsmen

South King County Multi-Service Center; 1200 South 336 St., PO Box 23699, Federal Way, WA 98903-0699; 206-838-6810, 800-422-1384

State Government Banking Commissioner

Supervisor of Banking; PO Box 41200, Olympia, WA 98504-1200; 360-902-8700
http://www.wa.gov/dfi/

State Office on Aging

Aging and Adult Services; PO Box 45050, Olympia, WA 98504-5600; 360-586-8753

State Utility Commission

Utilities and Transportation Commission; 1300 South Evergreen Park Dr. SW, Olympia, WA 98504; 360-753-6423, 800-562-6150 (WA only)
http://www.wutc.wa.gov/

WEST VIRGINIA

Federal Information Center

All Locations; 800-688-9889

State Information Office

304-558-3456
http://www.state.wv.us

Cooperative Extension Office

Robert Maxwell, Interim Director; Cooperative Extension; 8th Floor, Knapt Hall, PO Box 6031, West Virginia University, Morgantown, WV 26506-6031; 304-293-3408
http://www.wvu.edu/~exten

Attorney Grievances and Client Security Trust Fund

West Virginia State Bar; 2006, Kanawha Blvd. East, Charleston, WV 25311; 304-558-2456
http://www.wvbar.org

State Consumer Protection Office

Consumer Protection Division, Office of Attorney General; 812 Quarrier St., 6th Floor, Charleston, WV 25301; 304-558-8986, 800-368-8808 (WV only)

HUD Field Office

405 Capitol St., Suite 708; Charleston, WV 25301; 304-347-7000
http://www.hud.gov

State Insurance Commissioner

Insurance Commissioner; 1124 Smith St., PO Box 50540, Charleston, WV 25305-0540; 304-558-3394, 800-642-9004

Nursing Home Ombudsmen

Commission on Aging; State Capitol-Holly Grove, 1900 Kanawha Blvd. East, Charleston, WV 25305; 304-558-3317

State Government Banking Commissioner

Commissioner of Banking;

State Capitol Complex, Bldg. 3, Room 311, Charleston, WV 25305; 304-558-2294, 800-642-9056

State Office on Aging
Aging Commission; 1900 Kanawha Blvd., State Capitol Holly Grove, Charleston, WV 25305; 304-558-3317 http://www.wvdhhr.org/pages/bcs/aging.htm

State Utility Commission
Public Service Commission; 201 Brooks St., PO Box 812, Charleston, WV 25323-0812; 304-340-0300, 800-344-5113 (WV only) http://www.state.wv.us/psc/default.htm

WISCONSIN

Federal Information Center
All Locations; 800-688-9889

State Information Office
608-266-2211 http://www.state.wi.us

Cooperative Extension Office
Dr. Aeyse Somersan, Director; 432 N. Lake St., Room 601, Madison, WI 53706; 608-262-7966 http://www.uwex.edu/ces/

Attorney Grievances
Board of Attorneys Professional Responsibility; Tenney Bldg., 110 E. Main St., Room 410, Madison, WI 53703; 608-267-7274

Client Security Trust Fund and Fee Arbitration
State Bar of Wisconsin; PO

Box 7158, Madison, WI 53707; 608-257-3838, 800-728-7788 http://www.wisbar.org

State Consumer Protection Office
Office of Consumer Protection and Citizen Advocacy, Department of Justice; PO Box 7856, Madison, WI 53707-7856; 608-266-1852

HUD Field Office
Henry Rouss Federal Plaza; 310 W. Wisconsin Ave., Milwaukee, WI 53203; 414-297-3214 http://www.hud.gov

State Insurance Commissioner
Commissioner of Insurance; PO Box 7873, Madison, WI 53707-7873; 608-266-3585, 800-236-8517 (WI only) http://badger.state.wi.us/agencies/oci/oci_home.htm

Nursing Home Ombudsmen
Board on Aging and Long Term Care; 214 N. Hamilton St., Madison, WI 53703; 608-266-8944

State Government Banking Commissioner
Commissioner of Banking; 345 W. Washington Ave., 4th Floor, Madison, WI 53703; 608-266-1621 http://badger.state.wi.us/agencies/dfi

State Office on Aging
Aging and Long Term Care Board; 217 S. Hamilton St.,

Suite 300, Madison, WI 53703; 608-266-2536

State Utility Commission
Public Service Commission; 610 North Whitney Way, Madison, WI 53707; 608-266-2001, 800-225-7729
http://badger.state.wi.us/agencies/psc

WYOMING

Federal Information Center
All Locations; 800-688-9889

State Information Office
307-777-7011
http://www.state.wy.us

Cooperative Extension Office
Darryl Kautzman, Director CES; University of Wyoming, Box 3354, Laramie, WY 82071-3354; 307-766-5124
http://www.uwyo.edu/ag/ces/ceshome.htm

Attorney Grievances, Client Security Trust Fund, & Fee Arbitration
Wyoming State Bar; PO Box 109, Cheyenne, WY 82003-0109; 307-632-9061
http://www.wyomingbar.org

State Consumer Protection Office
Consumer Affairs, Office of Attorney General; 123 State Capitol Bldg., Cheyenne, WY 82002; 307-777-7841,

800-438-5799 (WY only)

HUD Field Office
4225 Federal Office Bldg., 100 East 8th St., PO Box 120, Casper, WY 82602-1919; 307-261-6254
http://www.hud.gov

State Insurance Commissioner
Commissioner of Insurance; Herschler Bldg., 122 W. 25th St, Cheyenne, WY 82002; 307-777-7401, 800-438-5768 (WY only)

Nursing Home Ombudsmen
Long Term Care Ombudsman; 756 Gilchrist St., Wheatland, WY 82201; 307-322-5553

State Government Banking Commissioner
Manager, Division of Banking; Herschler Bldg., 122 West 25th St., Cheyenne, WY 82002; 307-777-6600
http://audit.state.wy.us

State Office on Aging
Division on Aging, Department of Health; 117 Hathaway Bldg. Room 139, Cheyenne, WY 82002; 307-777-7986
http://wdhfs.state.wy.us/wdh/default.htm

State Utility Commission
Public Service Commission; 2515 Warren Ave., Hansen Bldg., Suite 300, Cheyenne, WY 82002; 307-777-7427

Index

A

AARPm 2, 9, 101, 303, 305
AFL-CIO, 201-202
Age discrimination, 233, 246
Age Pages, 136
Agency for Health Care Policy and Research, 163
Aging, 125
AIDS, 176
Air travel, 21
Airlines, 23
Allergies, 122, 157-158
Alzheimer's disease, 166-167
American Quarter Horse Association, 322
AMTRAK, 24
Apartment, 85
Archaeology, 58
Area Agencies on Aging, 305, 318
Army Corps of Engineers, U.S., 61
Arthritis, 145-146
quackery, 116
Asthma, 158
Automobile Insurance, 306

B

Back pain, 146
Banking, 213, 215
Baseball, 71
Bathroom, 111
Boating safety hotline, 65
Bones, 146
Book signings, 65
Books, 9
Botanic Garden, 32

Breast Cancer, 141
Brokerage firms, 220
Bureau of Engraving and Printing, 30
Burns, 106

C

Caffeine, 144
Calcium, 126,151
Cancer, 125, 139, 141
Capitol, U.S., 31
Car, 12
Carbon monoxide poisoning, 150-151
Carpeting, 246
Carpets, 113
Cat food, 120
Cat, 121
Catalogs, 55
Celebrities, 11
Charities, 224
Children, 319
CIC, 84, 241
Cleaning, 109-110
Clinical trials, 68
COBRA, 241
Coin collecting, 324
College, 255, 301
Commodities market, 222
Company tour, 39
Computer, 246
Concerts, 31
Congregate housing, 77, 78, 92
Congress, 31
Congressional Research Service (CRS), 77, 247
Conserving fuel, 87
Consumer Information Center (CIC), 81, 84, 108-109, 204, 240, 244, 317-318
Consumer Protection Office, 235
Cooking, 323
Cooperative Extension Service, 62

Country line dancing, 67
Coupons, 129
Crafts, 53
Credit report, 217
Credit unions, 214
Credit, 216
Crime Victims Fund, 236
Crochet, 54
Cross stitch, 54
Cruises, 24-25

D

Decorating, 112-113
Decorator, 112
Dental care resources, 179-190
Dental care, 177-190
Dental schools, 177-190
Dental Societies, 177-190
Dentures, 178-190
Department of Aging, 232
Department of Housing and Urban Development (HUD), 84
Department of Labor, 203-204
Depression, 160
Diabetes, 124, 143
Diet, 123, 136
Discrimination, 234
Disneyworld, 32
Dog food, 120
Dog, 117, 120
Down payment, 81
Drug companies, 197

E

ElderCare Locator, 59, 304
Elder Hostel, 28
Endangered species, 197
Environmental Protection Agency (EPA), 63, 103, 242, 324